o|s Ordnance Survey

STREET ATLAS
South Yorkshire

Contents

PHILIP'S

First edition published 1996 by

Ordnance Survey
Romsey Road
Maybush
Southampton SO16 4GU

and

George Philip Ltd.
an imprint of Reed Books
Michelin House, 81 Fulham Road, London SW3 6RB
and Auckland, Melbourne, Singapore and Toronto

ISBN 0-540-06330-4 (Philip's, hardback)
ISBN 0-540-06331-2 (Philip's, wire-o)

ISBN 0-319-00839-8 (Ordnance Survey, hardback)
ISBN 0-319-00840-1 (Ordnance Survey, wire-o)

Key to map symbols

Motorway		⇄	British Rail station
Primary Routes (Dual carriageway and single)		(locomotive symbol)	Private railway station
A Roads (Dual carriageway and single)		⬤	Bus, coach station
B Roads (Dual carriageway and single)		◆	Ambulance station
C Roads (Dual carriageway and single)		◆	Coastguard station
Minor Roads		◆	Fire station
Roads under construction		◆	Police station
County boundaries		✚	Casualty entrance to hospital
All Railways		✛	Churches, Place of worship
Track or private road		H	Hospital
Gate or obstruction to traffic (restrictions may not apply at all times or to all vehicles)		i	Information Centre
All paths, bridleways, BOAT's, RUPP's, dismantled railways, etc.		P	Parking
The representation in this atlas of a road, track or path is no evidence of the existence of a right of way		☐	Post Office
		⬤	Public Convenience
174 Adjoining page indicator			Important buildings, schools, colleges, universities and hospitals

Acad	Academy	Mon	Monument
Cemy	Cemetery	Mus	Museum
C Ctr	Civic Centre	Obsy	Observatory
CH	Club House	Pal	Royal Palace
Coll	College	PH	Public House
Ex H	Exhibition Hall	Resr	Reservoir
Ind Est	Industrial Estate	Ret Pk	Retail Park
Inst	Institute	Sch	School
Ct	Law Court	Sh Ctr	Shopping Centre
L Ctr	Leisure Centre	Sta	Station
LC	Level Crossing	TH	Town Hall/House
Liby	Library	Trad Est	Trading Estate
Mkt	Market	Univ	University
Meml	Memorial	YH	Youth Hostel

River Soar	Water Name
	Stream
	River or canal (minor and major)
	Water Fill
	Tidal Water
	Woods
	Sheffield Tramway

0		¼		½		¾		1 mile

0		250 m		500 m		750 m		1 Kilometre

The scale of the maps is 5.52 cm to 1 km
(3¹/₂ inches to 1 mile)

The small numbers around the edges of the maps identify the 1 kilometre National Grid lines

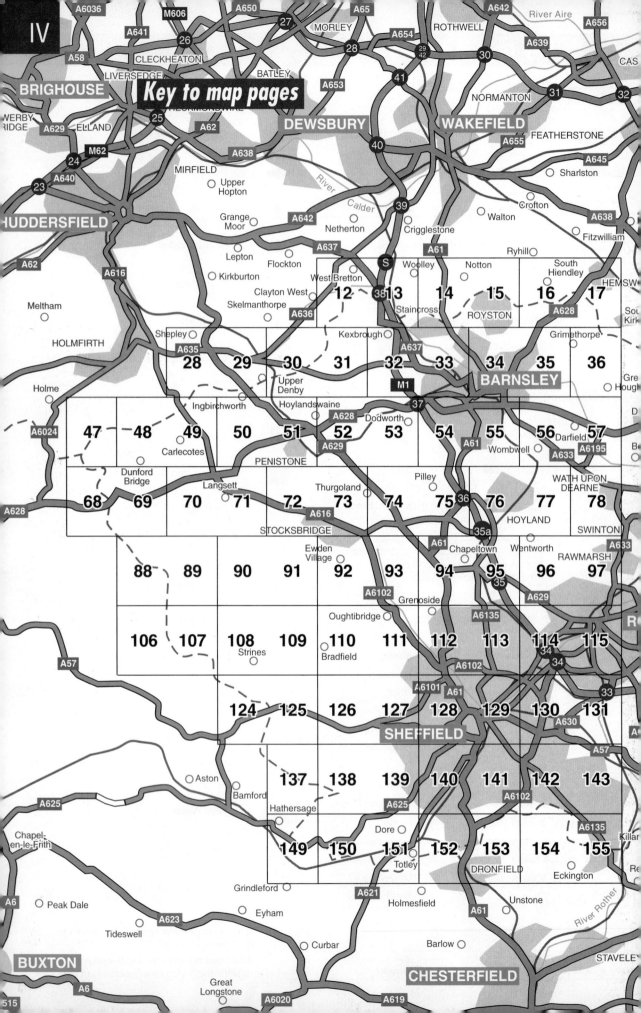

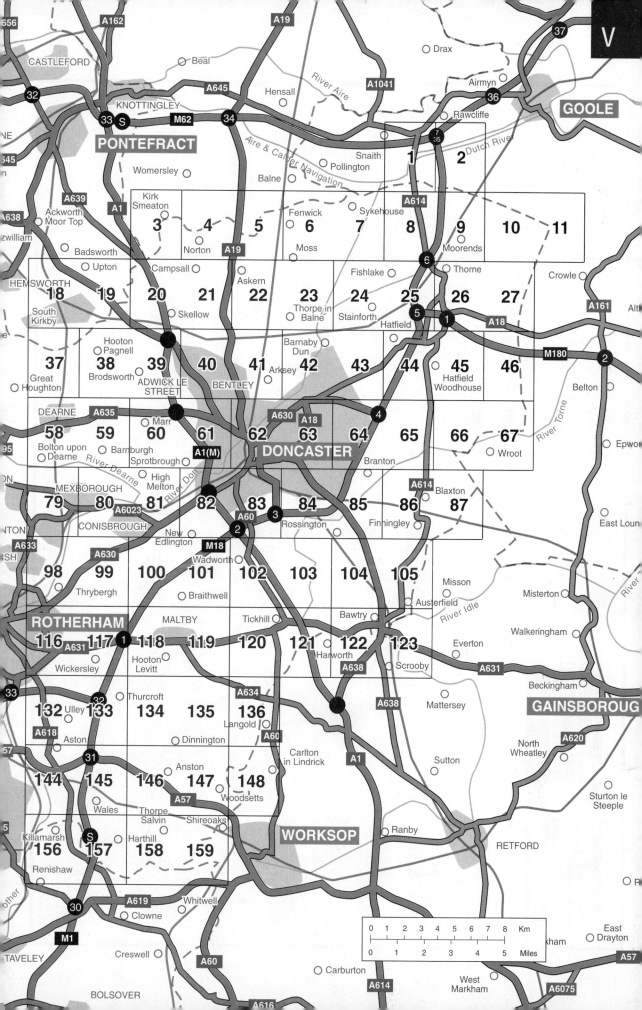

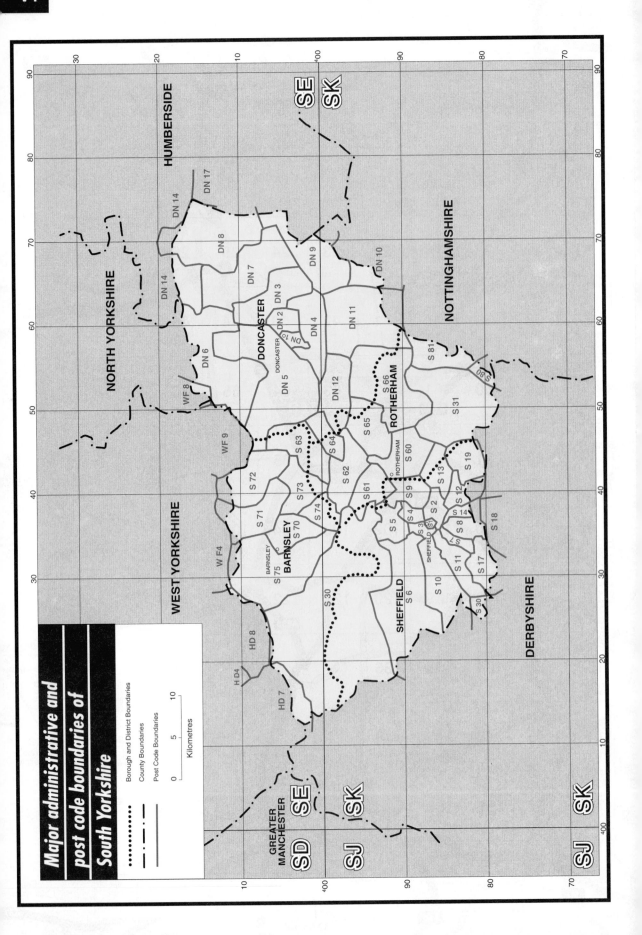

Major administrative and post code boundaries of
South Yorkshire

Borough and District Boundaries
County Boundaries
Post Code Boundaries

0   5   10
Kilometres

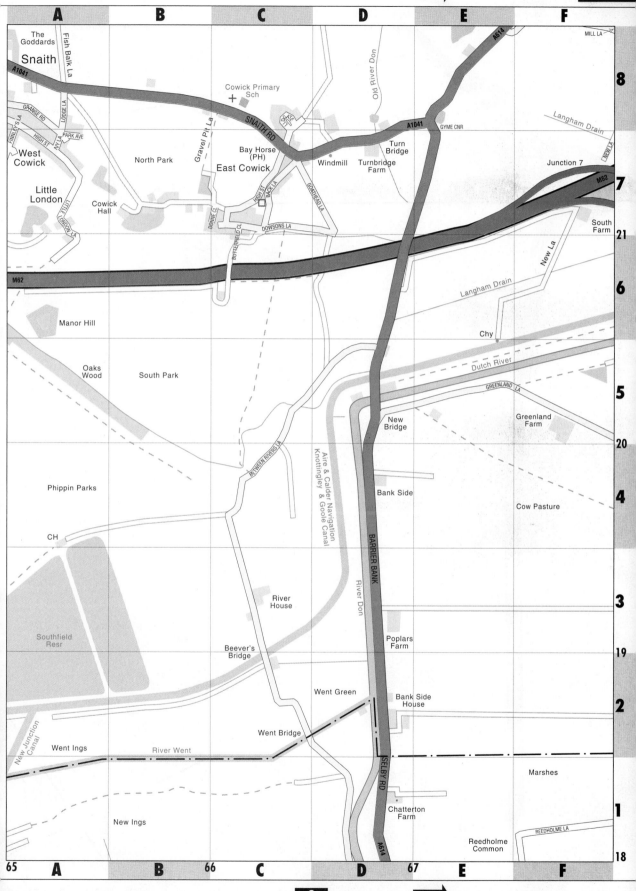

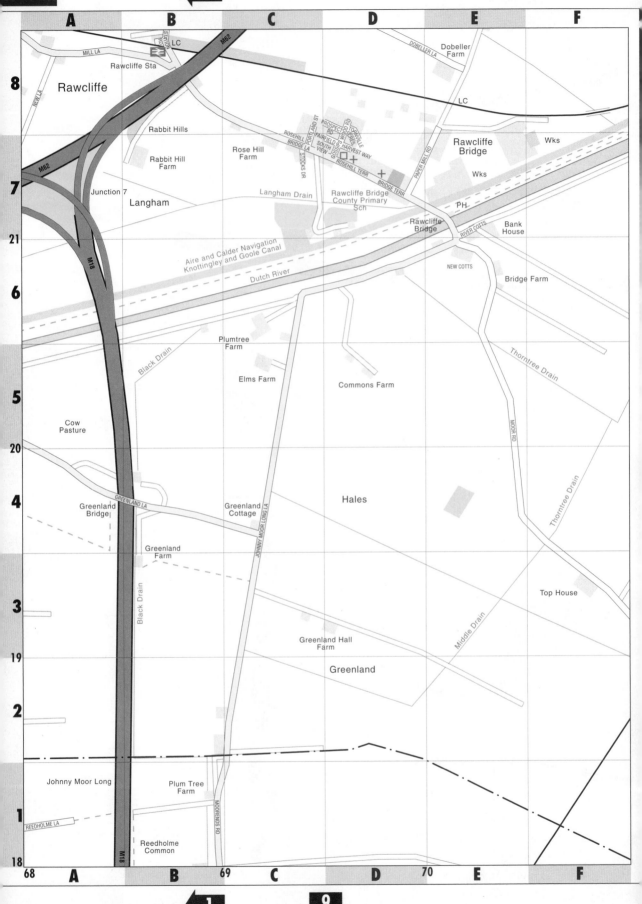

A B C D E F

8 Rawcliffe

MILL LA
NEW LA
Rawcliffe Sta
LC
STATION ROAD
M62

Rabbit Hills
Rabbit Hill Farm

Rose Hill Farm

DOBELLER LA
Dobeller Farm
LC

PROSPECT RD
FAIRFIELD RD
HARVEST WAY
SOUTH VIEW
ROSEHILL BRIDGE LA
ST ANN TERR
STOCKS DR

Rawcliffe Bridge
Wks
Wks
PAPER MILL RD

Rosehill Terr
Bridge Terr

7 Junction 7
M62
Langham

Langham Drain
Rawcliffe Bridge County Primary Sch

Rawcliffe Bridge
PH

21 Aire and Calder Navigation
Knottingley and Goole Canal

River Cotts
Bank House

New Cotts

6 Dutch River
M18

Bridge Farm

Black Drain

Plumtree Farm

Elms Farm

Commons Farm

Thorntree Drain

5 Cow Pasture

MOOR RD

20
Thorntree Drain

4 Greenland Bridge
GREENLAND LA
Greenland Cottage

JOHNNY MOOR LONG LA
Hales

Greenland Farm

Top House

3 Black Drain

Greenland Hall Farm

Middle Drain

19 Greenland

2

Johnny Moor Long
Plum Tree Farm
MOORENDS RD

1 REEDHOLME LA

18 M18
Reedholme Common

68 A B 69 C D 70 E F

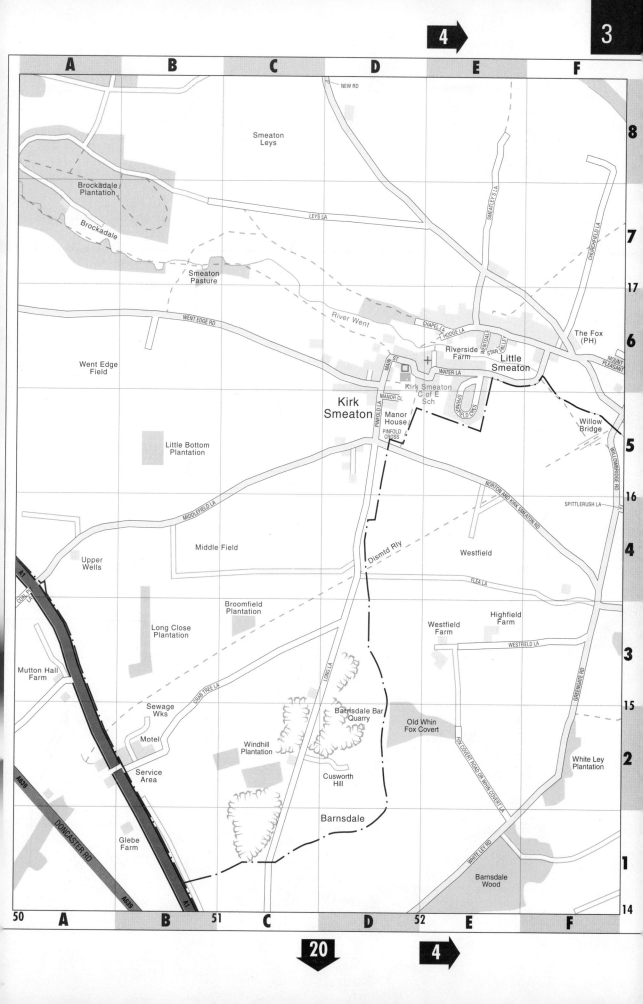

A   B   C   D   E   F

8

Smeaton
Leys

NEW RD

Brockadale
Plantation

7

Brockadale

LEYS LA

SMEATLEY'S LA

CHURCHFIELD LA

17

Smeaton
Pasture

River Went

WENT EDGE RD

CHAPEL LA

HODGE LA

The Fox
(PH)

6

Went Edge
Field

MAIN ST

WATER LA

Riverside
Farm

WENTDALE

STAN VALLEY

Little
Smeaton

MOUNT
PLEASANT

Kirk Smeaton
C of E
Sch

SPRINGFIELD CRES

Kirk
Smeaton

MANOR CL

PINFOLD LA

Manor
House

PINFOLD
CROSS

Willow
Bridge

WILLOWBRIDGE RD

5

Little Bottom
Plantation

NORTON AND KIRK SMEATON RD

SPITTLERUSH LA

16

MIDDLEFIELD LA

Middle Field

Dismtd Rly

Westfield

4

Upper
Wells

A1

COAL PIT LA

FLEA LA

Broomfield
Plantation

Long Close
Plantation

LONG LA

CRAB TREE LA

Westfield
Farm

Highfield
Farm

WESTFIELD LA

GREENGATE RD

3

Mutton Hall
Farm

Sewage
Wks

Barnsdale Bar
Quarry

Old Whin
Fox Covert

15

Motel

Windhill
Plantation

FOX COVERT ROAD OR WHIN COVERT LA

White Ley
Plantation

2

A638

Service
Area

Cusworth
Hill

Barnsdale

WHITE LEY RD

DONCASTER RD

Glebe
Farm

A1

A638

Barnsdale
Wood

1

14

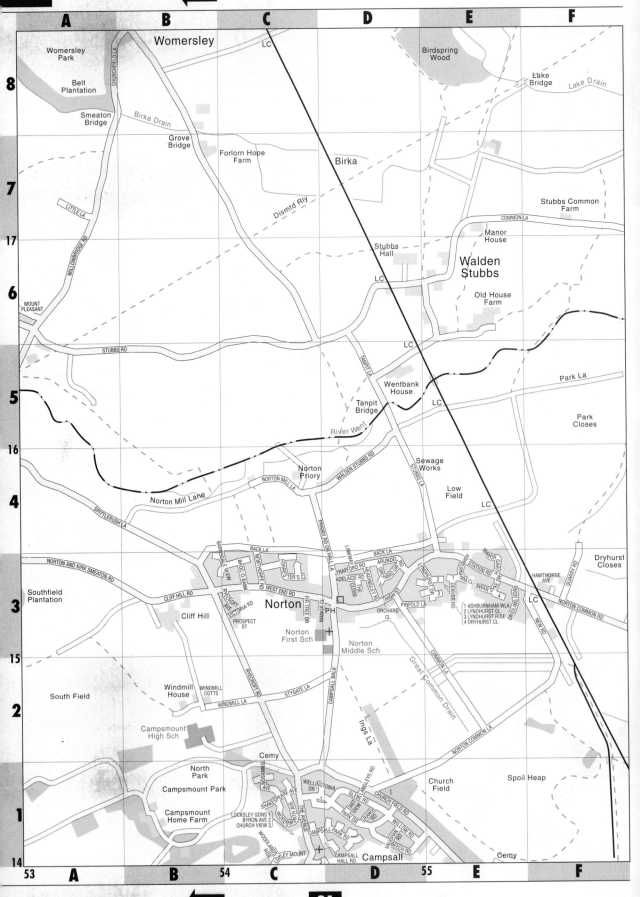

3

A   **B**   **C**   **D**   **E**   **F**

Womersley

Womersley
Park

Belt
Plantation

8

Birdspring
Wood

Lake
Bridge

Lake Drain

Smeaton
Bridge

Birka Drain

Grove
Bridge

Forlorn Hope
Farm

Birka

7

CHURCHFIELD LA

LITTLE LA

Dismtd Rly

Stubbs Common
Farm

COMMON LA

17

Manor
House

Stubbs
Hall

Walden
Stubbs

6

WILLOWBRIDGE RD

MOUNT
PLEASANT

LC

Old House
Farm

STUBBS RD

LC

Park La

5

Wentbank
House

Tanpit
Bridge

LC

Park
Closes

TANPIT LA

River Went

16

Norton
Priory

Sewage
Works

Norton Mill Lane

NORTON MILL LA

WALDEN STUBBS RD

STUBBS LA

Low
Field

4

SPITTLERUSH LA

LC

Southfield
Plantation

NORTON AND KIRK SMEATON RD

BACK LA

BACK LA

LINKWAY

Dryhurst
Closes

BARNSDALE V'EW

NEWTHORPE RD

FORRES

TER'S CL

TRAFFORD RD

ARUNDEL

HEADINGLEY RD

STATION RD

MANOR

GARTH

HAWTHORNE
AVE

CLIFF HILL RD

BROG-O-BANK

WEST END RD

ADELAIDE CL

THE CLOSE

HIGH ST

LYNDHURST DR

BURNHAM CL

SWAN

QUARRY RD

Cliff Hill

RYECROFT
AVE

VICTORIA RD

Norton

PH

PINFOLD LA

DENVER RD

3

FIR TREE DR

PRIORY RD OR HALL LA

ORCHARD
CL

1 ASHBURNHAM WLK
2 LYNDHURST CL
3 LYNDHURST RISE
4 DRYHURST CL

NORTON COMMON RD

LC

PROSPECT
ST

Norton
First Sch

NEW RD

Norton
Middle Sch

15

RYECROFT RD

Windmill
House

Windmill
Cotts

STYGATE LA

CAMPSALL BALK

Great Common Drain

COMMON LA

South Field

WINDMILL LA

2

Campsmount
High Sch

INGS LA

NORTON COMMON LA

Spoil Heap

Cemy

1

North
Park

Campsmount Park

TENNYSON AVE

WELLINGTONIA
DR

LANGLERS RD

GLEBE RD

CHURCH FIELD RD

Church
Field

SHAKESPEARE AVE

WORDSW'TH

THE AVENUE

PARK DR

EAST VIEW

GRANGE RD

WILLOW RD

Campsmount
Home Farm

LOCKSLEY GDNS 1
BYRON AVE 2
CHURCH VIEW 3

WOODLANDS RISE

LOXLEY MOUNT

CAMPSALL PARK RD

VAUGHAN

BEECH RD

Cemy

14

CAMPSALL HALL RD

Campsall

53   **A**   **B**   **54**   **C**   **D**   **55**   **E**   **F**

3

21

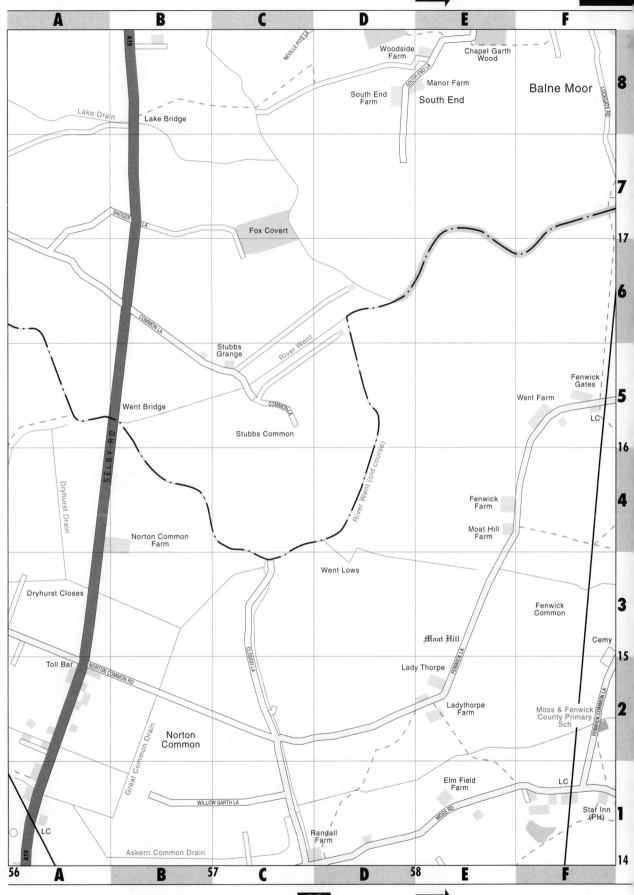

A19

Lake Drain

Lake Bridge

8

NEVILLE PIT STA

Woodside Farm

Chapel Garth Wood

SOUTH END LA

South End Farm

Manor Farm

South End

Balne Moor

LOCKGATE RD

7

BADGER LA

17

Fox Covert

COMMON LA

6

Stubbs Grange

River Went

Fenwick Gates

Went Farm

LC

5

Went Bridge

COMMON LA

Stubbs Common

16

SELBY RD

River Went (old course)

Dryhurst Drain

Fenwick Farm

4

Norton Common Farm

Moat Hill Farm

Dryhurst Closes

Went Lows

Fenwick Common

3

Moat Hill

Cemy

Toll Bar

NORTON COMMON RD

Lady Thorpe

FENWICK LA

15

Great Common Drain

Norton Common

Ladythorpe Farm

Moss & Fenwick County Primary Sch

FENWICK COMMON LA

2

CLOUGH LA

LC

Elm Field Farm

Star Inn (PH)

WILLOW GARTH LA

MOSS RD

1

A19

LC

Randall Farm

Askern Common Drain

14

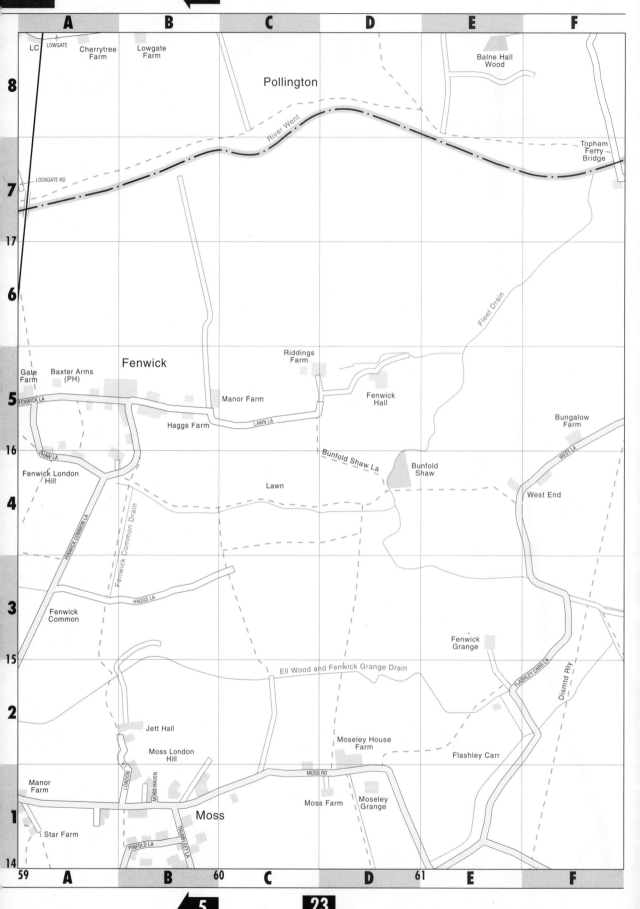

A   B   C   D   E   F

8

LC   LOWGATE   Cherrytree Farm   Lowgate Farm

Pollington

Balne Hall Wood

River Went

Topham Ferry Bridge

LOCKGATE RD

7

17

6

Fleet Drain

Gate Farm   Baxter Arms (PH)   Fenwick

Riddings Farm

Manor Farm   Fenwick Hall

5   FENWICK LA

Haggs Farm   LAWN LA

Bungalow Farm

16   SHAW LA

WEST LA

Fenwick London Hill

Bunfold Shaw La   Bunfold Shaw

Lawn

West End

4

FENWICK COMMON LA

Fenwick Common Drain

HAGGS LA

3   Fenwick Common

Fenwick Grange

15   Ell Wood and Fenwick Grange Drain

FLASHLEY CARR LA

Dismtd Rly

2

Jett Hall

Moseley House Farm

Moss London Hill

Flashley Carr

Manor Farm

LONDON LA

MOSS HAVEN

MOSS RD

Moss Farm   Moseley Grange

1

Moss

Star Farm

PINFOLD LA   TRUMFLEET LA

14

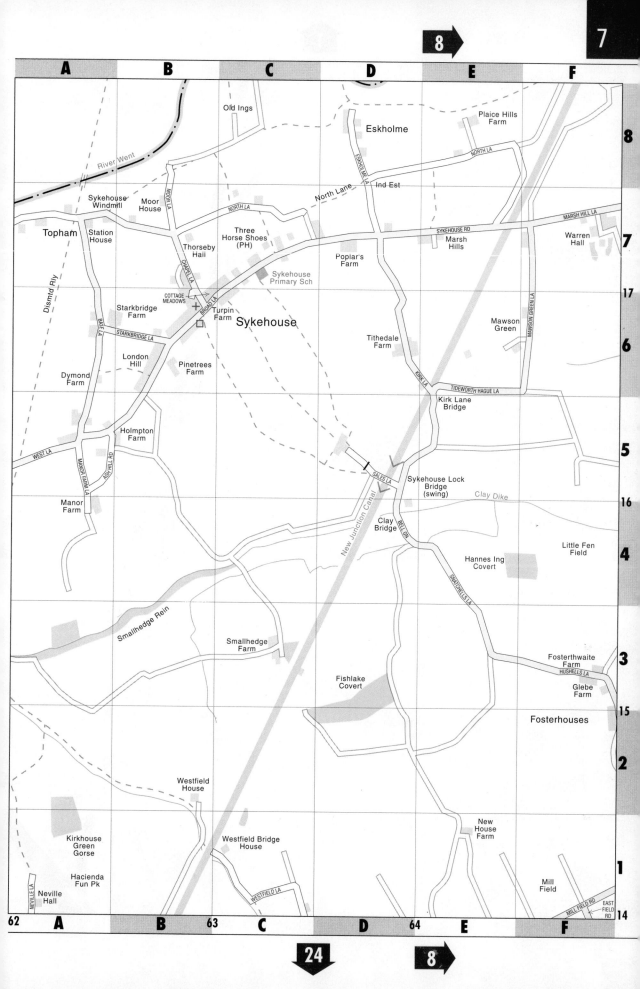

A B C D E F

17
16
15
14

Old Ings

Eskholme

Plaice Hills Farm

North La

River Went

Sykehouse Windmill

Moor House

North La

North Lane

Ind Est

Sykehouse Rd

Marsh Hill La

Topham

Station House

Thorseby Hall

Three Horse Shoes (PH)

Poplar's Farm

Marsh Hills

Warren Hall

Moor La

Chapel La

Sykehouse Primary Sch

Dismtd Rly

Cottage Meadows

Turpin Farm

Sykehouse

Starkbridge Farm

Broad La

Mawson Green La

Mawson Green

Bafe La

Starkbridge La

Tithedale Farm

London Hill

Pinetrees Farm

Dymond Farm

Kirk La

Tideworth Hague La

Kirk Lane Bridge

Holmpton Farm

West La

Manor Farm La

Ash Hill Rd

Sales La

Sykehouse Lock Bridge (swing)

Clay Dike

Manor Farm

New Junction Canal

Clay Bridge

Bel Gn

Little Fen Field

Hannes Ing Covert

Smallhedge Rein

Smitchells La

Smallhedge Farm

Fosterthwaite Farm

Hushells La

Fishlake Covert

Glebe Farm

Fosterhouses

Westfield House

New House Farm

Kirkhouse Green Gorse

Westfield Bridge House

Mill Field

Neville La

Hacienda Fun Pk

Neville Hall

Westfield La

Mill Field Rd

East Field Rd

7 ◀   ▲ **1**

A   B   C   D   E   F

8

New Ings

Bank House

Reedholme Common   Reedholme

Sykehouse Main Drain

Wood Villa

REEDHOLME LA

Oak Tree Farm

MARSH HILL LA

PINCHEON GREEN LA

Banks Farm

Pincheon Green Farm

7

Pincheon Green

Dikes Marsh Farm

17

Durham's Warping Drain

Warwick Field Drain

6

Ivy House Farm

Bank Side Farm

HADDS LA

RUDGATE LA

Warwick Field

Green Farm

Hadds

Wormley Hill Farm

WORMLEY HILL LA

Wormley Hill

5

SELBY RD

16

Tideworth Hague Gorse

4

Fen Carr

BLACK SYKE LA

Low Ings

HADDS NOOK RD

Marsh Farm

COWICK RD

River Don

NORTH COMMON RD

3

The Elms

GEESENESS LA

North Common

Poplars Farm

15

WENCHURST LA

HASPELLS LA

Fern Farm

2

SORRELL LA

Thorne Round Wlk

WOOD LA

FERRY RD

LAND ENDS RD

HAYES LA

Sandhall Farm

Thorninghurst Farm

Sewage Works

Field House Farm

PINFOLD LA

Hangsman Hill

LOWHILL

Junction 6

A614

1

MILL FIELD RD

Grange Farm

QUAYSIDE

WATERSIDE RD

QUAY RD

M18

Gyme

14

Hayes

SOUR LA

PH

65   A   B   66   C   D   67   E   F

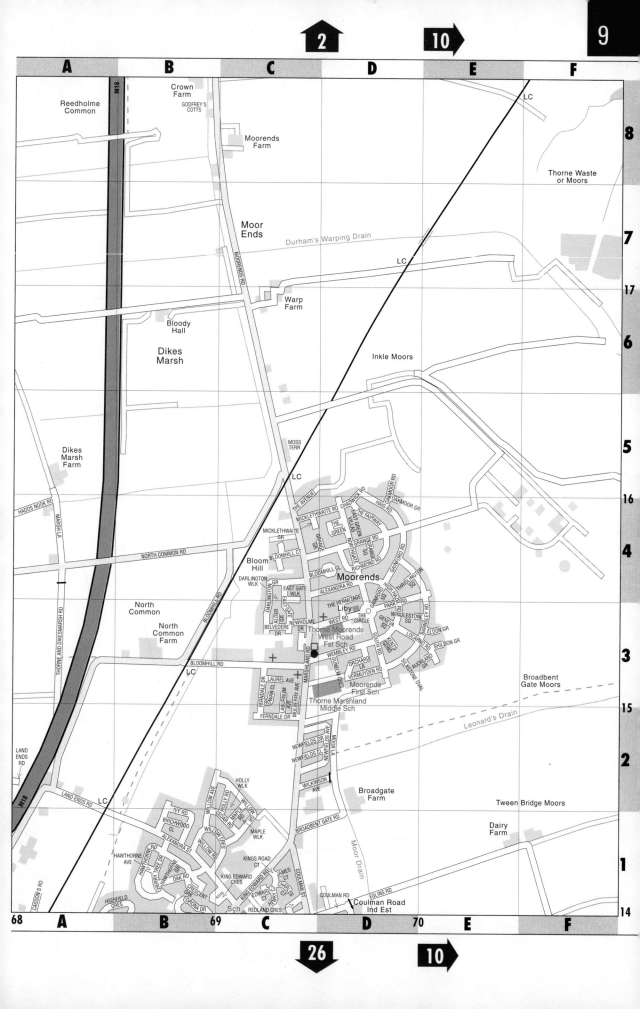

9

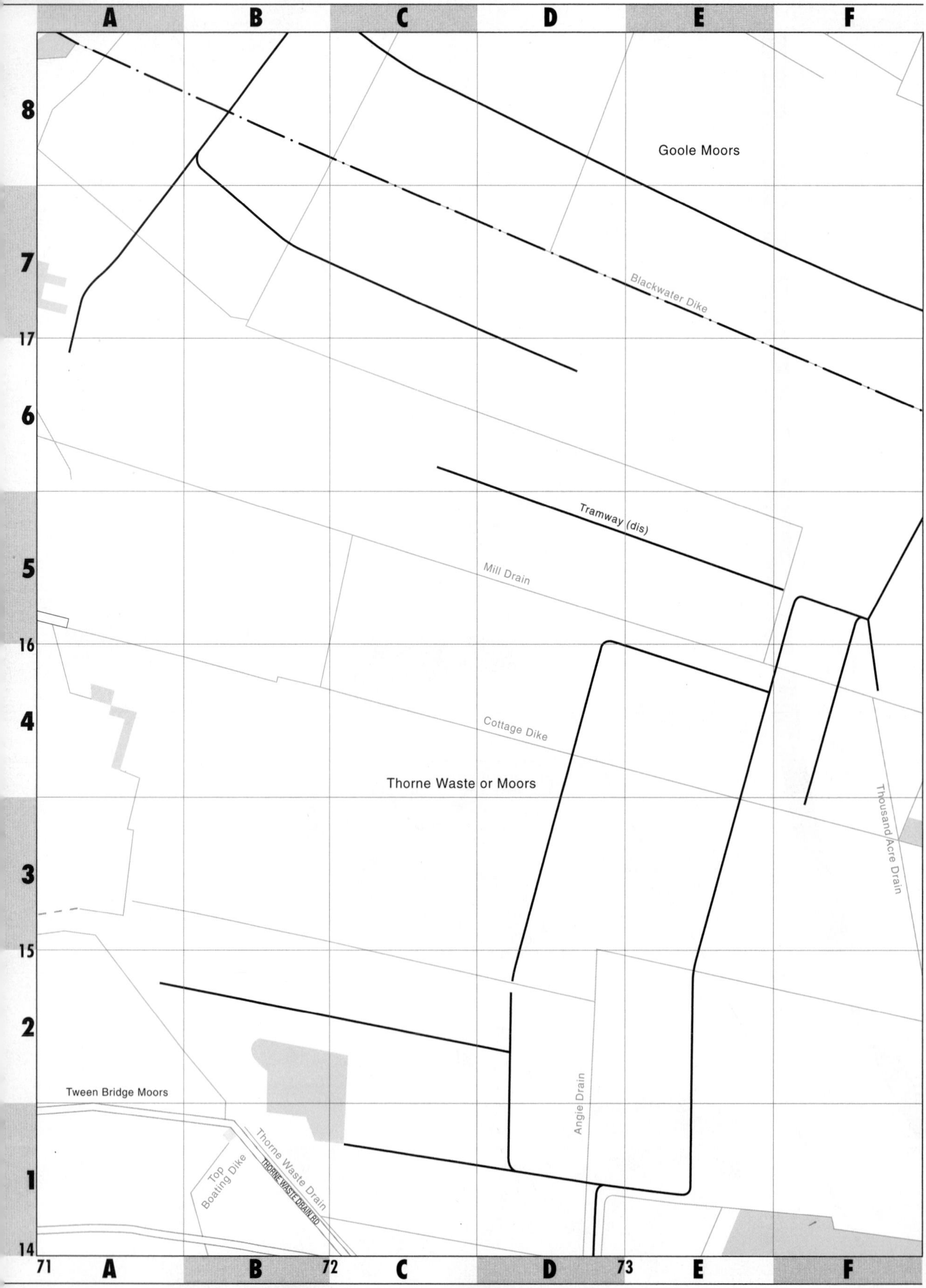
A
B
C
D
E
F
8
7
17
6
5
16
4
3
15
2
1
14
71
72
73
Goole Moors
Blackwater Dike
Tramway (dis)
Mill Drain
Cottage Dike
Thorne Waste or Moors
Thousand Acre Drain
Angie Drain
Tween Bridge Moors
Top Boating Dike
Thorne Waste Drain
THORNE WASTE DRAIN RD

9
27

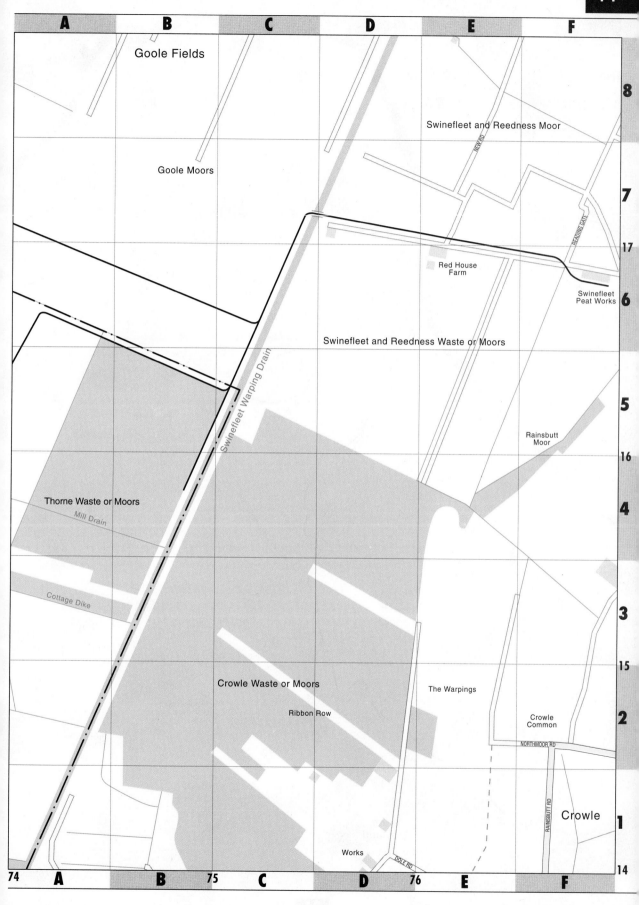

Goole Fields

Swinefleet and Reedness Moor

Goole Moors

Red House
Farm

Swinefleet
Peat Works

Swinefleet and Reedness Waste or Moors

Rainsbutt
Moor

Thorne Waste or Moors

Mill Drain

Cottage Dike

Crowle Waste or Moors

The Warpings

Ribbon Row

Crowle
Common

NORTHMOOR RD

Crowle

Works

DOLE RD

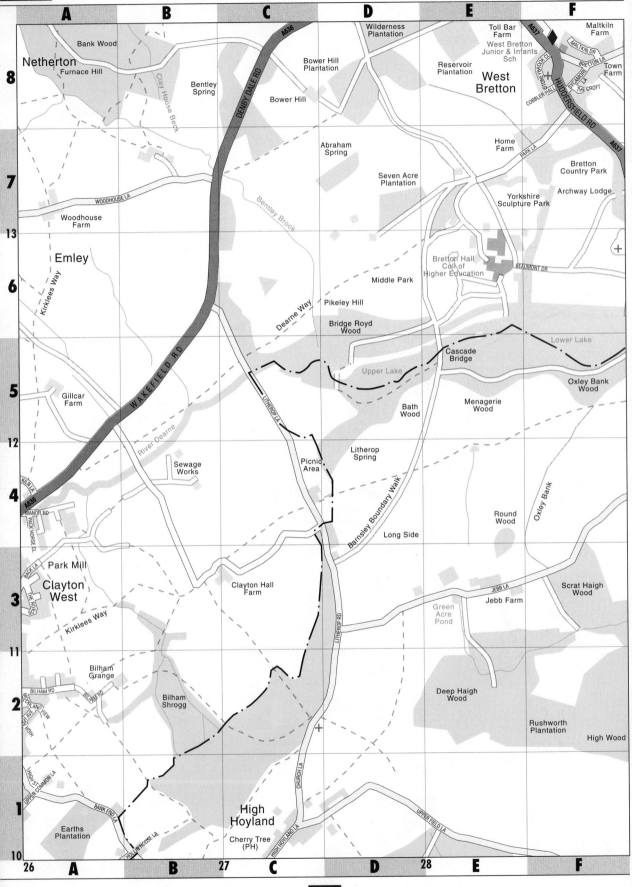

A · B · C · D · E · F

8 Netherton
Bank Wood
Furnace Hill
Clay House Beck
Bentley Spring
DENBY DALE RD
A636
Bower Hill Plantation
Bower Hill
Wilderness Plantation
Reservoir Plantation
Toll Bar Farm
West Bretton Junior & Infants Sch
Maltkiln Farm
A637
MALTKIN DR
BRETTON LA
Town Farm
West Bretton
COBBLER HALL
STONEY BROOK CL
HUDDERSFIELD RD
SYCAMORE LA
THE CROFT

7 WOODHOUSE LA
Abraham Spring
Seven Acre Plantation
A636
Home Farm
PARK LA
Bretton Country Park
Archway Lodge
A637

13 Woodhouse Farm
Bentley Brook
Yorkshire Sculpture Park

6 Emley
Kirklees Way
WAKEFIELD RD
Middle Park
Dearne Way
Pikeley Hill
Bridge Royd Wood
Bretton Hall Coll of Higher Education
BEAUMONT DR

Lower Lake
Cascade Bridge
Upper Lake
Oxley Bank Wood

5 Gillcar Farm
LITHEROP LA
Bath Wood
Menagerie Wood

12 River Dearne
Picnic Area
Litherop Spring
Barnsley Boundary Walk
Oxley Bank

4 KILN LA
A636
MANOR RD
PACK HORSE CL
Sewage Works
Long Side
Round Wood

3 BACK LA
THE HOLLS
Park Mill
Clayton West
Kirklees Way
Clayton Hall Farm
LITHEROP RD
Green Acre Pond
JEBB LA
Jebb Farm
Scrat Haigh Wood

11 Bilham Grange
BILHAM RD
BILHAM RD
Bilham Shrogg
Deep Haigh Wood

2 HIGH ST
MOORLAND VIEW
Rushworth Plantation
High Wood

1 UPPER COMMON LA
HIGH ST
BANK END LA
High Hoyland
CHURCH LA
HIGH HOYLAND LA
UPPER FIELD LA

10 Earths Plantation
HOLLINHOUSE LA
Cherry Tree (PH)

26 · A · B · 27 · C · D · 28 · E · F

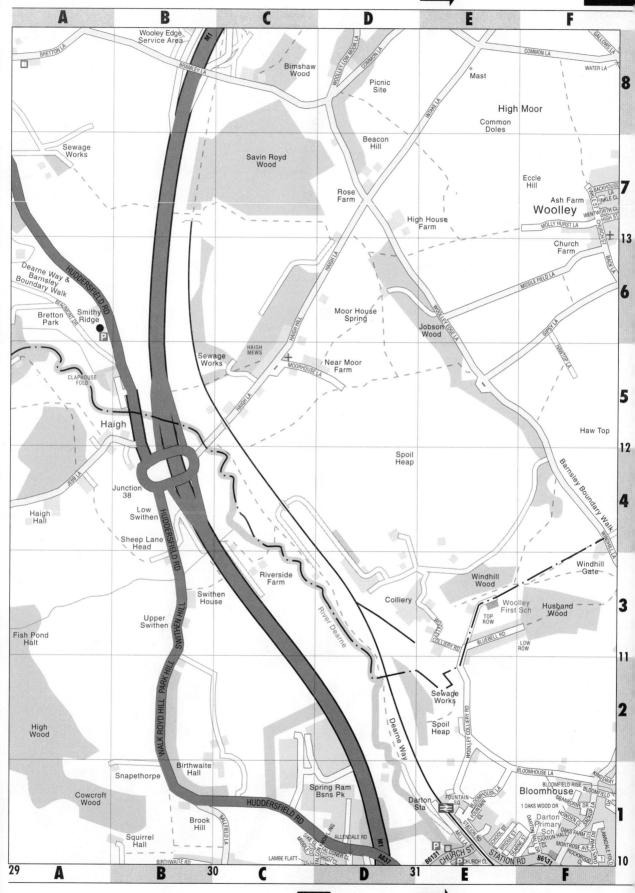

A   B   C   D   E   F

Bretton La
Wooley Edge Service Area
Bramley La
Bimshaw Wood
Woolley Low Moor La
Common La
Common La
Water La
Gallows La
Picnic Site
Mast
8
High Moor
Common Doles
Sewage Works
Savin Royd Wood
Intake La
Beacon Hill
Eccle Hill
Backhouse La
Hales St
Finkle Cl
7
Rose Farm
High House Farm
Ash Farm
Woolley
Wentworth Cl
Molly Hurst La
High St
Church St
13
Dearne Way & Barnsley Boundary Walk
Haigh La
Church Farm
Back La
Beaumont Dr
Huddersfield Rd
Bretton Park
Smithy Ridge
P
Moor House Spring
Woolley Edge La
Middle Field La
6
Jobson Wood
Gipsy La
Haigh Mews
Haigh La
Haigh Hill
Sewage Works
Near Moor Farm
Moorhouse La
Haw Top
5
Claphouse Fold
Haigh
Spoil Heap
12
Barnsley Boundary Walk
Jebb La
Junction 38
Low Swithen
Haigh Hall
Windhill La
Windhill Gate
4
Sheep Lane Head
Huddersfield Rd
Swithen Hill
Riverside Farm
Windhill Wood
Husband Wood
3
Fish Pond Halt
Upper Swithen
Swithen House
River Dearne
Colliery
Woolley First Sch
Woolley Colliery Rd
Bluebell Rd
Top Row
Low Row
High Wood
Walk Royd Hill
Park Hill
Swithen Hill
Dearne Way
Sewage Works
Woolley Colliery Rd
11
Spoil Heap
2
Cowcroft Wood
Snapethorpe
Birthwaite Hall
Spring Ram Bsns Pk
Darton Sta
Bloomhouse La
Bloomfield Rise
Bloomhouse
Kingsway
Bloomfield Cl
1
Huddersfield Rd
Fountain
Fountain La
Granborne Dr
1 Oaks Wood Dr
Howden Cl
Oaks Farm Cl Dr
Lawndale Fold
Squirrel Hall
Brook Hill
Balfield La
Allendale Rd
Middle Cl
Falconer Cl
Spring
High Cl
Mill La
Station Rd
School St
Bridge St
Dearne St
Darton Hall Cl
Darton Primary Sch
Montrose Ave
Rockwood Cl
10
Lambe Flatt
Church Cl
B6131
Church St
P
Station Rd
B6131
29   A   B   30   C   D   31   E   F   10

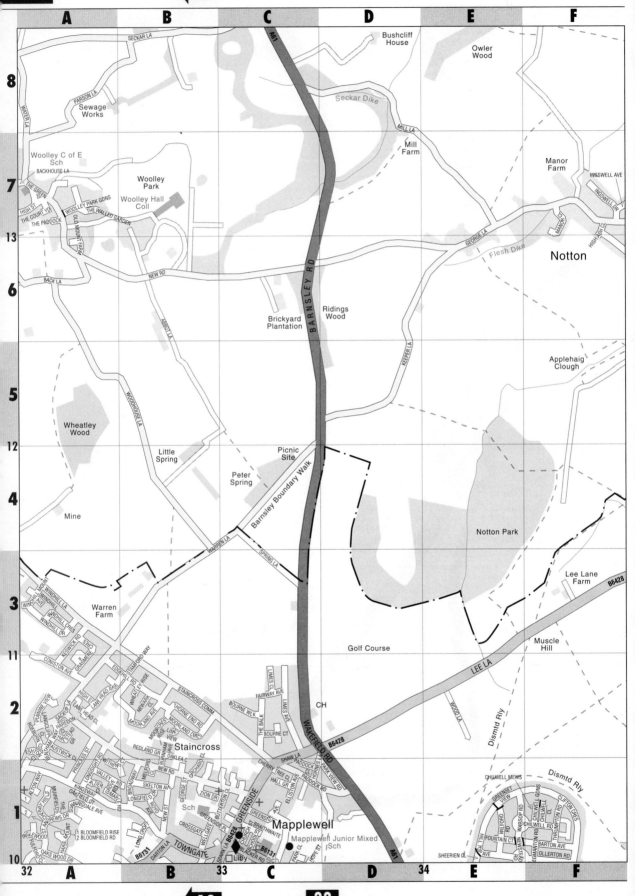

ROYSTON

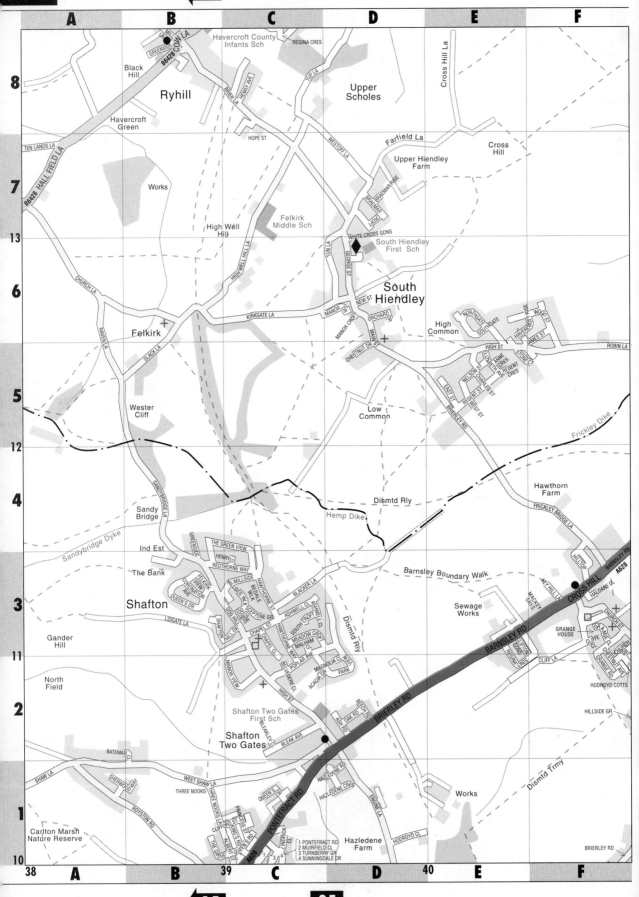

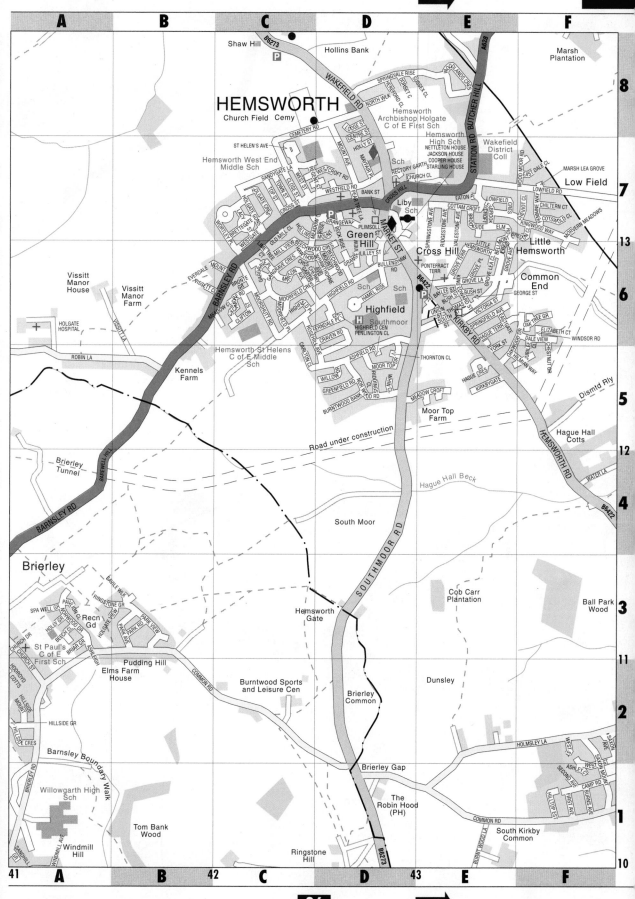

HEMSWORTH

Brierley

17

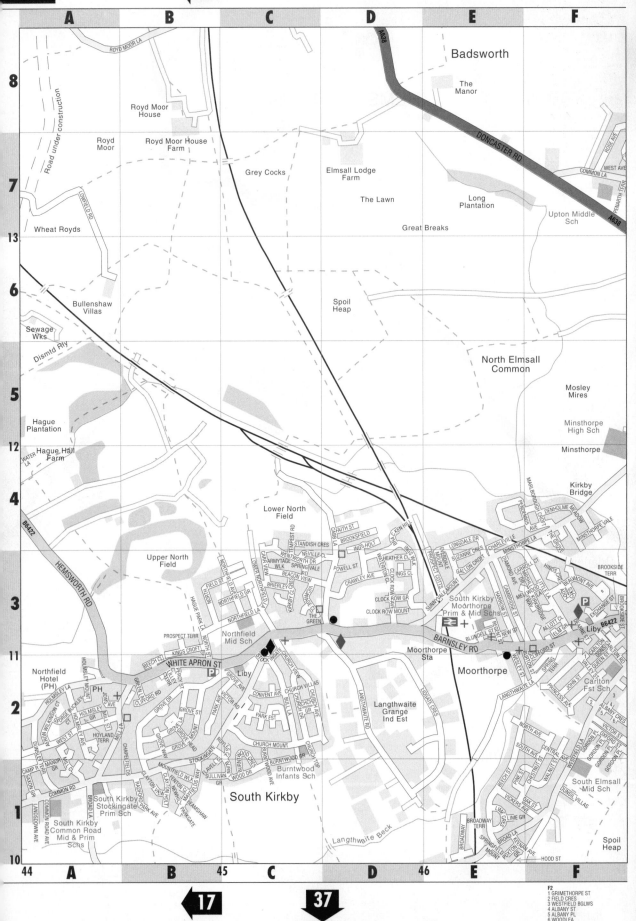

A B C D E F

8

7

13

6

5

12

4

3

11

2

1

10

44 A 45 B C 46 D E F

17
37

Badsworth

The Manor

DONCASTER RD

Royd Moor House

Royd Moor

Royd Moor House Farm

Grey Cocks

Elmsall Lodge Farm

The Lawn

Long Plantation

Upton Middle Sch

A638

WEST AVE
COMMON LA
PENARTH TERR
ROSS AVE

Wheat Royds

Road under construction

ROYD MOOR LA

LOWFIELD RD

Great Breaks

Spoil Heap

North Elmsall Common

Mosley Mires

Minsthorpe High Sch

Minsthorpe

Bullenshaw Villas

Sewage Wks

Dismtd Rly

Hague Plantation

Hague Hall Farm

WATER LA

B6422

HEMSWORTH RD

Kirkby Bridge

Lower North Field

Upper North Field

FAITH ST
STANDISH CRES
BROOKSFIELD
INGS HOLT
KEN HILL
INGS WLK
WEATHER CL
INGS CL
CARR LA
NEVILLE CL
WENTWORTH DR
ARMYTAGE WLK
SPRING VALE
POWELL ST
CRAWLEY AVE
CLOCK ROW AVE
CLOCK ROW GR
CLOCK ROW MOUNT
SUNNYVALE MOUNT
BARNSLEY RD

LONGDALE DR
CHARLEVILLE
MINSTHORPE LA
SUZANNE CRES
GALLON CROFT
PROSPECT COTTS
RIVENDALE
MEDINA
CAMBRIDGE ST
CARROLL CT
DIAMOND AVE
MELWOOD CL
NORTHRIDGE
HARRON ST
CAMBRIDGE ST
BLUNDELL CT
REGENT ST
ALLOTT CL
MARLBOROUGH CROFT
FERNDINGS AVE
DENHOLME AVE
MINSTHORPE VALE
THE GROVE
BROADMEAD
HINDS CRES
NORBRIDGE
BEAUMONT AVE
EXCHANGE ST
BROOKSIDE TERR
BROWNSMITH
B6422

South Kirkby Moorthorpe Prim & Mid Schs

Moorthorpe Sta

Moorthorpe

Liby

Northfield Mid Sch

NORTHFIELD GR
NORTHFIELD LA
HAGUE PARK LA
KINGS CROFT
PROSPECT TERR
BEECH CL
LOWER NORTHFIELD LA
TEMPEST RD
CARR VIEW
KIRKBY CRES
BRIERLEY
BEACON VIEW
VICTORIA ST
THE GREEN

Northfield Hotel (PH)

WHITE APRON ST

Liby

HOLMSLEY LA
LEDGER BUCKLEY
HOLMSLEY MOUNT
LEDSON CT
HOLMSLEY
HURON
JOHN AVE
GREEN LA
CLIFFORD RD
GROVE DR
KINGS TERR
PERCY ST
PARK AVE
VICTOR RD
GROVE ST
CONVENT AVE
CHURCH VILLAS
BULLA
CHURCH TERR
BLOCK WALK
CHURCH LA

NORTHFIELD AVE

Langthwaite Grange Ind Est

PH
WEST LA
HOYLAND TERR
CHAPELFIELDS
MOUNTFIELD WLK
GROVE WAY
GROVE END
STOCKINGATE
FENTON CL
CLAYTON CT
FLAVELL CL
SULLIVAN GR
WOOD CL
WOOD DR
ROYAL CL
PARK EST
CHURCH MOUNT
BURNTWOOD AVE
BURNTWOOD GR
LANGTHWAITE LA
LIDGATE CRES

Burntwood Infants Sch

South Kirkby

Carlton Fst Sch

South Elmsall Mid Sch

NORTH AVE
SOUTH AVE
CENTRAL AVE
BEECH ST
PINE ST
CHESTNUT ST
WALNUT ST
OAK ST
VICKERS AVE
LILAC GR
LIME GR
CRAB TREE AVE
JOHN ST
QUEEN ST
CARLTON ST
BURTON ST
CLIFFORD ST
PRINCESS AVE
WESLEY ST
SPRING TERR
ALBANY CRES
VICTOR ST
GORDON ST
DUNSIL VILLAS

CAMP RD
MANOR GR
MILL LA
SAXON GR
DANSLEY GR
COMMON RD
LANDSDOWN AVE
COMMON ROAD AVE
BROAD LA
RADFORD PARK AVE
STOCKINGATE
BROAD LA
TREAMSHAW
TERRYWILL
FIRGATE

South Kirkby Stockingate Prim Sch

South Kirkby Common Road Mid & Prim Schs

Langthwaite Beck

BROADWAY
BROADWAY TERR
SPRINGFIELD MOUNT
POXTON GR
KERNHAM GR
HOOD ST

Spoil Heap

F2
1 GRIMETHORPE ST
2 FIELD CRES
3 WESTFIELD BGLWS
4 ALBANY ST
5 ALBANY PL
6 WOODLEA

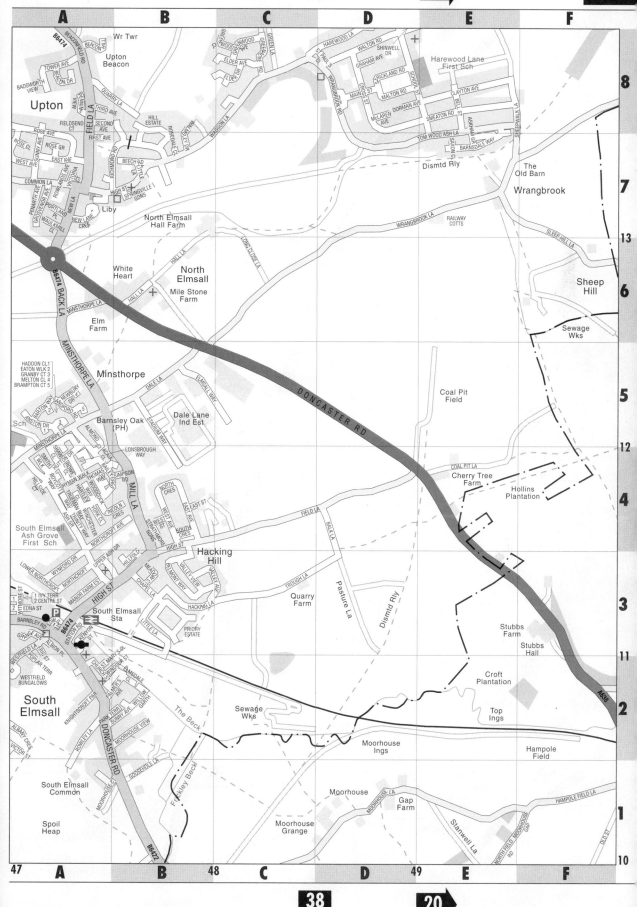

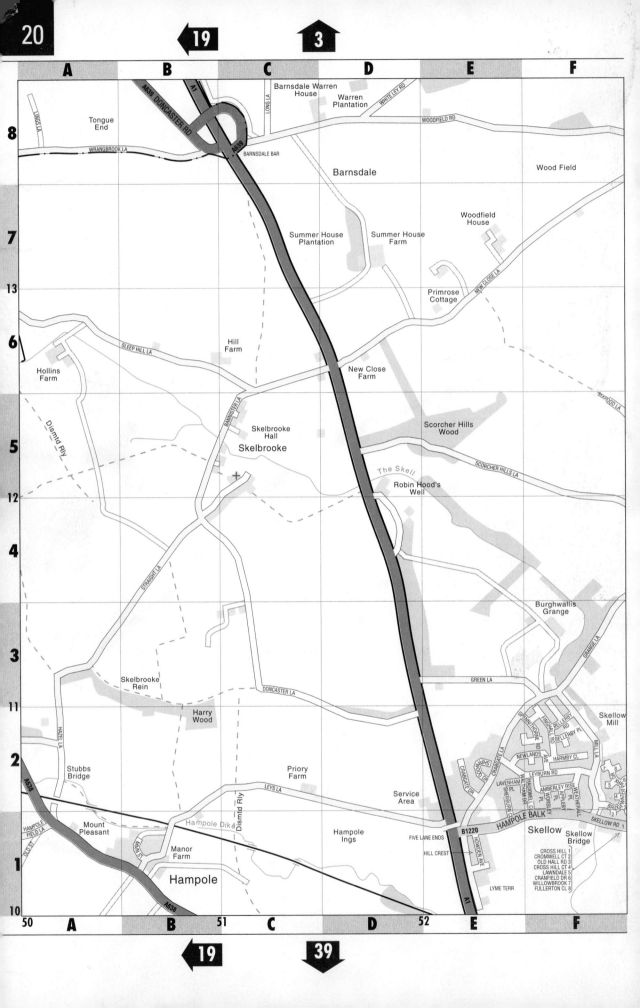

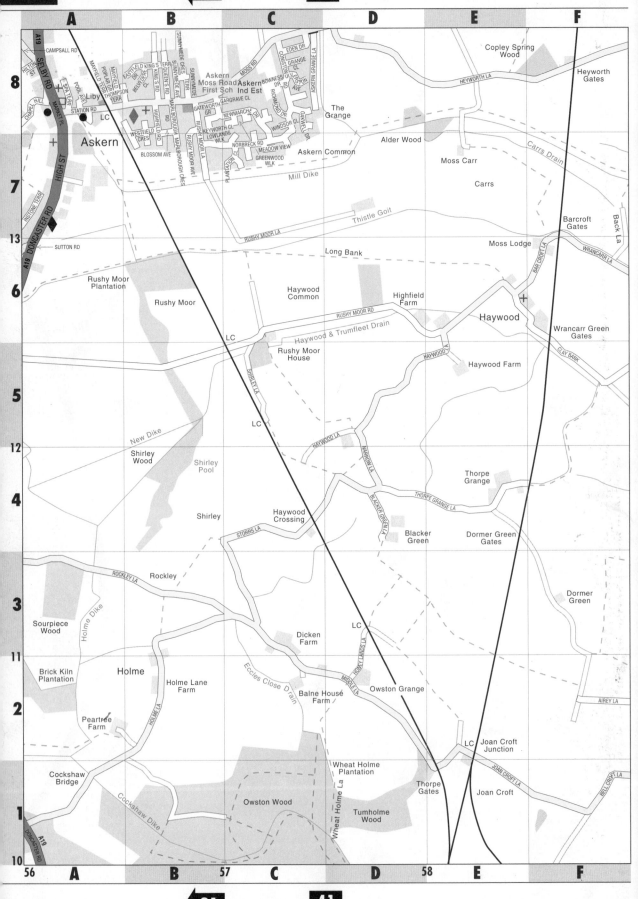

A B C D E F

8
7
13
6
5
12
4
3
11
2
1
10

CAMPSALL RD
SELBY RD
HILTON ST
A19
CHAPEL HILL
MARKET PL
STATION RD
POOL AVE
SPA TERR
Liby
LC
+
Askern
WESTFIELD CRES
BLOSSOM AVE
EASTFIELD DR
MAYFIELD TERR
POPLAR GR
MAYFIELD DR
THOMPSON TERR
KING'S TERR
KING'S RD
BELVEDERE CL
QUEEN'S RD
SUNNYMEDE TERR
SUNNYMEDE AVE
SUNNYMEDE CRES
MARLBOROUGH RD
HIGHFIELD RD
RUSHY MOOR LA
MARLBOROUGH CRES
PLANTATION
GATEWORTH GR
NEWMARCHE DR
KEYWORTH CL
LOWLANDS WLK
NORBRECK RD
MEADOW VIEW
GREENWOOD WLK
Askern Moss Road First Sch Ind Est
MOSS RD
EDEN DR
GRANGE CL
CONISTON DR
BOWNESS DR
RICHMOND DR
CRISPON AVE
OAKWELL DR
ASKERN GRANGE LA
CARGRAVE CL
WINDSOR DR
The Grange
Askern Common
Alder Wood
Moss Carr
Carrs
Copley Spring Wood
HEYWORTH LA
Heyworth Gates
Carrs Drain
Back La
Barcroft Gates
Moss Lodge
WRANCARR LA
BAR CROFT LA
INSTONE TERR
A19 DONCASTER RD
SUTTON RD
Mill Dike
Thistle Golf
RUSHY MOOR LA
Long Bank
Rushy Moor Plantation
Rushy Moor
Haywood Common
RUSHY MOOR RD
Highfield Farm
Haywood
Wrancarr Green Gates
CLAY BANK
+
LC
SHIRLEY LA
Haywood & Trumfleet Drain
Rushy Moor House
HAYWOOD LA
Haywood Farm
LC
New Dike
Shirley Wood
Shirley Pool
HAYWOOD LA
NARROW LA
Thorpe Grange
Shirley
Haywood Crossing
STORRS LA
BLACKER GREEN LA
THORPE GRANGE LA
Blacker Green
Dormer Green Gates
ROCKLEY LA
Rockley
Dormer Green
Sourpiece Wood
HOLME DIKE
Brick Kiln Plantation
Holme
Holme Lane Farm
HOLME LA
Dicken Farm
ECCLES CLOSE DRAIN
LC
HONEY LANDS LA
MIDDLE LA
AIREY LA
Peartree Farm
Balne House Farm
Owston Grange
LC
Joan Croft Junction
Cockshaw Bridge
COCKSHAW DIKE
Wheat Holme Plantation
WHEAT HOLME LA
Thorpe Gates
JOAN CROFT LA
Joan Croft
BELL CROFT LA
A19 DONCASTER RD
Owston Wood
Tumholme Wood

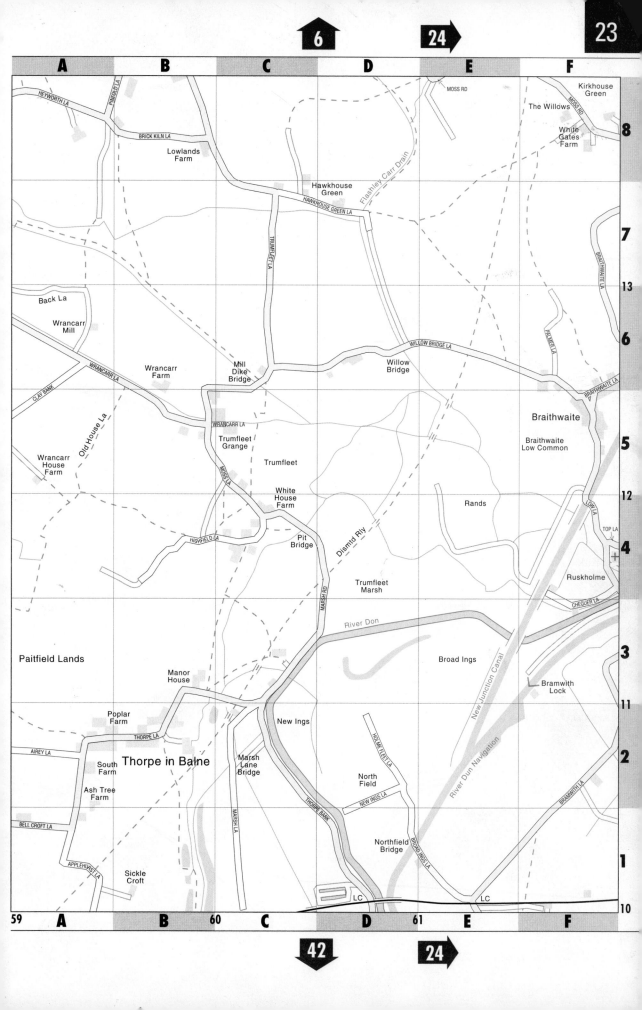

A   B   C   D   E   F

HEYWORTH LA
PINFOLD LA
BRICK KILN LA
Lowlands Farm

MOSS RD
The Willows
Kirkhouse Green
White Gates Farm

Hawkhouse Green
HAWKHOUSE GREEN LA

Flashley Carr Drain

8

TRUMFLEET LA

7

BRAITHWAITE LA

13

Back La
Wrancarr Mill

WRANCARR LA
Wrancarr Farm

Mill Dike Bridge

WILLOW BRIDGE LA

Willow Bridge

PALMER LA

6

CLAY BANK

Old House La

Wrancarr House Farm

WRANCARR LA
Trumfleet Grange

Trumfleet

Braithwaite
Braithwaite Low Common

BRAITHWAITE LA

5

MOSS LA

White House Farm

Rands

LOW LA

12

TOP LA

HIGHFIELD LA

Pit Bridge

Dismtd Rly

Trumfleet Marsh

Ruskholme

4

CHEQUER LA

Paitfield Lands

Manor House

River Don

Broad Ings

New Junction Canal

Bramwith Lock

3

Poplar Farm
THORPE LA

New Ings

11

AIREY LA

Thorpe in Balne

South Farm

Marsh Lane Bridge

HOLME FLEET LA

River Dun Navigation

BRAMWITH LA

2

Ash Tree Farm

MARSH LA

North Field

NEW INGS LA

BELL CROFT LA

THORPE BANK

BROAD INGS LA

1

APPLEHURST LA

Sickle Croft

Northfield Bridge

LC
LC
10

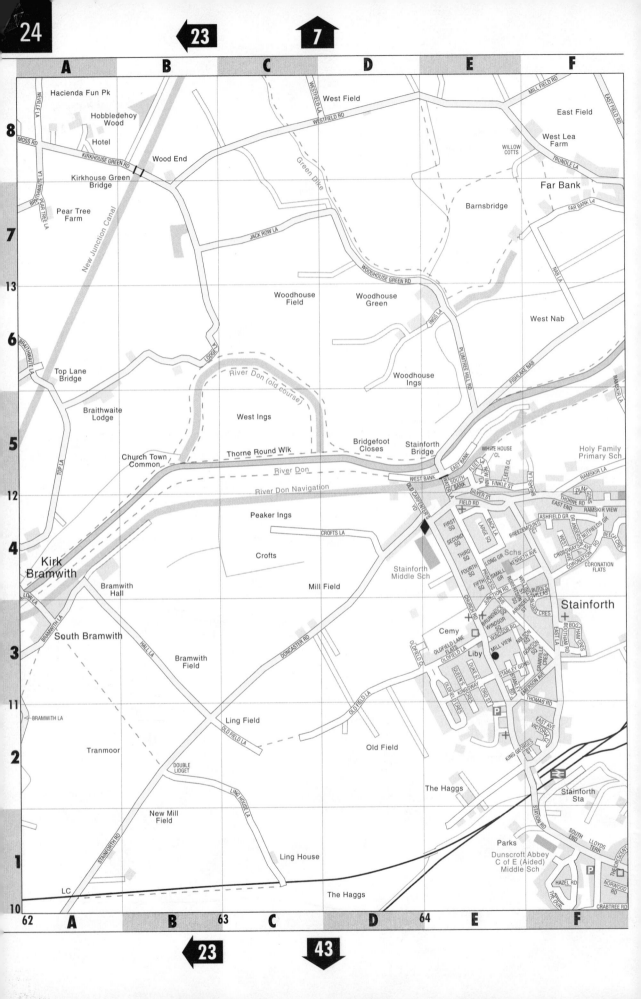

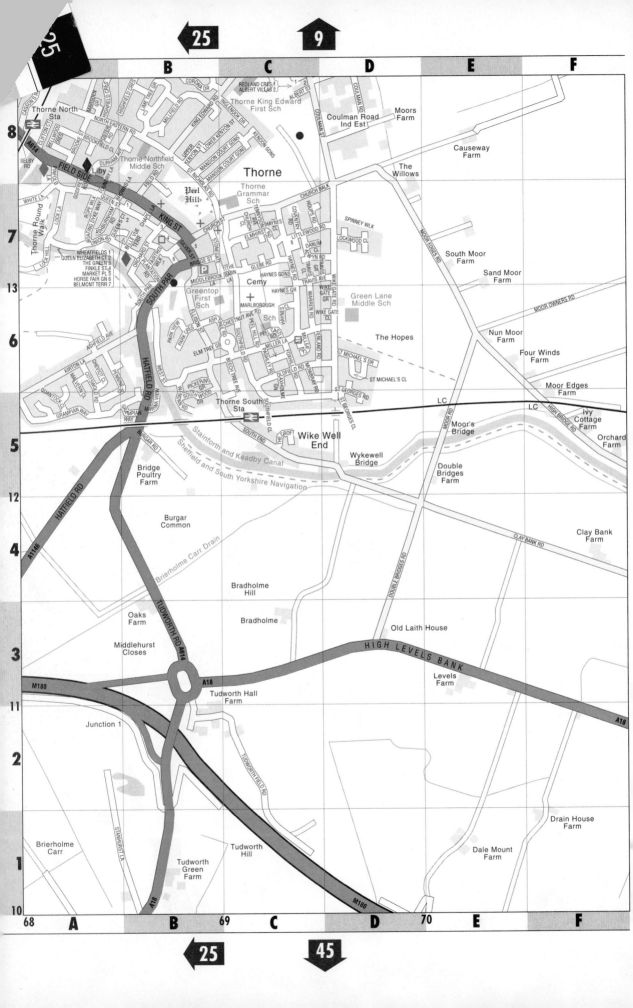

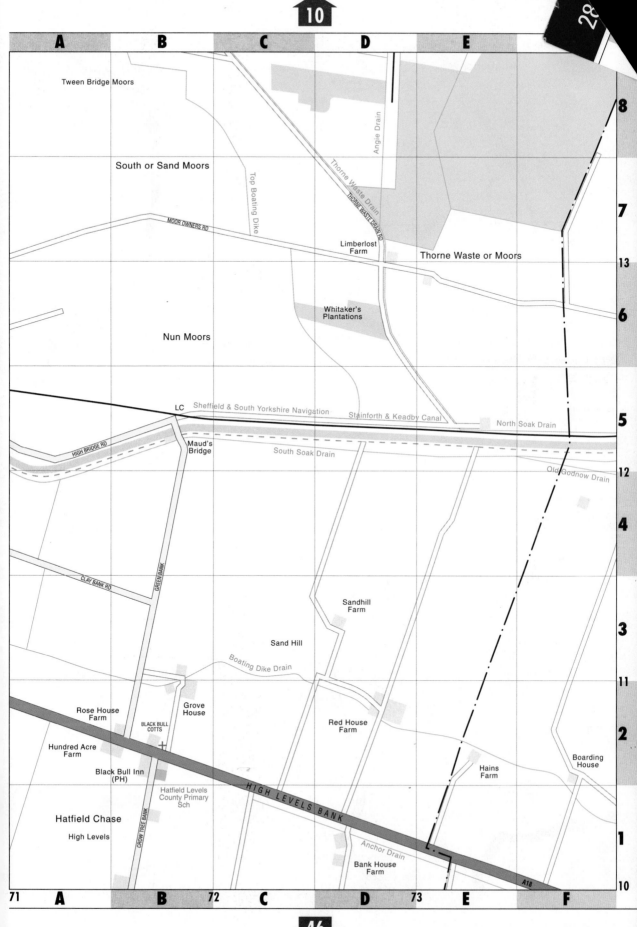

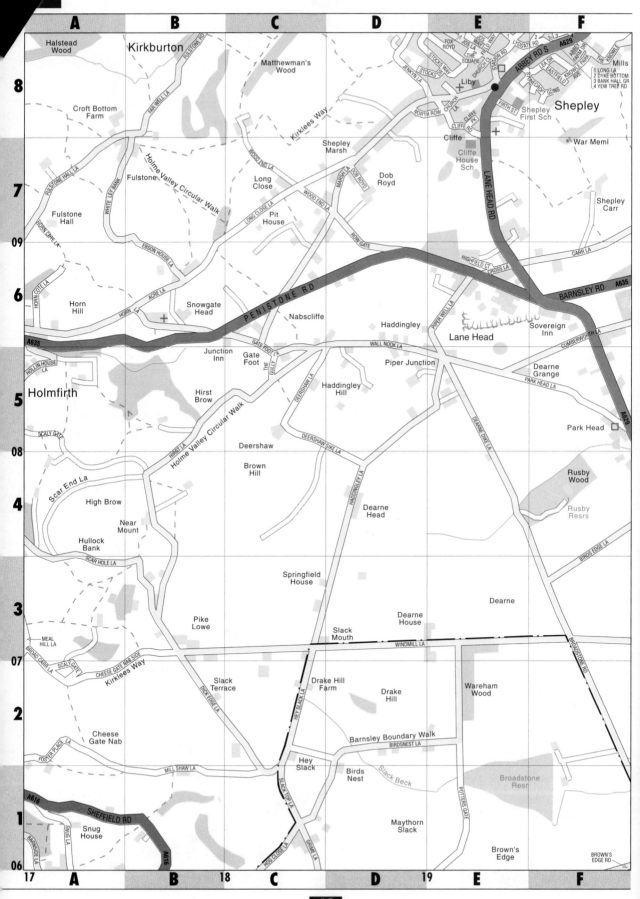

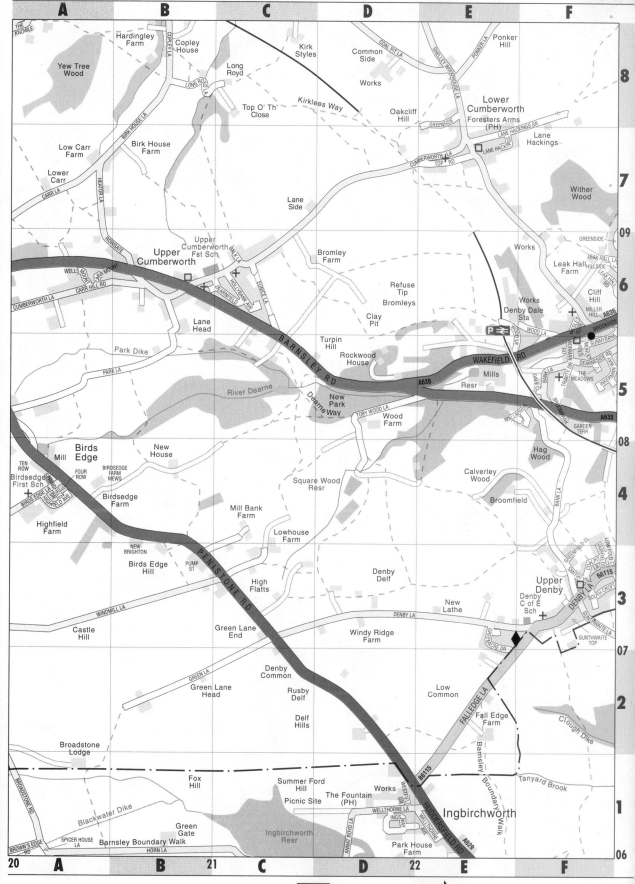

THE KNOWLE

Yew Tree Wood

Hardingley Farm

Copley House

Kirk Styles

Long Royd

Common Side

Works

COAL PIT LA

Ponker Hill

Lower Cumberworth

Foresters Arms (PH)

Lane Hackin

Lane Hackings

SHELLEY WOODHOUSE LA

PONKER LA

GREENSIDE

Oakcliff Hill

Kirklees Way

Top O' Th' Close

BIRK HOUSE LA

COPLEY LA

LONG ROYD LA

Low Carr Farm

Birk House Farm

Lower Carr

CARR LA

HEATON LA

RONGATE

CUMBERWORTH LA TOP RD

Wither Wood

GREENSIDE

LEAK HALL LA

Lane Side

Upper Cumberworth

Upper Cumberworth Fst Sch

Bromley Farm

HILLSIDE

Leak Hall Farm

LEAK HALL RD

Cliff Hill

WELLS MOUNT

CARR MOUNT

CARR HILL RD

BALK LA

DEARNFIELD

HOLLYBANK AVE

EUNICE LA

Works

MILLER HILL

A636

CUMBERWORTH LA

Refuse Tip Bromleys

Works

Denby Dale Sta

SUNNYBANK

BROOKSIDE

Lane Head

Clay Pit

NORMAN RD

TRINITY DR

DEARNESIDE RD

WESLEY

WOOD LA

Park Dike

BARNSLEY RD

Turpin Hill

Rockwood House

A636

Resr

Mills

WAKEFIELD RD

INKERMAN

THE MEADOWS

PARK LA

River Dearne

DEARNE WAY

New Park Way

TOBY WOOD LA

Wood Farm

WALLROYDE

DALE CL

BROOMLIN

GARDEN TERR

A635

A635

TEN ROW

Mill

Birds Edge

New House

BIRDSEDGE FARM MEWS

Square Wood Resr

Calverley Wood

Hag Wood

Broomfield

BANK LA

FOUR ROW

Birdsedge First Sch

SPRINGFIELD TER

HIGHFIELD AVE

Birdsedge Farm

Mill Bank Farm

Lowhouse Farm

Denby Delf

GREENFIELD CL

LOW FOLD

COLD

PARK VIEW

BIRDS EDGE LA

Highfield Farm

NEW BRIGHTON

Birds Edge Hill

PUMP ST

PENISTONE RD

High Flatts

SMITHY

DENBY LA

Upper Denby

SOUTH CROFT

B6115

GUNTHWAITE LA

Denby C of E Sch

New Lathe

Windy Ridge Farm

GUNTHWAITE TOP

WINDMILL LA

Castle Hill

Green Lane End

GREEN LA

Green Lane Head

Denby Common

Rusby Delf

Delf Hills

Low Common

GREENACRE DR

FALLEDGE LA

Fall Edge Farm

Clough Dike

Broadstone Lodge

Fox Hill

Summer Ford Hill

Picnic Site

The Fountain (PH)

Works

WESTFIELD GR

B6115

Barnsley Boundary Walk

Tanyard Brook

BROADSTONE RD

Blackwater Dike

Green Gate

SPICER HOUSE LA

Barnsley Boundary Walk

HORN LA

Ingbirchworth Resr

WELLTHORNE LA

ANNAT ROYD LA

INGS WAY

WELLTHORNE AVE

Park House Farm

HUDDERSFIELD RD

A629

Ingbirchworth

BROWN'S EDGE RD

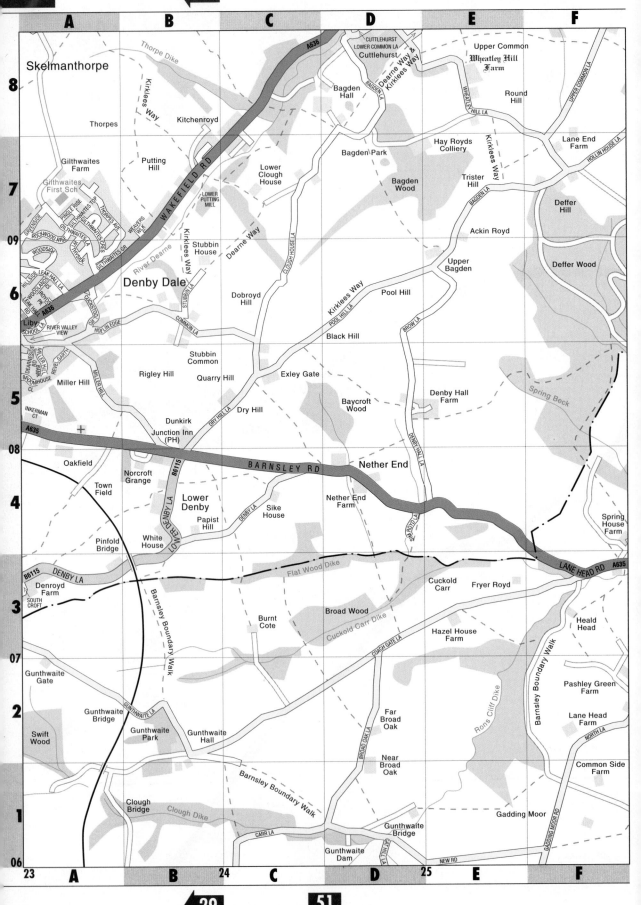

Skelmanthorpe

Thorpe Dike

Kirklees Way

Thorpes

Kitchenroyd

Putting Hill

Gilthwaites Farm

Gilthwaites First Sch

PINGLE RISE
THORPES AVE
GILTHWAITES TOP
GILTHWAITES LA
GILTHWAITES CRES
WEAVERS WLK
GILTHWAITES GR

GREENSIDE
ROCK-WOOD RD
SOUTHSIDE
WOODSIDE

LEAK HALL LA
WOODLANDS
ROYDE PK
CLARKSON ST
HOLLIN EDGE
HILLSIDE
OAK HILL LA
A636

River Dearne

Denby Dale

Liby
SCHOOL
RIVER VALLEY VIEW

MILLER HILL
BANK
REEVE GARTH
DEARNESIDE
BROOMHOUSE
CL

INKERMAN CT

Miller Hill

A635

WAKEFIELD RD

A636

Cuttlehurst

CUTTLEHURST
LOWER COMMON LA
Cuttlehurst

Dearne Way & Kirklees Way

Upper Common

Wheatley Hill Farm

Bagden Hall

Bagden Park

Round Hill

Lower Clough House

Bagden Wood

Hay Royds Colliery

Trister Hill

Lane End Farm

HOLLIN HOUSE LA

UPPER COMMON LA

WHEATLEY HILL LA

Deffer Hill

Deffer Wood

Ackin Royd

Upper Bagden

Dearne Way

Kirklees Way

Stubbin House

LOWER PUTTING MILL

KIRKLEES WAY

STUBBIN

CLOUGH HOUSE LA

Dobroyd Hill

Kirklees Way

Pool Hill

POOL HILL LA

BAGDEN LA

KIRKLEES WAY

BROW LA

COMMON LA

Black Hill

Stubbin Common

Rigley Hill

Quarry Hill

Exley Gate

DRY HILL LA

Dry Hill

Baycroft Wood

Denby Hall Farm

Spring Beck

A635

BARNSLEY RD

Dunkirk Junction Inn (PH)

Nether End

DENBY HALL LA

Oakfield

Town Field

Norcroft Grange

Lower Denby

B6115

Papist Hill

White House

Pinfold Bridge

LOWER DENBY LA

DENBY LA

Sike House

Nether End Farm

SIKE ROYD LA

Spring House Farm

LANE HEAD RD

A635

B6115

DENBY LA

Denroyd Farm

SOUTH CROFT

Barnsley Boundary Walk

Flat Wood Dike

Cuckold Carr

Fryer Royd

Heald Head

Gunthwaite Gate

Burnt Cote

Broad Wood

Cuckold Carr Dike

Hazel House Farm

Barnsley Boundary Walk

Pashley Green Farm

Swift Wood

Gunthwaite Bridge

Gunthwaite Park

Gunthwaite Hall

GUNTHWAITE LA

Barnsley Boundary Walk

Far Broad Oak

Near Broad Oak

Rons Cliff Dike

BROAD OAK LA

COACH GATE LA

Lane Head Farm

NORTH LA

Common Side Farm

Clough Bridge

Clough Dike

Barnsley Boundary Walk

CARR LA

Gunthwaite Dam

Gunthwaite Bridge

CAT HILL LA

NEW RD

Gadding Moor

GADDING MOOR RD

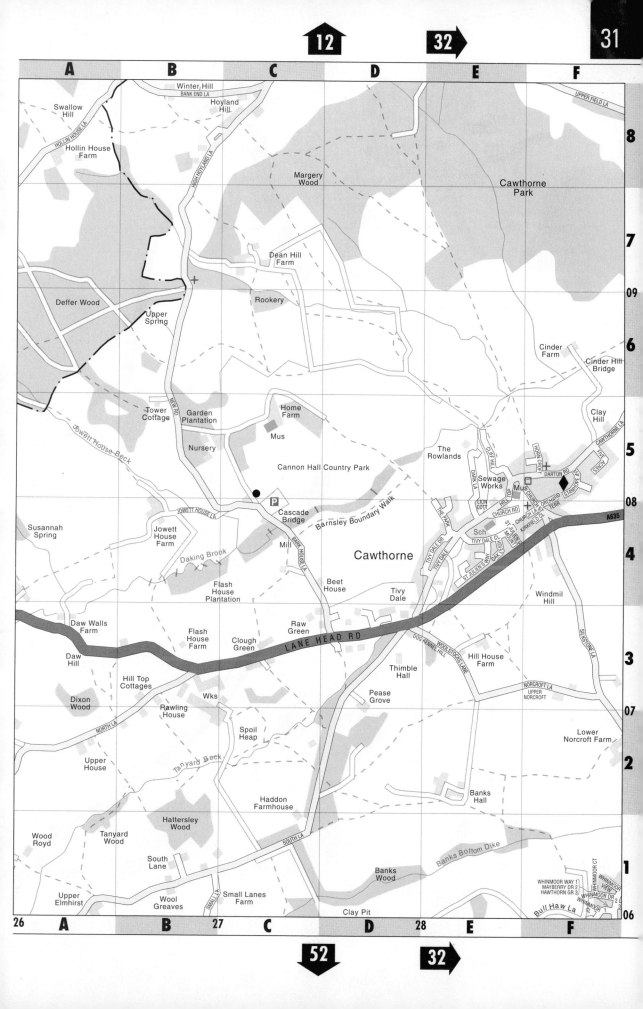

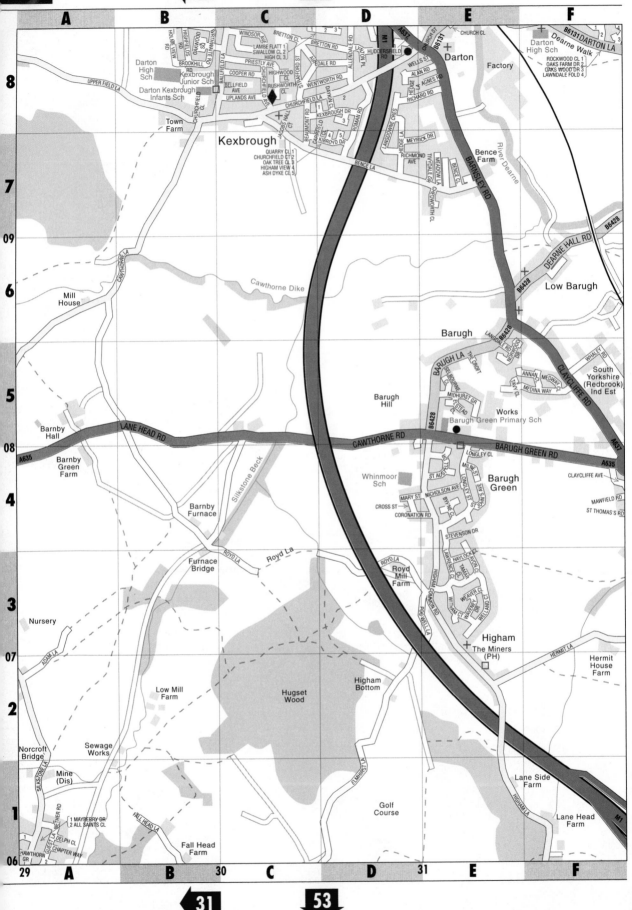

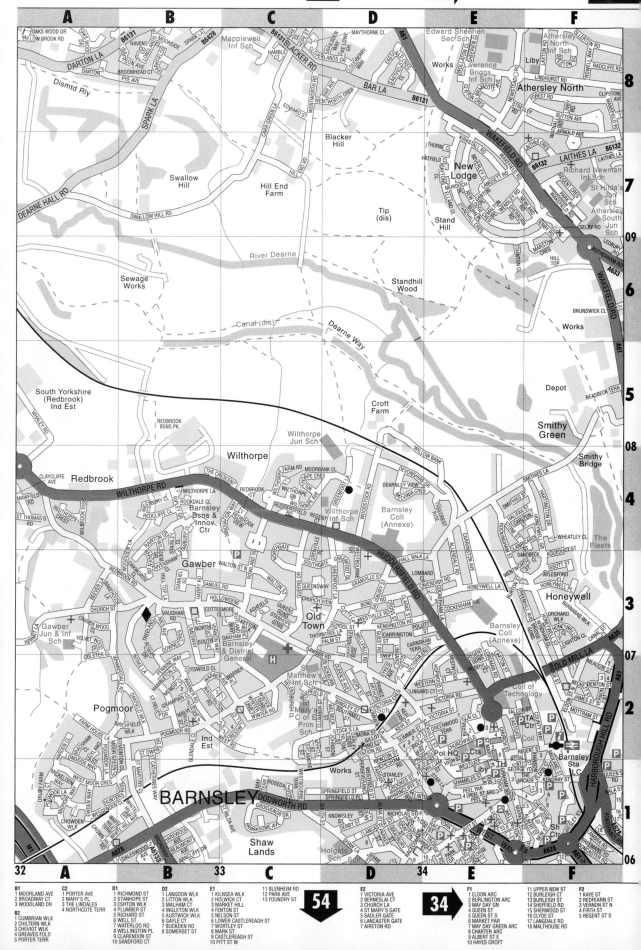

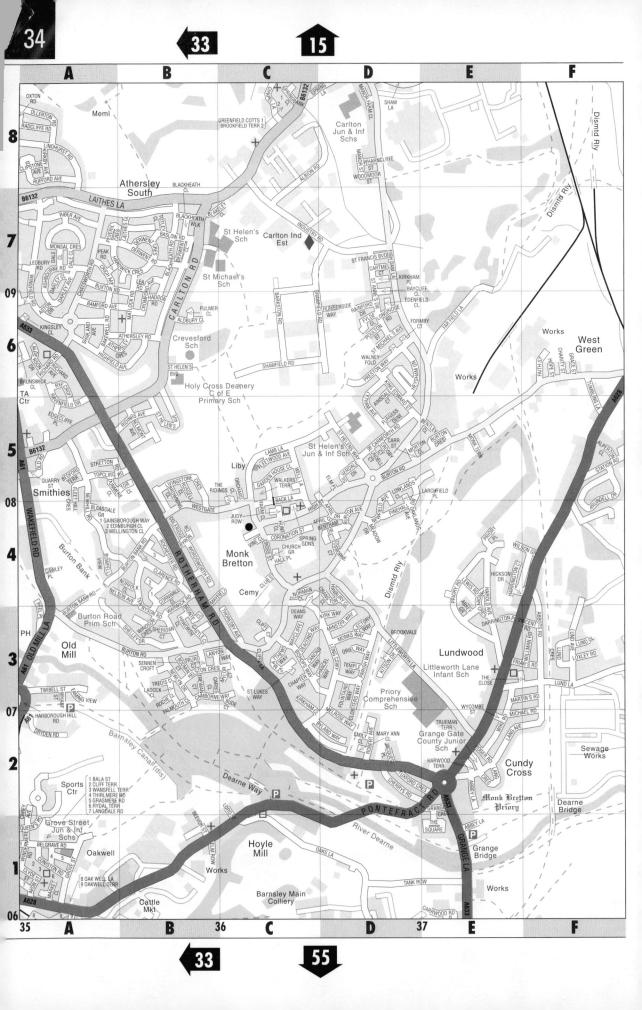

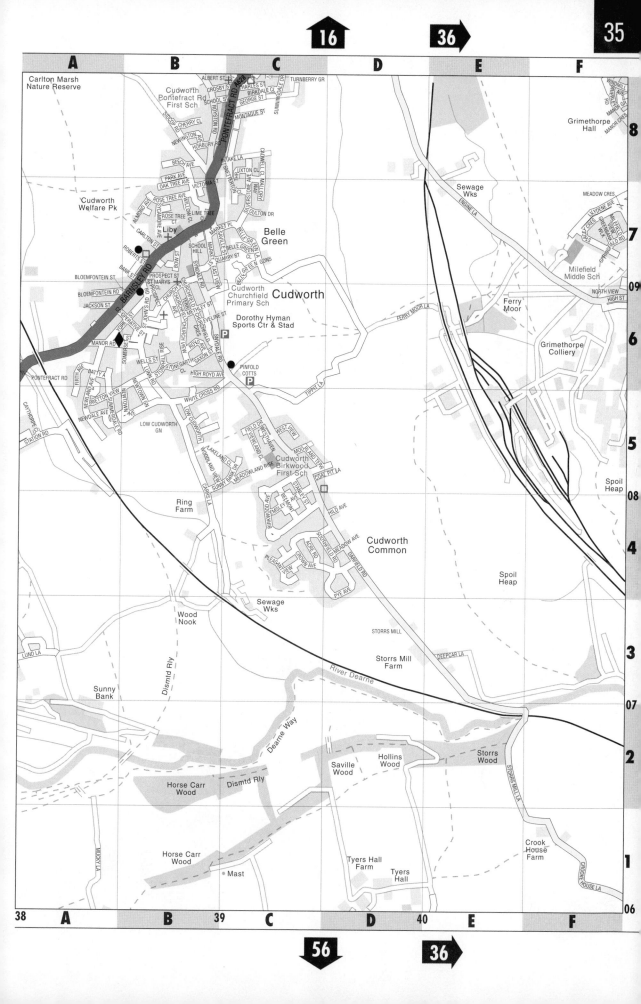

A   B   C   D   E   F

Carlton Marsh
Nature Reserve

Cudworth
Pontefract Rd
First Sch

ALBERT ST
CROSBY DR
CHARLES ST
BIRKDALE CL
GEORGE ST
Turnberry Gr

SCHOOL LA
ROYSTON RD
SUNNINGDALE DR

SIDCOP RD
CHERRY CL
Newington Ave
HORBURY RD
MONTAGUE ST

PONTEFRACT RD A628

M'TAKE LA
CROWELL CL
BUXTON CL
MALLORY
MW

BEECH AVE
PARK AVE
OAK TREE AVE
Victoria St
SMEATERTON
SILVERSTONE AVE
DULTON DR

ROSE TREE AVE
LIME TREE
ROSE TREE
CT

ALMOND AVE
SYCAMORE AVE
WILLOW CL
LIME TREE

CARLTON ST
Liby
MARKET PL
BELLE GR REN LA

Belle
Green

ROBERTS ST

BANK ST
BARNSLEY RD

BELLE GREEN GDNS
QUARRY ST
EAST VIEW

SCHOOL
HILL
SAVILLE ST

Bloemfontein St
PROSPECT ST

Cudworth
Churchfield
Primary Sch

Cudworth

Bloemfontein Rd
ST MARYS
RCL
CHURCHFIELD
TERRACE
CHURCH VIEW

ST JOHN'S RD
CO OPERATIVE ST

Jackson St
SMITHY RISE
STONEGARTH
SAXON CL

EVELINE ST
METHLEY CL
CHURCHFIELD CRES
ROYD LA

Dorothy Hyman
Sports Ctr & Stad

SKY DALE RD

P

FERRY MOOR LA

Sewage
Wks

ENGINE LA

MEADOW CRES

CLYDENE AVE
MILLFIELD
GREENLAND
WALK
SPRINGFIELD RD

STACEY CRES

Milefield
Middle Sch

Grimethorpe
Hall

WINDMILL
PRIESTLEY CL
RD
MANOR GR
MANOR CRES

8

7

NORTH VIEW
HIGH ST

09

Ferry
Moor

Grimethorpe
Colliery

6

MANOR RD
SOMERSET ST
YORK ST
WELLS ST
LUMN RD
STH TYNE RISE

PINFOLD
COTTS
P

Pontefract Rd
FIRTH AVE
BATTY A
NEWLAND AVE
BRETTON VIEW
NEWTOWN
AVE

NEWDALE AVE
NEWTOWN GN
SUMMERDALE RD

WHITE CROSS RD
LOW CUDWORTH

Low Cudworth
GN

TIPPIT LA

Spoil
Heap

5

08

CAYTHORPE CL
STATION RD

Ring
Farm

CARRS LA
WOODLAND VIEW
SUNNY BANK DR
LAKELAND CL
MEADOWLAND RISE
BIRKWOOD AVE
BELMONT
FIELD DR
WEST VIEW
NEW HAVEN
NEW HAVEN CL

Cudworth
Birkwood
First Sch

STANLEY ST
MOO-
R-LAND TERR
COAL PIT LA

HILD AVE

Cudworth
Common

Spoil
Heap

4

Wood
Nook

Sewage
Wks

WOODLAND DR
PLEASANT
VIEW
CROWN AVE
ACRE RD
SOUTHFIELD RD
CROWN AVE
MEADOW AVE
PYE AVE
DARFIELD RD

STORRS MILL

Storrs Mill
Farm

DEEPCAR LA

3

LUND LA

Sunny
Bank

Dismtd Rly

River Dearne

07

Horse Carr
Wood

Dearne Way

Dismtd Rly

Saville
Wood

Hollins
Wood

Storrs
Wood

STORRS MILL LA

2

MUCKY LA

Horse Carr
Wood

Mast

Tyers Hall
Farm

Tyers
Hall

Crook
House
Farm

CROOKE HOUSE LA

1

38   A   B   39   C   D   40   E   F   06

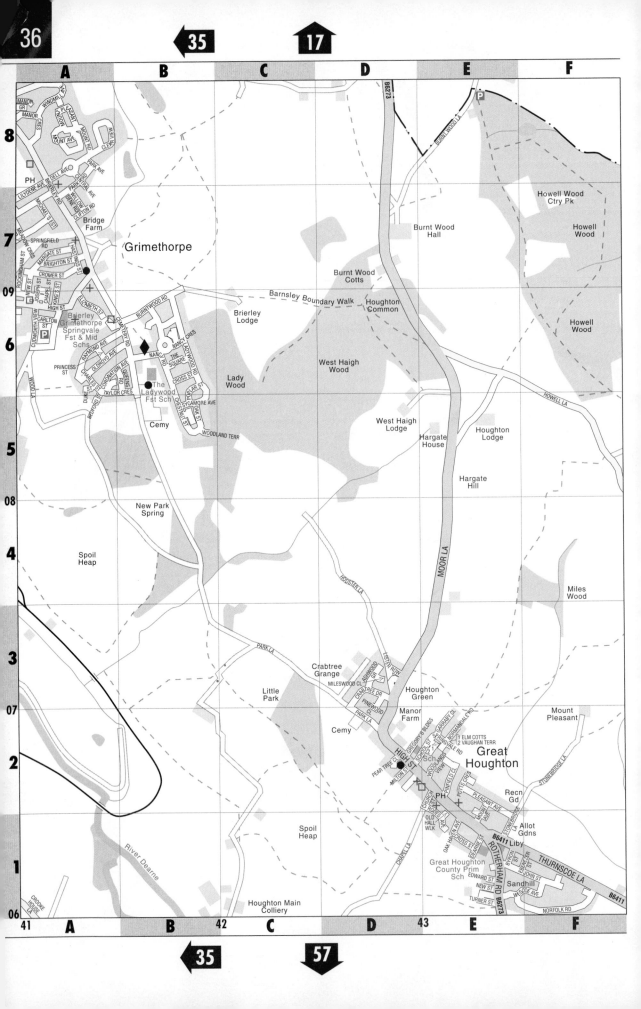

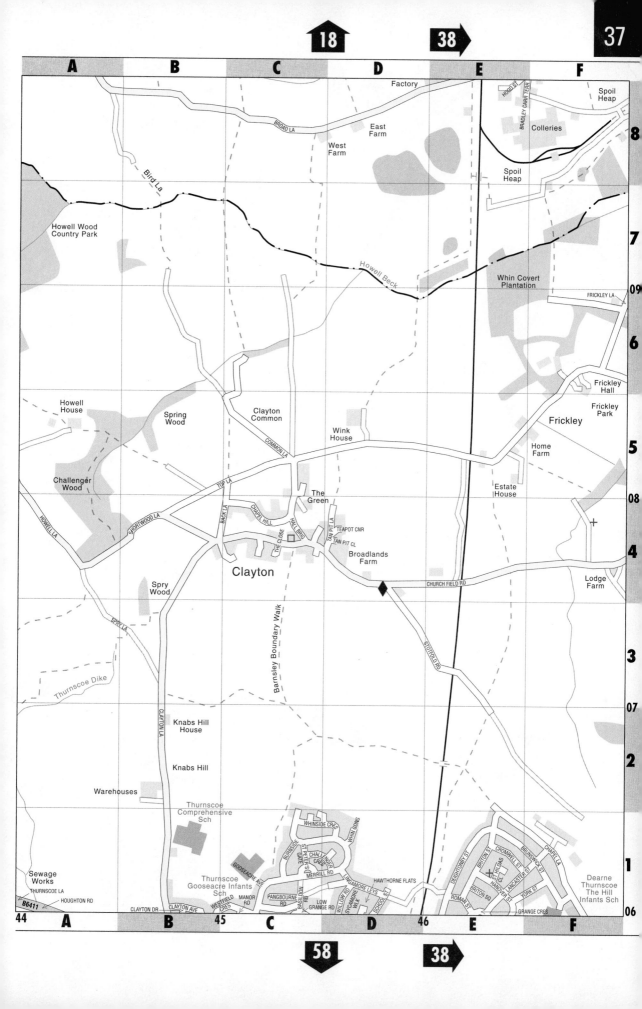

A   B   C   D   E   F

Factory

Spoil
Heap

8

BROAD LA

East
Farm

HOOD ST

BRADLEY CARR TERR

Colleries

West
Farm

Spoil
Heap

Bird La

Howell Wood
Country Park

7

Howell Beck

Whin Covert
Plantation

FRICKLEY LA

09

6

Frickley
Hall

Howell
House

Spring
Wood

Clayton
Common

Frickley
Park

Frickley

Wink
House

Home
Farm

5

Challenger
Wood

COMMON LA

Estate
House

08

HOWELL LA

SHORTWOOD LA

TOP LA

BACK LA

CHAPEL HILL

THE CLOSE

HILL BRIG

TAN PIT LA

The
Green

TEAPOT CNR

TAN PIT CL

Broadlands
Farm

4

Clayton

CHURCH FIELD RD

Lodge
Farm

Spry
Wood

Barnsley Boundary Walk

STOFOLD RD

3

07

SPRY LA

Thurnscoe Dike

CLAYTON LA

Knabs Hill
House

2

Knabs Hill

Warehouses

Thurnscoe
Comprehensive
Sch

WHINSIDE CRES

WHIN GDNS

Sewage
Works

THURNSCOE LA

B6411

HOUGHTON RD

Thurnscoe
Gooseacre Infants
Sch

GOOSEACRE AVE

BURNSIDE GATE

ST PETER'S CL

CHALLENGER
CRES

MERRILL RD

LINGAMORE LEYS

Hawthorne Flats

BEIGHTON BY ST

BRITON ST

CROMWELL ST

ST HILDAS
CL

BRUNSWICK ST

CHAPEL LA

Dearne
Thurnscoe
The Hill
Infants Sch

1

CLAYTON DR

CLAYTON AVE

WESTFIELD
CRES

MANOR
RD

PANGBOURNE
RD

BASILDON RD

LOW
GRANGE RD

WILLOW RD

SYCAMORE WLK

SCHOOL ST

ROMAN ST

BRITON SQ

HANOVER ST

LANCASTER ST

YORK ST

GRANGE CRES

06

44   A   B   45   C   D   46   E   F

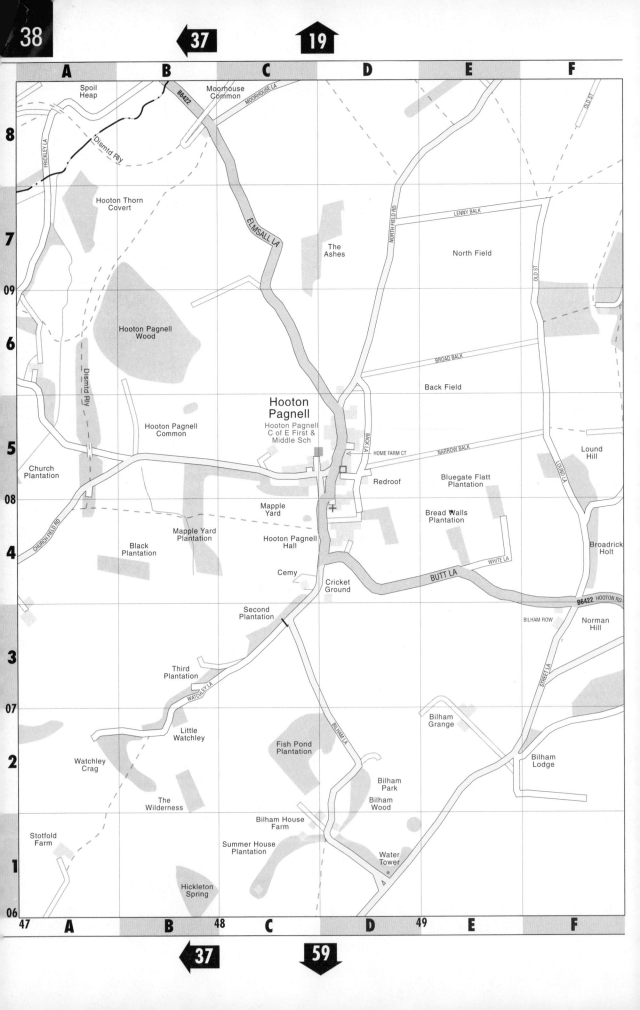

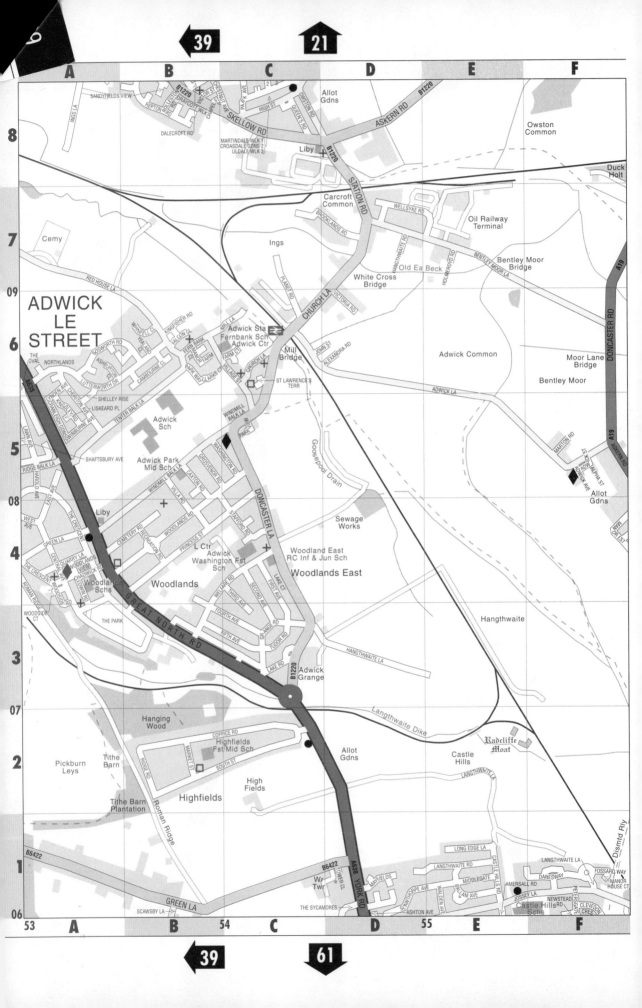

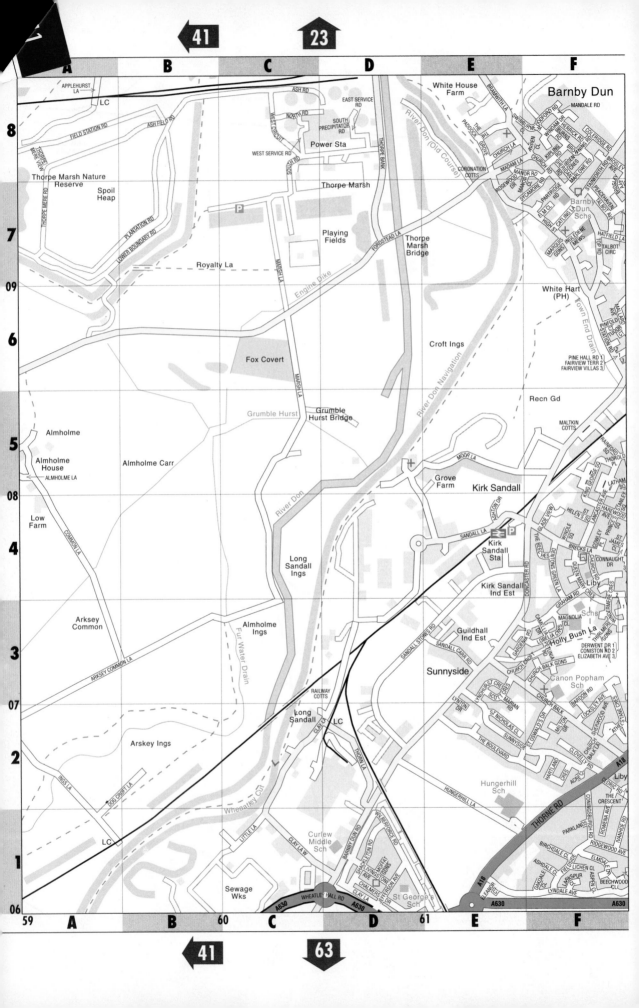

Barnby Dun

Applehurst La
LC
Field Station Rd
Ash Field Rd
Ash Rd
North Rd
East Service Rd
West Circuit Rd
West Service Rd
South Precipitator Rd
Power Sta
Thorpe Mere View
Thorpe Marsh Nature Reserve
Spoil Heap
Plantation Rd
Lower Boundary Rd
Royalty La
Marsh La
Thorpe Bank
Fordstead La
Thorpe Marsh
Playing Fields
Thorpe Marsh Bridge
River Don (Old Course)
White House Farm
Bramwith La
Swinburne Dr
Paddock Grove
The Phil
Church La
Coronation Cotts
Rosewood Dr
Madam La
Manor Rd
Sycamore Rd
Elm Cl
Pinfold Gdns
High St
Catling La
Maypole Gdns
Ingledene Mews
Hatfield La
Talbot Circ
Top Rd
Station Rd
Pinfold La
Mallard Ave

White Hart (PH)
Engine Dike
Croft Ings
Fox Covert
Town End Drain
Pine Hall Rd 1
Fairview Terr 2
Fairview Villas 3
Recn Gd
Maltkin Cotts

Grumble Hurst
Grumble Hurst Bridge
Marsh La
River Don Navigation
Moor La
Ranford Rd
Thorold Pl
King George's Sq
Latham Sq

Almholme
Almholme House
Almholme La
Almholme Carr
River Don
Grove Farm
Kirk Sandall
St Helen's Sq
Cowley Sq
Windle Prince Cl
Harewood Ave
St James Cl
The Glade View
Deltons Green La
Ash Ton Dr
Connaught Dr
Liby
Brecks Cl
The Beeches

Low Farm
Common La
Sandall La
Kirk Sandall Sta
P
Doncaster Rd
Graham La
Magnolia Cl
Lobelia Cres
Gardenia Rd
Camellia La
Kirk Sandall Ind Est
Church Rd
Queen Mary Cres
Tanbridge Cres
Holly Bush La
Derwent Dr 1
Coniston Rd 2
Elizabeth Ave 3

Arksey Common
Arksey Common La
Almholme Ings
Fur Water Drain
Railway Cotts
Long Sandall
Guildhall Ind Est
Sandall Stores Rd
Sandall Carr Rd
Sandall Balk La
Sunnyside
Vinehurst Cres
Scott Rd
Marian Rd
Canon Popham Sch
Bardon Rd
Locksley Ave
Sherwood Ave
Church Balk
Atheretone Cres

Arksey Ings
Ings La
Dog Croft La
Clay La
LC
Wheatley Cott
Little La
Clay La W
Long Sandall
Thorn La
St Nicholas Cl
Lynton Dr
St Oswald's St
St Oswald's Dr
The Boulevard
Sunnyside
Clovelly Rd
Hartland Cres
Balfour Rd
Acre Rd
Hungerhill Sch
Hungerhill La
Thorne Rd
A18
Liby
The Crescent
Coningsburgh Rd
Parklands
Cedric Rd

LC
Sewage Wks
Barnby Town Rd
Shacklton Rd
Livingstone Rd
Robins
Clay La
Chalmers Rd
Nessfield Ave
St George's Sch
Curlew Middle Sch
Wilberforce Rd
St George's
A630
Wheatley Hall Rd
A630
A630
A18
A630
Birchdale Cl
Ashdale Cl
Oakdale Cl
Lyndale Ave
Larkspur
Lichen Cl
Elmdale Cl
Aspen Cl
Ridgewood Ave
Rowena Ave
Ivanhoe Rd
Beechwood Cl

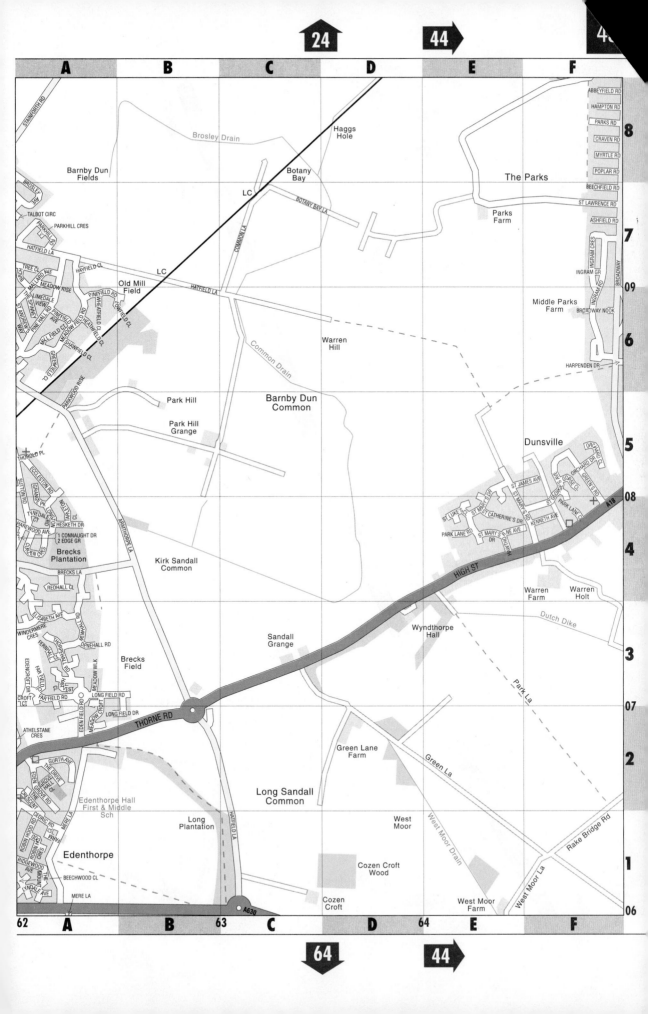

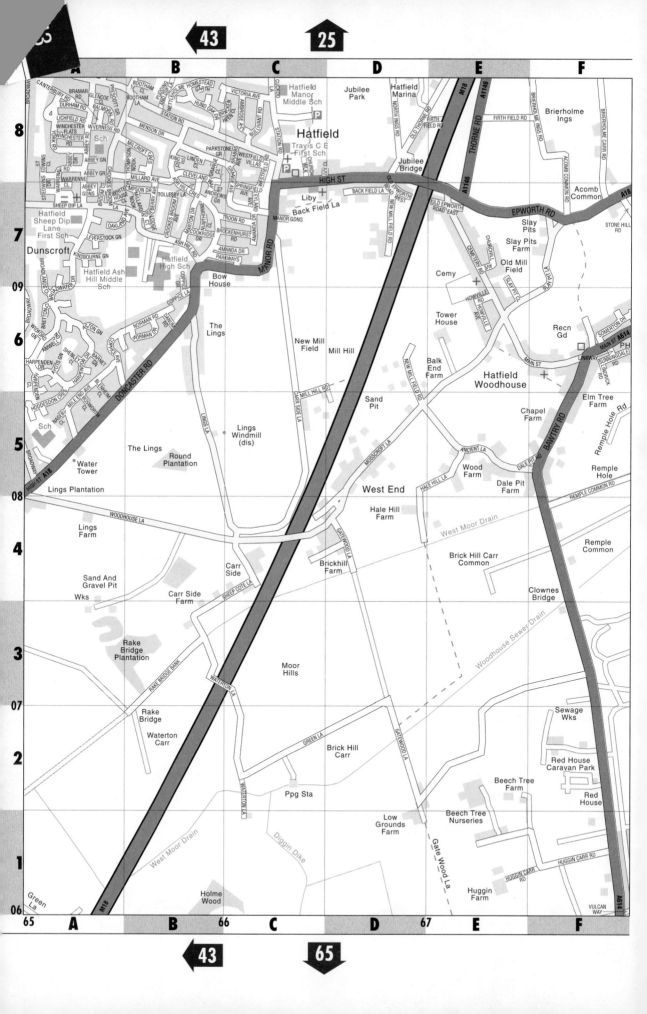

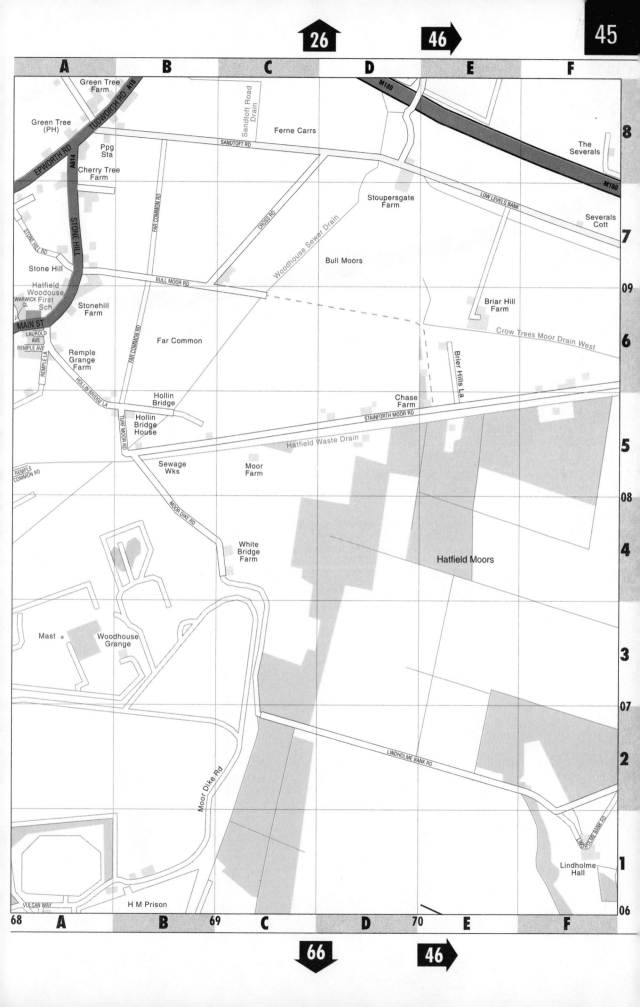

A   B   C   D   E   F

8

Green Tree
Farm
Green Tree
(PH)
TUDWORTH RD A18
Ppg
Sta
EPWORTH RD
Cherry Tree
Farm
A614
STONE HILL
STONE HILL RD
Stone Hill
Hatfield
Woodouse
WARWICK CL
First Sch
MAIN ST
LAUROLD
AVE
REMPLE AVE
REMPLE LA
Stonehill
Farm
HOLLIN BRIDGE LA
Remple
Grange
Farm
REMPLE
COMMON RD

FAR COMMON RD
Sandtoft Road
Drain
SANDTOFT RD
CROSS RD
Ferne Carrs

Woodhouse Sewer Drain
Bull Moors
BULL MOOR RD
Far Common
FAR COMMON RD

Hollin
Bridge
TURF MOOR RD
Hollin
Bridge
House
Sewage
Wks
MOOR DIKE RD
Moor
Farm
White
Bridge
Farm

Mast
Woodhouse
Grange

Moor Dike Rd

VULCAN WAY
H M Prison

M180
The
Severals
M180

LOW LEVELS BANK
Stoupersgate
Farm
Severals
Cott

09

Briar Hill
Farm
Crow Trees Moor Drain West

6

Brier Hills La
Chase
Farm
STAINFORTH MOOR RD
Hatfield Waste Drain

5

08

4
Hatfield Moors

3

07

LINDHOLME BANK RD

2

LINDHOLME BANK RD
Lindholme
Hall
1

06

45
27

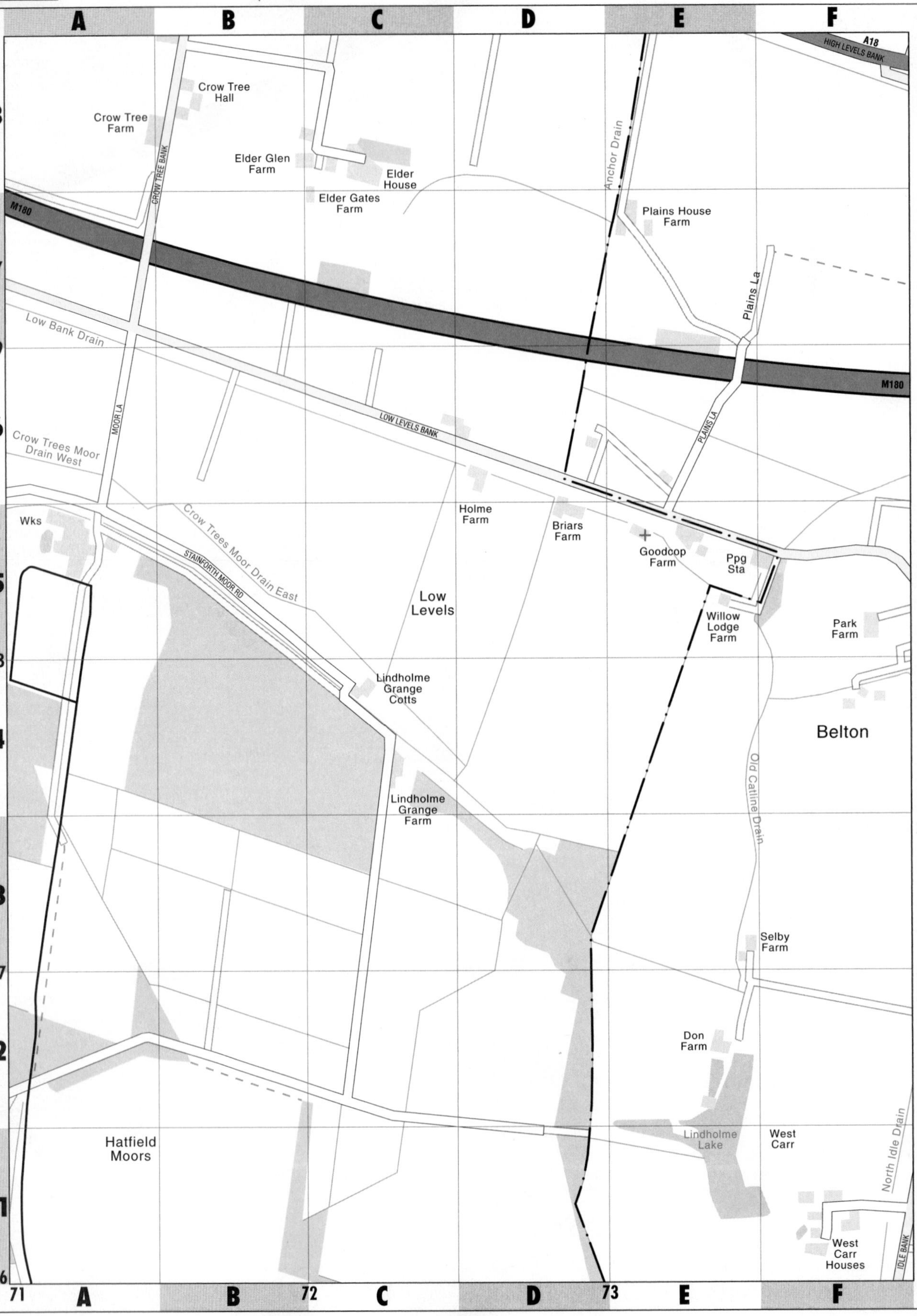
A
B
C
D
E
F
8
7
09
6
5
08
4
3
07
2
1
06
71
72
73
A18
HIGH LEVELS BANK
Crow Tree Hall
Crow Tree Farm
CROW TREE BANK
Elder Glen Farm
Elder House
Elder Gates Farm
Anchor Drain
Plains House Farm
M180
Plains La
Low Bank Drain
MOOR LA
LOW LEVELS BANK
PLAINS LA
Crow Trees Moor Drain West
Holme Farm
Briars Farm
Goodcop Farm
Ppg Sta
Wks
Crow Trees Moor Drain East
STAINFORTH MOOR RD
Low Levels
Willow Lodge Farm
Park Farm
Lindholme Grange Cotts
Belton
Old Catline Drain
Lindholme Grange Farm
Selby Farm
Don Farm
Hatfield Moors
Lindholme Lake
West Carr
North Idle Drain
IDLE BANK
West Carr Houses

45
67

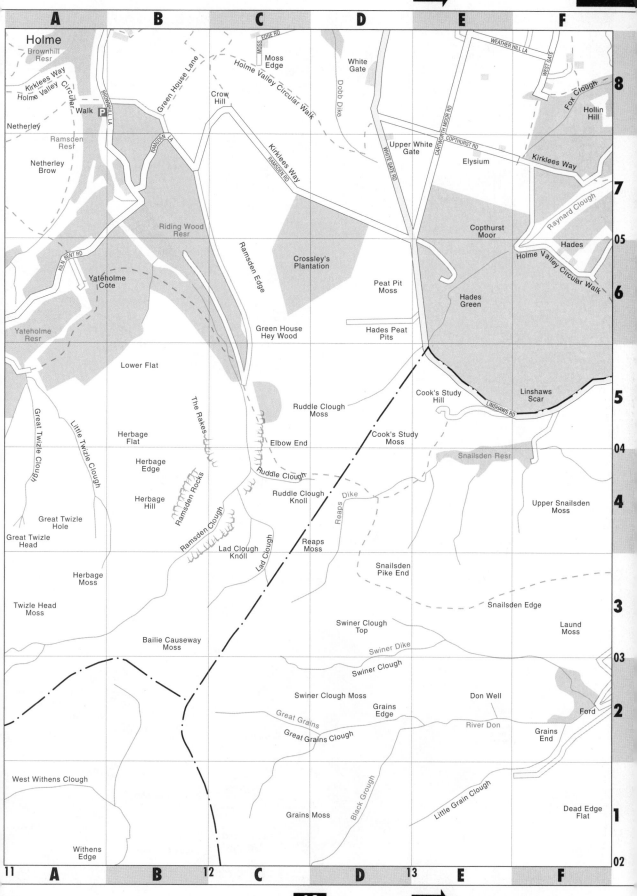

Holme
Brownhill Resr

Kirklees Way
Holme Valley Circular Walk

Netherley

Ramsden Resr

Netherley Brow

Kiln Bent Rd

Yateholme Cote

Yateholme Resr

Great Twizle Clough
Little Twizle Clough

Great Twizle Hole
Great Twizle Head

Herbage Moss

Twizle Head Moss

West Withens Clough

Withens Edge

Green House Lane
Brownhill La

Crow Hill

Ramsden La
Ramsden Rd

Riding Wood Resr

Ramsden Edge

The Rakes

Ramsden Rocks

Ramsden Clough

Lower Flat

Herbage Flat

Herbage Edge

Herbage Hill

Lad Clough Knoll
Lad Clough

Bailie Causeway Moss

Moss Edge Rd

Moss Edge

Holme Valley Circular Walk

Kirklees Way

Crossley's Plantation

Green House Hey Wood

Ruddle Clough Moss

Elbow End

Ruddle Clough

Ruddle Clough Knoll

Reaps Moss

Reaps Dike

Swiner Clough Top

Swiner Dike

Swiner Clough

Swiner Clough Moss

Great Grains

Great Grains Clough

Grains Edge

Grains Moss

Black Grough

White Gate

Dobb Dike

White Gate Rd

Upper White Gate

Copthurst Rd
Cartworth Moor Rd

Elysium

Copthurst Moor

Peat Pit Moss

Hades Green

Hades Peat Pits

Cook's Study Hill

Cook's Study Moss

Linshaws Rd

Snailsden Resr

Snailsden Pike End

Snailsden Edge

Don Well

River Don

Little Grain Clough

Weather Hill La
West Gate

Fox Clough

Hollin Hill

Kirklees Way

Raynard Clough

Hades

Holme Valley Circular Walk

Linshaws Scar

Upper Snailsden Moss

Laund Moss

Ford

Grains End

Dead Edge Flat

47

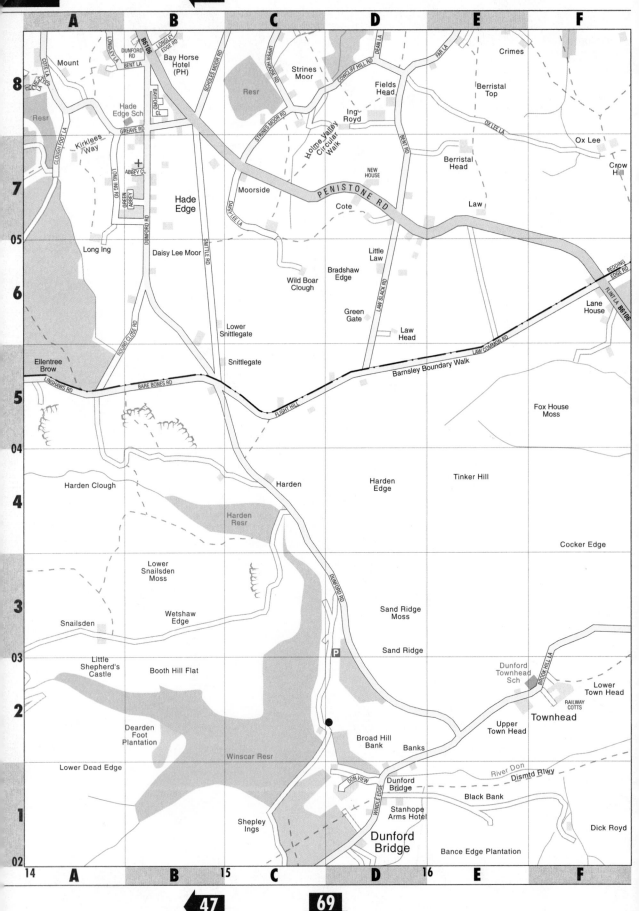

A   B   C   D   E   F

8

Mount

B6106
DUNFORD RD
LONGLEY EDGE RD
BENT LA
Bay Horse Hotel (PH)
SCHOLES MOOR RD
UPPER MOSS RD

Strines Moor

DEAN LA
CONCLIFF HILL RD
FAR LA

Crimes

Berristal Top

COTE LA
HOLL LA

Resr

Hade Edge Sch

BAYFORD CL

Resr

Fields Head

Ing Royd

Berristal Head

OX LEE LA

Ox Lee

Crow Hill

CLOUGH FOOT LA

Kirklees Way

GREAVE RD

ABBEY CL

GREEN ABBEY

DUNFORD RD

Hade Edge

Moorside

DAISY LEE LA

Holme Valley Circular Walk

PENISTONE RD

NEW HOUSE

Cote

BENT RD

Law

7

Long Ing

LONG ING RD

Daisy Lee Moor

SNITTLE RD

05

Lower Snittlegate

Wild Boar Clough

Bradshaw Edge

Little Law

LAW SLACK RD

Green Gate

Law Head

REDDING EDGE RD

FLINT LA
B6106

Lane House

6

ROUND CLOSE RD

Ellentree Brow

Snittlegate

LINSHAWS RD

BARE BONES RD

FLIGHT HILL

Barnsley Boundary Walk

LAW COMMON RD

Fox House Moss

5

04

Harden Clough

Harden

Harden Edge

Tinker Hill

Harden Resr

Cocker Edge

4

Lower Snailsden Moss

DUNFORD RD

Snailsden

Wetshaw Edge

Sand Ridge Moss

3

03

Little Shepherd's Castle

Booth Hill Flat

Sand Ridge

P

Dunford Townhead Sch

BROOK HILL LA

Lower Town Head

Dearden Foot Plantation

Upper Town Head

RAILWAY COTTS

Townhead

2

Broad Hill Bank

Banks

Winscar Resr

River Don

Dismtd Rlwy

Lower Dead Edge

DON VIEW

Dunford Bridge

Black Bank

WINDLE EDGE

Shepley Ings

Stanhope Arms Hotel

Dick Royd

1

Dunford Bridge

Bance Edge Plantation

02

14   A   B   15   C   D   16   E   F

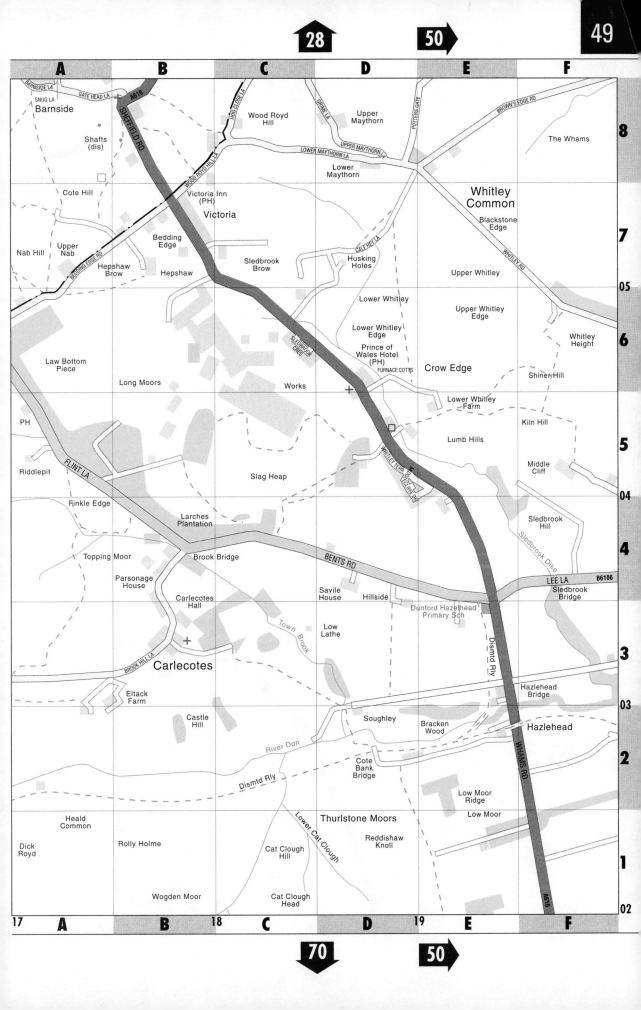

49
29

A B C D E F

8

Brown's Edge Farm

HORN LA

Ingbirchworth Resr

Works

PARK HOUSE CT

BACK LA

A629

HUDDERSFIELD RD

Rose & Crown (PH)

A629

Spicer House

Ingbirchworth Moor

ANNAT ROYD LA

ANNAT ROYD LA

MILL LA

NEW ROW LA

Green Farm

Broadfield Farm

Cockle Edge

7

Barnsley Boundary Walk

HIGH LA

INGBIRCHWORTH LA

Scout Dike Resr

Greenley Carr

SPICER HOUSE LA

Maze Brook

05

Spicer Hill

Annat Royd Farm

Far Royd Moor

Royd Moor Resr

Folly

Bell Royd

6

Royd Moor

FOLLY LA

NORWOOD LA

WHITLEY RD

Small Shaw Bank

Whitley House

Royd Moor Farm

ROYD MOOR RD

5

Eagle Nest

Small Shaw

Royd Moor Hill

Royd Moor House

04

The Knoll

Royd

ROYD LA

SLANT GATE

HIGH BANK LA

Westfield Farm

Illions

Flash House Farm

Little Royd Farm

High Bank

WESTFIELD LA

4

HOLLIN LA

B6106

Works

Rough Brow

NEW ROYD

COPPERS CL

CROFT DR

The Croft

A628

Hazelhead Hall

Catshaw Cross

LEE LA

Millhouse Primary Sch

ROYD AVE

WEST END RD

BIRKS AVE

BIRKS COTTS

Plumpton Mills

MILL LA

SAVILE LA

Ford

3

CATSHAW LA

Catshaw House

Lee Lane Dike

B6106

MANCHESTER RD

MOLAND CL

KENNEDY CL

BIRKS LA

Millhouse Green

Eckland Bridge Works

LEAPINGS LA

HORBURY WILL RD

CROSS LA

03

Bullhouse Mill

River Don

Bullace Grange Farm

Starling Bridge

Bank House Farm

HILL SIDE LA

Mill

Bullhouse Bridge

SHORE HALL LA

2

Ranah Stones

Bullhouse Hall

BULLHOUSE LA

Dismtd Rly

Ecklands Bridge

PARKIN HOUSE LA

Hill Side

HARTCLIFF LA

Works

1

Ranah Stones Farm

Cranberry Holes

Opencast Workings

ECKLANDS LONG LA

LILEY LA

FIELD LA

Ecklands

A628

Hartcliff Brow

Bella Vista

02

20 A B 21 C D 22 E F

49
71

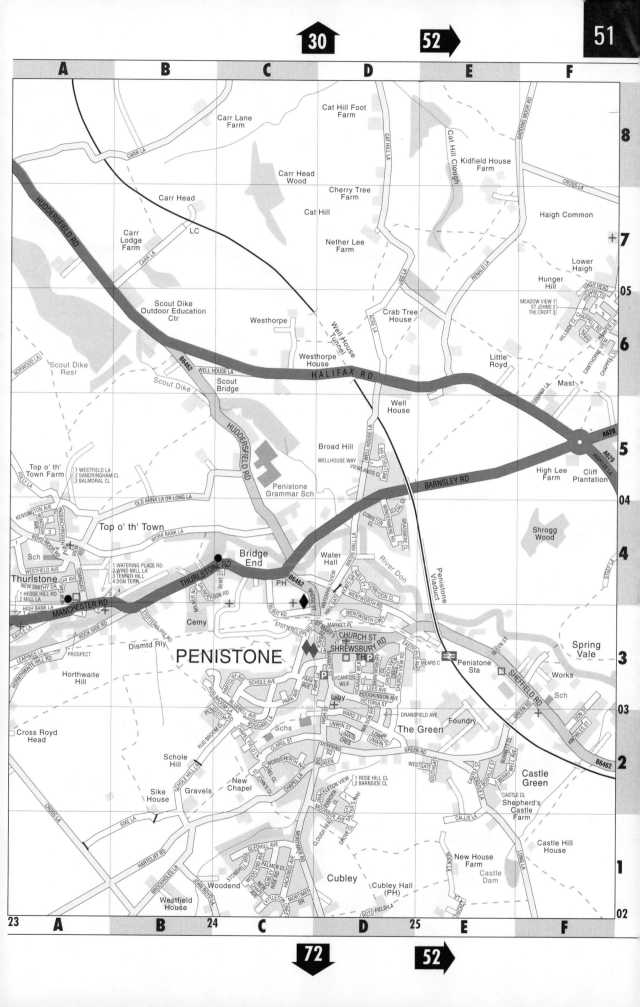

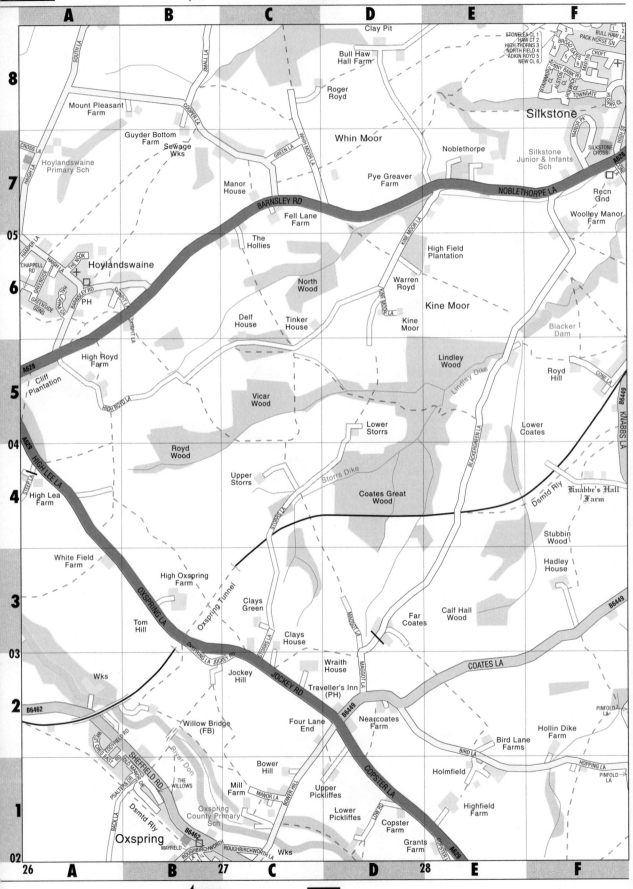

51 31

A B C D E F

8

Mount Pleasant Farm

Clay Pit

Bull Haw Hall Farm

Roger Royd

STONELEA CL 1
HAW CT 2
HIGH THORNS 3
NORTH FIELD 4
ADKIN ROYD 5
NEW CL 6

BROAD GATES

CROFT

MARTIN

BULL HAW LA
PACK HORSE GN

Silkstone

7

Guyder Bottom Farm

Sewage Wks

Whin Moor

Noblethorpe

Silkstone Junior & Infants Sch

Silkstone Cross

COOPER LA

SMALL LA

GREEN LA

WHIN MOOR LA

SOUTH LA

Hoylandswaine Primary Sch

CROSS LA

HAIGH LA

Manor House

Pye Greaver Farm

NOBLETHORPE LA

MANOR PK

Woolley Manor Farm

Recn Gnd

05

Hoylandswaine

Fell Lane Farm

The Hollies

High Field Plantation

A628

SILKSTONE CROSS

HIGH ST

6

CHAPPELL RD

GREENSIDE GDNS

GREENSIDE

HAIGH LA

THE NOOK

PH

BARNSLEY RD

SYKEFIT LA

North Wood

Warren Royd

Kine Moor

KINE MOOR LA

KINE MOOR LA

Kine Moor

Blacker Dam

BARNSLEY RD

Delf House

Tinker House

Lindley Wood

Royd Hill

5

A628

Cliff Plantation

High Royd Farm

HIGH ROYD LA

Vicar Wood

Lindley Dike

BLACKERGREEN LA

Lower Coates

CONE LA

B6449

KNABBS LA

04

A629

HIGH LEE LA

STEEP LA

Royd Wood

Lower Storrs

Storrs Dike

Coates Great Wood

Dsmtd Rly

Knabbe's Hall Farm

4

High Lea Farm

Upper Storrs

STORRS LA

Stubbin Wood

White Field Farm

High Oxspring Farm

Oxspring Tunnel

Clays Green

Far Coates

Calf Hall Wood

Hadley House

B6449

3

OXSPRING LA

Tom Hill

OXSPRING LA

JOCKEY RD

Clays House

MAGGOT LA

03

Wks

JOCKEY RD

Jockey Hill

Wraith House

COATES LA

2

B6462

Willow Bridge (FB)

STORRS LA

BOWER HILL

Traveller's Inn (PH)

B6449

Four Lane End

Nearcoates Farm

BIRD LA

Bird Lane Farms

Hollin Dike Farm

PINFOLD LA

HOPPING LA

PINFOLD LA

River Don

SHEFFIELD RD

OLD MANOR DR

THE WILLOWS

Bower Hill

MANOR LA

Mill Farm

Upper Pickliffes

LOW RD

Holmfield

Highfield Farm

1

PSALTERS DR

BACK LA

Dsmtd Rly

Oxspring County Primary Sch

Lower Pickliffes

COPSTER LA

A629

COPSTER LA

Copster Farm

02

Oxspring

MAYFIELD

B6462

ROUGHBIRCHWORTH LA

ROUGHBIRCHWORTH LA

Wks

Grants Farm

26 A B 27 C D 28 E F

51 73

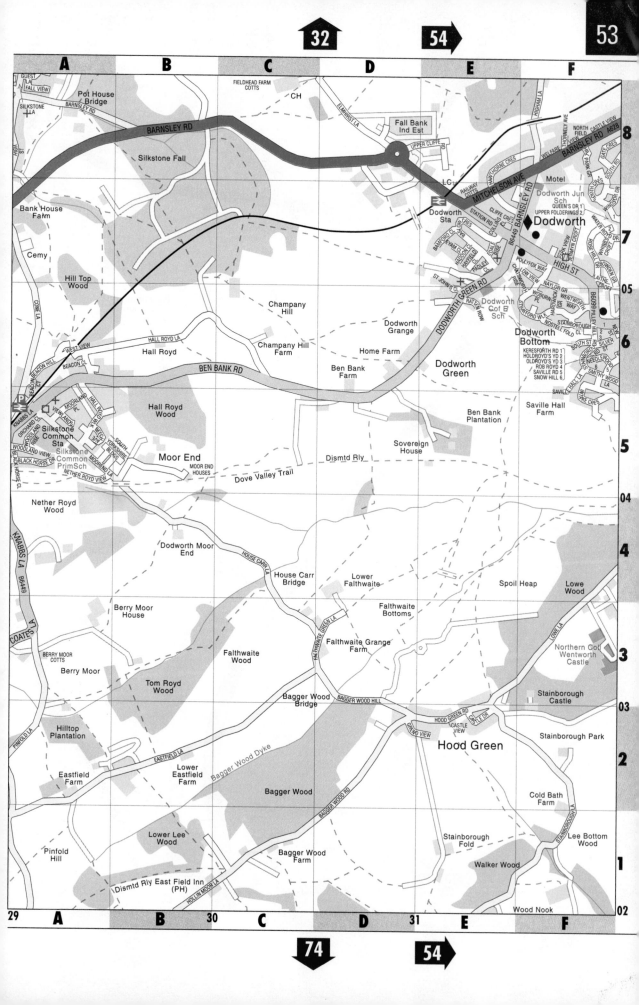

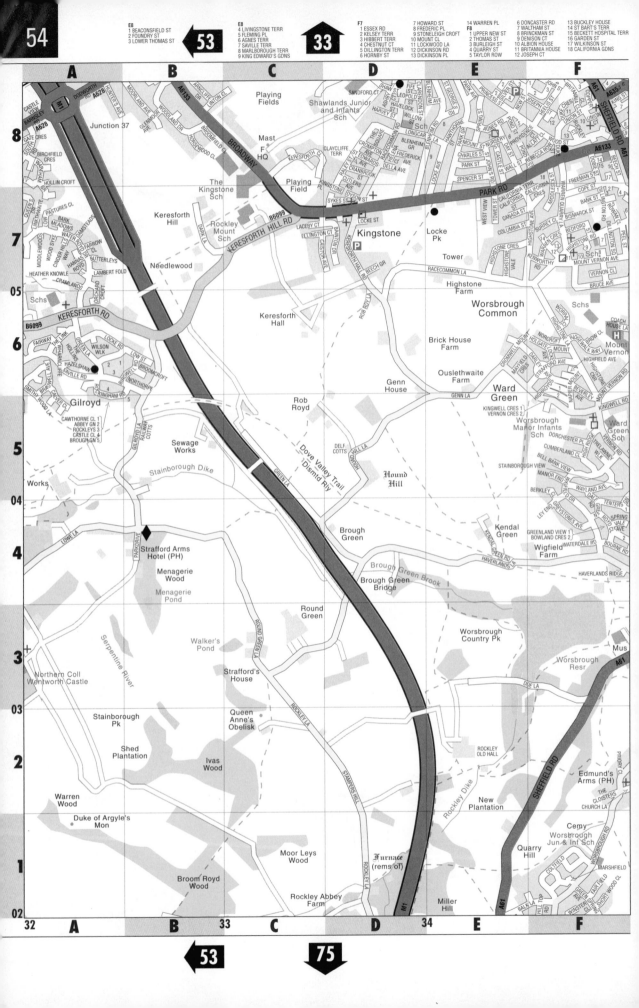

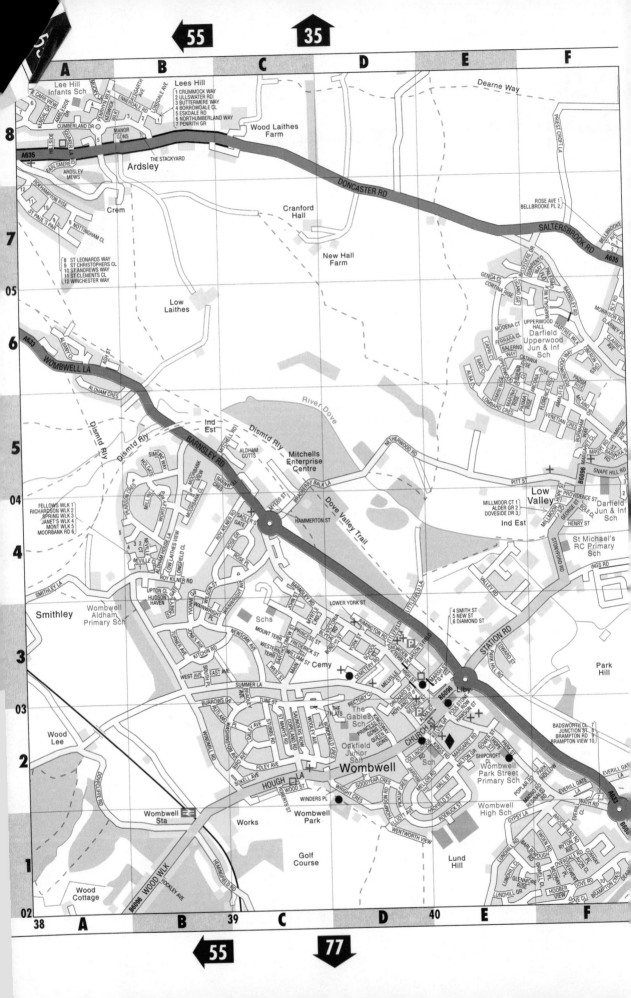

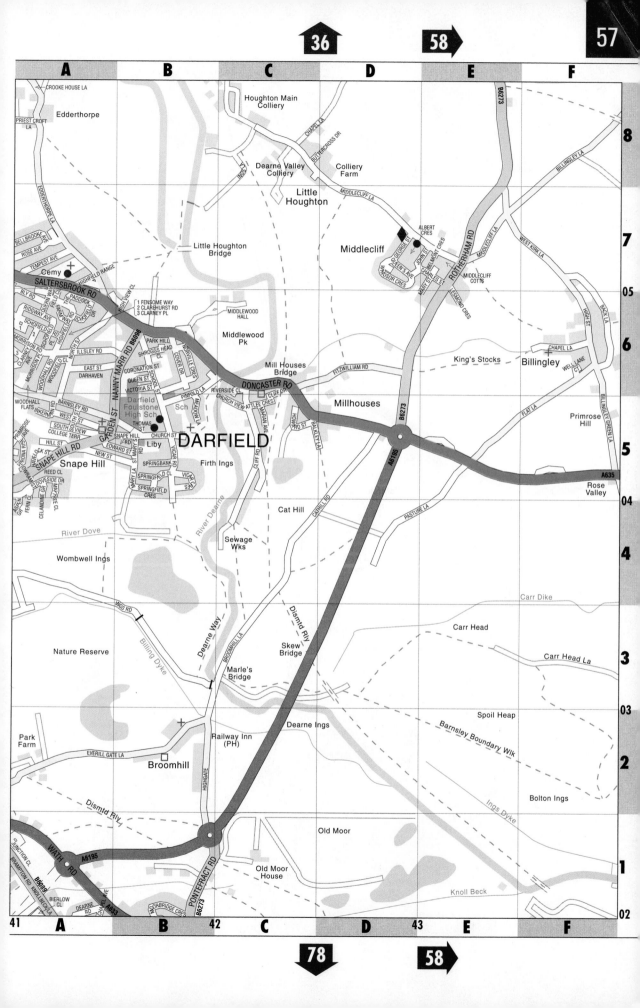

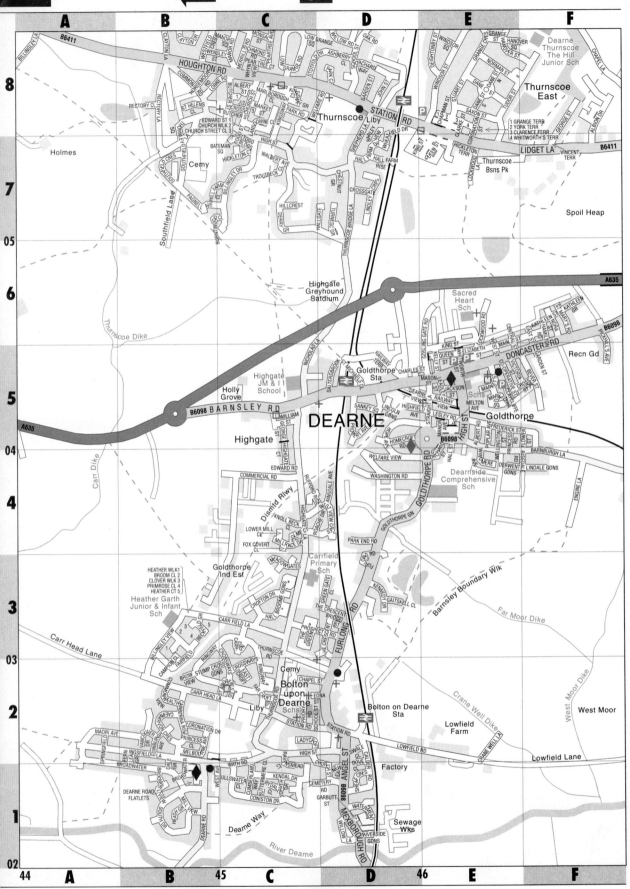

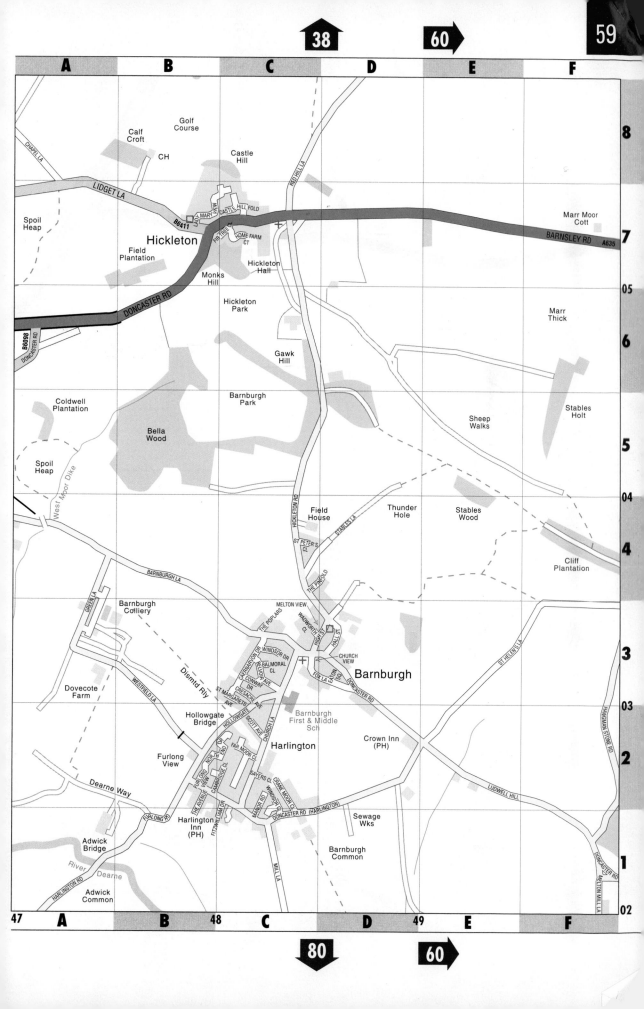

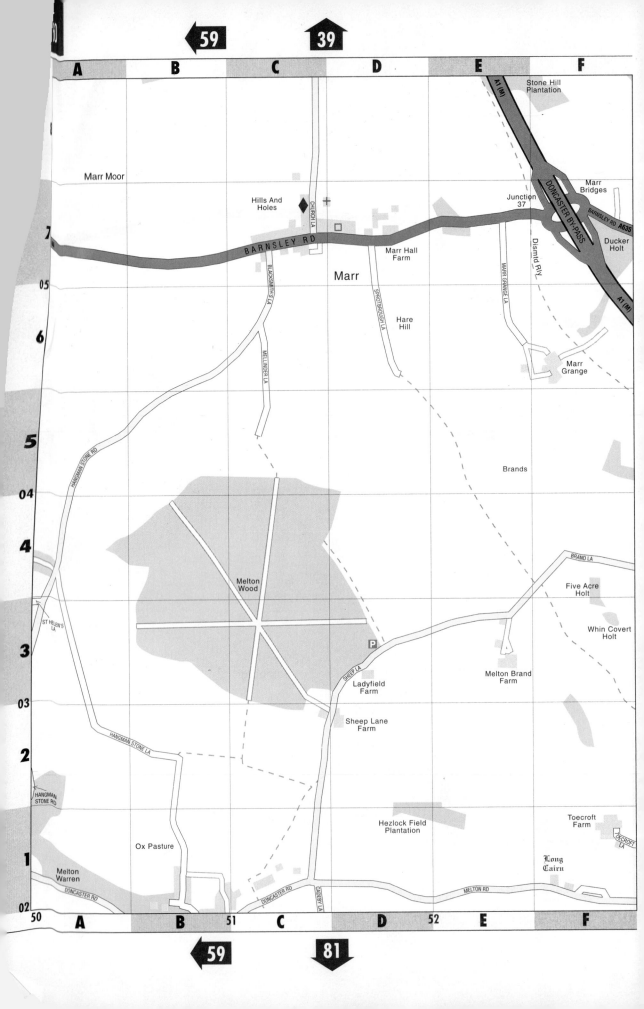

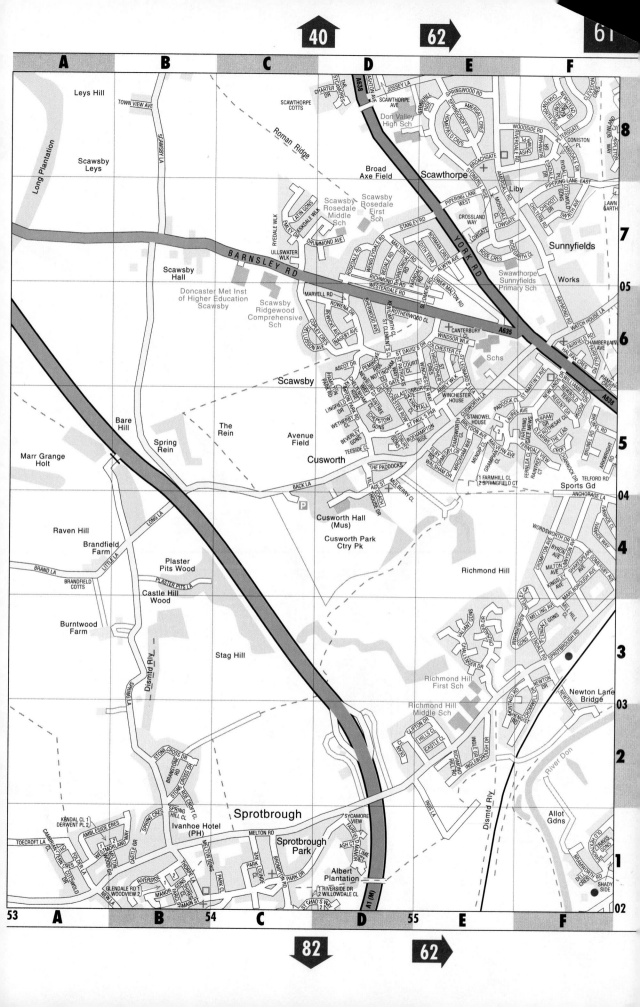

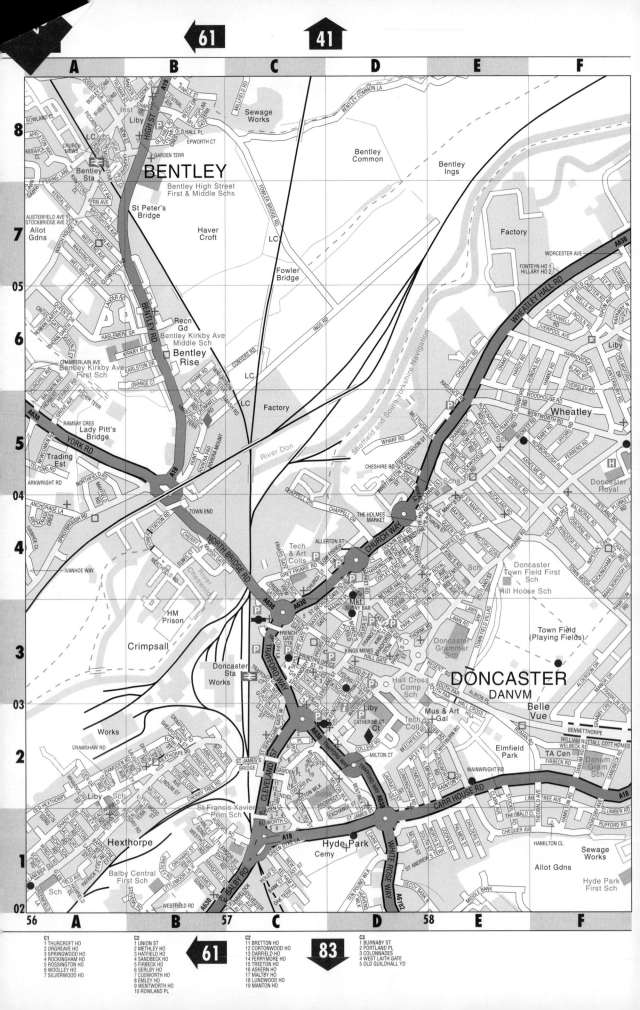

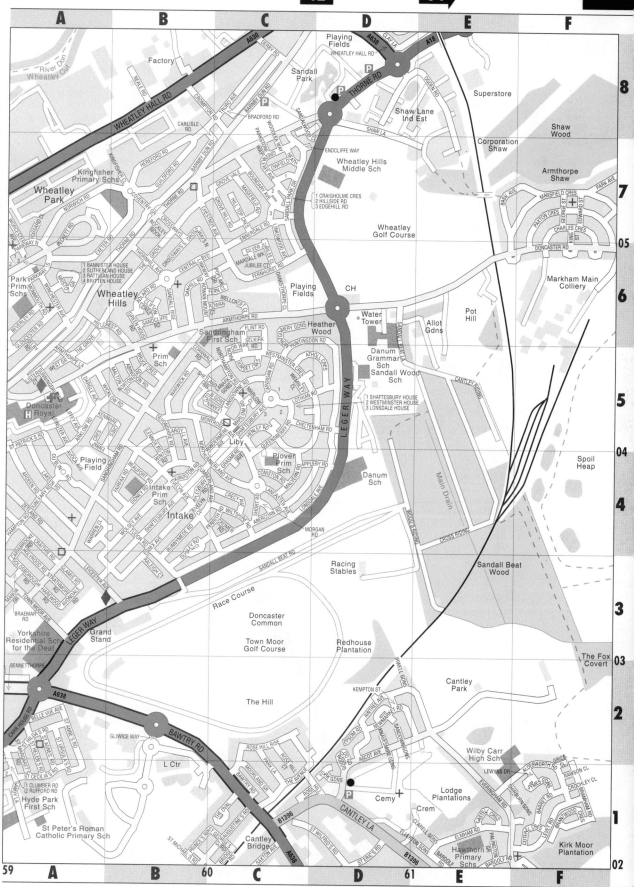

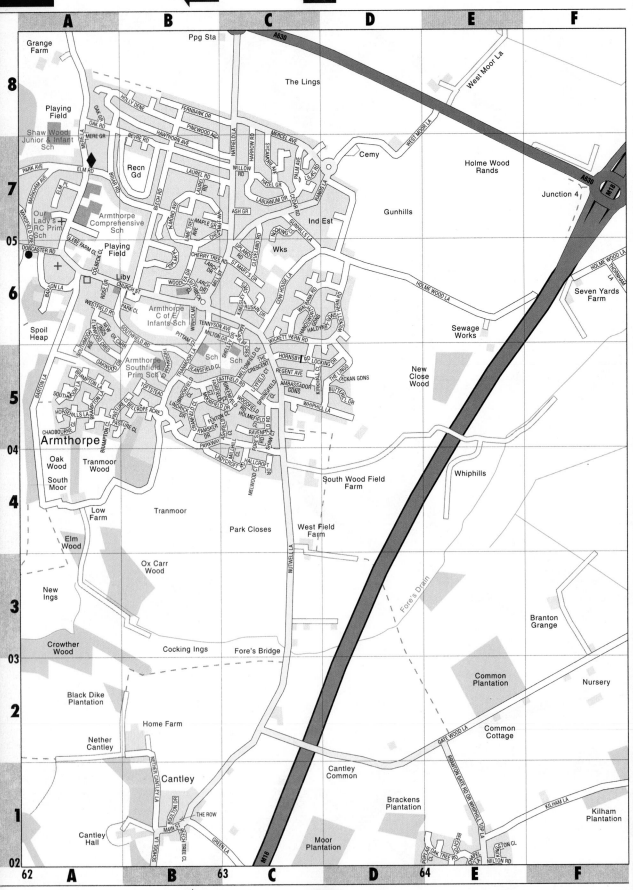

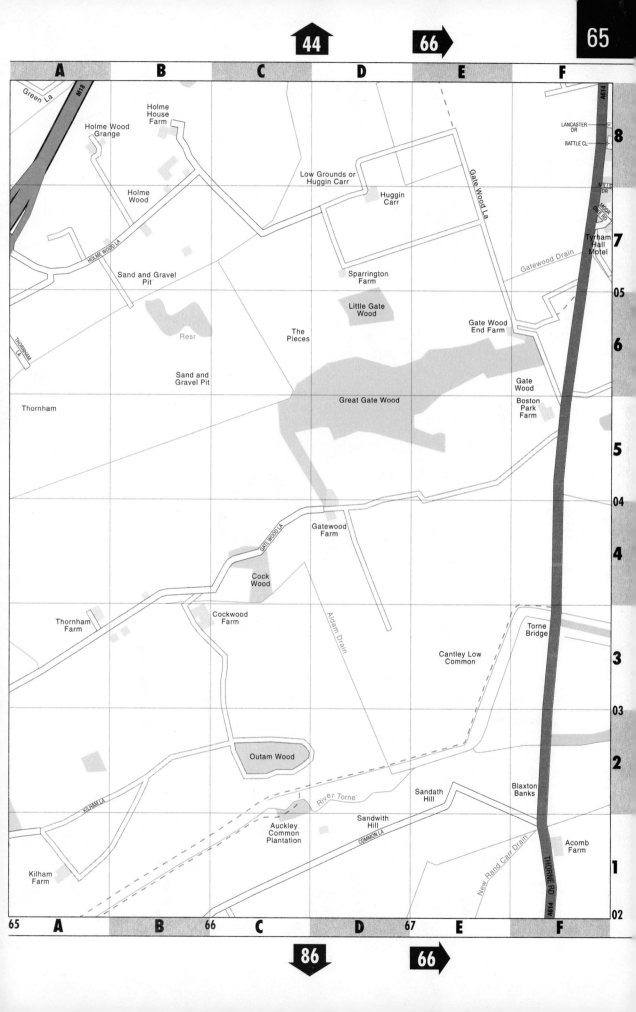

A   B   C   D   E   F

Green La
M18
Holme Wood Grange
Holme House Farm
Holme Wood
HOLME WOOD LA
THORNHAM LA
Sand and Gravel Pit
Resr
Sand and Gravel Pit
Thornham

Low Grounds or Huggin Carr
Huggin Carr
Sparrington Farm
Little Gate Wood
The Pieces
Great Gate Wood

Gate Wood La
Gatewood Drain
A614
LANCASTER DR
BATTLE CL
MILLS DR
MOOR DIKE RD
Tyrham Hall Motel
Gate Wood End Farm
Gate Wood
Boston Park Farm

8
7
05
6
5
04
4
3
03
2
1
02

GATE WOOD LA
Gatewood Farm
Cock Wood
Cockwood Farm
Thornham Farm
Aldam Drain
Cantley Low Common
Torne Bridge

KILHAM LA
Outam Wood
River Torne
Sandath Hill
Sandwith Hill
Auckley Common Plantation
COMMON LA
Blaxton Banks
New Rand Carr Drain
Acomb Farm
THORNE RD
A614
Kilham Farm

A   B   C   D   E   F

HAMPDEN CRES
LANCASTER DR
1   2
BLENHEIM RD
WELLINGTON RD
1 CUNNINGHAM RD
2 GIBSON RD

H M Prison

Moor Dike Rd

8

Playing Fields

MILLS DR
VARSITY CL
CANBERRA AVE
MOOR DIKE RD
LINCOLN RD

Canberra
Cottage Farm

7

05

Sand &
Gravel Pit

6

Old Moor Drain

Hatfield Moors

Poor
Piece

Ellerholme
Farm

5

Middle Ring Drain

North Ring Drain

04

MOOR LA

ACRES LA

SAND LA

Sewage
Wks

Chester
Cottage
Farm

4

Southlands
Farm

HIGH ST

Dolwood Drain

Glebe
Farm

South Ring Drain

3

River Torne

Candy
Farm

03

God's Cross

Long Plantation

Godscross Drain

Old Thatch Carr
Drain

2

Long Plantation

CANDY BANK

1

Blaxton
Common

Sand &
Gravel Pit

NAN SAMPSON BANK

New Thatch Carr Drain

Thatch Carr
Plantation

02

68   A   B   69   C   D   70   E   F

A B C D E F

8

7

05

6

Hatfield
Moors

Roe
Carr

The
Roe

Porters Drain

Moor Bank

Old Moor Drain

Epworth

Wroot
Acres

East Ring Drain

River Torne

Tunnel
Pits

Riverside
Farm

Chestnut
Farm

5

ACRES LA

Ppg
Sta

04

Common La

4

Brook House
Farm

HIGH ST

IDLE BANK

BROOK TERR

POLES BANK

Wroot

Rectory

Cross Keys Inn
(PH)

Auchlands
Farm

South Engine Drain

3

Sandhill
Farm

Woodside

Eastfield
Farm

03

FIRTH LA

WOODSIDE LA

Woodside
Farm

Wroot Travis
Charity Sch
(Junior Mixed
& Infants)

WOODSIDE
VILLAS

WATER BANK

Thatch Carr
Farm

Franklins Drain

South Idle Drain

2

Field House
Farm

FIELD LA

Load Drain

1

Wroot Church Drain

02

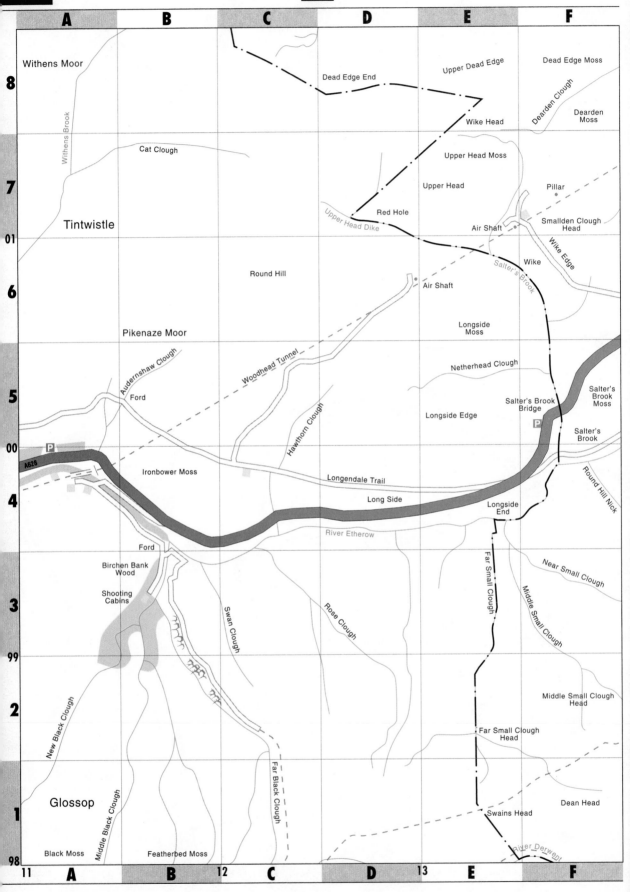

A   B   C   D   E   F

8 Withens Moor

Dead Edge End   Upper Dead Edge   Dead Edge Moss

Wike Head   Dearden Clough   Dearden Moss

Cat Clough   Upper Head Moss

7 Tintwistle   Upper Head   Pillar

Red Hole   Smallden Clough Head

01   Air Shaft   Wike

Round Hill   Wike Edge

6   Air Shaft   Salter's Brook

Pikenaze Moor   Longside Moss

Woodhead Tunnel   Netherhead Clough   Salter's Brook Moss

5   Audernshaw Clough   Salter's Brook Bridge   Salter's Brook Moss

Ford   Hawthorn Clough   Longside Edge   P   Salter's Brook

00   P   Longendale Trail   Round Hill Nick

A628   Ironbower Moss   Long Side   Longside End

4   River Etherow

Ford   Near Small Clough

Birchen Bank Wood   Far Small Clough   Middle Small Clough

3 Shooting Cabins   Swan Clough   Rose Clough

99   Middle Small Clough Head

2   Far Small Clough Head

New Black Clough   Far Small Clough

1 Glossop   Middle Black Clough   Far Black Clough   Dean Head

Swains Head   River Derwent

98 Black Moss   Featherbed Moss

11 A   B   12   C   D   13   E   F

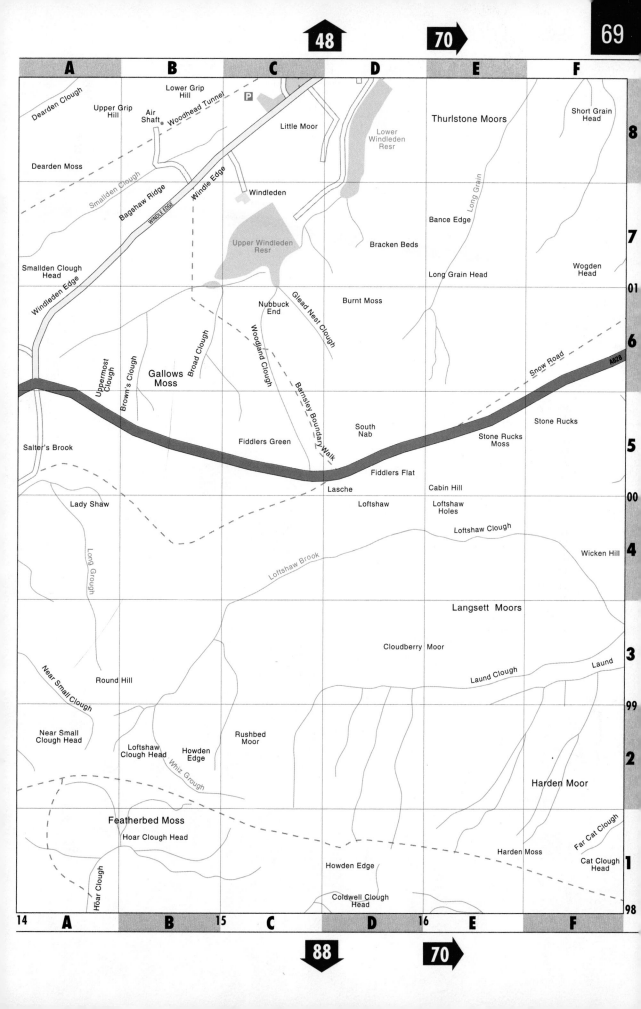

A B C D E F

Dearden Clough

Upper Grip Hill

Lower Grip Hill

Air Shaft

Woodhead Tunnel

P

Little Moor

Lower Windleden Resr

Thurlstone Moors

Short Grain Head

8

Dearden Moss

Smallden Clough

Bagshaw Ridge

Windle Edge

WINDLE EDGE

Windleden

Bance Edge

Long Grain

7

Smallden Clough Head

Windleden Edge

Broad Clough

Nubbuck End

Glead Nest Clough

Burnt Moss

Long Grain Head

Wogden Head

01

Uppermost Clough

Brown's Clough

Gallows Moss

Woodland Clough

Barnsley Boundary Walk

Snow Road

A628

6

Salter's Brook

Fiddlers Green

South Nab

Stone Rucks Moss

Stone Rucks

5

Fiddlers Flat

Lasche

Cabin Hill

Lady Shaw

Long Grough

Loftshaw

Loftshaw Holes

Loftshaw Clough

Wicken Hill

00

4

Loftshaw Brook

Langsett Moors

Cloudberry Moor

Round Hill

Laund Clough

Laund

3

Near Small Clough

99

Near Small Clough Head

Loftshaw Clough Head

Howden Edge

Whiz Grough

Rushbed Moor

Harden Moor

2

Featherbed Moss

Hoar Clough Head

Harden Moss

Far Cat Clough

Cat Clough Head

1

Hoar Clough

Howden Edge

Coldwell Clough Head

98

14 A B 15 C D 16 E F

A   B   C   D   E   F

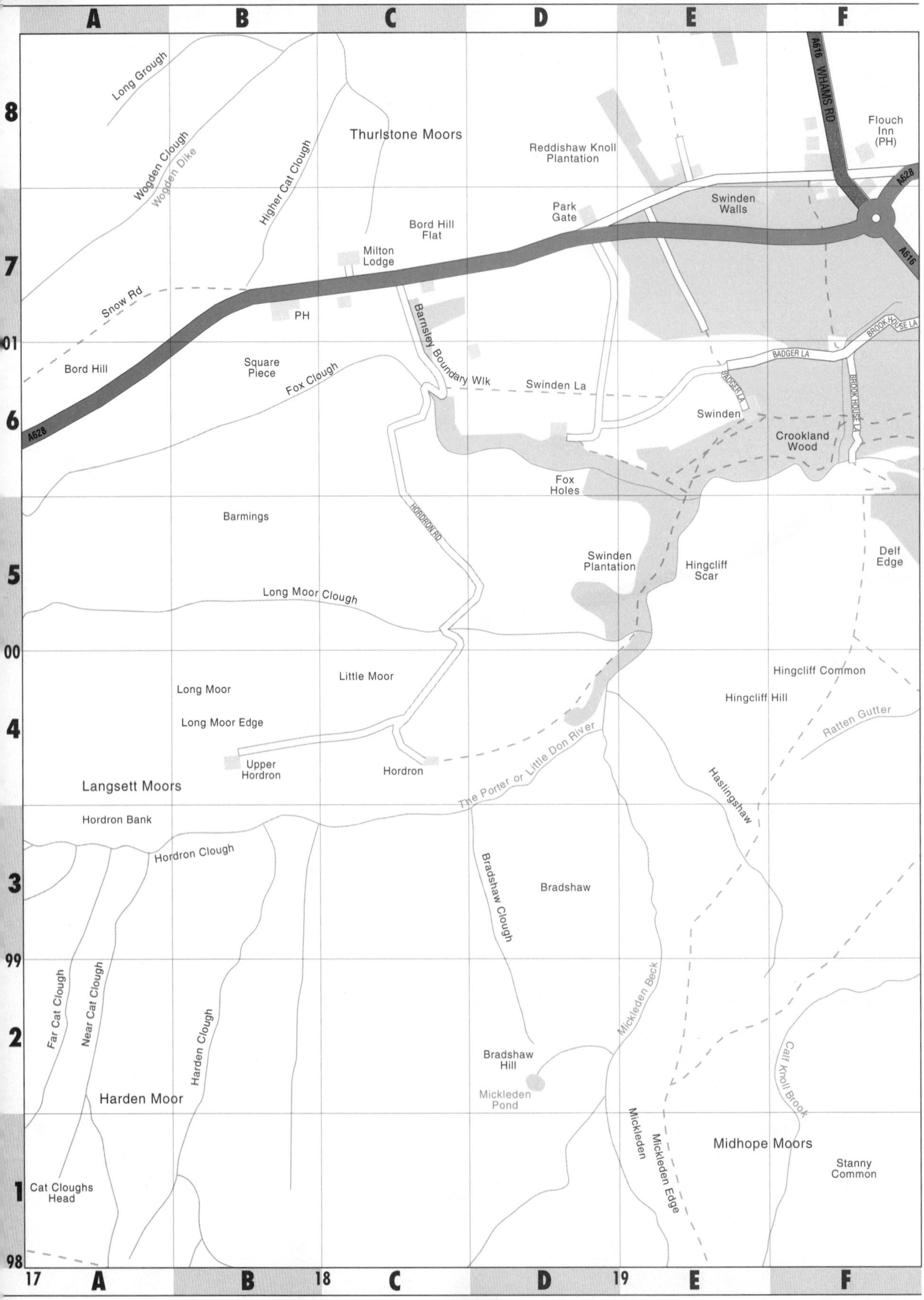

8

Long Grough

Thurlstone Moors

Reddishaw Knoll
Plantation

Flouch
Inn
(PH)

A628

A616 WHAMS RD

Wogden Clough

Wogden Dike

Higher Cat Clough

Bord Hill
Flat

Park
Gate

Swinden
Walls

A616

7

Milton
Lodge

Snow Rd

PH

Square
Piece

Fox Clough

Barnsley Boundary Wlk

Swinden La

BADGER LA

BADGER LA

BROOK HOUSE LA

BROOK HOUSE LA

01

Bord Hill

Swinden

Crookland
Wood

6

A628

Fox
Holes

Barmings

HORDRON RD

Swinden
Plantation

Hingcliff
Scar

Delf
Edge

5

Long Moor Clough

Hingcliff Common

00

Little Moor

Hingcliff Hill

Ratten Gutter

Long Moor

4

Long Moor Edge

Upper
Hordron

Hordron

The Porter or Little Don River

Haslingshaw

Langsett Moors

Hordron Bank

Hordron Clough

Bradshaw Clough

Bradshaw

Mickleden Beck

3

99

Far Cat Clough

Near Cat Clough

Harden Clough

Bradshaw
Hill

Mickleden

Calf Knoll Brook

2

Mickleden Edge

Midhope Moors

Mickleden
Pond

Harden Moor

Stanny
Common

1

Cat Cloughs
Head

98

17   A   B   18   C   D   19   E   F

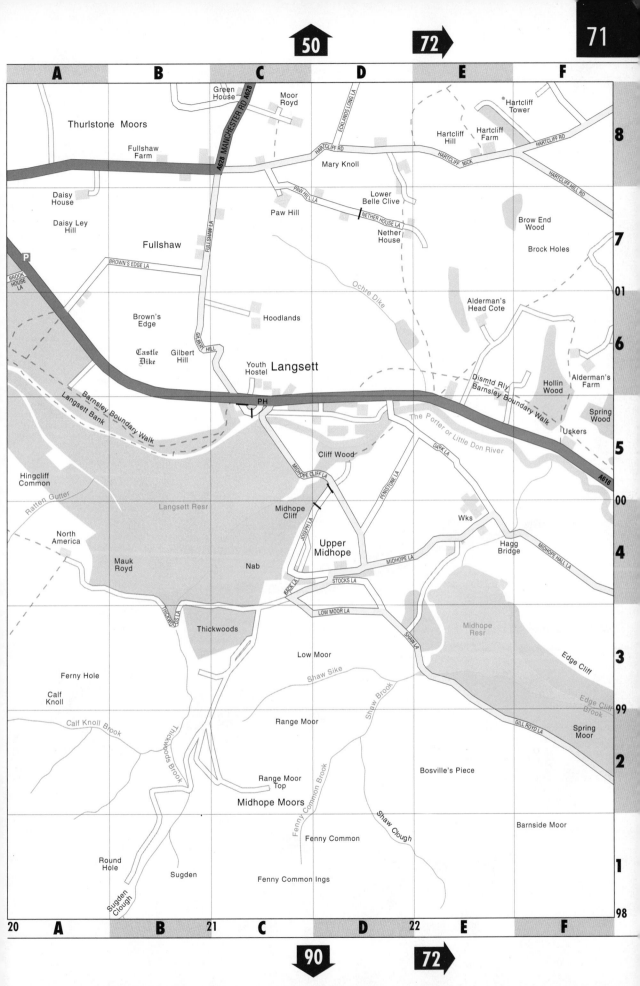

50
72

A B C D E F

8

Thurlstone Moors

Green
House

Moor
Royd

Hartcliff
Tower

Fullshaw
Farm

A628 MANCHESTER RD A628

Hartcliff
Hill

Hartcliff
Farm

HARTCLIFF RD

ECKLANDS LONG LA

HARTCLIFF RD

Mary Knoll

HARTCLIFF NICK

HARTCLIFF HILL RD

Daisy
House

PAW HILL LA

Lower
Belle Clive

Brow End
Wood

7

Daisy Ley
Hill

Paw Hill

NETHER HOUSE LA

Nether
House

Brock Holes

FULLSHAW LA

Fullshaw

Ochre Dike

01

BROWN'S EDGE LA

Alderman's
Head Cote

6

P

Brown's
Edge

Hoodlands

GILBERT HILL

Dismtd Rly
Barnsley Boundary Walk

Hollin
Wood

Alderman's
Farm

BROOK
HOUSE LA

Castle
Dike

Gilbert
Hill

Youth
Hostel

Langsett

Spring
Wood

Barnsley Boundary Walk
Langsett Bank

PH

The Porter or Little Don River

Uskers

5

Hingcliff
Common

Cliff Wood

MIDHOPE CLIFF LA

DARK LA

FENNISTONE LA

A616

Ratten Gutter

Langsett Resr

Midhope
Cliff

Wks

00

North
America

JOSEPH LA

Upper
Midhope

MIDHOPE LA

Hagg
Bridge

MIDHOPE HALL LA

4

Mauk
Royd

Nab

STOCKS LA

BACK LA

Midhope
Resr

THICKWOODS LA

LOW MOOR LA

Thickwoods

SHAW LA

Edge Cliff

3

Ferny Hole

Low Moor

Shaw Sike

Shaw Brook

Edge Cliff
Brook

99

Calf
Knoll

Calf Knoll Brook

Thickwoods Brook

Range Moor

GILL ROYD LA

Spring
Moor

2

Range Moor
Top

Fenny Common Brook

Bosville's Piece

Midhope Moors

Shaw Clough

Barnside Moor

Round
Hole

Fenny Common

1

Sugden

Fenny Common Ings

Sugden Clough

98

20 A B 21 C D 22 E F

90
72

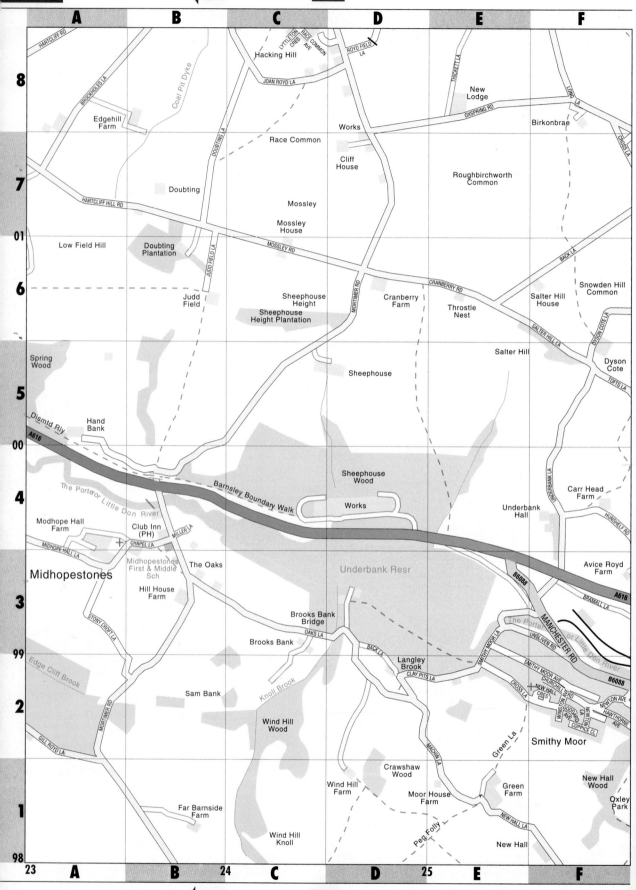

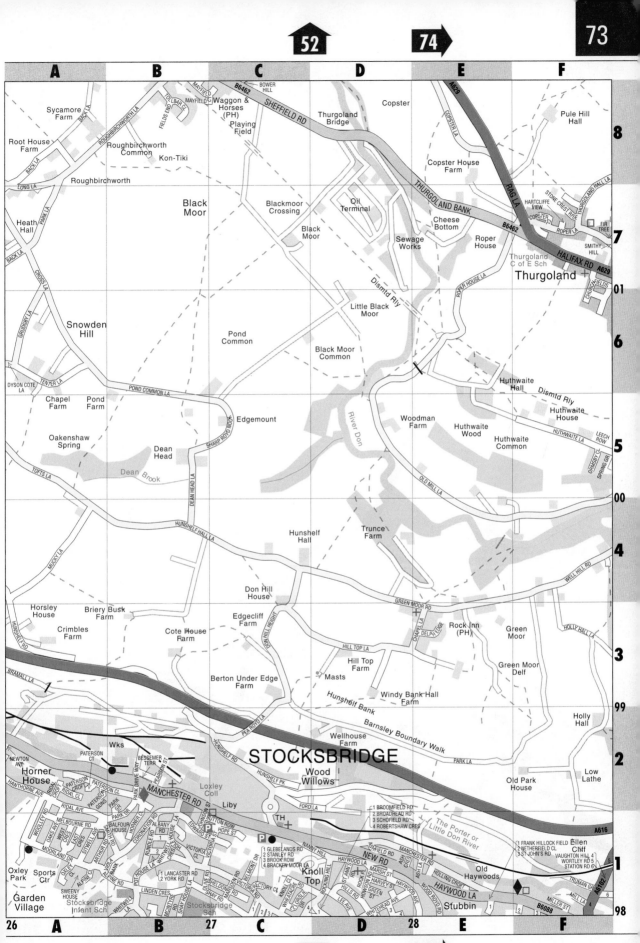

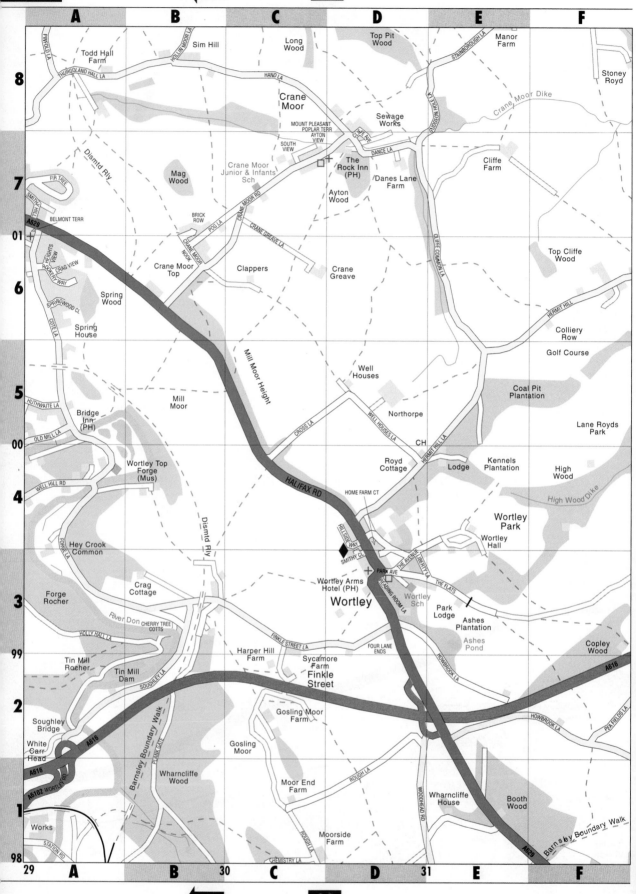

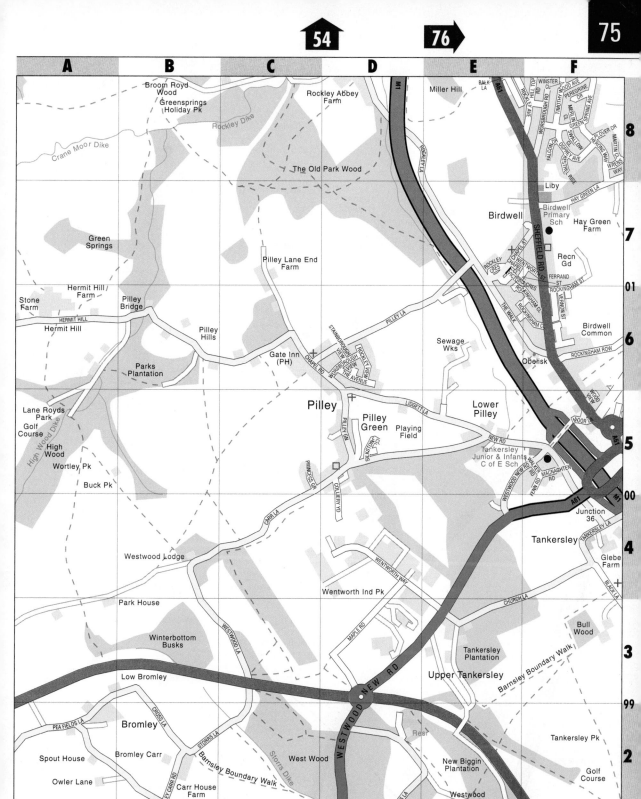

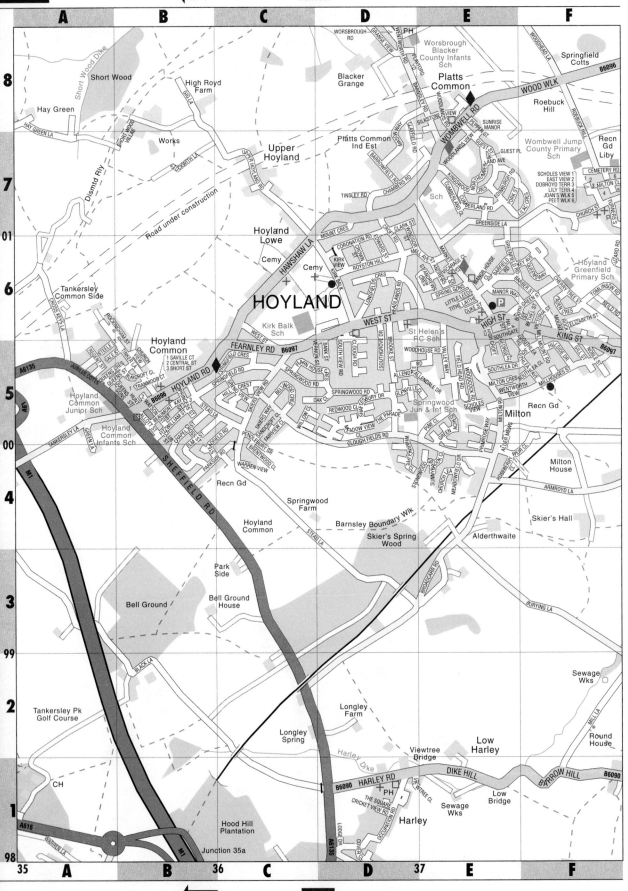

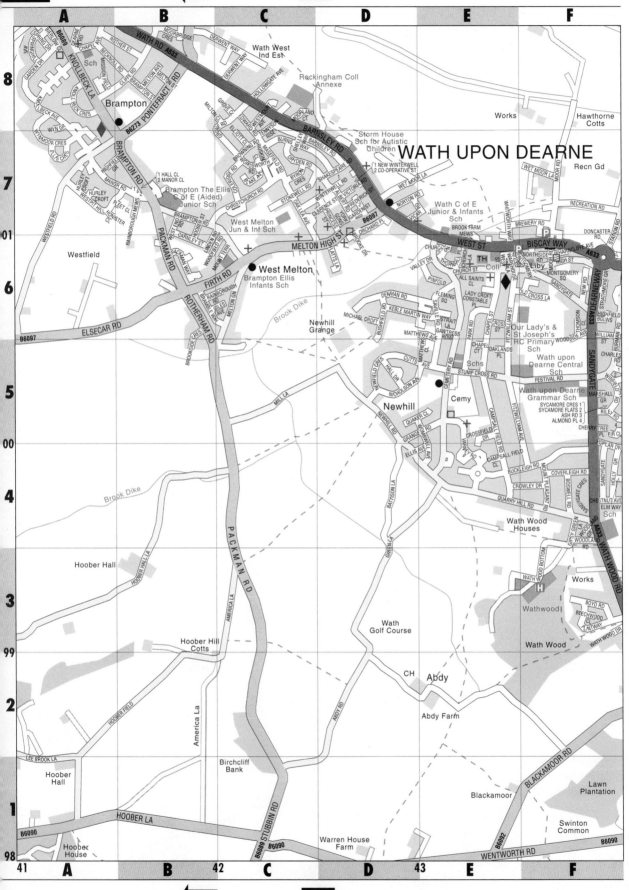

77
57

A   B   C   D   E   F

8

WATH RD A633

Wath West Ind Est

Rockingham Coll Annexe

Brampton

B6273

Works

Hawthorne Cotts

KNOLLBECK LA

PONTEFRACT RD

Storm House Sch for Autistic Children

WATH UPON DEARNE

BARNSLEY RD

Recn Gd

7

1 NEW WINTERWELL
2 CO-OPERATIVE ST

WET MOOR LA

RECREATION RD

Brampton The Ellis C of E (Aided) Junior Sch

Wath C of E Junior & Infants Sch

Brewery RD

Doncaster RD

01

BRAMPTON RD

West Melton Jun & Inf Sch

B6097

Brook Farm Mews

WEST ST

BISCAY WAY

A633

Westfield

PACKMAN RD

West Melton

MELTON HIGH ST

TH Coll

Libv

6

FIRTH RD

Brampton Ellis Infants Sch

All Saints CL

Lady Croft Constable

Sandygate

OLD CROSS LA

ROTHERHAM RD

Brook Dike

Newhill Grange

DENMAN RD

KEBLE MARTIN WAY

Our Lady's & St Joseph's RC Primary Sch

DEARNE WAY

ELSECAR RD

B6097

Wath upon Dearne Central Sch

Charles ST

5

MILL LA

Newhill

NEWHILL RD

Cemy

Wath upon Dearne Grammar Sch

SYCAMORE CRES 1
SYCAMORE FLATS 2
ASH RD 3
ALMOND PL 4

SANDYGATE

MARSHALL

RILEY

00

Campsall Field

4

PACKMAN RD

Brook Dike

BATTISON LA

GREEN LA

QUARRY HILL RD

Wath Wood Houses

A633 WATH WOOD RD

3

Hoober Hall

HOOBER HALL LA

Wath Golf Course

Wathwood

BOYD RD

Works

BEECHWOOD

Hoober Hill Cotts

CH Abdy

Wath Wood

BLACKAMOOR RD

99

AMERICA LA

Lawn Plantation

2

HOOBER FIELD

America La

Abdy Farm

Blackamoor

Swinton Common

1

LEE BROOK LA

Hoober Hall

STUBBIN RD

Birchcliff Bank

HOOBER LA

B6089 B6090

Warren House Farm

WENTWORTH RD

B6092

B6090

98

B6090

Hoober House

41   A   B   42   C   D   43   E   F

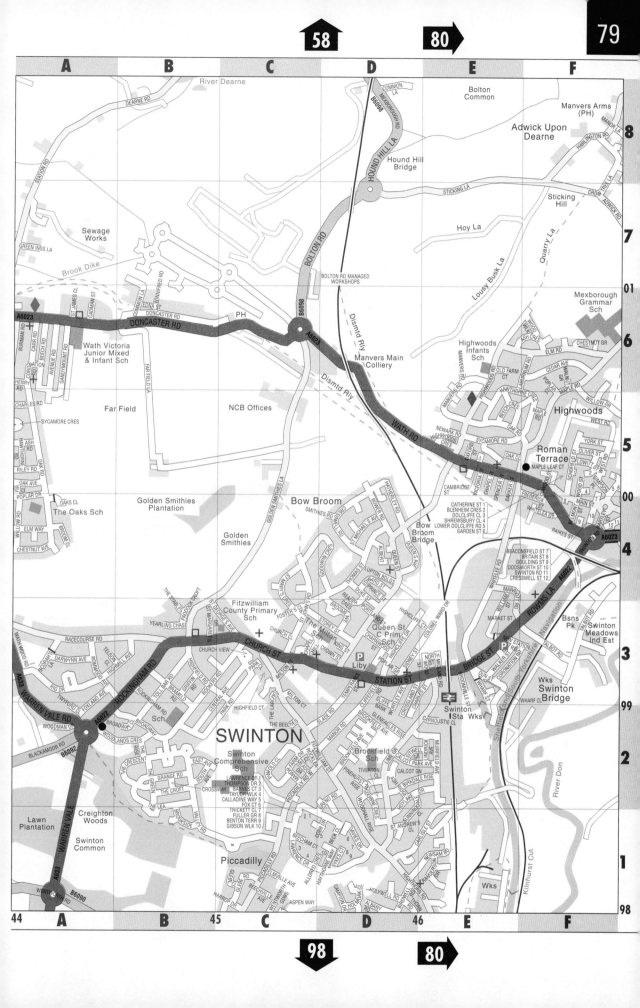

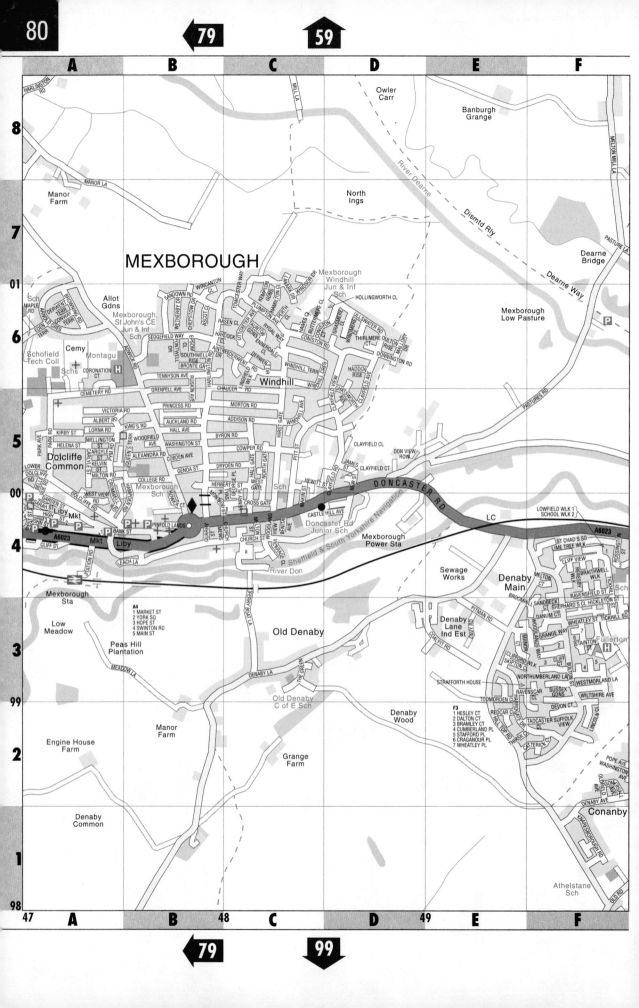

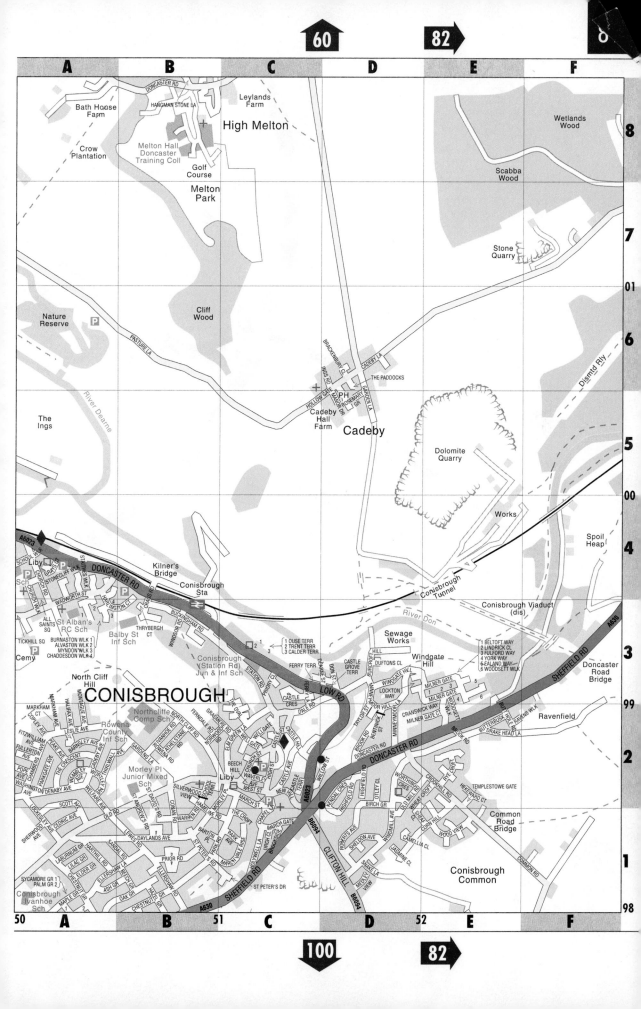

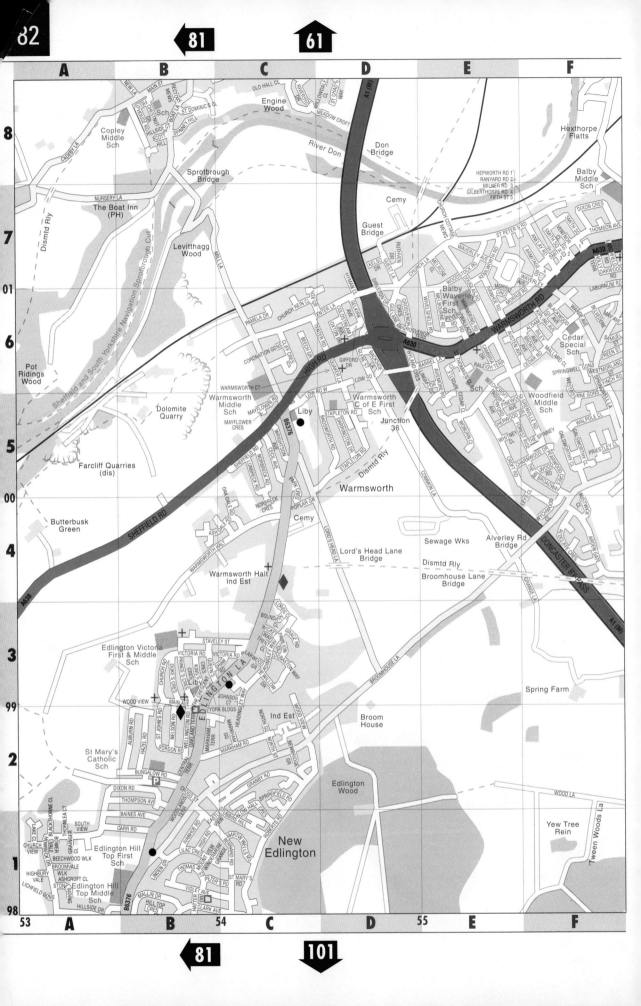

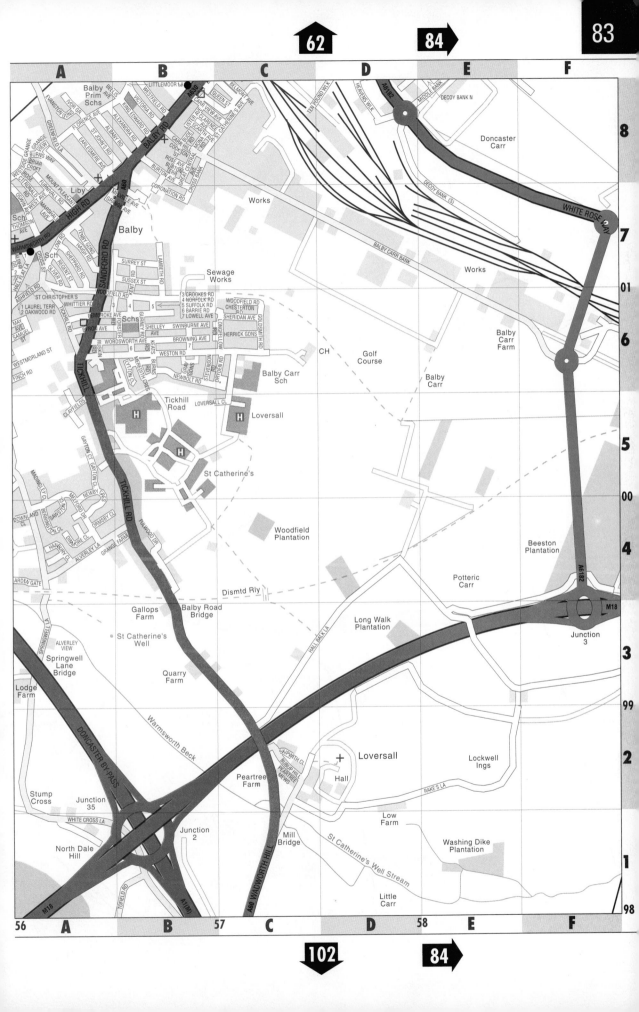

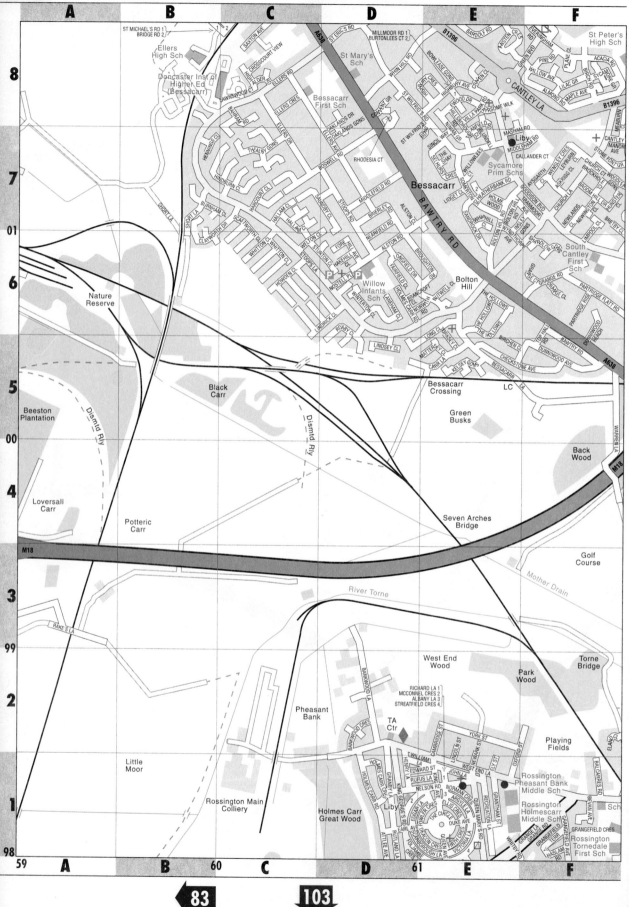

83
63

A B C D E F

8

7

01

6

5

00

4

3

99

2

1

98

59 A B 60 C D 61 E F

St Peter's High Sch

B1396

St Michael's Rd 1
Bridge Rd 2

Ellers High Sch

Doncaster Inst of Higher Ed (Bessacarr)

SAXTON AVE
CROSSCOURT VIEW

St Eric's Rd
Millmoor Rd 1
Burtonlees Ct 2

St Mary's Sch

Bessacarr First Sch

Bessacarr

CANTLEY LA

B1396

CANTLEY MANOR AVE

Liby

Sycamore Prim Schs

South Cantley First Sch

Rhodesia Ct

BAWTRY RD

Bolton Hill

Willow Infants Sch

Nature Reserve

Black Carr

Dismtd Rly

Beeston Plantation

Loversall Carr

Potteric Carr

M18

Bessacarr Crossing

LC

Green Busks

Back Wood

M18

A638

Seven Arches Bridge

Golf Course

Mother Drain

River Torne

West End Wood

Park Wood

Torne Bridge

RAKE'S LA

Pheasant Bank

Richard La 1
McConnel Cres 2
Albany La 3
Streatfield Cres 4

TA Ctr

Playing Fields

Rossington Pheasant Bank Middle Sch

Little Moor

Rossington Main Colliery

Holmes Carr Great Wood

Liby

Rossington Holmescarr Middle Sch

Grangefield Cres

Rossington Tornedale First Sch

Sch

St Peter's High Sch
Four Lane Ends Plantation
1 MEABURN CL
2 STONE FONT GR
CANTLEY LA
Catherine McAuley Upper Sch
Convent
DONCASTER RD
SANDPIT HILL
MOOR GAP
Branton
Branton C of E Sch
Great Hakehill Field
QUARRY LA
LANGTON GDNS
SUNNYSIDE
DONCASTER RD
Folly Plantation
Brockholes Farm
Millhouse Farm
Auckley Bridge
Dam End
MAIN ST B1396
Black Carr Plantation
Old Springs Wood
Eagle & Child (PH)
South Cantley Middle Sch
Short Plats Plantation
Black Carr
Sewage Works
The Carrs
Crow Pool Plantation
Insley Plantation
Hatchell Wood
Hatchell Wood
HATCHELLWOOD VIEW
Mother Drain
Mill Hill
WARNINGTON DR
BAWTRY RD
Hayfield Comprehensive Sch
CH
The Warren
Hay Field
Twelve Months Carr
OAK TREE AVE 1
WALNUT AVE 2
WILLOW CRES 3
Finningley Camp County Primary Schs
Golf Course
Rossington Bridge
River Torne
Rossington Bridge Farm
Hayfield Lodge Farm
HAYFIELD LA
Hanging Carr Farm
B6463
Castle Hills
Marr Flats
Poor's Land
Savage Wood
Torne Valley Farm
Sheep Bridge
SHEEP BRIDGE LA
Gelster Wood
GREAT NORTH RD
Hurst Plantation
Savage Wood End
Poplars Farm
Hurst Wood
Gelster Lane Holt
Pithill
LITTLEWORTH CL
LITTLEWORTH LA
Littleworth
Gipsy Plantation
Warren House Farm
STRIPE RD B6463
PLOVER CT
Wr Twr
A638
Rossington

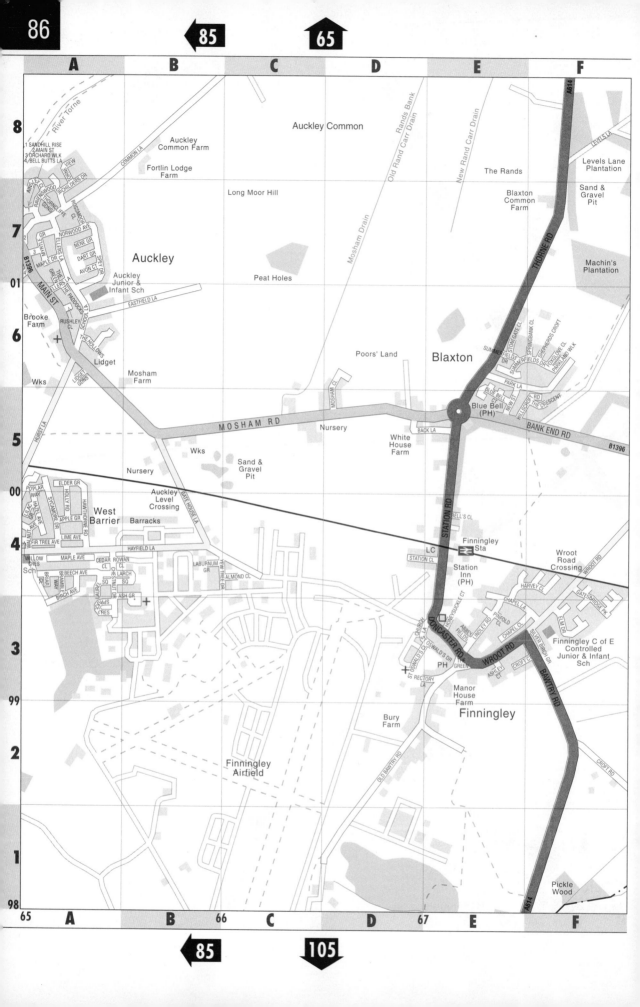

A B C D E F

8

River Torne

Auckley Common

Rands Bank

Old Rand Carr Drain

New Rand Carr Drain

Levels Lane
Plantation

1 SANDHILL RISE
2 MAIN ST
3 ORCHARD WLK
4 BELL BUTTS LA

Auckley
Common Farm

The Rands

Sand &
Gravel
Pit

Fortlin Lodge
Farm

COMMON LA

Blaxton
Common
Farm

7

Long Moor Hill

Machin's
Plantation

THORNE RD

Auckley

NORWOOD AVE
NENE GR
DART GR
AVON CT

Peat Holes

Mosham Drain

01

Auckley
Junior &
Infant Sch

EASTFIELD LA

6

Brooke
Farm

Poors' Land

Blaxton

SUMMERFIELDS DR
STONEGATE CL
SPRINGBANK CL
SHEPHERDS CROFT
FOXGLOVE CL
PARKLAND WLK

Lidget

Park La

Blue Bell
(PH)

HILLSCROFT RD
NEW ST
THE CRESCENT

Mosham
Farm

5

HURST LA

MOSHAM RD

Nursery

BACK LA

BANK END RD

B1396

Wks

White
House
Farm

Nursery

Sand &
Gravel
Pit

STATION RD

00

POPLAR
WAY
ELDER GR

Auckley
Level
Crossing

GATE HOUSE LA

BELL'S CL

Wroot
Road
Crossing

WROOT RD

4

West
Barrier

HAWTHORNE RD
HOLLY RD
LIME RD

Barracks

HAYFIELD LA

LC

STATION CL

Finningley
Sta

Finningley C of E
Controlled
Junior & Infant
Sch

GATESBRIDGE PK

WILLOW
CRES
Sch

MAPLE AVE

CEDAR
CL
ROWAN
CL

LABURNUM
GR

YEW TREE DR

ALMOND CL

Station
Inn
(PH)

HARVEY CL

CHAPEL LA

ELM DR

3

BEECH AVE
BRAMBLE WAY
BIRCH AVE

LARCH
SQ
ASH GR

HONEYSUCKLE CT

MOLEY RD
PINFOLD
CL
CHAPEL CL

SILVER BIRCH GR

CROFT CL

DONCASTER RD

ABBEY FIELDS

CHURCH

PH
GREEN

WROOT RD

ASHLEY
CT

BANTRY RD

99

ST OSWALD'S DR

RECTORY
LA

Manor
House
Farm

Finningley

2

Finningley
Airfield

Bury
Farm

OLD BANTRY RD

CROFT RD

1

A614

Pickle
Wood

98

65 A 66 B C 67 D E F

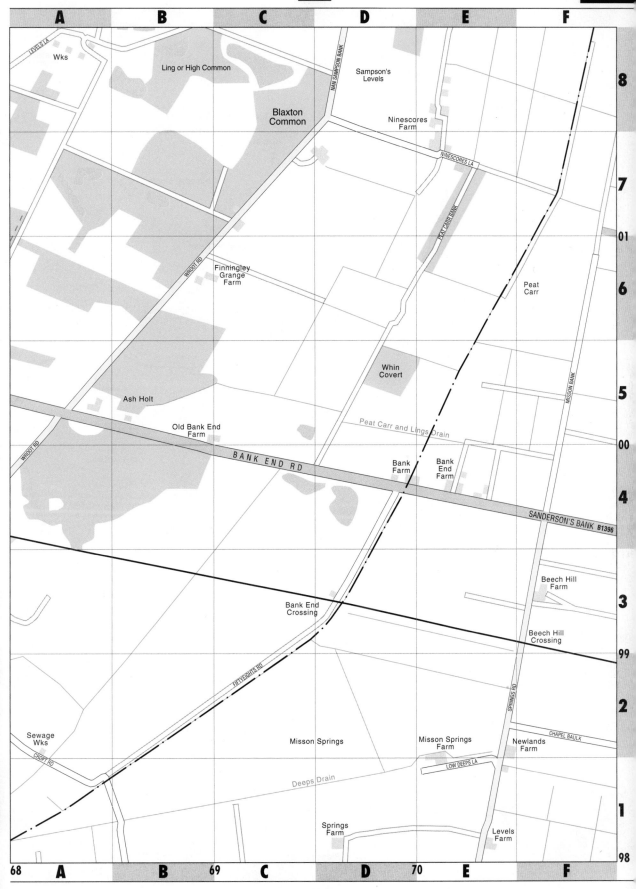

A   B   C   D   E   F

8
01
7
6
5
00
4
3
99
2
1
98

Wks

LEVELS LA

Ling or High Common

Blaxton
Common

MAN SAMPSON BANK

Sampson's
Levels

Ninescores
Farm

NINESCORES LA

PEAT CARR BANK

Peat
Carr

MISSON BANK

WROOT RD

Finningley
Grange
Farm

Ash Holt

WROOT RD

Old Bank End
Farm

Whin
Covert

Peat Carr and Lings Drain

BANK END RD

Bank
Farm

Bank
End
Farm

SANDERSON'S BANK   B1396

Beech Hill
Farm

Beech Hill
Crossing

Bank End
Crossing

HEYEIGHTS RD

SPRINGS RD

Sewage
Wks

CROFT RD

Misson Springs

Deeps Drain

Misson Springs
Farm

LOW DEEPS LA

CHAPEL BAULK

Newlands
Farm

Springs
Farm

Levels
Farm

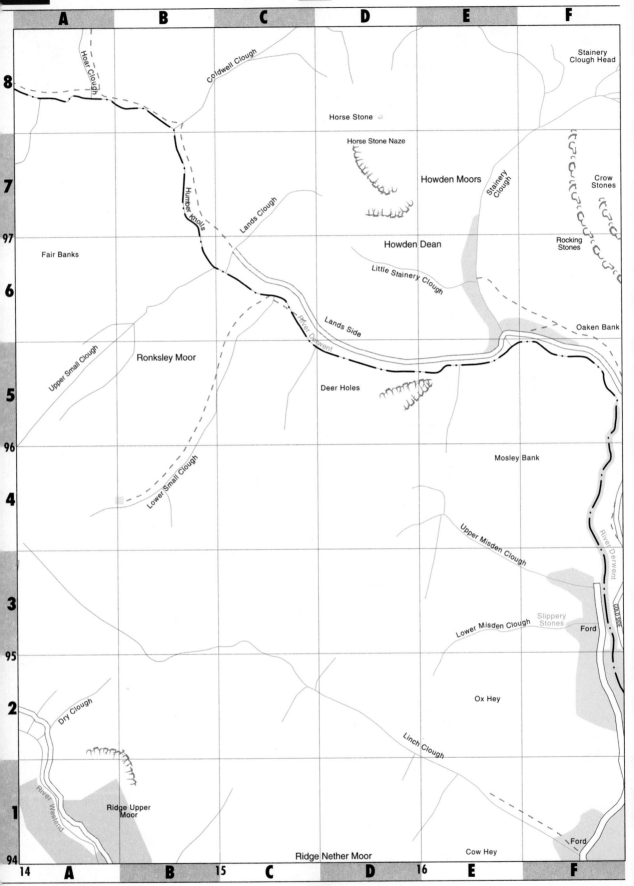

A B C D E F

8

Hoar Clough

Coldwell Clough

Stainery
Clough Head

Horse Stone

Horse Stone Naze

7

Humber Knolls

Lands Clough

Howden Moors

Stainery
Clough

Crow
Stones

97

Fair Banks

Howden Dean

Rocking
Stones

Little Stainery Clough

6

River Derwent

Lands Side

Oaken Bank

Upper Small Clough

Ronksley Moor

Deer Holes

5

96

Lower Small Clough

Mosley Bank

4

Upper Misden Clough

River Derwent

3

Lower Misden Clough

Slippery
Stones

Ford

COLD SIDE

95

Ox Hey

2

Dry Clough

Linch Clough

1

River Westend

Ridge Upper
Moor

Cow Hey

Ford

94

Ridge Nether Moor

14 A B 15 C D 16 E F

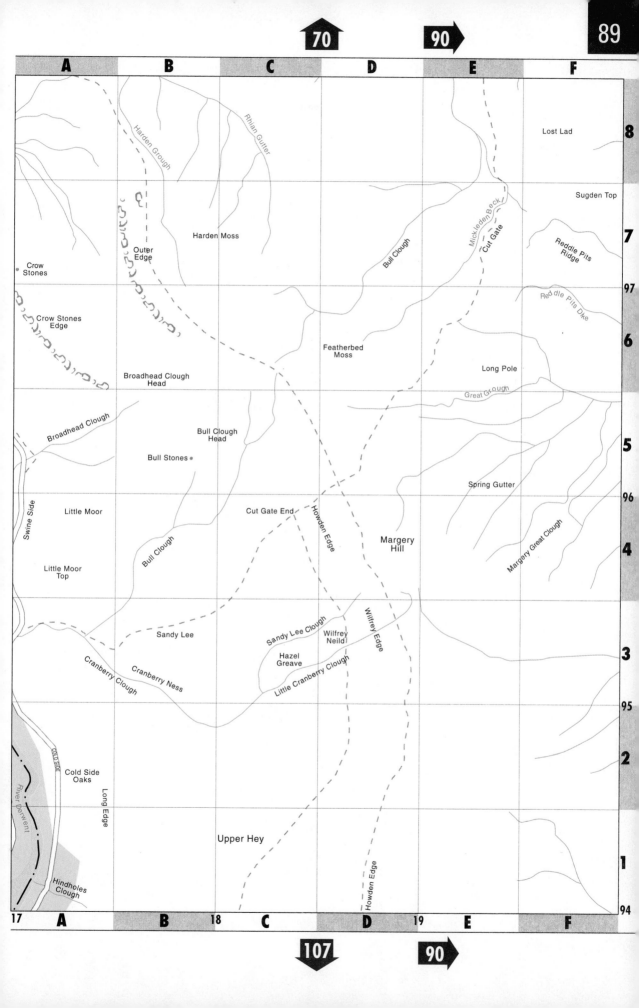

Lost Lad

Sugden Top

Harden Moss

Rhian Gutter

Harden Grough

Outer Edge

Crow Stones

Crow Stones Edge

Broadhead Clough Head

Broadhead Clough

Bull Clough Head

Bull Stones

Little Moor

Swine Side

Little Moor Top

Bull Clough

Cut Gate End

Howden Edge

Sandy Lee

Sandy Lee Clough

Cranberry Clough

Cranberry Ness

Hazel Greave

Wilfrey Neild

Little Cranberry Clough

Wilfrey Edge

Margery Hill

Bull Clough

Featherbed Moss

Mickleden Beck

Cut Gate

Reddle Pits Ridge

Reddle Pits Dke

Long Pole

Great Grough

Spring Gutter

Margery Great Clough

Cold Side

Cold Side Oaks

Long Edge

River Derwent

Upper Hey

Hindholes Clough

Howden Edge

89
71

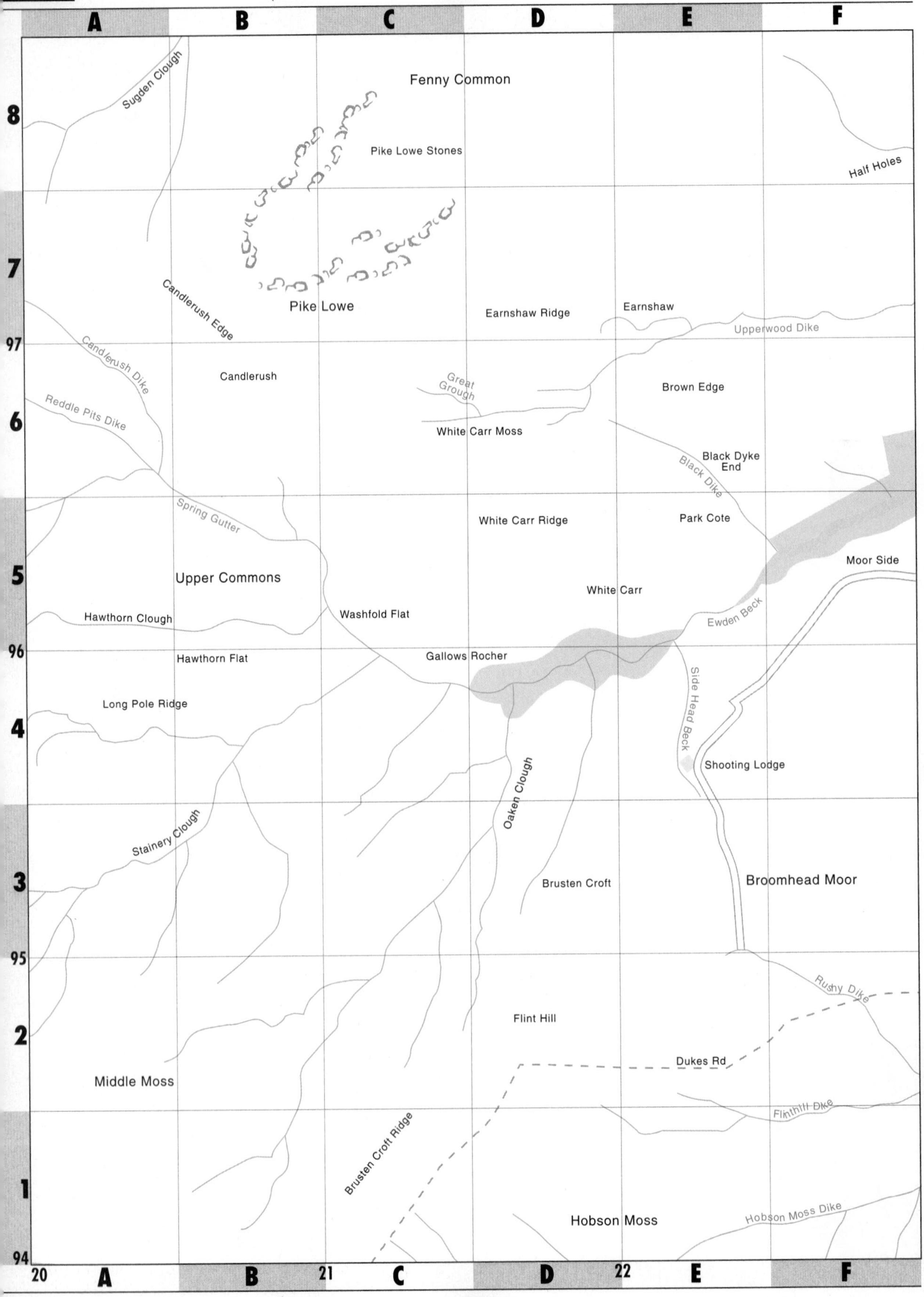

A　　　B　　　C　　　D　　　E　　　F

Fenny Common

8

Sugden Clough

Pike Lowe Stones

Half Holes

7

Candlerush Edge

Pike Lowe

Earnshaw Ridge

Earnshaw

Upperwood Dike

97

Candlerush Dike

Candlerush

Great Grough

Brown Edge

6

Reddle Pits Dike

White Carr Moss

Black Dike End

Black Dike

Spring Gutter

White Carr Ridge

Park Cote

Moor Side

5

Upper Commons

White Carr

Ewden Beck

Hawthorn Clough

Washfold Flat

96

Hawthorn Flat

Gallows Rocher

Side Head Beck

Long Pole Ridge

4

Shooting Lodge

Oaken Clough

Stainery Clough

3

Brusten Croft

Broomhead Moor

95

Rushy Dike

2

Flint Hill

Dukes Rd

Middle Moss

Flinthill Dike

Brusten Croft Ridge

1

Hobson Moss

Hobson Moss Dike

94

20　　A　　　B　　21　　C　　　D　　22　　E　　　F

89
108

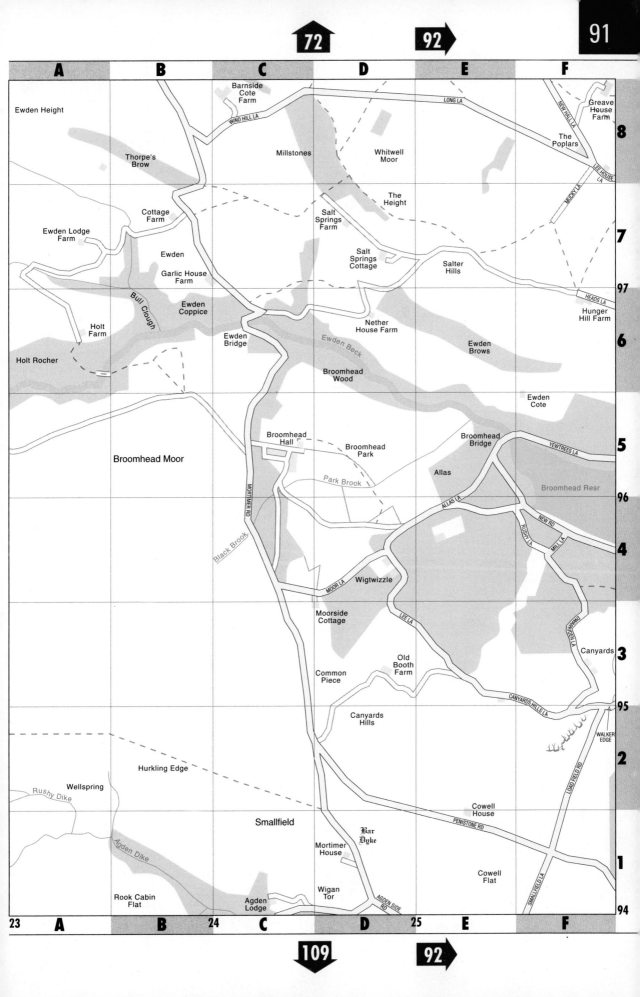

A   B   C   D   E   F

Ewden Height

Barnside
Cote
Farm

WIND HILL LA

LONG LA

NEW HALL LA

Greave
House
Farm

8

The
Poplars

LEE HOUSE
LA

Thorpe's
Brow

Millstones

Whitwell
Moor

MUCKY LA

Cottage
Farm

The
Height

7

Ewden

Salt
Springs
Farm

Ewden Lodge
Farm

Garlic House
Farm

Salt
Springs
Cottage

Salter
Hills

97

HEADS LA

Ewden
Coppice

Bull Clough

Nether
House Farm

Ewden
Brows

Hunger
Hill Farm

6

Holt
Farm

Ewden
Bridge

Ewden Beck

Holt Rocher

Broomhead
Wood

Ewden
Cote

Broomhead
Hall

Broomhead
Park

Broomhead
Bridge

YEWTREES LA

5

Broomhead Moor

Allas

Broomhead Resr

Park Brook

ALLAS LA

96

MORTIMER RD

NEW RD

RUSHY LA

MILL LA

4

Black Brook

MOOR LA

Wigtwizzle

OWLER LA

WARREN LA

Canyards

3

Moorside
Cottage

LEE LA

Old
Booth
Farm

CANYARDS HILLS LA

95

Common
Piece

Canyards
Hills

WALKER
EDGE

2

Hurkling Edge

Wellspring

Rushy Dike

Cowell
House

PENISTONE RD

LOAD FIELD RD

Smallfield

Bar
Dyke

Mortimer
House

Agden Dike

Cowell
Flat

1

Rook Cabin
Flat

Agden
Lodge

Wigan
Tor

AGDEN SIDE
RD

SMALLFIELD LA

94

23   A   B   24   C   D   25   E   F

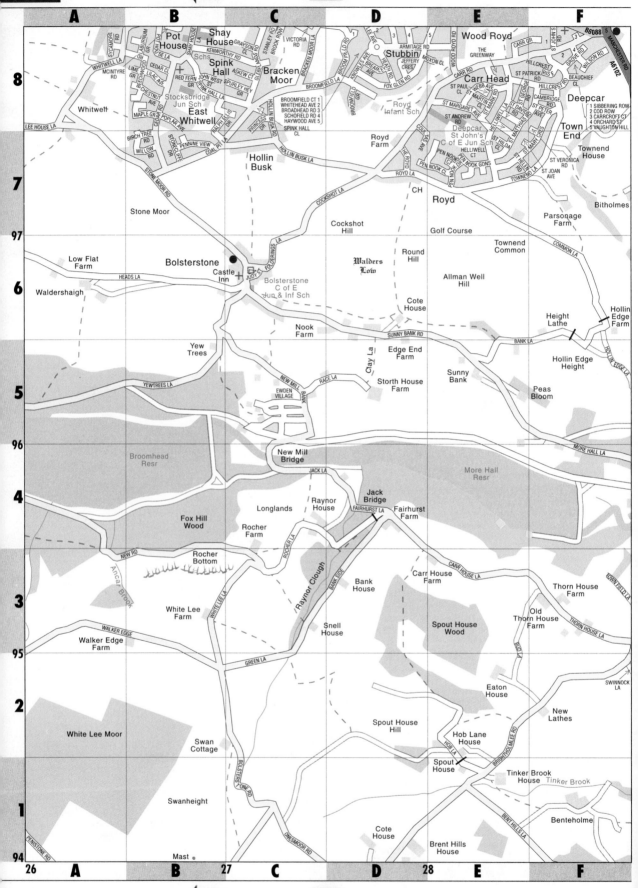

A B C D E F

8

Whitwell

Pot House
Shay House
Spink Hall
Stocksbridge Jun Sch
East Whitwell

Bracken Moor

Victoria Rd

BROOMFIELD CT 1
WHITEHEAD AVE 2
BROADHEAD RD 3
SCHOFIELD RD 4
HAYWOOD AVE 5

Stubbin

Wood Royd

THE GREENWAY

Carr Head

Deepcar
1 SIBBERING ROW
2 COD ROW
3 CARRCROFT CL
4 ORCHARD ST
5 VAUGHTON HILL

Town End

Townend House

Royd Infant Sch

Royd Farm

Deepcar St John's C of E Jun Sch

HELLIWELL CT

7

Stone Moor

Hollin Busk

Hollin Busk

CH

Royd

Bitholmes

Parsonage Farm

97

Low Flat Farm

Bolsterstone

Castle Inn

Bolsterstone C of E Jun & Inf Sch

Cockshot Hill

Walders Low

Round Hill

Golf Course

Townend Common

6

Waldershaigh

HEADS LA

Cote House

Allman Well Hill

Height Lathe

Hollin Edge Farm

Hollin Edge Height

Nook Farm

SUNNY BANK RD

BANK LA

Yew Trees

YEWTREES LA

Edge End Farm

Sunny Bank

Peas Bloom

5

EWDEN VILLAGE

NEW MILL BANK

RACE LA

Clay La

Storth House Farm

96

Broomhead Resr

New Mill Bridge

JACK LA

More Hall Resr

MORE HALL LA

4

Longlands

Rocher Farm

Raynor House

Jack Bridge

FAIRHURST LA

Fairhurst Farm

Fox Hill Wood

NEW RD

Rocher Bottom

Raynor Clough

BANK SIDE

Bank House

CARR HOUSE LA

Carr House Farm

Thorn House Farm

3

White Lee Farm

WHITE LEE LA

Snell House

Spout House Wood

Old Thorn House Farm

THORN HOUSE LA

WALKER EDGE

95

Walker Edge Farm

GREEN LA

Eaton House

SWINNOCK LA

2

White Lee Moor

Swan Cottage

Spout House Hill

Hob Lane House

Spout House

New Lathes

Tinker Brook House

Tinker Brook

Benteholme

1

Swanheight

BOLSTERS TONE RD

ONESMOOR RD

Cote House

Brent Hills House

BENT HILLS LA

94

PENISTONE RD

Mast

26 A B 27 C D 28 E F

93
75

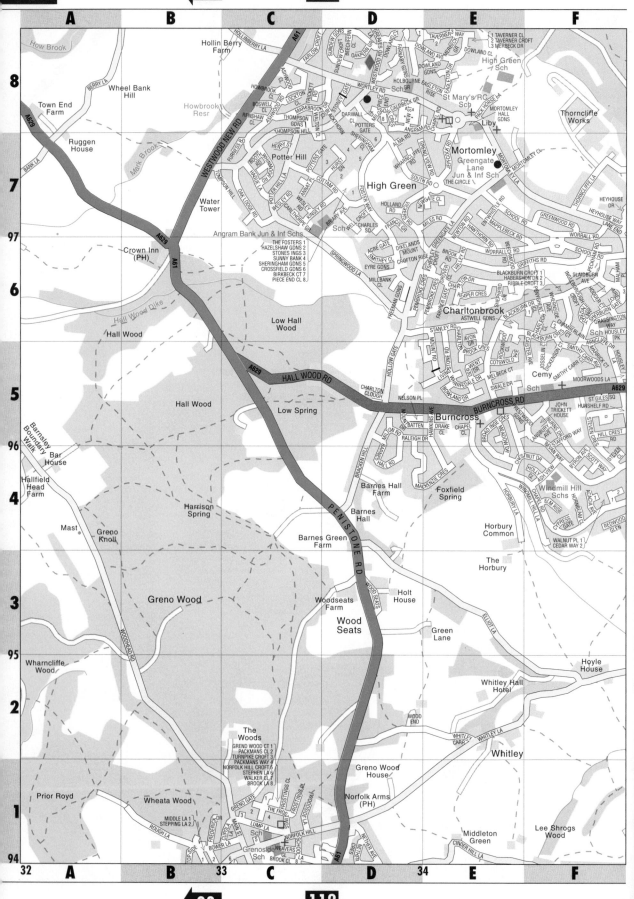

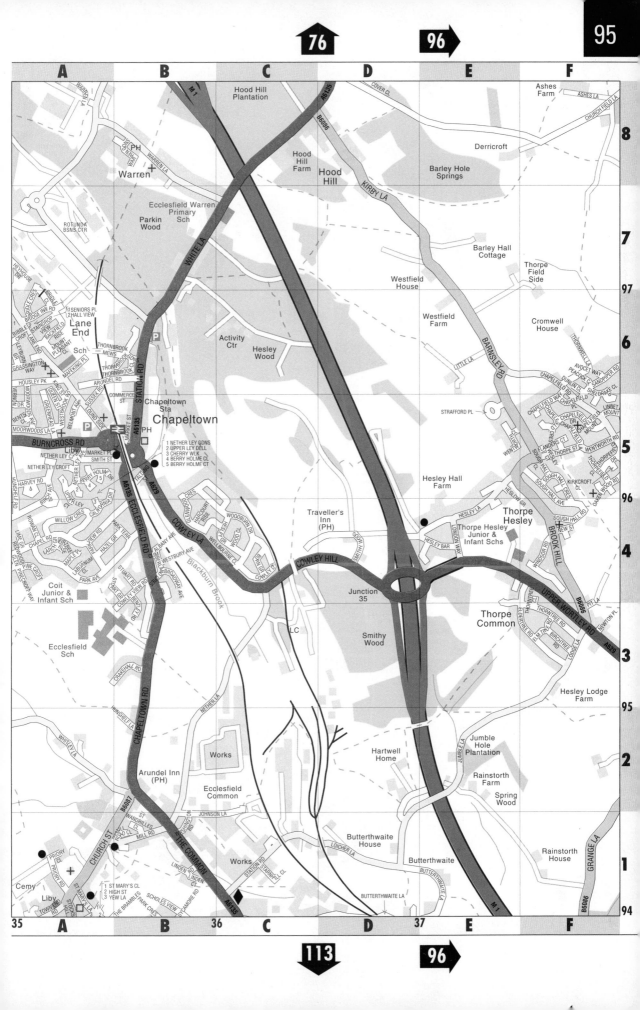

95
77

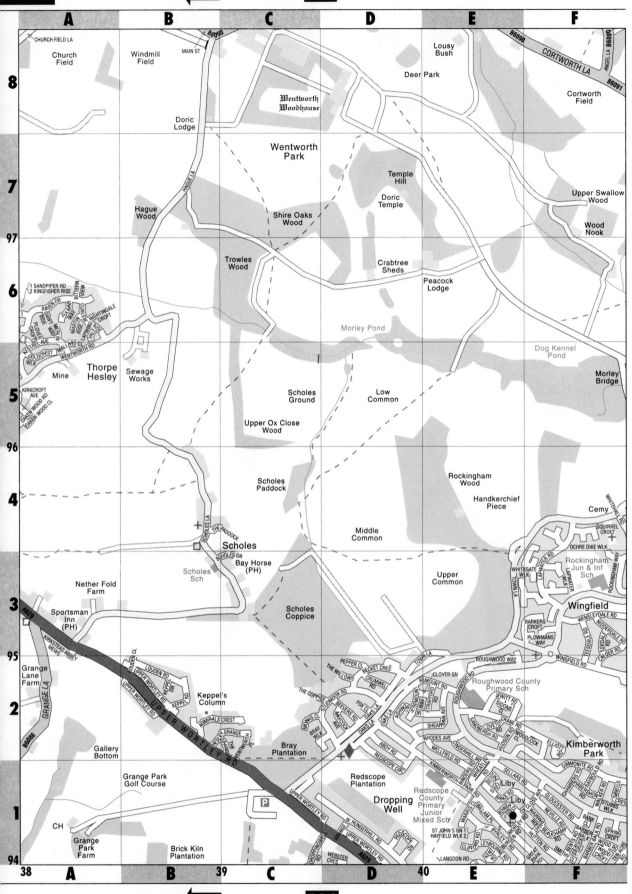

95
114

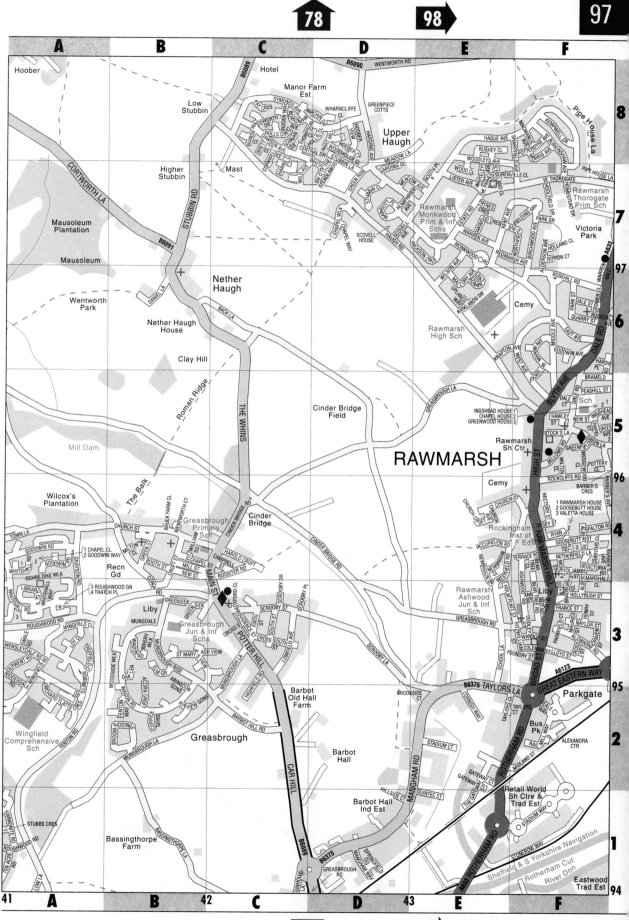

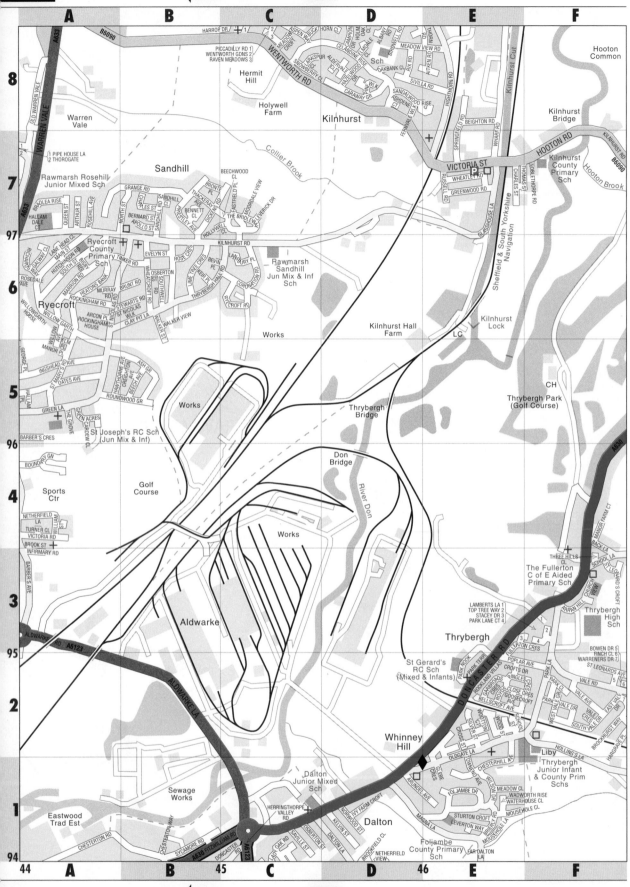

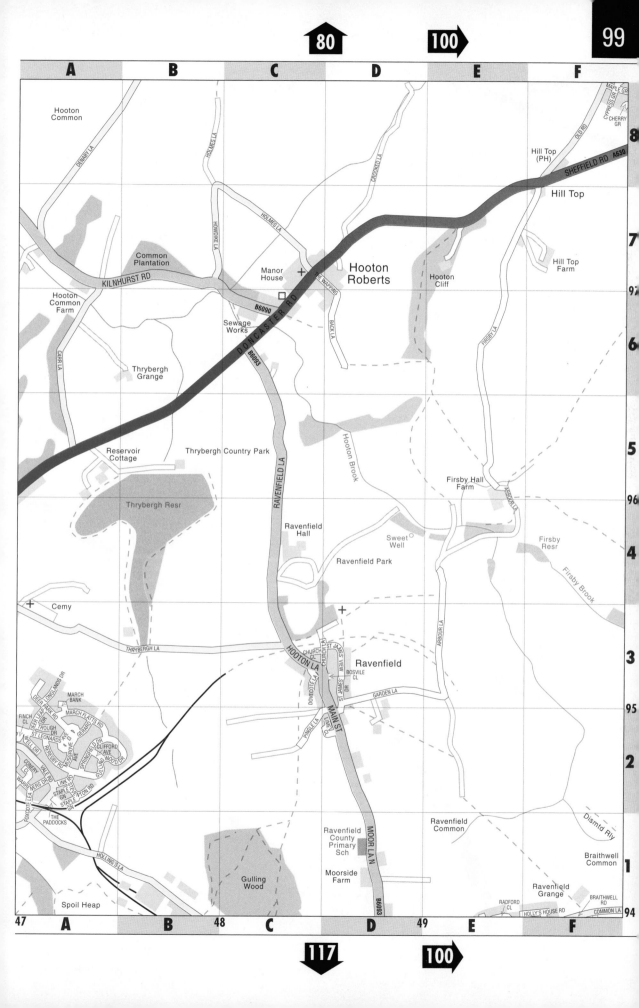

99
81

A B C D E F

8

HAWTHORN GR
LARCH GR
CEDAR GR
CHERRY GR
MAPLE GR
PINE GR
ACACIA GR
MICKLEBRING GR
DANETHORPE GR
PALM GR
CHESTNUT GR
OAK GR
POPLAR GR
SHEFFIELD RD
A630
A630
Cemy
SPRING BANK RD
Spring
Bank
Conisbrough Parks
KEARSLEY LA
Manor
Farm
Clifton Hill
Bridge
B6094
CLIFTON HILL
Den Brook
SNAKE LA
COMMON RD
CARR LA

7

Conisbrough Parks
Clifton
Common
Crookhill Park
Municipal
Golf Course
CH
B6094

'7

Parks Farm
Cotts
COMMON LA
Lidgets
Hill

6

Conisbrough Parks
Farm
Pearson
Holt
PARK LA
Beech House
Farm
Clifton
CLIFTON B'TRS
CHURCH LA
BACK LA
BEACON SQ
GREEN BALK
SHIPMAN BALK

5

Beacon
Hill
• Mast
BEACON LA

96

Conisbrough Lodge
Farm
Dismtd Rly
M18
RUDDLE LA

4

Birk Lodge
Farm
Micklebring
Gorse
Firsby Brook
The Beck
NEW RD

3

95

Micklebring
MICKLEBRING LA
Manor
House

2

Conisbrough Grange
Farm
Braithwell
Common
PARK LA
COAL PIT LA
GREAVES SIKE LA
Well
Farm
Plough
Inn
(PH)
ALDERNS CL
BACK LA
Back La
ASHTON LA

1

BRAMLEY LA
M18
HELLABY LA
MOOR LA
FORDOLES HEAD LA
Foredoles
Farm
MARSH HILL
Fieldhouses
Farm
MOYLE CROFT LA

94

COMMON LA

50 A B 51 C D 52 E F

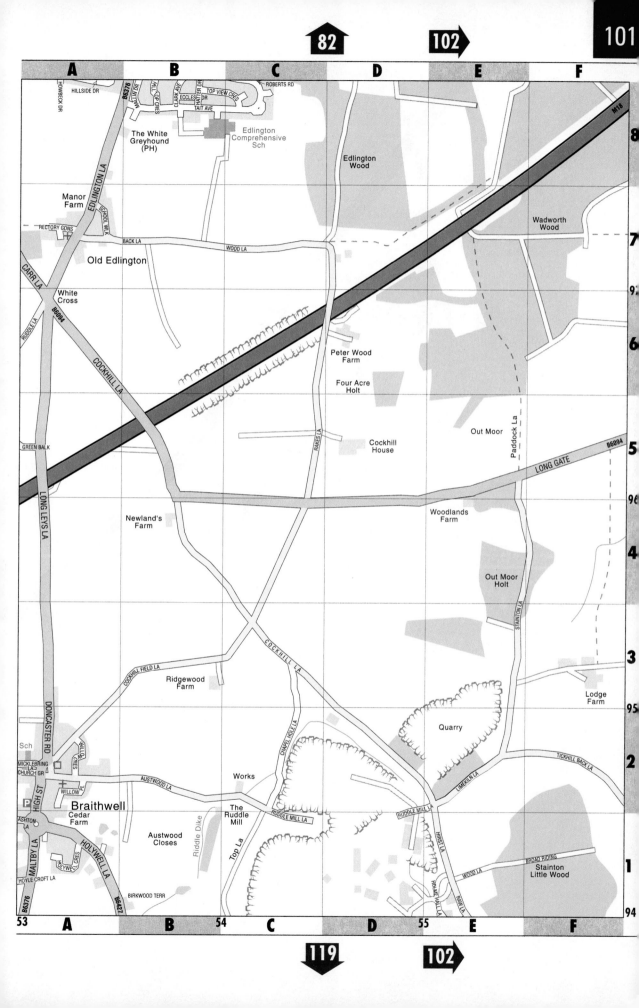

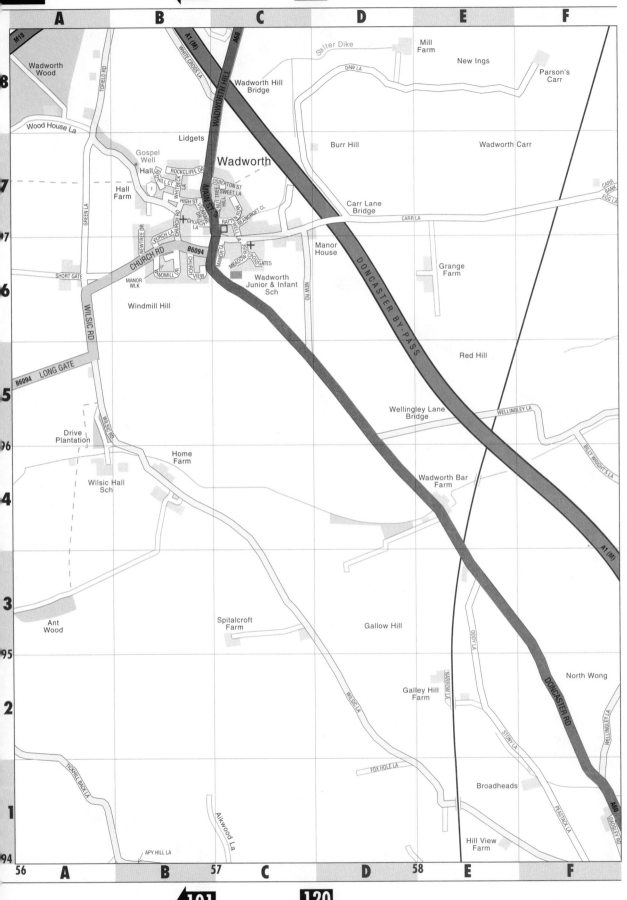

101
83

A   B   C   D   E   F

8

Wadworth Wood

M18

Wood House La

TOFIELD RD

A1 (M)

WHITE CROSS LA

WADWORTH HILL

A60

Salter Dike

DAW LA

Mill Farm

New Ings

Parson's Carr

Lidgets

Wadworth Hill Bridge

Burr Hill

Wadworth Carr

7

Gospel Well

Hall

HILL CT

ROCKCLIFFE DR

OSBERTON ST

SWEET LA

Wadworth

CARR BANK

EGG LA

Hall Farm

WHITBECK

HIGH ST

VICARAGE DR

MAIN ST

BEANCROFT CL

Carr Lane Bridge

GREEN LA

7'

CHURCH RD

CHURCH LA

RATTEN ROW

WELL LA

CROSS GATES

Manor House

CARR LA

NEWTREE DR

CHURCH CL

B6094

CHURCH VIEW

MANOR CL

MEADOW DR

NUNT HILL

Grange Farm

6

SHORT GATE

MANOR WLK

WINDMILL DR

Wadworth Junior & Infant Sch

NEW RD

Windmill Hill

WILSIC RD

DONCASTER BY-PASS

Red Hill

5

B6094 LONG GATE

Wellingley Lane Bridge

WELLINGLEY LA

96

Drive Plantation

WILSIC RD

Home Farm

BILLY WRIGHT S LA

4

Wilsic Hall Sch

Wadworth Bar Farm

A1 (M)

3

Ant Wood

Spitalcroft Farm

Gallow Hill

ODDY LA

95

North Wong

2

WILSIC LA

Galley Hill Farm

NARROW LA

DONCASTER RD

WELLINGLEY LA

STONY LA

FOX HOLE LA

Broadheads

1

TICKHILL BACK LA

AIKWOOD LA

PEASACK LA

A60

DADSLEY RD

APY HILL LA

Hill View Farm

94

56   A   57   B   C   57   D   58   E   F

101
120

Parson's Carr

Wadworth Carr

Refuse Tip

River Torne

Little Mother Drain

Holmes Carr Great Wood

Rossington Grange La Fst Sch

FOLJAMBE CRES 1
SKIPWITH GDNS 2
QUEEN MARY'S RD 3

SKIPWITH GDNS

MORRISON DR

GRANGEFIELD AVE

HESLEY CRES

GRANGE LA

RUTLAND LA

KING GEORGE'S RD

ATTLEE AVE

BARRAM GR

ABERCONWAY CRES

JUNCTION RD

WHITBY RD

CENTRAL DR

CROSS ST

DOOR ST

HUNSTER GR

WAYFIELDS

CRISTLE WY

CLAY FLAT LA

8

MEADOW CT 1
BOSWELL CL 2
HYPERION WAY 3

Cemy

ORMONDE GR WAY

HAIG CRES

SCEPTRE GR

MEMOIR GR

ALLENBY CRES

SOLARIO WAY

HETHERSETT WAY

CORONACH WAY

RADBURN RD

CHANDOSSAIRE

CANTELLO CT

TROUTBECK WAY

BAYARDO WALK

TULCAR CL

PERSIMMON CL

MELD CL

WILDFLOWER

RAGUSA DR

WHITAKER CL

OAKDENE

WHITCOMB DR

PORTLAND

BOND ST

BRUNI WAY

KEPPLE

Rossington Grange Farm

Hunster Flat La

ELMFIELD RD 1
FARRINGDON DR 2
SEATON GDNS 3

7

97

CARR BANK

EGG LA

Egg La

STANCIL LA

South Seats Drain

Reedy Holmes Plantation

Carr Doles

6

Stancil Carr

Wellingley Low Grounds

Wellingley Grange

5

96

Park Wood

BILLY WRIGHT'S LA

FOUR LANE ENDS

WELLINGLEY LA

Stancil

Wellingley Holt

STANCIL LA

Hesley Hall Farm

Hesley Hall Sch

4

Wellingley Farm

Broomhills Wood

Nursery

Hesley Park

Dadsley Well Bridge

Goole Dike or River Torne

Bog Wood

3

Middle Drain

Coneyborough Plantation

95

Dadsley Well Stream

Limpool Farm

B6463

STRIPE RD

2

Eastfield Wood

Tickhill Low Common

Tickhill High Common

Dumpling Castle Covert

Sawney Hill

1

Eastfield

A60

DONCASTER RD

DADSLEY RD

A1 (M)

HOPYARD LA

COMMON LA

SHEEPWASH LA

Sheepwash Bridge

B6463

Dumpling Castle Farm

94

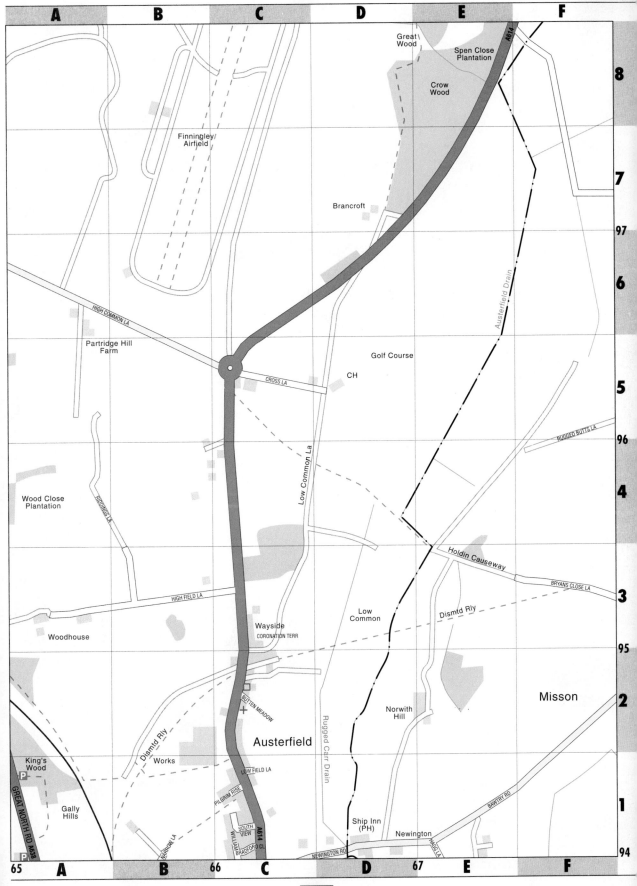

A B C D E F

8
97
7
6
5
96
4
3
95
2
94
1

Great Wood
Spen Close Plantation
Crow Wood
A614
Finningley Airfield
Brancroft
Austerfield Drain
HIGH COMMON LA
Partridge Hill Farm
CROSS LA
Golf Course
CH
Low Common La
RUGGED BUTTS LA
Wood Close Plantation
BIDDINGS LA
Holdin Causeway
BRYANS CLOSE LA
HIGH FIELD LA
Dismtd Rly
Woodhouse
Wayside
CORONATION TERR
Low Common
Misson
BUTTEN MEADOW
Norwith Hill
Dismtd Rly
Works
Austerfield
Rugged Carr Drain
King's Wood
P
GREAT NORTH RD A638
LOW FIELD LA
PILGRIM RISE
NARROW LA
Gally Hills
SOUTH VIEW
WILLIAM
BRADFORD CL
A614
Ship Inn (PH)
Newington
HAGG LA
BAWTRY RD
P
NEWINGTON RD

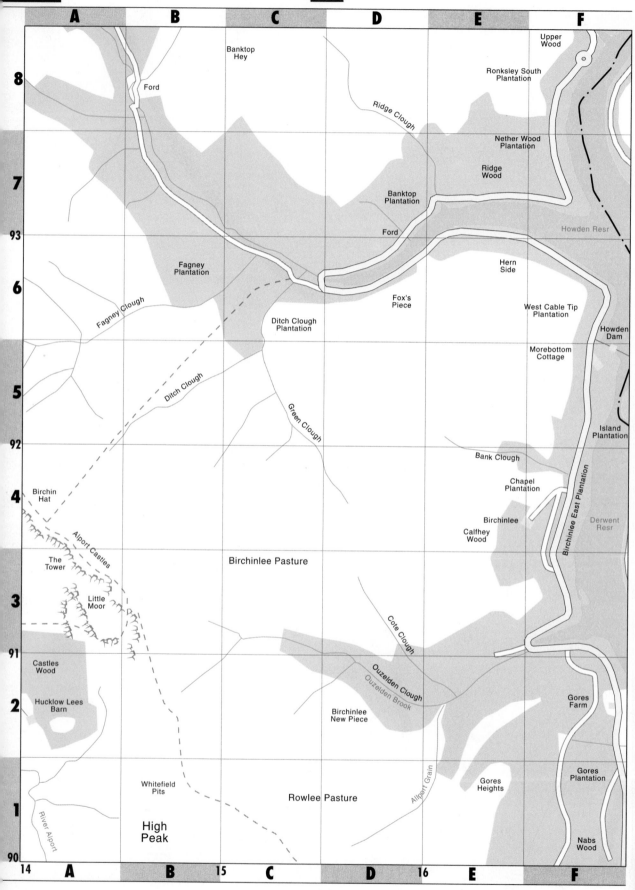

A   B   C   D   E   F

8

Banktop
Hey

Ford

Upper
Wood

Ronksley South
Plantation

Ridge Clough

Nether Wood
Plantation

7

Ridge
Wood

Banktop
Plantation

93

Ford

Howden Resr

Hern
Side

6

Fagney
Plantation

Fox's
Piece

West Cable Tip
Plantation

Howden
Dam

Fagney Clough

Ditch Clough
Plantation

Morebottom
Cottage

5

Ditch Clough

Green Clough

92

Island
Plantation

Bank Clough

4

Birchin
Hat

Chapel
Plantation

Derwent
Resr

Alport Castles

Birchinlee

Birchinlee East Plantation

The
Tower

Calfhey
Wood

3

Little
Moor

Birchinlee Pasture

Cote Clough

91

Castles
Wood

Ouzelden Clough

Ouzelden Brook

Gores
Farm

2

Hucklow Lees
Barn

Birchinlee
New Piece

Allport Grain

Gores
Heights

Gores
Plantation

1

Whitefield
Pits

Rowlee Pasture

River Alport

Nabs
Wood

High
Peak

90

14   A   B   15   C   D   16   E   F

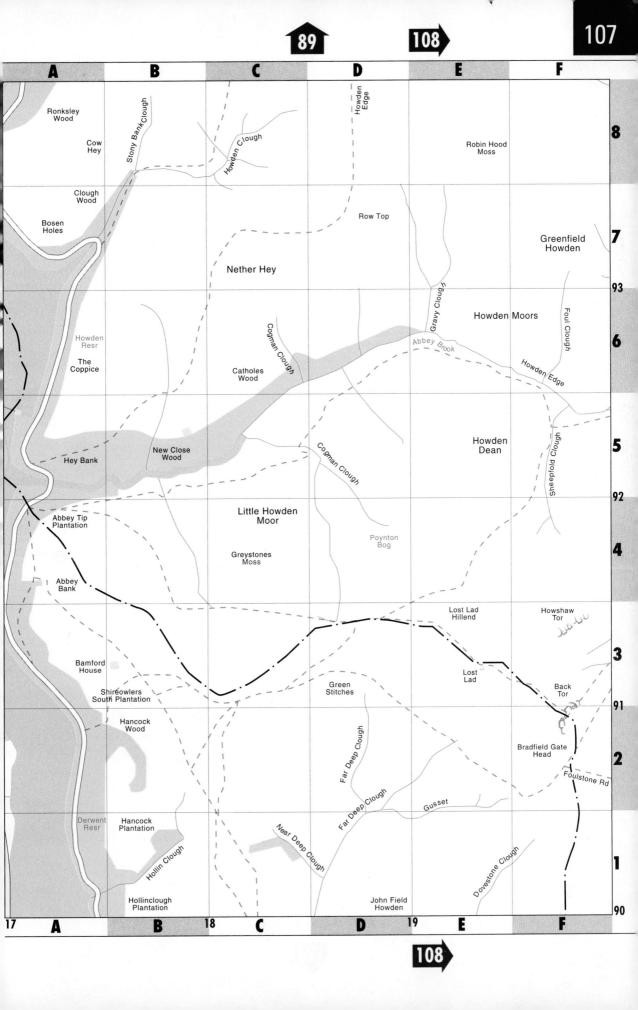

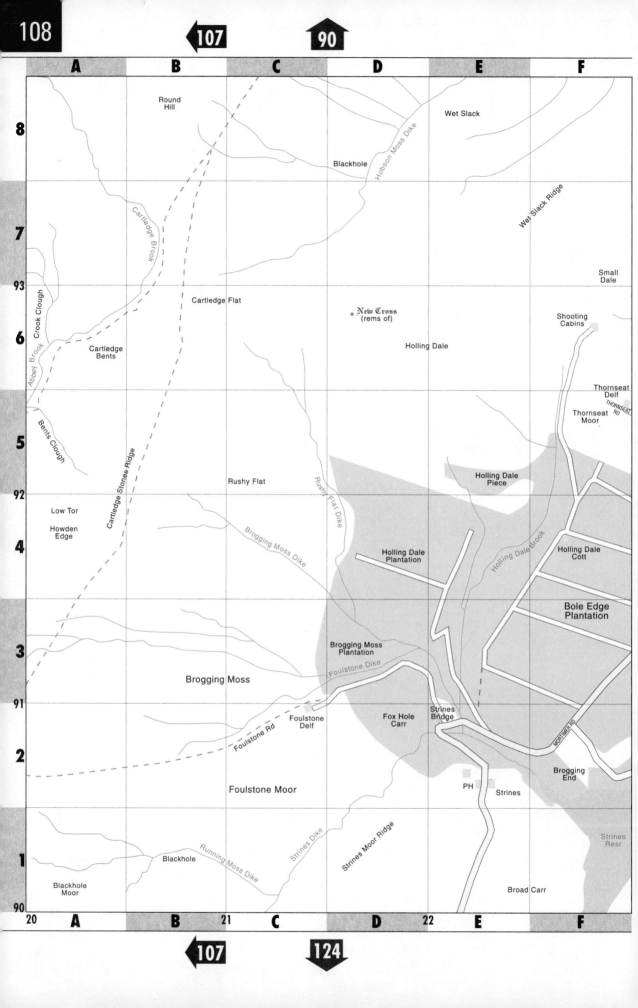

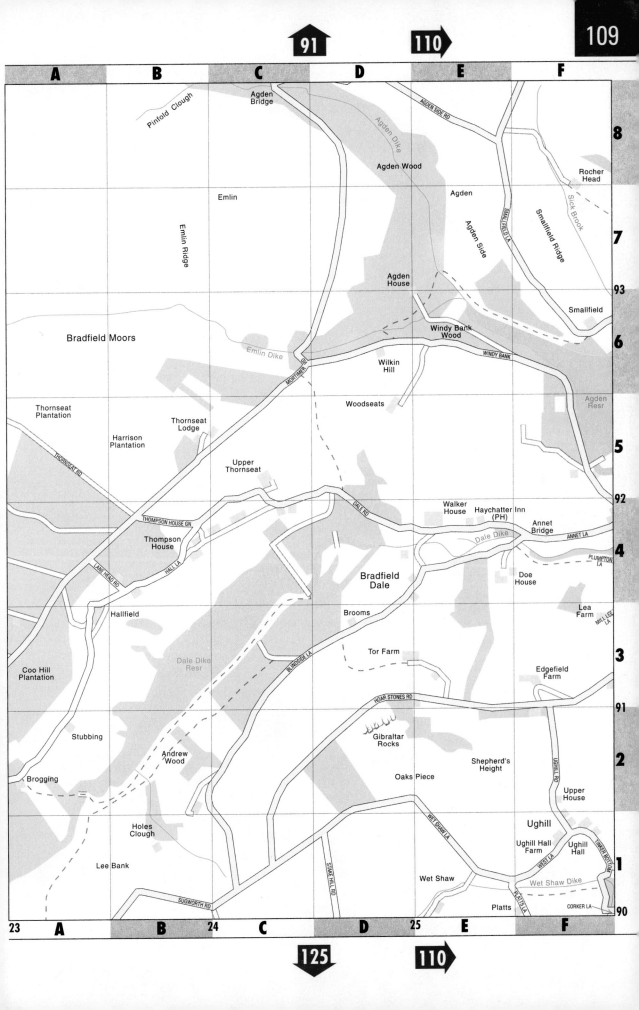

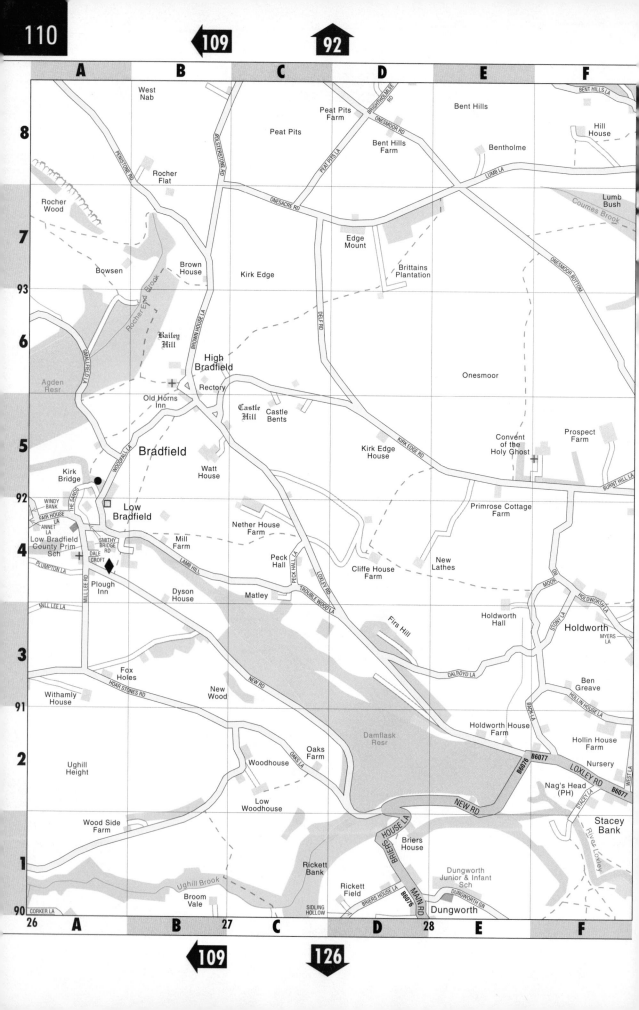

111
94

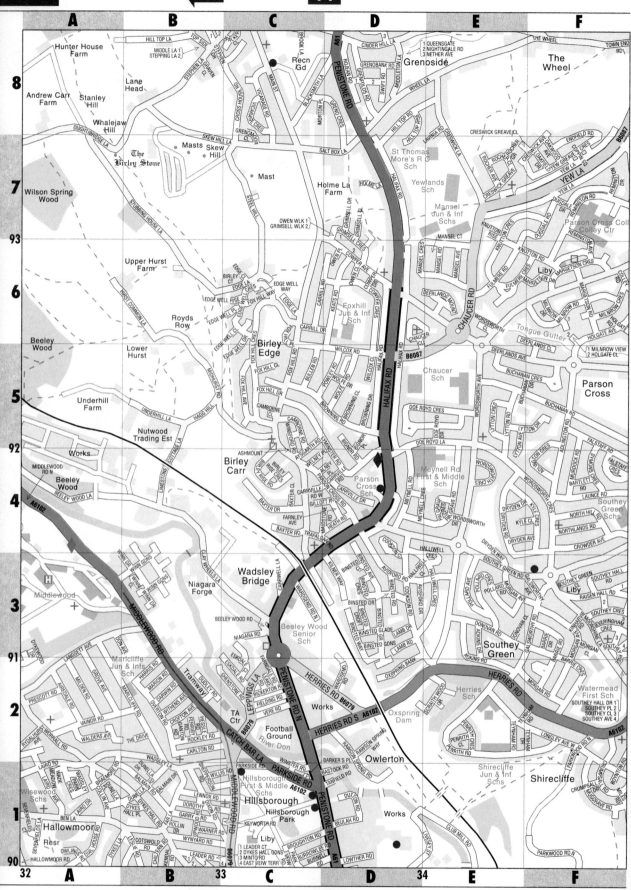

111
128

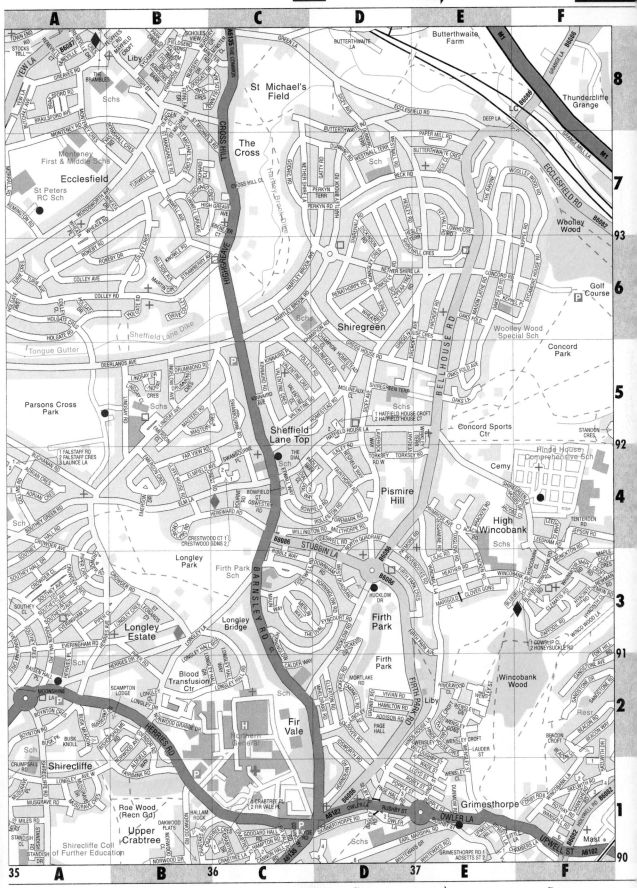

95 114

129 114

D1
1 BOLSOVER RD E
2 HEATHCOTE ST
3 BARRETTA ST
4 EARL MARSHAL CL
5 EARL MARSHAL DR
6 WHITEWAYS RD

F1
1 FARCROFT GR
2 SKELWITH CL
3 BRATHAY CL
4 BRATHAY RD
5 BIRDWELL RD
6 SOUTHWELL RD
7 CARLISLE ST E
8 WINCO RD

113
96

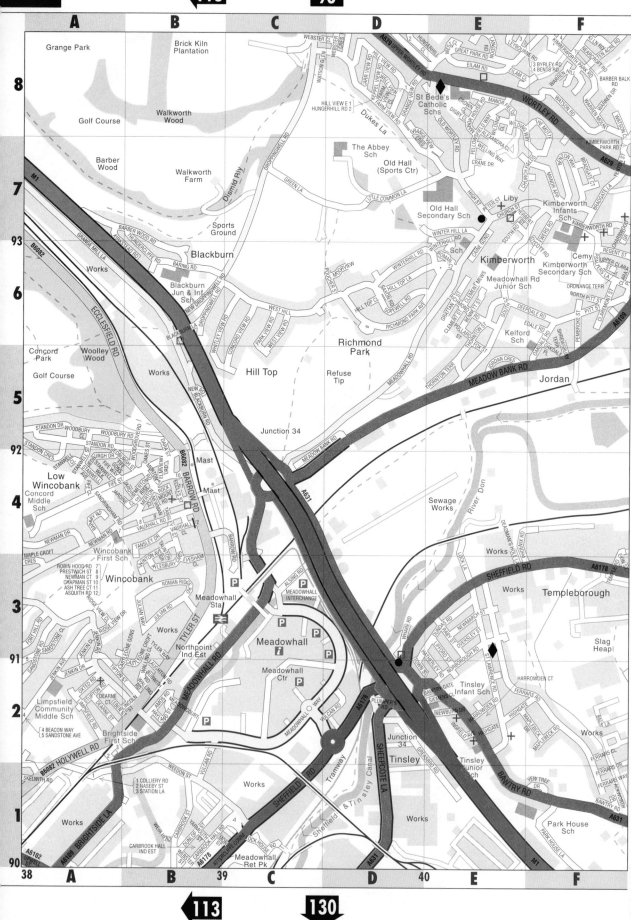

113
130

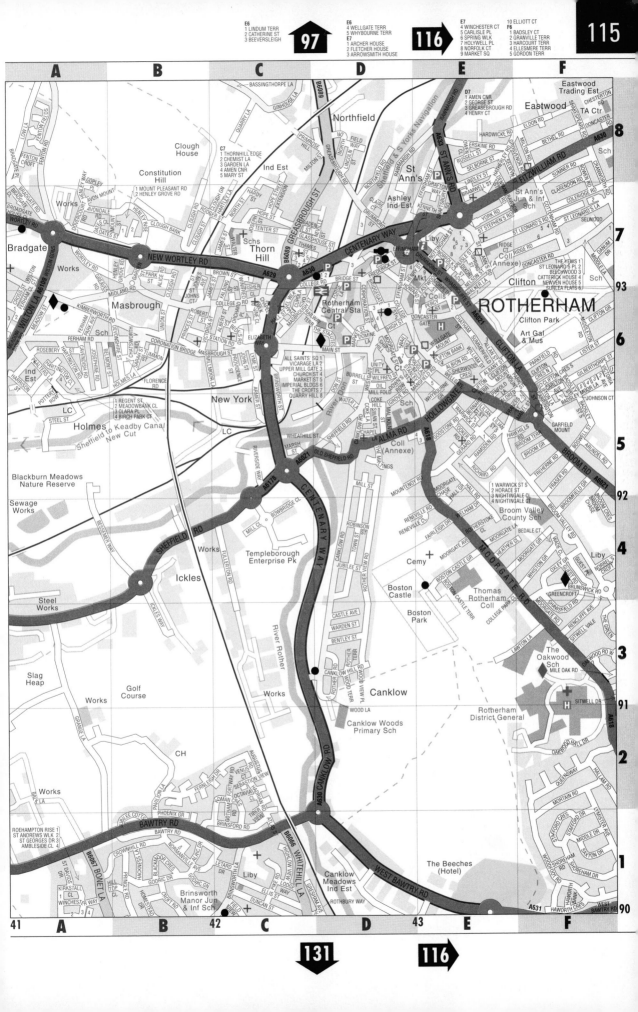

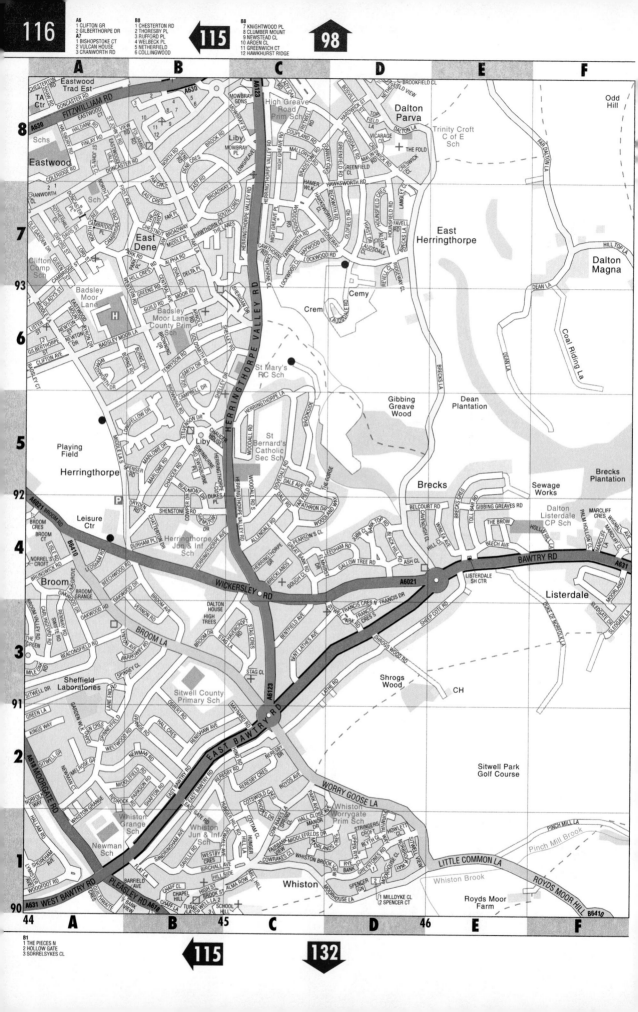

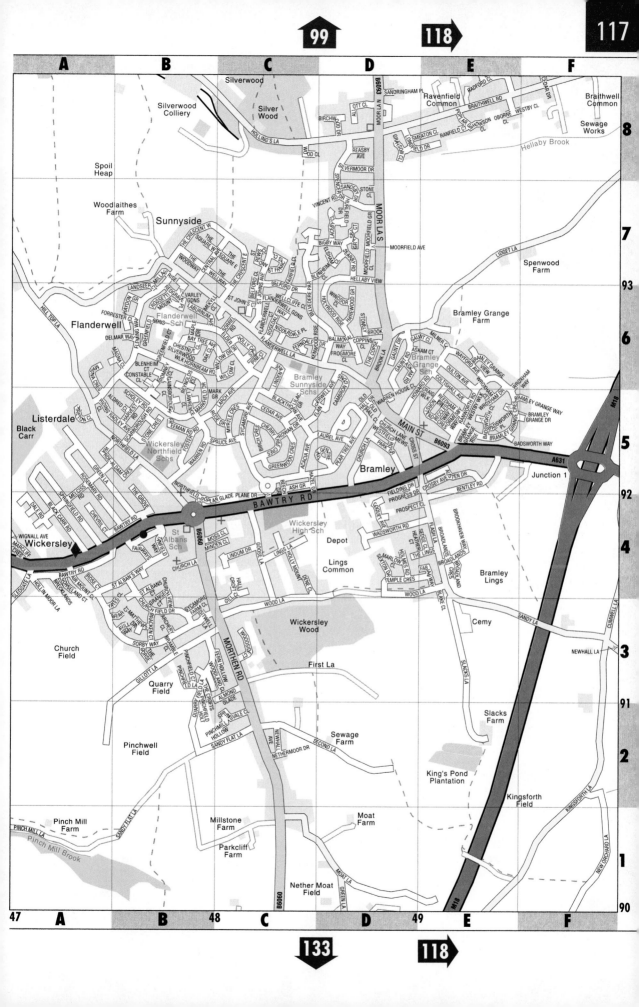

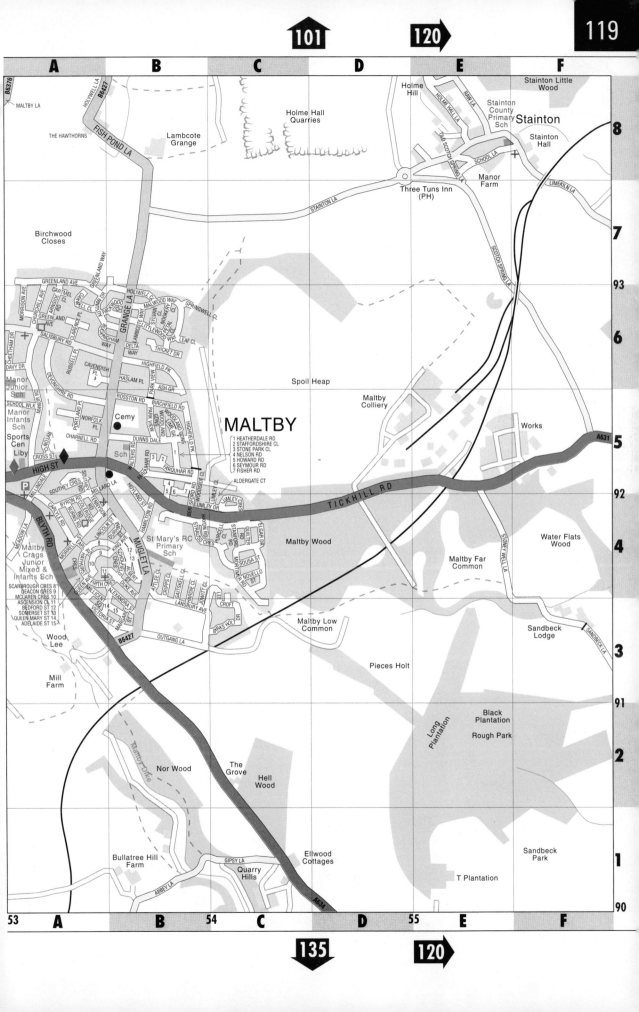

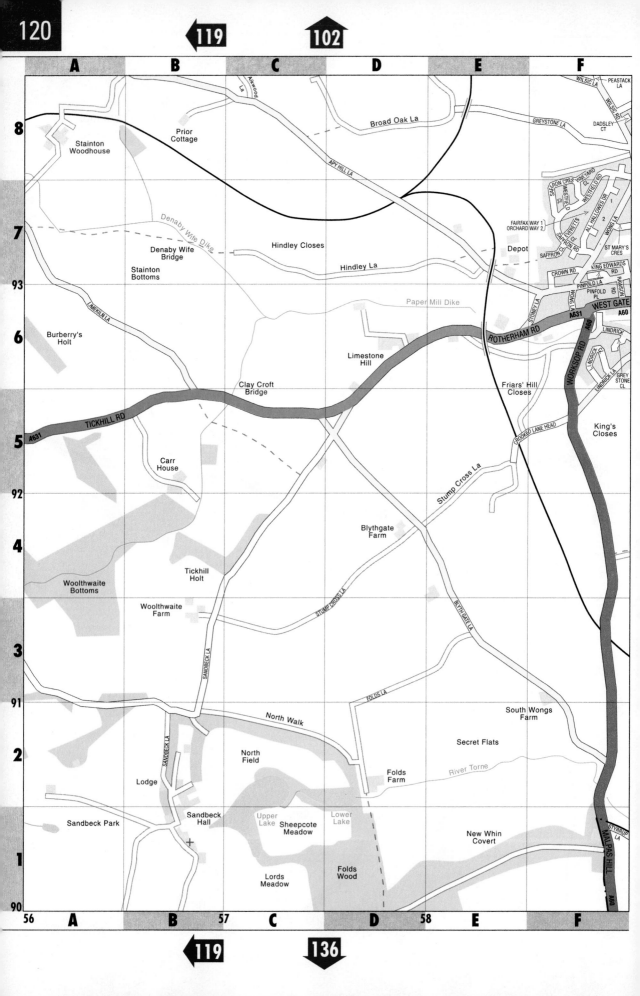

119
102

A   B   C   D   E   F

8   Stainton Woodhouse   Prior Cottage   Broad Oak La   WILSIC LA   PEASTACK LA
                                                                    WILSIC RD   DADSLEY CT
                                         APY HILL LA   GREYSTONE LA

SAFFRON CRES   VINEYARD CL
WESTFIELD   WESTFIELD RD
CL

FAIRFAX WAY 1   1
ORCHARD WAY 2   2   WONG LA

7   Denaby Wife Dike   Hindley Closes   Depot   ST MARY'S CRES
    Denaby Wife Bridge   SAFFRON   EVERETTS CL
    Stainton Bottoms   Hindley La   SAFFRON CL   ALL HALLOWES DR
                                    SAFFRON RD   KING EDWARDS RD

93   CROWN RD   PINFOLD LA   RAWSON RD
                                              PINFOLD PL
                                    Paper Mill Dike   WEST GATE
    LIMEKILN LA   STONEY LA   A631   A60

6   Burberry's Holt   Limestone Hill   ROTHERHAM RD   LINDRICK
                                                  WORKSOP RD   LINDRICK
                                                               GREY STONE CL
    Clay Croft Bridge   Friars' Hill Closes   King's Closes

5   A631   TICKHILL RD   CROOKED LANE HEAD

    Carr House   Stump Cross La

92

4   Blythgate Farm

    Tickhill Holt
    Woolthwaite Bottoms
    Woolthwaite Farm   STUMP CROSS LA   BLYTHGATE LA

3   FOLDS LA   South Wongs Farm

91
    North Walk   North Field   Secret Flats
2   Folds Farm   River Torne
    Lodge
    Sandbeck Park   Sandbeck Hall   Upper Lake   Lower Lake   New Whin Covert   STYRRUP LA
    SANDBECK LA   Sheepcote Meadow
1   Folds Wood   MALPAS HILL
    Lords Meadow
90   A60
    56   A   B   57   C   D   58   E   F

119
136

Bog Hill

Warehouses

Sewage Works

Sandrock Plantation

Sandrock Park

Spital Hill

Sandrock Farm

Tollbar Bridge

Goole Bridge

TICKHILL SPITAL

Moorhouse Farm

West Bank Farm

Tickhill

Castle Folds Farm

1 PINFOLD LA
2 ST MARY'S GATE
3 BRIDE CHURCH LA

WEST GATE

Lindrick

Tickhill Low Common

Water La

Bagley Green

Bagley Farm

Banks Carr Wood

Rose Cottage

Harworth

Sewage Works

Grey Gables

Cemy

Dismtd Rly

Crow Wood

Styrrup Carr

Grange Farm

White Swan (PH)

Styrrup

Raker Field

Ind Est

Refuse Tip

Dismtd Rly

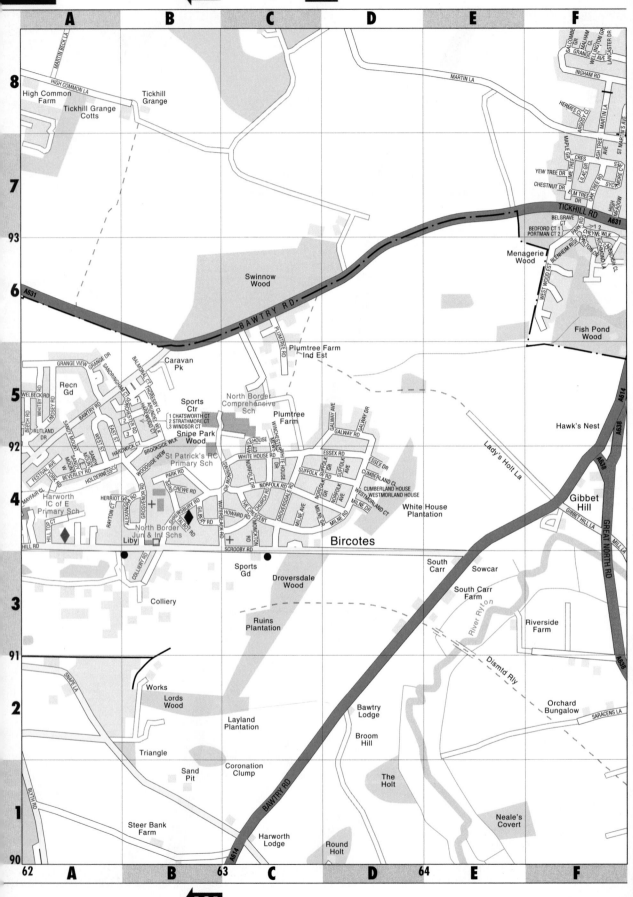

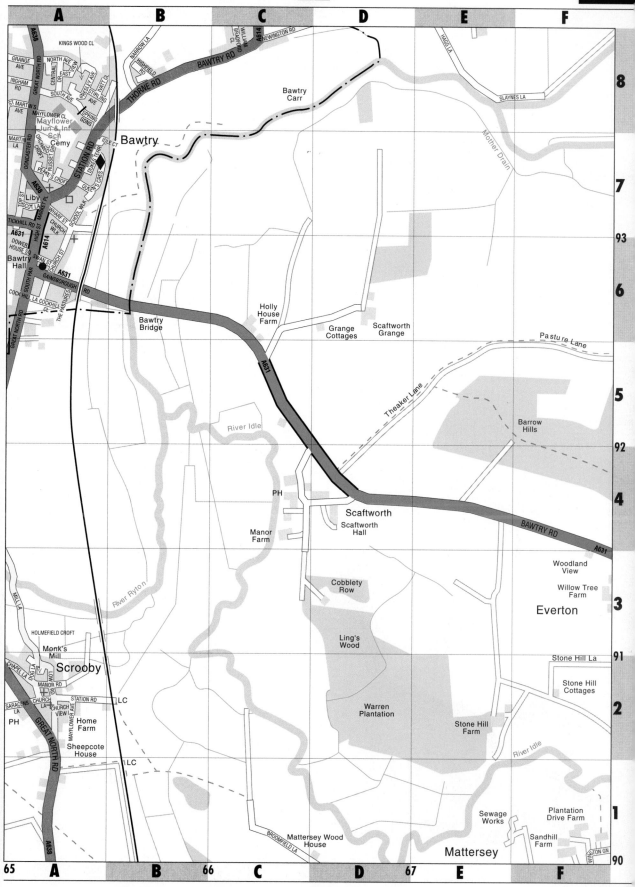

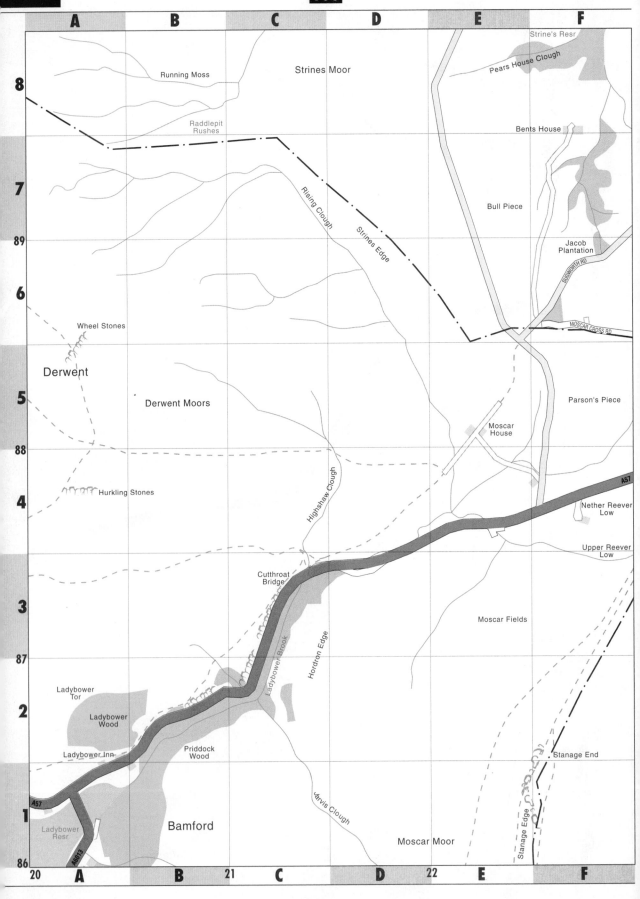

A B C D E F

8

Running Moss

Strines Moor

Strine's Resr

Pears House Clough

Raddlepit Rushes

Bents House

7

Rising Clough

Strines Edge

Bull Piece

Jacob Plantation

89

SUGWORTH RD

6

MOSCAR CROSS RD

Wheel Stones

Derwent

Derwent Moors

Parson's Piece

5

Moscar House

88

Highshaw Clough

Hurkling Stones

Nether Reever Low

4

Upper Reever Low

Cutthroat Bridge

3

Moscar Fields

Ladybower Brook

Hordron Edge

87

Ladybower Tor

2

Ladybower Wood

Ladybower Inn

Priddock Wood

Stanage End

Jarvis Clough

Stanage Edge

1

A57

Ladybower Resr

A6013

Bamford

Moscar Moor

86

20 A B 21 C D 22 E F

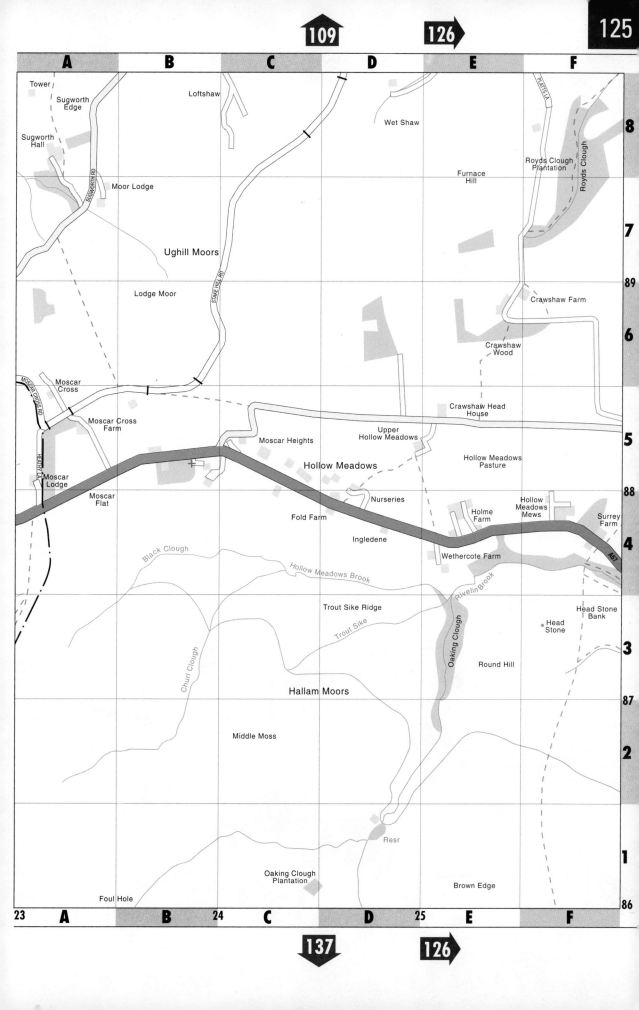

A   B   C   D   E   F

Tower
Sugworth Edge
Loftshaw
Wet Shaw
8
PLATT'S LA
Royds Clough
Sugworth Hall
Royds Clough Plantation
Moor Lodge
SUGWORTH RD
Furnace Hill
7
Ughill Moors
STAKE HILL RD
89
Lodge Moor
Crawshaw Farm
6
Crawshaw Wood
Moscar Cross
MOSCAR CROSS RD
Crawshaw Head House
Moscar Cross Farm
5
Moscar Heights
Upper Hollow Meadows
Hollow Meadows
Hollow Meadows Pasture
HEATH LA
Moscar Lodge
88
Moscar Flat
Nurseries
Hollow Meadows Mews
Fold Farm
Holme Farm
Surrey Farm
Ingledene
A57
4
Black Clough
Wethercote Farm
Hollow Meadows Brook
Rivelin Brook
Head Stone Bank
Trout Sike Ridge
Oaking Clough
Head Stone
Churl Clough
Trout Sike
Round Hill
3
87
Hallam Moors
Middle Moss
2
Resr
1
Oaking Clough Plantation
Brown Edge
Foul Hole
86

23   A   B   24   C   D   25   E   F

← 125   110

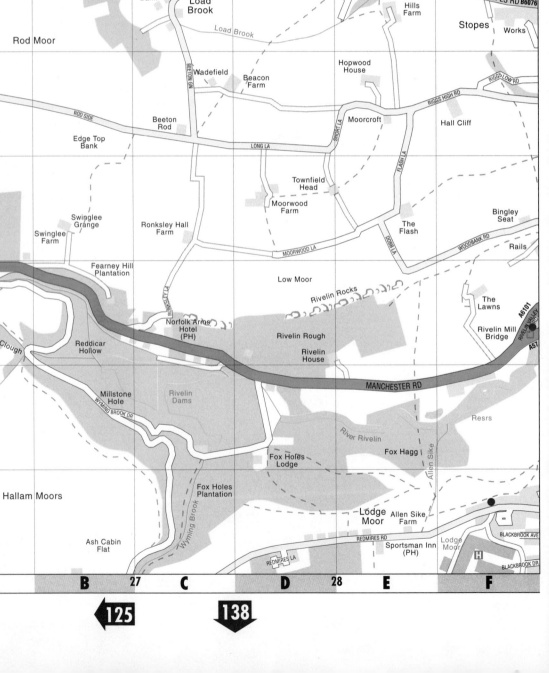

A B C D E F

8 7 89 6 5 88 4 3 87 2 86 1

26 27 28

Corker Walls
CORKER LA
Hall Broom
Hall Broom Wood
Hall Brown Cote
Works
Rod Moor
Heather Bank
Load Brook
Load Brook
Cemy
Crawshaw Lodge
ROD SIDE
Edge Top Bank
Beeton Rod
BEETON GN
Wadefield
Beacon Farm
LONG LA
Swinglee Grange
Swinglee Farm
Ronksley Hall Farm
Fearney Hill Plantation
A57
Head Stone Bank
Reddicar Clough
Reddicar Hollow
New Hagg
Millstone Hole
WYMING BROOK DR
Rivelin Dams
White Rake
Hallam Moors
Ash Cabin Flat
Wyming Brook
Fox Holes Plantation
REDMIRES LA
Fox Holes Lodge
RONKSLEY LA
Norfolk Arms Hotel (PH)
Rivelin Rough
Rivelin House
Rivelin Rocks
MANCHESTER RD
River Rivelin
Fox Hagg
Low Moor
MOORWOOD LA
Moorwood Farm
Townfield Head
The Flash
DOBB LA
Rails
WOODBANK RD
Bingley Seat
Hall Cliff
Moorcroft
SHORT LA
FLASH LA
Hopwood House
RIGGS HIGH RD
RIGGS LOW RD
Riggs Low Rd
The Lawns
Rivelin Mill Bridge
RIVELIN VALLEY RD
A6101
A57
Resrs
Allen Sike
Lodge Moor
Allen Sike Farm
REDMIRES RD
Sportsman Inn (PH)
Lodge Moor
BLACKBROOK AVE
BLACKBROOK RD
H
Tom Hill
Dungworth
B6076
MAIN RD
YEWS LA
Royal Hotel (PH)
Syke
DUNGWORTH LN
Storrs Grange Farm
STORRS CARR
Syke House Farm
SYKEHOUSE LA
CLIFFE HILL
Hill Top
Nether Cliffe
STORRS GN
STORRS LA
Hazelhurst Farm
LEE MOOR LA
COW GAP LA
Cow Gap
HILL TOP RD
BENTS LA
RYE LA
Bents Farm
Brookside Bank
Brookside
BROOKSIDE LA
BROOKSIDE BANK RD
Brookside Bridge
Storrs Brook
STOPES RD
B6076
Hills Farm
Stopes
Works
GAME LA
SIDLING HOLLOW

111
128
139
128

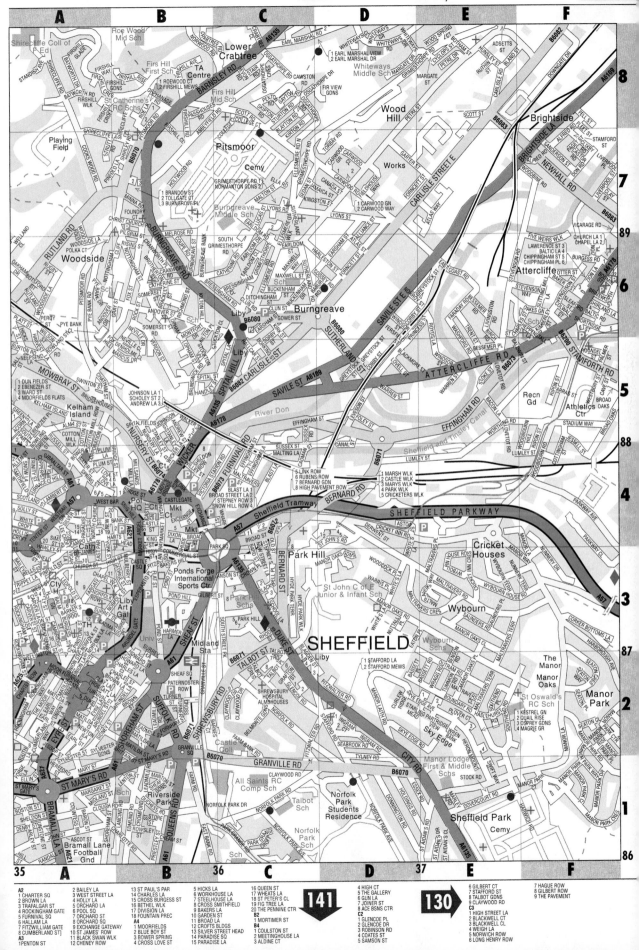

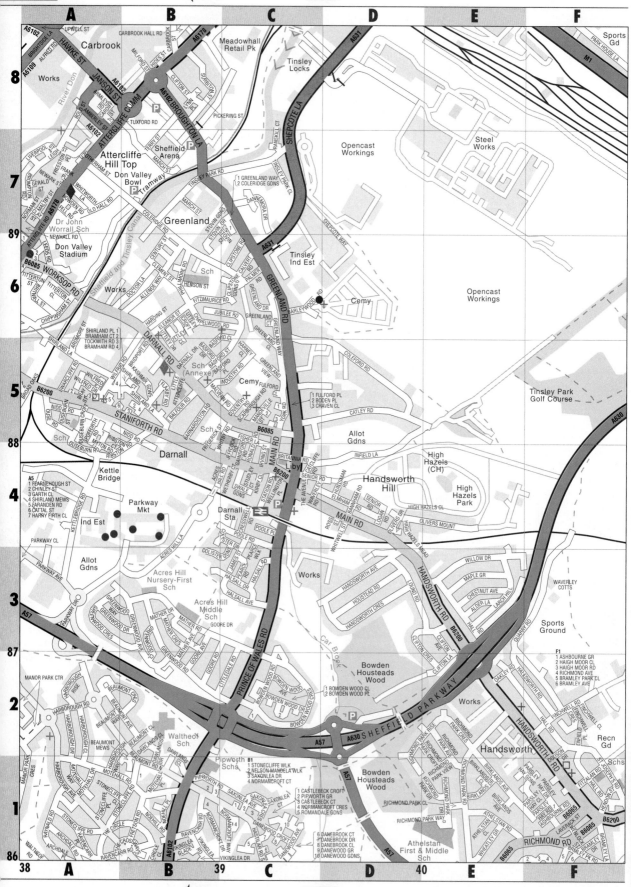

130

A6
1 VICARAGE RD
2 BEVERLEY ST
3 BOOTLE ST
4 CHAPEL LA

129   114

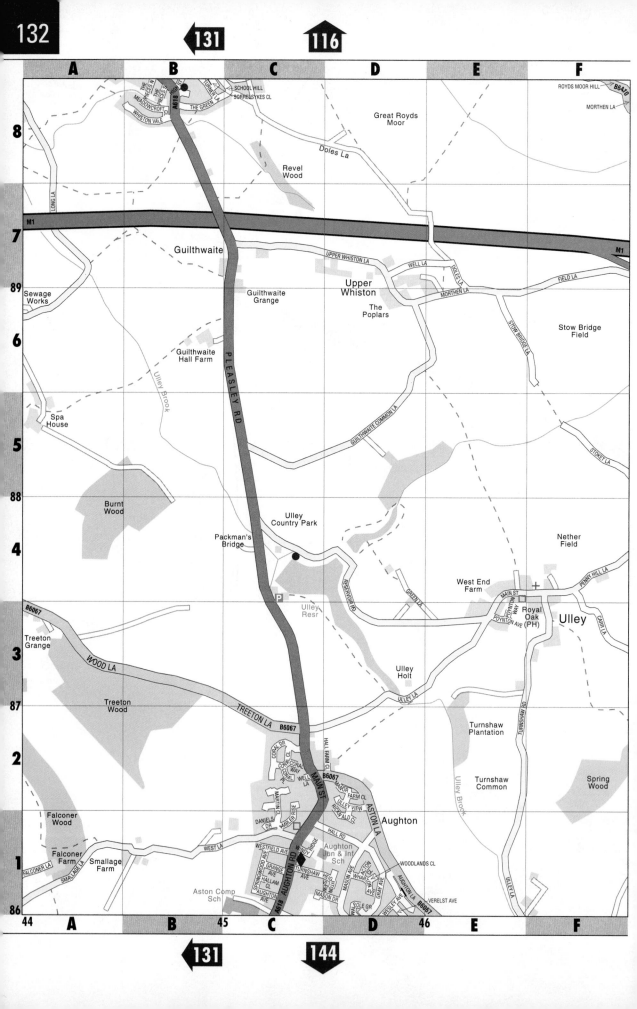

	A	B	C	D	E	F

8 Spoil Heap · The Terrace · Green La

7 Thurcroft Hall · Brook House · Manor Farm · Slade Hooton · Abbey La · Carr La · Home La · High Hooton Rd

89 Brookhouse Dike · Brookhouse · Coldwell Green · Slade View

6 Arbour Cres · Arbour Dr · The Crescent End · Steadfolds Rise · The Crest · Steadfolds · Clark Ave · Booth Cl · Autumn Cl · Howard Cl · Steadfolds La · Thurcroft · Laughton Rd · Rose La · Brookhouse La · The Travellers (PH) · Mill Cl · Hooton Bridge · Hooton La · Sewage Works · Hooton Dike

5 Rotherham La · All Saints C of E (Aided) Primary Sch · Castle Hill · Church Cmn · High St · Abbey Cl · Laughton en le Morthen · PH · Field Cres · Hooton Cl · East Field La

88 Holmlea Farm · Common La · Old Hall Cl · Mellow Fields Rd · School Rd · Castle Gn · St John's St · New St · Firbeck La · Orchard Cl · Grangewood Rd · Longthwaite · Kingswood · Lingodell Cl · Kingswood Ave

4 B6060 · Side Farm · Laughton Common Rd · Laughton Common Farm · Sandall House · Allotment Gardens · St John's Rd · St John's

3 Laughton Common · Sandall View · Passdale Cl · Recn Gnd · Hangsman La · Little Moor · Throapham · Oldcoates Rd · B6463 · Hunters Way · Hunters Pk · Hunters Cl · Hunters Gdns · Hunters Chase

87 Station Way · Station Rd · PH · Lumley St · St Leger Ave · Beckwith Rd · Hatfield Cres · Meadow St · Common Rd · Throapham Common · Dinnington Bsns Ctr · Anne St · Breck La · Chestnut Gr · Charles St · Recn Gnd · Manor Rd · Duke St

2 Dinnington · Rotherham Rd · Meadow Rd · Monk's Bridge Trad Est · Princess St · Park La · Monk's Bridge Rd · Outgang La · Dinnington Colliery · Collier Cl · Queen St · Dinnington Comprehensive Sch · Doe Quarry La · School St · East St

1 Common Farm · Booker's La · Bookers Way · Works · Todwick Rd · Marbeck's Bridge · Church La · Broadoaks Rd 1 · Broadoaks Cl 2 · Coronation Ave · Plantation Ave · South St · Carlisle Terr · Laughton Rd · Cemy · Liby · P · Doe Quarry Terr · New St · Addison

86 Common Rd · Holborn Rd · Abbey Way · B6463 · Whitehead · Athorpe Gr · Limes Ave · Tiercel Mews · Littlefield Rd · West Edward St · Garth Cl · B6060 · Leopold · Lidgett La · Sch

	A	B	C	D	E	F
50			51		52	

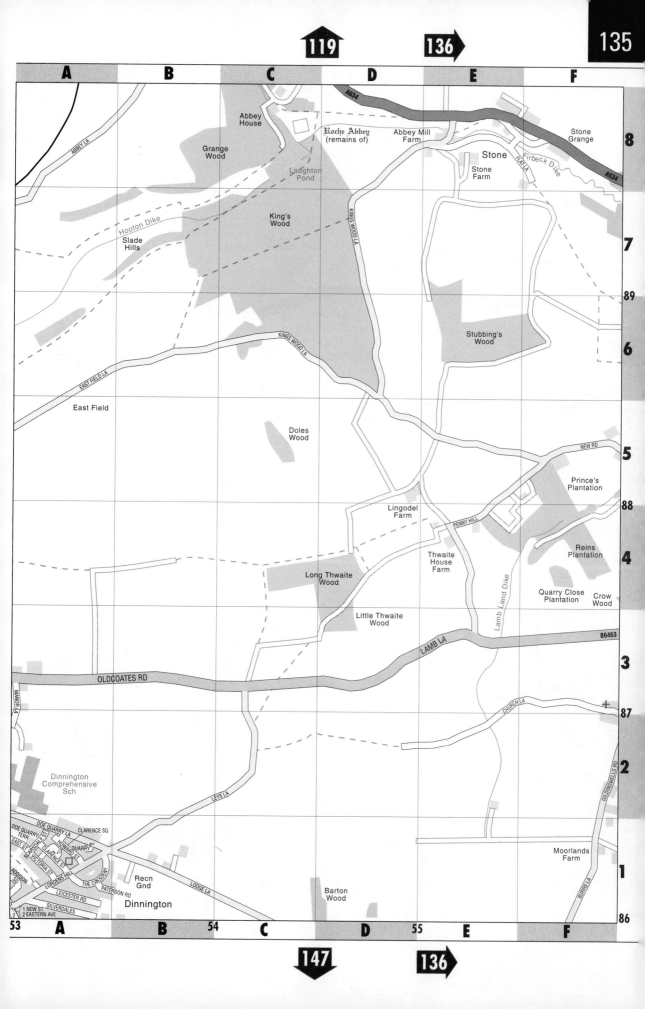

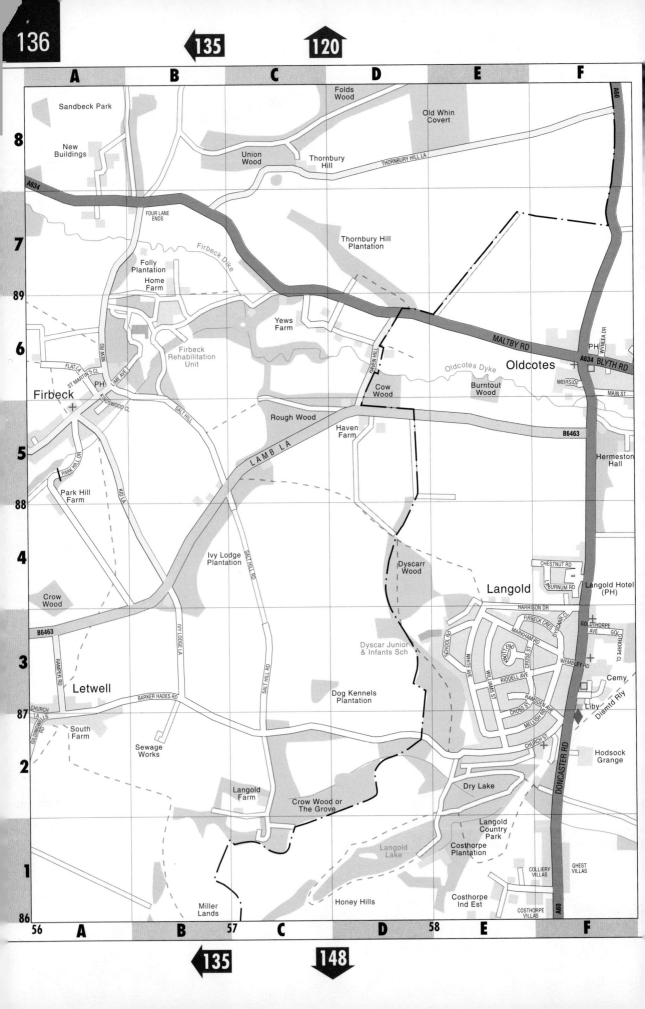

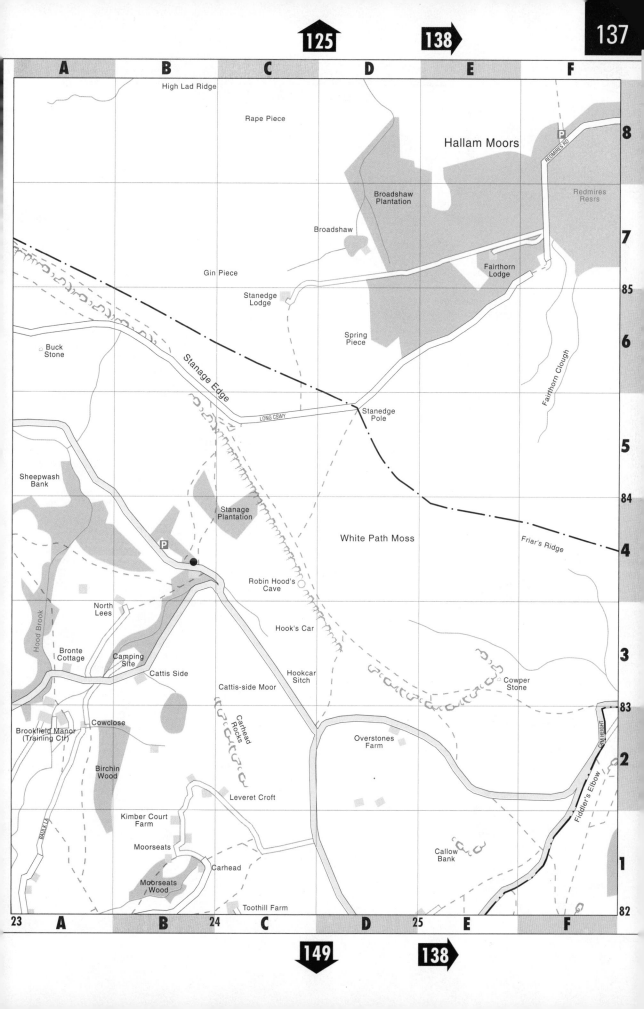

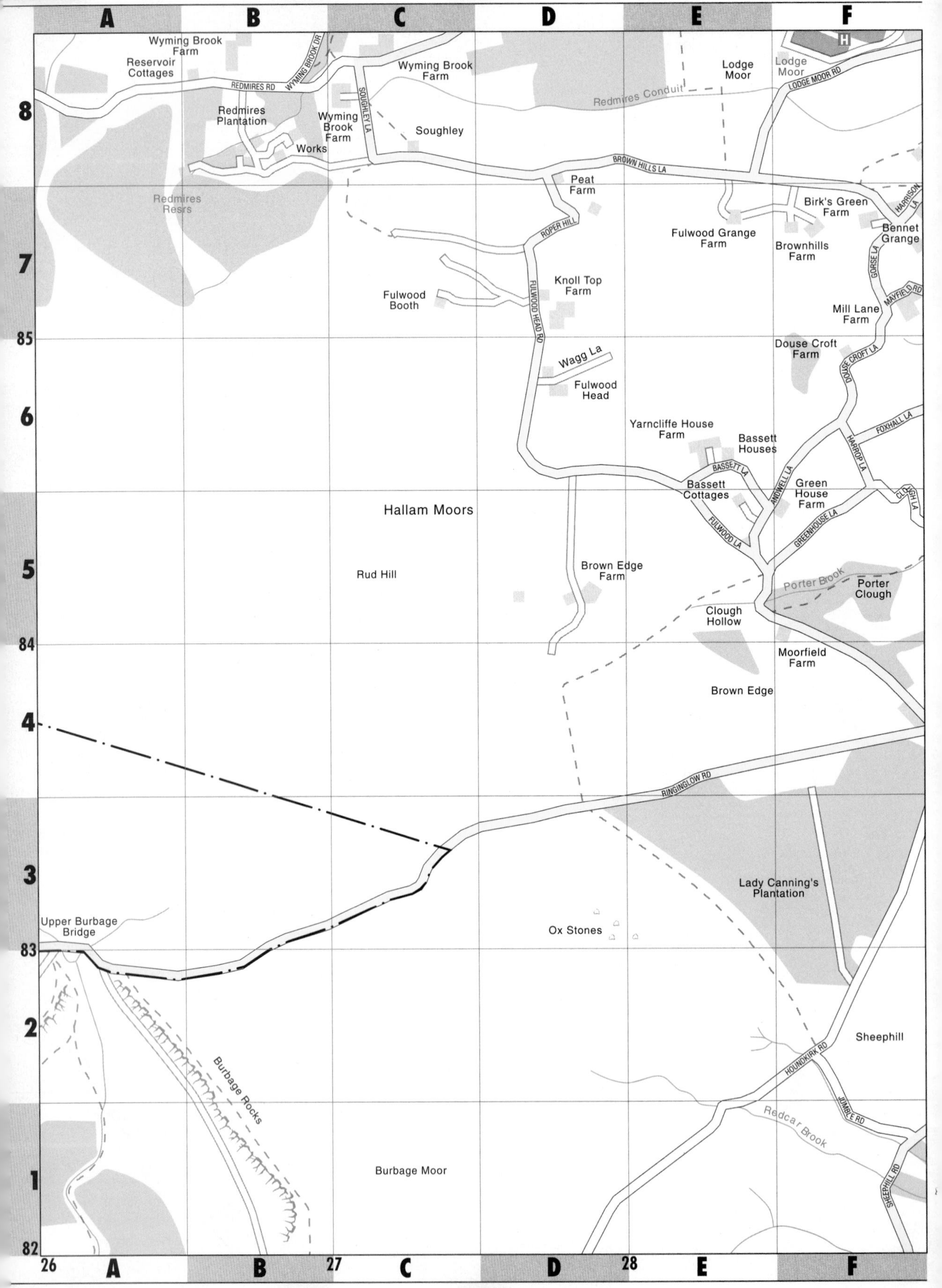

A B C D E F

8

Wyming Brook Farm
Reservoir Cottages
Redmires Plantation
REDMIRES RD
WYMING BROOK DR
Wyming Brook Farm
Wyming Brook Farm
Works
SOUGHLEY LA
Soughley
Wyming Brook Farm
Redmires Conduit
Lodge Moor
Lodge Moor
LODGE MOOR RD
H

Redmires Resrs
Peat Farm
BROWN HILLS LA
Birk's Green Farm
Fulwood Grange Farm
Brownhills Farm
Bennet Grange
HARRISON LA
GORSE LA

7

ROPER HILL
Knoll Top Farm
Fulwood Booth
FULWOOD HEAD RD
Mill Lane Farm
MAYFIELD RD

85

Wagg La
Fulwood Head
Douse Croft Farm
DOUSE CROFT LA

6

Yarncliffe House Farm
Bassett Houses
Green House Farm
FOXHALL LA
HARROP LA
CRIMICLE HILL LA

Hallam Moors
Bassett Cottages
BASSETT LA
ANDWELL LA
GREENHOUSE LA
FULWOOD LA

5

Rud Hill
Brown Edge Farm
Porter Brook
Porter Clough

84

Clough Hollow
Moorfield Farm

Brown Edge

4

RINGINGLOW RD
Lady Canning's Plantation

3

Upper Burbage Bridge
Ox Stones

83

Burbage Rocks
HOUNDKIRK RD
Sheephill
JUMBLE RD
Redcar Brook

2

1

Burbage Moor
SHEEPHILL RD

82

26 A B 27 C D 28 E F

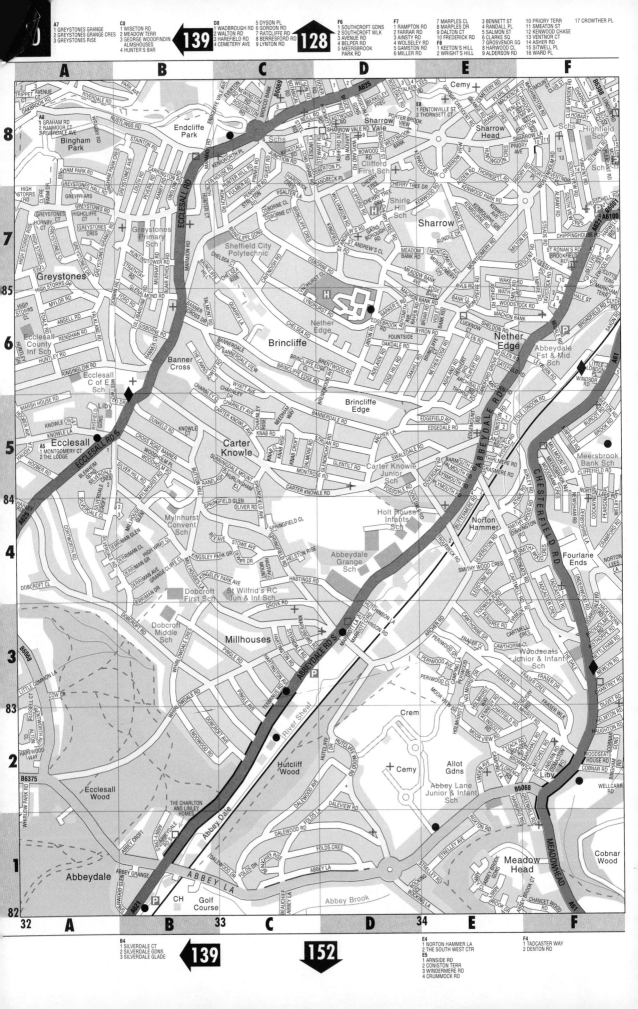

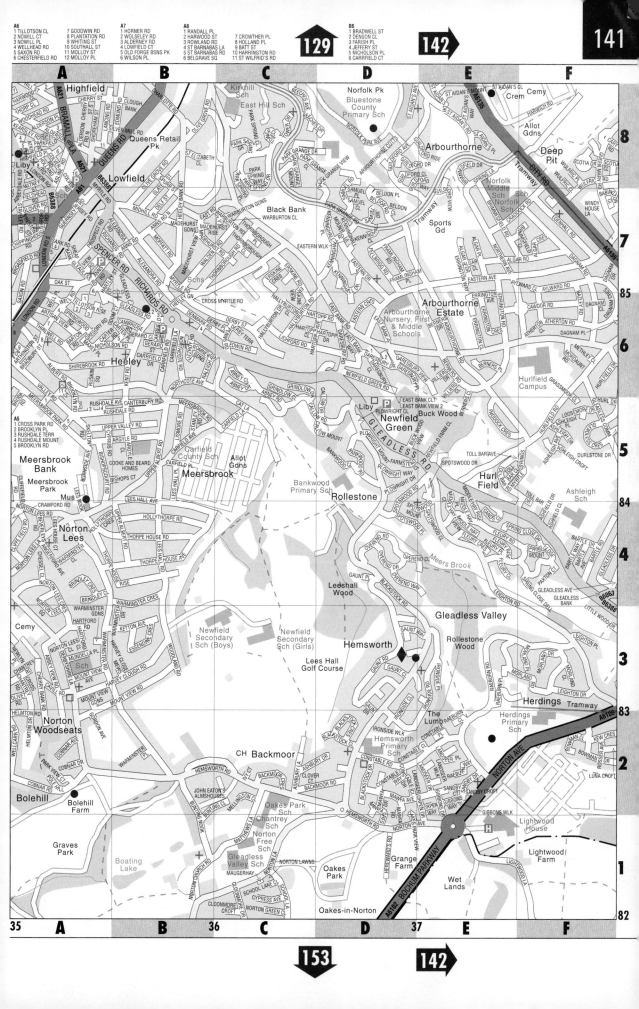

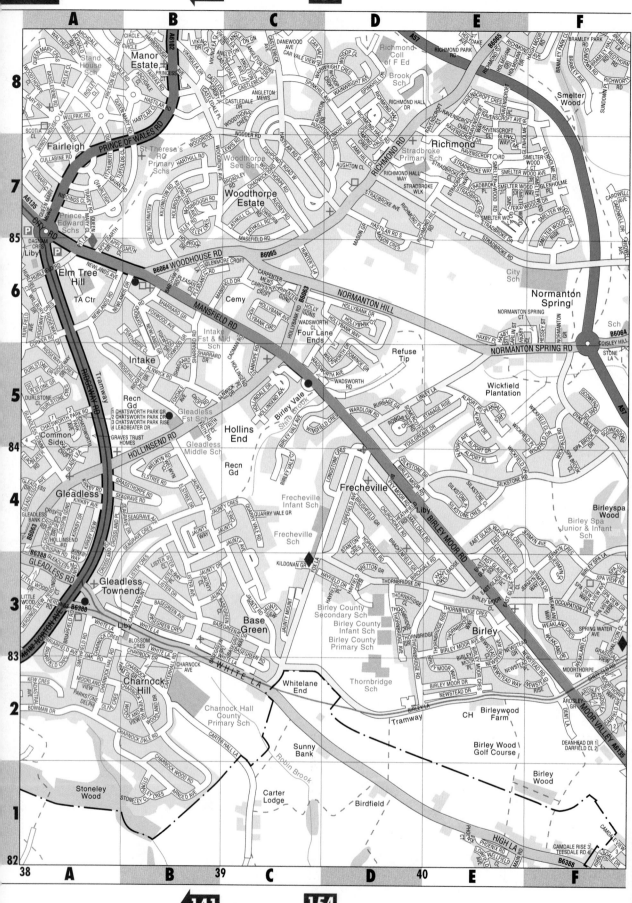

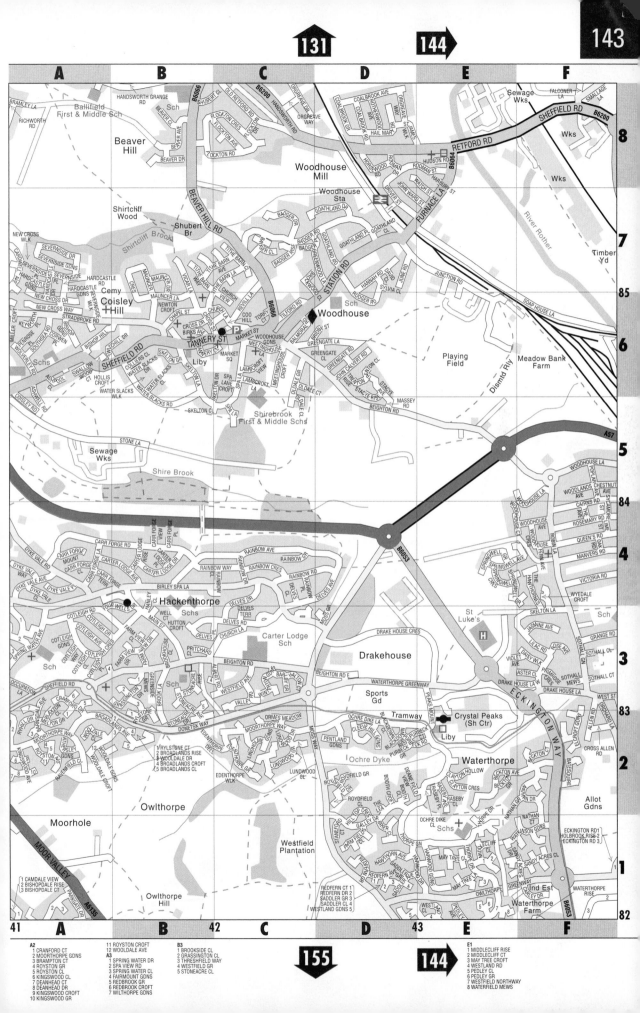

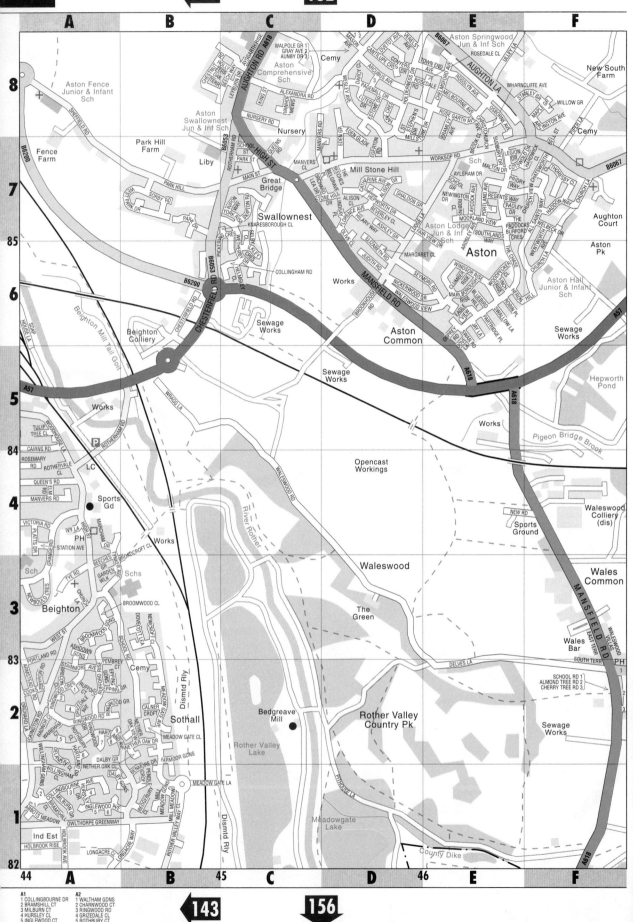

A1
1 COLLINGBOURNE DR
2 BRAMSHILL CT
3 MILBURN CT
4 HURSLEY CL
5 INGLEWOOD CT
6 INGLEWOOD DELL

A2
1 WALTHAM GDNS
2 CHARNWOOD CT
3 RINGWOOD RD
4 GRIZEDALE CL
5 ROTHBURY CT
6 HARTLAND CT
7 WYCHWOOD GLENN
8 WYCHWOOD CROFT
9 WYCHWOOD GR

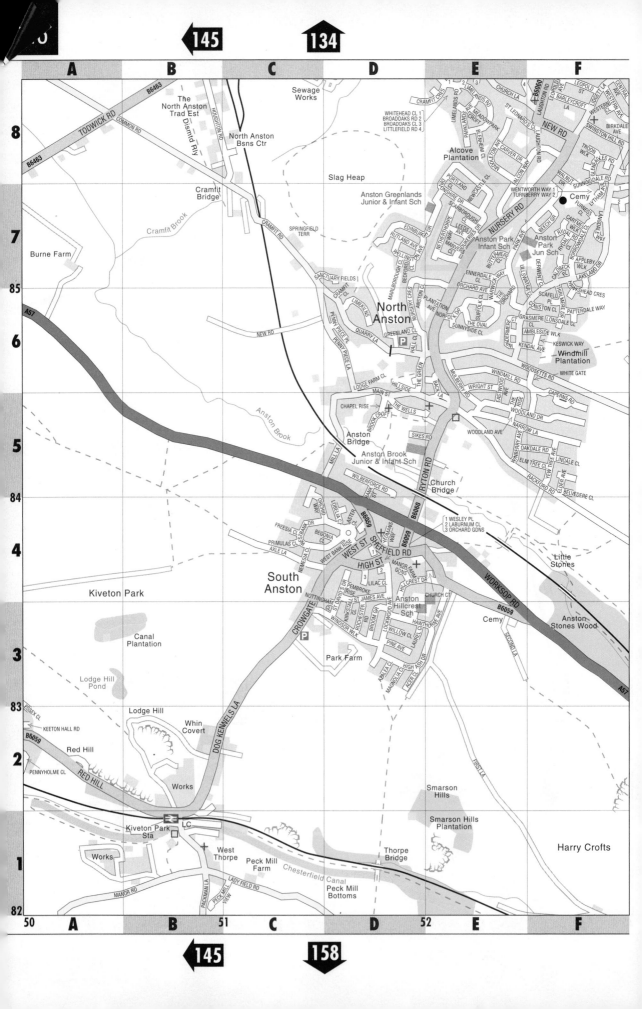

A B C D E F

EASTERN CL
EASTERN AVE
BYRON RD
SHAKESPEARE DR
KEATS DR
TENNYSON CL
BYRON CL
HIGH NOOK RD
CHASEFIELD CT
SHELLEY DR
CENTRAL AVE
MILTON RD
BURNS RD
WESTERN AVE
WORDSWORTH AVE
BIRKDALE AVE
BELFRY WAY
MOORTOWN AVE
WENTWORTH WAY
TURNBERRY WAY

Lodge
Plantation
Lodge Farm

LODGE LA

Red Quarry
Plantation

RED QUARRY LA

Burrs
Farm
North Farm
8
Pear Tree Farm
BURRS LA
ROTHERHAM BAULK

White Walls Farm
Laneside
Farm

Gildingwells
Sunny Bank
Farm
7
Home
Farm
WOODSETTS RD
WALLINGWELLS LA
85

SWINSTON HILL RD
BRAND'S LA
Brand's Wood
Wellswood
Farm
6

Swinston
Hill
Bradshaw
Wood

Swinston Hill
Wood

Owlands Wood Dike

The Clump
Brand's
Farm
Oakland House
Oakland
CL
BRANDS CL
GILDINGWELLS RD
OSMERE DR
Owlands
Wood
5

WOODSETTS RD
Hoades Farm
DINNINGTON RD
HOADES AVE
NORTHFIELD CL
SPRINGFIELD CL
84

Rackford Farm
Cross La
BERNE CL
PH
Woodsetts
Inf Sch
Woodsetts
4
RACKFORD RD
Dewidales Wood
Woodsetts
Lindrick Road
Jun Sch
PEAR TREE CL
WARREN CL
CROSS FIELD DR
LINDRICK CT

Manor
Farm
WELLFIELD
GREN
SCHLEY AVE
LIMESTONE
CL
ROCKFIELD DR
GRANGE AVE
WORKSOP RD

Grange
Farm
LINDRICK RD
STAMBERS
CL

Anston Stones
Wood
Rackford La
Lofties
Plantation
GRANGE FARM
CT
TAYLOR CRES
TAYLOR DR
Socheage
Hill
Cotterhill
Woods
3

Black La
83

Lindrick Hill
Farm
Anston Brook
Lindrick
House
Birkett
House
Cotterhill
Woods
Farm

WORKSOP RD
Birket Wood
2

Lindrick Dale
Lindrick Golf Course
CH
Deep Carrs
Deep Carr
Farm
A57

Lindrick Common
Anston Grange
Stubbings
Lathe
Stubbings

River Ryton
Monk
Bridge

Moses'
Seat
1
82

53 A B 54 C D 55 E F 82

A B C D E F

8

Acorn Piece
Miller Lands
Woodland Farm
Langold Holt

Costhorpe Ind Est
Sports Field
Costhorpe

1 WEST VIEW
2 INGHAM BGLWS
3 HIGHFIELD VILLAS

Riddell Arms (PH)

7

Buckwood Farm
ROTHERHAM BAULK

PENTLAND DR   1
HAMBLETON CT   2
CHILTERN WAY   3
LOWTHER SQ   4
BEVERLEY WLK   5
CHICHESTER WLK 6
SALISBURY WLK 7
CANTERBURY WLK 8
CHEVIOT CT   9
MENDIP CT   10
LICHFIELD WLK 11
COTSWOLD CT   12

NORTH WAY
DADLEY RD
A60
DONCASTER RD
NORTHUMBERLAND AVE
SUTHERLAND
CUMBERLAND CL
WEST MARLAND
LAWN RD

CLEVELAND CL
LILAC GR
HAWTHORN WAY
WILLOW AVE
BEECH GR
SYCAMORE RD
LIME
TREE AVE
BECKETT RD
QUEENS RD
RAMS-DEN CRES
MULBERRY CRES
KNATON RD
KINGSTON RD
STEWART CL
AMANDA AVE
OXFORD RD
LINDRICK CL
Liby

85

WALLINGWELLS LA

6

STEWART RD
LONG LA
WINDSOR GDNS
CARISBROOK RD
CRAITHIE RD
CRAGSTON RD
GLAMIS RD
PEMBROKE DR
RICHMOND RD
CONWAY DR
BALMORAL
STRATHAVON DR
STRATHMORE
KENILWORTH DR
WARWICK AVE
WINDSOR RD
ARUNDEL DR

Carlton Park Infants Sch
Kingston Junior Sch

Carlton in Lindrick

Castle Garden

Wallingwells Wood
Carlton Wood

5

Wallingwells Park
Hollin Hills

OSBERTON HALL LA
CHURCH LA
A60

The Lawns

Owlands Wood

84

The Ashes
Holme Wood
Carlton Lake
Field House Farm

4

Corn Mill Farm

Sewage Works
The Bottoms
Owlands Wood Dike

Holme House Farm

3

OWDAY LA

Hardwick Ashes

83

Owday Wood

Broom Farm

2

WORKSOP RD
The Homestead
Owday Plantation
Little Broom Wood
Nab's Ashes Wood
Sand Hill Plantation
A60
CARLTON RD

Rough Piece

Whipman Wood
Cocked Hat Wood

WORKSOP RD
A57
Fox Covert
GATEFORD RD
WOODSETTS LA

1

Ashes Wood
Dog Kennel Plantation

ASHES PARK AVE
EDDISON PARK AVE
EASTWOOD

82

56 A B 57 C D 58 E F

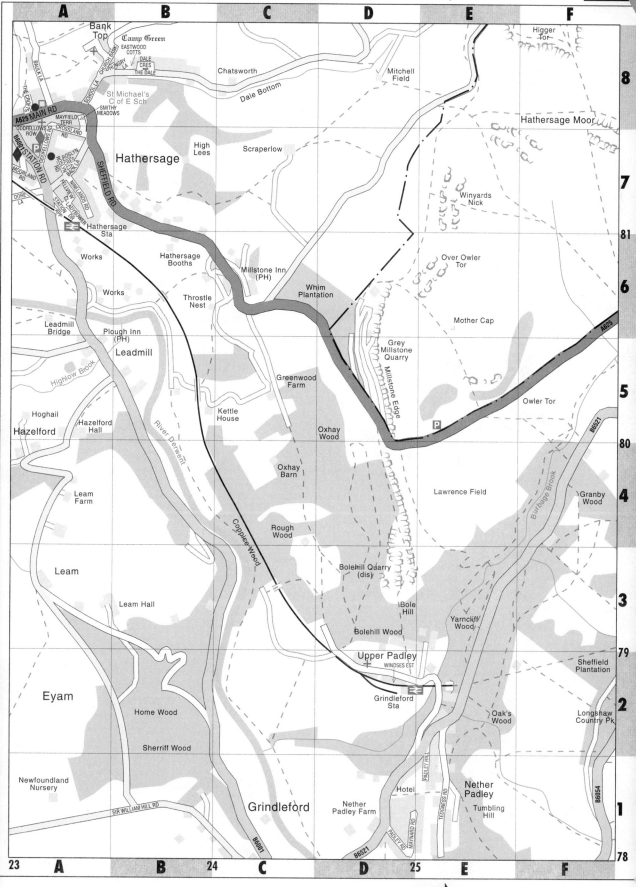

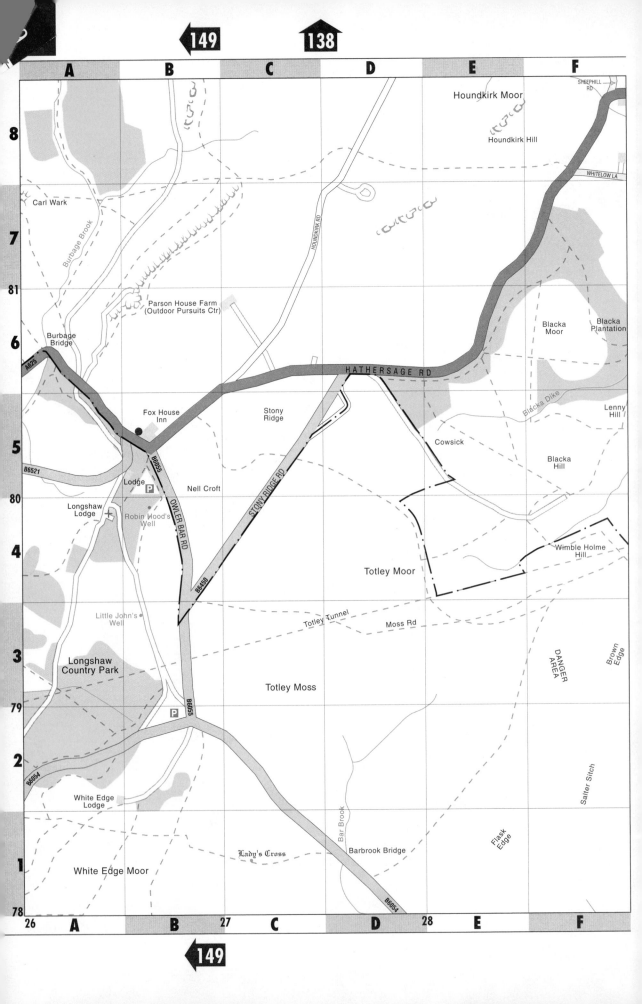

Houndkirk Moor

SHEEPHILL RD

Houndkirk Hill

WHITELOW LA

Carl Wark

Burbage Brook

HOUNDKIRK RD

Parson House Farm
(Outdoor Pursuits Ctr)

Blacka
Moor

Blacka
Plantation

Burbage
Bridge

A625

HATHERSAGE RD

Blacka Dike

Lenny
Hill

Fox House
Inn

Stony
Ridge

Cowsick

Blacka
Hill

B6055

B6521

STONY RIDGE RD

Lodge

P

Nell Croft

Wimble Holme
Hill

Longshaw
Lodge

OWLER BAR RD

Robin Hood's
Well

Totley Moor

B6450

Little John's
Well

Totley Tunnel

Moss Rd

DANGER
AREA

Brown
Edge

Longshaw
Country Park

B6055

Totley Moss

79

P

B6054

Salter Sitch

White Edge
Lodge

Lady's Cross

Bar Brook

Barbrook Bridge

Flask
Edge

White Edge Moor

B6054

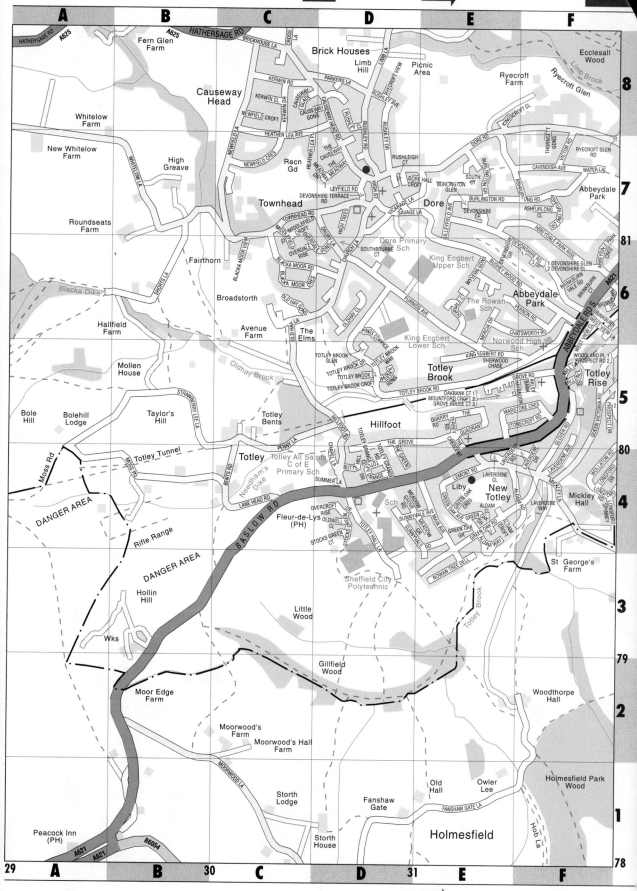

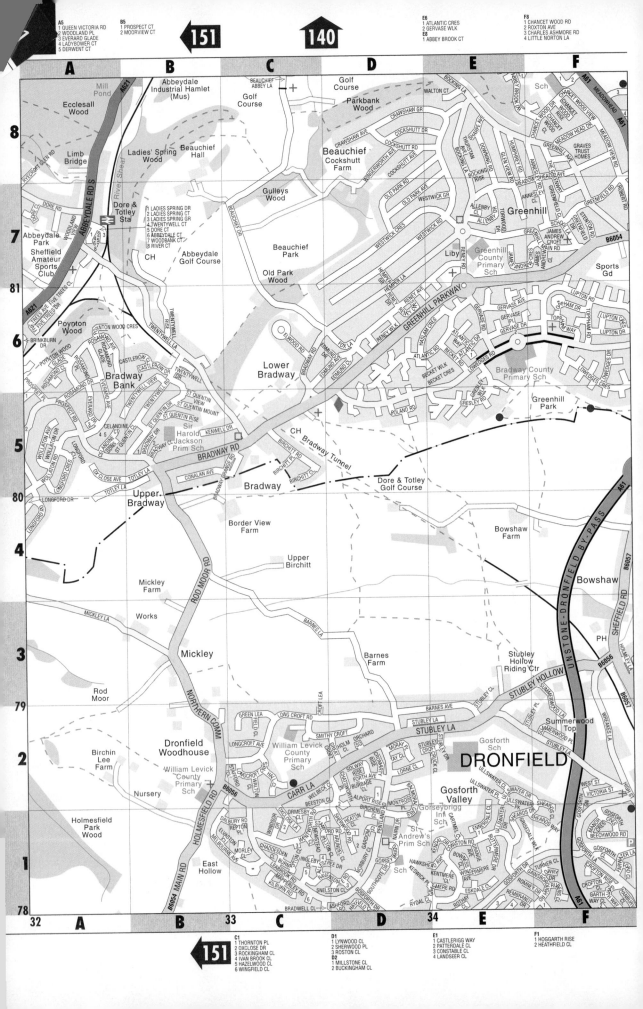

A   B   C   D   E   F

Graves Park
Little Norton
CHARLES ASHMORE RD
CLOONMORE DR
Lightwood
Farm
Lightwood
GRAVES
TRUST
HOMES
SERPENTINE WLK
HENLEY AVE
Oakes
Park
Broomfield
Wood
HAZLEHURST LA
LIGHTWOOD LA

Norton
BROCKLEHURST AVE
THE MEADS
NORTON LA
SCHOOL LA
A6102
8

LITTLE NORTON RD
BIRCH FARM AVE
GREENFIELD RD
LITTLE NORTON DR
NORTON PARK VIEW
NORTON PARK AVE
NORTON PARK DR
NORTON PARK RD
NORTON PARK CRES
CINDERHILL LA
BOCHUM PARKWAY

HUNSTONE AVE
LITTLE MSK
LITTLE NORTON LA
3
ROBERT RD
MEADOWHEAD
NORTON LA
Mossbrook
Sch
Hazlebarrow
Farm
Newfield
Spring
Wood
7

A6102
4
BOCHUM PARKWAY
B6157
Graves
Tennis
& L Ctr
HAZLEBARROW DR
Jordanthorpe
Plantation
81

Jordanthorpe
Sch
Norton
Coll
Rawlinson
Sch
Jordanthorpe
A7
1 LITTLE NORTON WAY
2 HAIGH MEMORIAL HOMES
3 GREENHILL MAIN RD
4 GREENHILL PARKWAY
ORMOND RD
HAZLEBARROW CT
HAZLEBARROW DR
HAZLEBARROW RD
HAZLEBARROW CRES
HAZLEBARROW GR
SELLY OAK GR
JORDANTHORPE PARKWAY
Hazlebarrow
Primary
Schs
7

Sports
Ground
Hotel
Jordanthorpe Sch
LOWEDGES PL
ORMOND DR
ORMOND CL
DYCHE DR
DYCHE PL
DYCHE RD
LINGFOOT PL
MEETHOUSE
Coalpit
Wood
6

Lowedges
Liby
P
WHITE THORNS
WHITE THORNS VIEW
WHITE THORNS CL
WHITE THORNS DR
LINGFOOT AVE
LINGFOOT CRES
JORDANTHORPE PARKWAY
Long
Wood
The Moss
Bridle
Road
Wood
6

LOWEDGES CRES
LOWEDGES RD
BATEMOOR PL
BATEMOOR VIEW
BATEMOOR DR
BATEMOOR CL
WHINACRE PL
WHINACRE CL
WHINACRE WLK
LINGFOOT WLK
Nor
Wood
Owler
Car
Wood
5

CHESTERFIELD RD S
A61
Sch
Batemoor
BOWSHAW AVE
BOWSHAW CL
BOWSHAW VIEW
B6158
White
Thorns
Nurseries
Ockley
Farm
CROSS LA
Whinacre
Wood
Hillside
Nurseries
SICKLEBROOK LA
Sicklebrook
Farm
OWLER CAR LA
5

B6157
Birchitt
Ppg Sta
JORDANTHORPE PARKWAY
Henpepper
Farm
80

SHEFFIELD RD
Holmefield
Farm
DYCHE LA
MEADOW CL
WILSON RD
Cross and
Birches
Farm
4

Coal
Aston
PIGHILLS LA
THORPE AVE
CUNLIFFE ST
FARM CL
WESTBANK CL
PIGHILLS LA
B6158
Rawlins
Ct
BIRCHES POND
P
ECKINGTON RD
Woodcock
Farm
Bentley
Hall
B6056
4

Holmley
Common
BROOKVIEW CT
HOLMLEY LA
HOLMLEY BANK
FORRESTER'S
BROWN LA
STONE CL
CROSS LA
DRURY
STONE RD
RIDGEWAY
ECKINGTON RD
PROSPECT RD
BARNARD AVE
FERNDALE CL
FERNDALE RISE
FIRTHWOOD CL
FIRTHWOOD AVE
FIRTHWOOD RISE
FIRTHWOOD RD
Nursery
3

BIRCHITT VIEW
SYCAMORE AVE
HAWTHORNE AVE
MARSH AVE
PLUM TREE
SNAPEHILL CL
SNAPE HILL LA
Lenthall
Co Inf
Sch
AVON LA
TRENT GR
DERWENT PL
DERWENT CT
DERWENT LA
ASTON CL
LANGDALE DR
WARREN RISE
DENTS LA
FALCON RD
FALCON RISE
THE KNOLL
DUCKET
Bentleyhall
Farm
Ibbotson's
Farm
ASH LA
Bentley
Farm
3

FAIRVIEW RD
ALMA CRES
SNAPEHILL CRES
CECIL RD
CHIVERTON CL
CECIL AVE
ALEXANDRA RD
SNAPE HILL LA
GREEN LA
FANSHAW RD
VIXEN LA
BEATS CRES
HOLMESDALE CL
Northfield Co Jun
Mixed
Sch
OAKHILL RD
HOLMESDALE RD
PADDOCK WAY
Gladys Buxton
Community Ed Ctr
Frith
Wood
Summerley
Farm
Elm Tree
Farm
SUMMERLEY RD
79

Snape
Hill
EGERTON RD
HARTINGTON RD
SNAPE HILL LA
FANSHAW RD
THE LAWN
HARDWICK CL
THE AVENUE
HADDON CL
Holmesdale
Infants
Sch
Holmesdale
STONELOW RD
STONELOW CRES
Summerley
SUMMERLEY LOWER RD
2

Ind
Est
THIRLMERE DR
SNAPE HILL
 PRINCESS RD
GREEN
CROSS
Henry
Fanshawe
Sch
Dronfield
Sta
Greendale
Sh Ctr
2
1 HARTINGTON CT
2 GREENDALE CT
3 STONELOW GN
PARK AVE
The Stonelow
County Junior Sch
SHIREOAKS RD
2

Liby
HIGH ST
APPERKNOWLE
HOLT LA
SNAPE HILL DR
CHURCH ST
HOLLIN BANK
TILFORD RD
B6158
B1
1 SCARSDALE CROSS
2 SCARSDALE RD
3 PALMER CRES
The Dronfield Sch
CALLYWHITE LA
Unstone
BACK RD
1

C Ctr
P
FAIRWATER
FANSHAW BANK
FAIRWINDS CL
SCHOOL LA
APPLE TREE
GREEN LA
TEA VALE
P
Quoit
Green
Schs
GLEDHILL CL
MOONPENNY WAY
GOMERSAL LA
ARCHER AVE
CHESTERFIELD RD
MILL LA
HALLOWES LA
GREEN LA N
Ind Est
Bridgefield
Wood
TOWN END
78

NETHERDENE RD
CROSS LA
B6057

A1
1 GOSFORTH LA
2 HILLSIDE AVE
3 NETHERDENE RD
4 PEMBROKE RD
5 UPPER SCHOOL LA

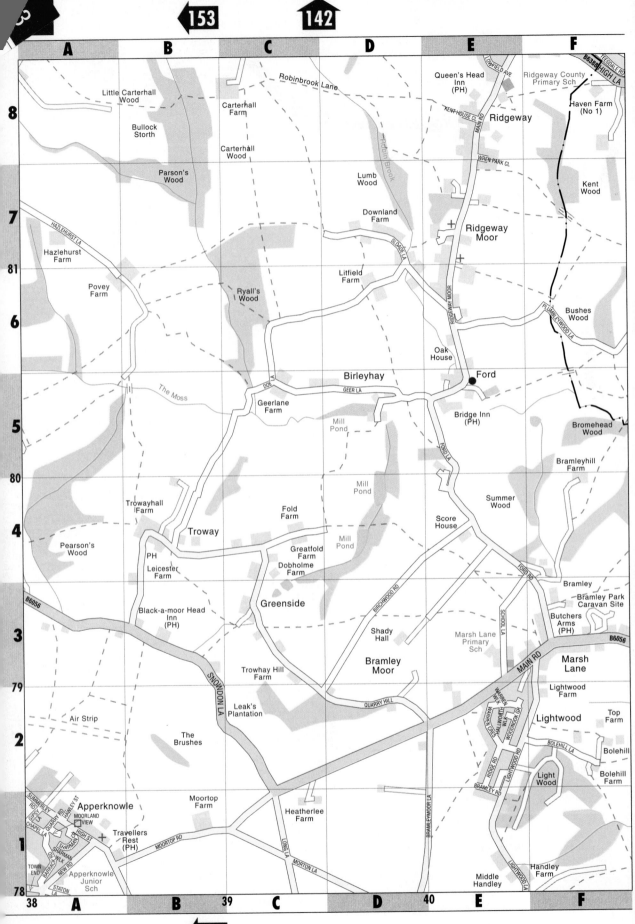

A   B   C   D   E   F

8

Little Carterhall Wood

Bullock Storth

Carterhall Farm

Robinbrook Lane

Carterhall Wood

Parson's Wood

Queen's Head Inn (PH)

KENT HOUSE CL

Ridgeway County Primary Sch

HIGH LA

Ridgeway

Haven Farm (No 1)

WREN PARK CL

Kent Wood

7

HAZLEHURST LA

Hazlehurst Farm

Lumb Wood

Downland Farm

Ridgeway Moor

81

Povey Farm

Ryall's Wood

Litfield Farm

SLOADE LA

RIDGEWAY MOOR

P LUMBLEY WOOD LA

Bushes Wood

6

The Moss

DOE LA

Birleyhay

GEER LA

Oak House

Ford

Bridge Inn (PH)

Bromehead Wood

5

Geerlane Farm

Mill Pond

Bramleyhill Farm

80

Trowayhall Farm

Fold Farm

Mill Pond

Score House

Summer Wood

FORD LA

4

Pearson's Wood

Troway

PH

Leicester Farm

Greatfold Farm

Dobholme Farm

Mill Pond

Bramley

FORD RD

SCHOOL LA

Bramley Park Caravan Site

Butchers Arms (PH)

3

B6056

Black-a-moor Head Inn (PH)

Greenside

Shady Hall

BIRCHWOOD RD

Bramley Moor

Marsh Lane Primary Sch

B6056

Marsh Lane

MAIN RD

79

SNOWDON LA

Trowhay Hill Farm

Leak's Plantation

QUARRY HILL

Lightwood Farm

WARREN WLK

WARREN CRES

HALLWORTH WLK

WOODNOOK GR

Lightwood

Top Farm

2

Air Strip

The Brushes

BOLEHILL LA

Bolehill

RIDGE RD

LIGHTWOOD RD

Light Wood

Bolehill Farm

1

SUMMERLEY RD

GIPSY LA

CHAPEL ST

HAWLEY ST

HIGH ST

MOORLAND VIEW

Apperknowle

Travellers Rest (PH)

SHARMAN WLK

NEW RD

BARTHOLG

Moortop Farm

MOORTOP RD

Heatherlee Farm

LONG LA

MORTON LA

BRAMLEY RD

BRAMLEYMOOR LA

Middle Handley

Handley Farm

LIGHTWOOD RD

TOWN END

STATON LA

Apperknowle Junior Sch

78

38   A   B   39   C   D   40   E   F

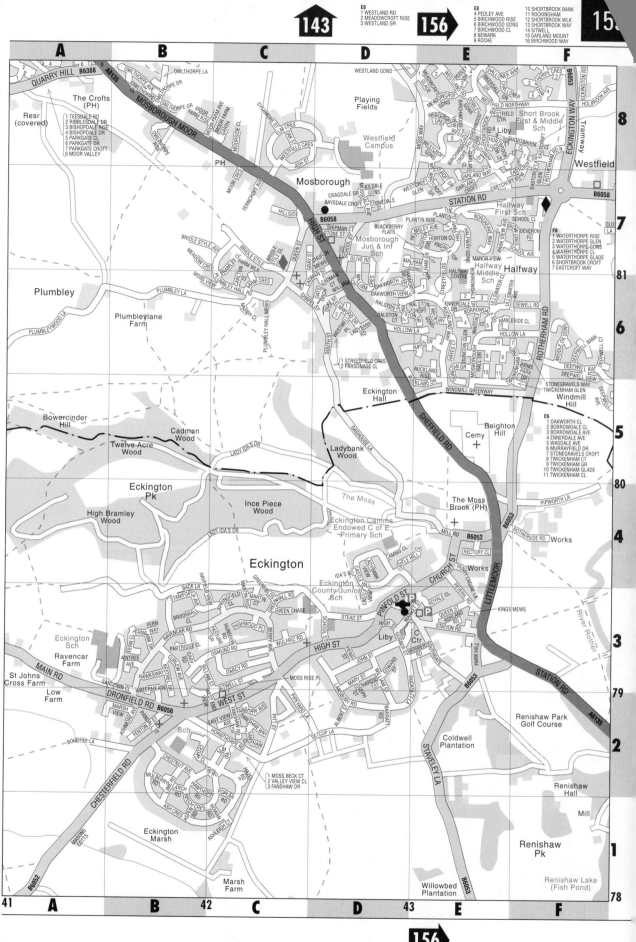

E8
1 WESTLAND RD
2 MEADOWCROFT RISE
3 WESTLAND GR

E8
4 PEDLEY AVE
5 BIRCHWOOD RISE
6 BIRCHWOOD GDNS
7 BIRCHWOOD CL
8 NEWARK
9 ROCHE

10 SHORTBROOK BANK
11 ROCKINGHAM
12 SHORTBROOK WLK
13 SHORTBROOK WAY
14 SITWELL
15 GARLAND MOUNT
16 BIRCHWOOD WAY

The Crofts
(PH)
1 TEESDALE RD
2 RIBBLESDALE DR
3 BISHOPDALE RISE
4 BISHOPDALE DR
5 PARKGATE CL
6 PARKGATE DR
7 PARKGATE CROFT
8 MOOR VALLEY

Resr
(covered)

Mosborough

Playing
Fields

Westfield
Campus

Short Brook
First & Middle
Sch

Westfield

Plumbley

Plumbleylane
Farm

Mosborough
Jun & Inf
Sch

Halfway
First Sch

Halfway

F8
1 WATERTHORPE RISE
2 WATERTHORPE GLEN
3 WATERTHORPE GDNS
4 WATERTHORPE CL
5 WATERTHORPE GLADE
6 SHORTBROOK CROFT
7 EASTCROFT WAY

Halfway
Middle
Sch

1 STREETFIELD CRES
2 PARSONAGE CL

Eckington
Hall

Windmill Greenway

Windmill
Hill

Bowercinder
Hill

Cadman
Wood

Twelve Acre
Wood

Ladybank
Wood

Cemy

Beighton
Hill

E6
1 OAKWORTH CL
2 BORROWDALE CL
3 BORROWDALE AVE
4 ENNERDALE AVE
5 WASDALE AVE
6 MURRAYFIELD DR
7 STONEGRAVELS CROFT
8 TWICKENHAM CT
9 TWICKENHAM GR
10 TWICKENHAM GLADE
11 TWICKENHAM CL

Eckington
Pk

High Bramley
Wood

Ince Piece
Wood

The Moss

The Moss
Brook (PH)

Eckington Camms
Endowed C of E
Primary Sch

Eckington

Eckington
County Junior
Sch

Eckington
Sch

Ravencar
Farm

St Johns
Cross Farm

Low
Farm

Works

Works

Renishaw Park
Golf Course

Coldwell
Plantation

Renishaw
Hall

Mill

Eckington
Marsh

Renishaw
Pk

Marsh
Farm

Willowbed
Plantation

Renishaw Lake
(Fish Pond)

1 MOSS BECK CT
2 VALLEY VIEW CL
3 FANSHAW DR

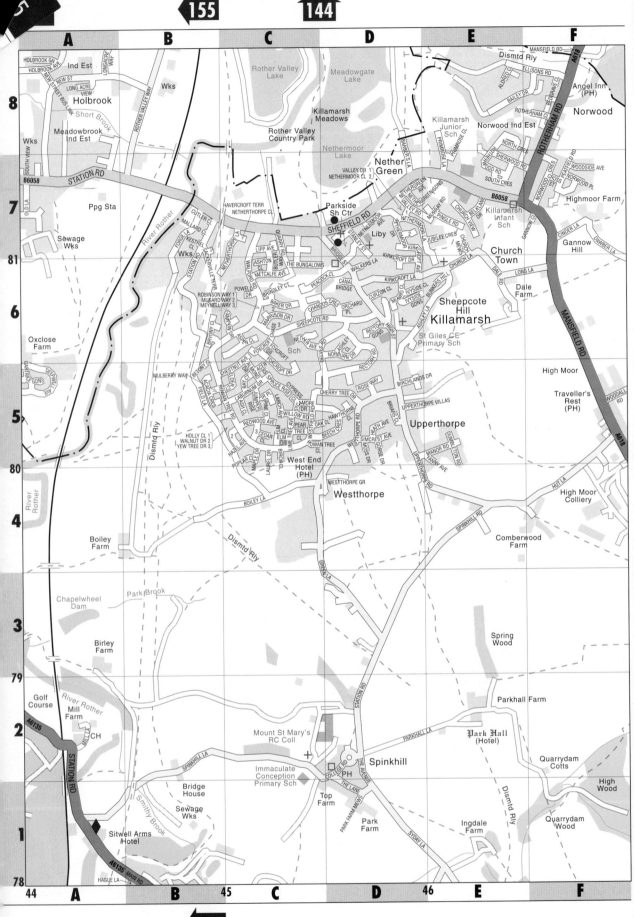

A   B   C   D   E   F

Holbrook Ga
Ind Est
Holbrook
NEW ST
NEW STREET BUS LNK
LONG ACRE VIEW
Short Brook
Meadowbrook Ind Est
Wks
Wks
LONGACRE WAY
ROTHER VALLEY WAY
Wks

Rother Valley Lake
Meadowgate Lake
Killamarsh Meadows
Rother Valley Country Park
Nethermoor Lake
Nether Green

Killamarsh Junior Sch
Norwood Ind Est
MANSFIELD RD
Dismtd Rly
Angel Inn (PH)
Norwood
ALFRED CL
ELLISONS RD
BAILEY DR
ROTHERHAM CL
NORTH CRES
SHERWOOD RD
WOOD RD
SOUTH CRES
NORWOOD PL
WOODSIDE AVE
Highmoor Farm
ROTHERHAM RD
BEDGRAVE CL
A618
NORWOOD CROSS
NORWOOD CRES
PEATFIELD RD

STATION RD
B6058
Ppg Sta
OLD LA

SOUTH VIEW

River Rother
Sewage Wks
Wks
MALLARD CL
FORGE LA
SACKERVILLE TERR
KESTREL CL
CUTLER CL
Havercroft Terr
Netherthorpe CL
QUARRY RD
NETHERTHORPE WAY
STATION RD
LIPP AVE
WALFORD RD
ASHTON CL
METCALFE AVE
POWELL RD
Robinson Way 1
Musard Way 2
Meynell Way 3
HARRISON DR
BRINDLEY CL
BAKER DR
The Bungalows
PEACOCK CL
CHANDOS CRES
SHEEPCOTE RD
ORCHARD PL
CHASE
NETHER AVE
SISLEY CL
NORBURN DR
RECTORY RD
Sch
FOXCROFT AVE
FOXCROFT GR
FOXCROFT DR
ASPEN CL
BETONY CL
CHESTNUT AVE
ELDER CT
ALMOND PL
SPRUCE RISE
ROWAN TREE RD
LABURNUM GR
JUNIPER RISE
LARCH WAY
LIME TREE AVE
WILLOW RD
SYCAMORE DR
PEAR TREE CL
BEECH CRES
OAK CL
ROWAN TREE CL
WESTFIELD RD
HAWTHORNE
SIMCREST AVE
MULBERRY WAY
FIELD LA
ACACIA CRES
MAPLE DR
HAZEL AVE
POPLAR CL
LAUREL DR
CEDAR
BEDWOOD AVE
HOLLY CL 1
WALNUT DR 2
YEW TREE DR 3
CYPRESS
ELM CL
West End Hotel (PH)

Parkside Sh Ctr
SHEFFIELD RD
Liby
BRIDGE ST
STANLEY ST
WALKERS LA
CANAL BRIDGE
KIRKCROFT DR
KIRKCROFT LA
KIRKCROFT AVE
CURZON CL
MILL LA
IVYSIDE
IVYSIDE GDNS
BUNKERS HILL
ASHLEY LA
RECTORY RD
St Giles CE Primary Sch
ROSE WAY
HEATH AVE
GORSE LA
BIRCHLANDS DR
Upperthorpe Villas
BRIARS CL
Upperthorpe
UPPERTHORPE
MANOR RD
LANNY AVE
WEST THORPE RD
WESTTHORPE GR
Westthorpe
BOILEY LA

Nethermoor
VALLEY DR 1
NETHERMOOR CL 2
NETHERGREEN AVE
NETHERGREEN GDNS
VALLEY RD
NETHERMOOR RD
MURRAY RD
PINGLE RD
CHURCH VIEW
BELKLANE
CHURCH LA
JUBILEE CRES
BARBER'S LA
PRIMROSE CL
PRIMROSE LA
NORTHFIELD
CHURCH ST
DALE RD
LONG LA
Sheepcote Hill
Killamarsh
Church Town
B6058
Killamarsh Infant Sch
GANNOW CL
CINDER LA
TAWBER CL
Gannow Hill
Dale Farm
Dale Rd
High Moor
Traveller's Rest (PH)
High Moor Colliery
Comberwood Farm
NUT LA
WOODALL RD
High Moor Colliery
RUMBLETON RD
SPINKHILL RD
MANSFIELD RD
A618

Oxclose Farm
GARTH AVE
DEEPWELL AVE
GARTH GDNS

Dismtd Rly
River Rother
Boiley Farm
Chapelwheel Dam
Park Brook
Birley Farm
Dismtd Rly
GREEN LA
STATION RD
Spring Wood
Parkhall Farm
Park Hall (Hotel)
Quarrydam Cotts
High Wood
Quarrydam Wood

Golf Course
River Rother
A6135
STATION RD
Mill Farm
CH
Mount St Mary's RC Coll
SPINKHILL LA
Immaculate Conception Primary Sch
COLLEGE RD
THE AVENUE
PH
Spinkhill
PARKHALL LA
Park Hall (Hotel)
Bridge House
Sewage Wks
Top Farm
THE LANE
PARK FARM MEWS
Park Farm
STORY LA
SYDNEY LA
Ingdale Farm
Dismtd Rly
Sitwell Arms Hotel
A6135 MAIN RD
HAGUE LA
Smithy Brook

8   7   81   6   5   80   4   3   79   2   1   78

44   A   B   45   C   D   46   E   F

A B C D E F

Nor
Wood

Spoil
Heap

Hard
Field

Baugy
Hill

North House

North
Farm Cl

Hudson Dr

North
House

Beehive
Farm

Thorpe Rd

Manor Rd

Killamarsh
Pond

Top
Farm

Poplar
Farm

Woodall
Pond

Woodall

Rectory Gdns

Street Farm Cl

Jackys La

Orchard Lee

Harthill

Killamarsh La

Sewage
Wks

Low
Plantation

Woodall La

Broad
Bridge

Kye La

South Farm Ave

Serlby La

De Warren Pl

Osborne Croft

Common Rd

Woodall
Bottoms

Stone
Hill

Harthill
Resr

Carver

Carver
Way

Priory
Ct

Peregrin Way

De Sutton Pl

Pryor Mede

Uswell La

Harthill
Jun & Inf
Sch

Winney Hill

The
Hop Inge

The Dinnings

Serlby Dr

Harthill Field Rd

Woodall
Rd

Woodall
Service Area

Crescent

Hewitt Pl

Firvale

Woodall
Common

Mansfield
Rd

Fir
Hill

Woodall
Common

Birkenhead
Wood

Carr Farm
Cottage

Winney La

Carr
Farm

Pebleygrove
Farm

The
Pebley
(PH)

Pebley
Oaks

Rotherham Rd

Pebley
Resr

Harthill
Field

Ward La

Crabtree
Wood

Car
Plantation

Hawke
Wood

Barlborough

Garden
Plantation

Nitticarhill
Wood

Harthill La

Butcherlawn
Pond

Barlborough Hall Sch
formerly
Barlborough Hall

Nitticarhill

Longrybank
Wood

M1

A618

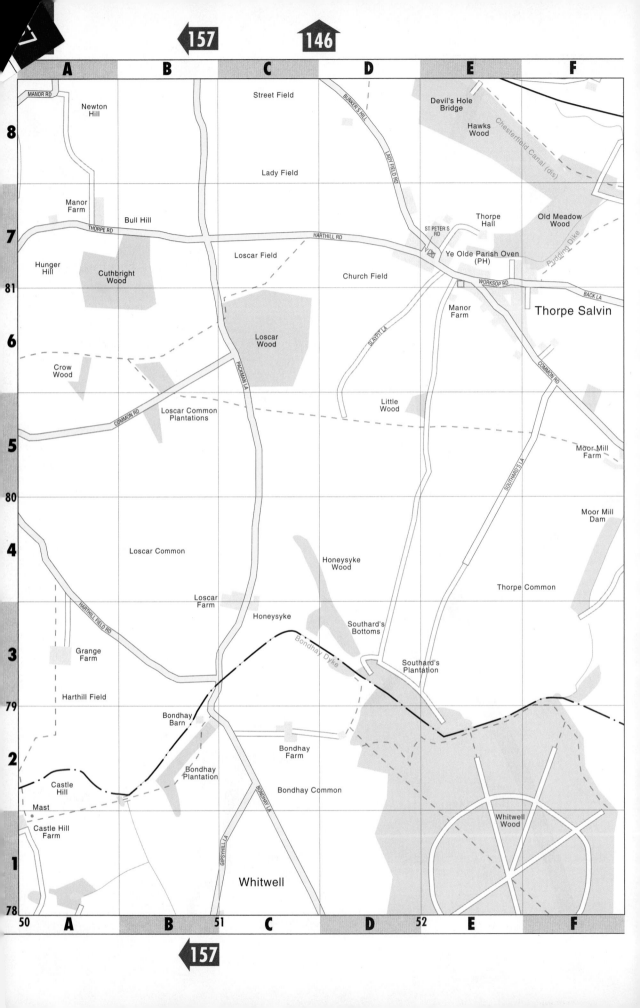

A B C D E F

8

Newton
Hill

MANOR RD

Street Field

BUNKER'S HILL

Devil's Hole
Bridge

Hawks
Wood

Chesterfield Canal (dis)

7

Manor
Farm

Bull Hill

THORPE RD

Lady Field

HARTHILL RD

LADY FIELD RD

ST PETER'S
RD

Thorpe
Hall

Old Meadow
Wood

Pudding Dyke

81

Hunger
Hill

Cuthbright
Wood

Loscar Field

Church Field

Ye Olde Parish Oven
(PH)

WORKSOP RD

Manor
Farm

BACK LA

Thorpe Salvin

6

Crow
Wood

Loscar
Wood

SLAYPIT LA

COMMON RD

5

COMMON RD

Loscar Common
Plantations

Little
Wood

Moor Mill
Farm

80

PACKMAN LA

SOUTHARD'S LA

Moor Mill
Dam

4

Loscar Common

Honeysyke
Wood

Thorpe Common

Loscar
Farm

Honeysyke

Southard's
Bottoms

3

HARTHILL FIELD RD

Grange
Farm

Bondhay Dyke

Southard's
Plantation

79

Harthill Field

Bondhay
Barn

2

Castle
Hill

Bondhay
Plantation

Bondhay
Farm

BONDHAY LA

Bondhay Common

Mast

Castle Hill
Farm

Whitwell
Wood

1

GIPSYHILL LA

Whitwell

78

50 A B 51 C D 52 E F

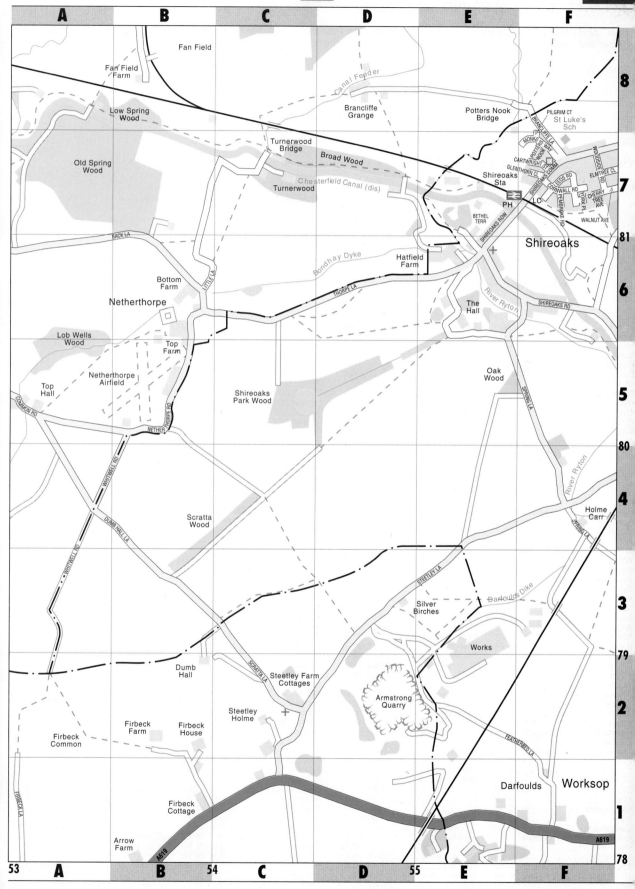

A B C D E F

Fan Field
Fan Field Farm
Canal Feeder
Low Spring Wood
Brancliffe Grange
Potters Nook Bridge
PILGRIM CT
St Luke's Sch
Turnerwood Bridge
Broad Wood
Old Spring Wood
Turnerwood
Chesterfield Canal (dis)
BRANCLIFFE LA
MONKS
POTTERS WAY
NOOK CL
CARTWRIGHT ST
GLENTHORN CL
SHIREOAKS COMM
LEEDS RD
WOODSIDE RD
CORNWALL RD
YORK PL
PEMBROKE RD
ELMTREE CL
CHERRY TREE AVE
WALNUT AVE
Shireoaks Sta
BETHEL TERR
PH
LC
Shireoaks
BACK LA
LITTLE LA
Bottom Farm
Bondhay Dyke
Hatfield Farm
THORPE LA
SHIREOAKS ROW
The Hall
River Ryton
SHIREOAKS RD
Netherthorpe
Lob Wells Wood
Top Farm
Oak Wood
SPRING LA
Netherthorpe Airfield
Shireoaks Park Wood
Top Hall
COMMON RD
THORPE RD
NETHER
NETHER
WHITWELL RD
River Ryton
Holme Carr
Scratta Wood
DUMB HALL LA
WHITWELL RD
STEETLEY LA
Darfoulds Dike
Silver Birches
SPRING LA
Works
Dumb Hall
SCRATTA LA
Steetley Farm Cottages
Armstrong Quarry
Firbeck Farm
Firbeck House
Steetley Holme
Firbeck Common
FEATHERBED LA
Darfoulds
Worksop
Firbeck Cottage
FIRBECK LA
A619
Arrow Farm
A619

53 A B 54 C D 55 E F 78

8
7
81
6
5
80
4
79
3
2
1

EXPLANATION OF THE STREET INDEX REFERENCE SYSTEM

Street names are listed alphabetically and show the locality, the Post Office Postcode District, the page number and a reference to the square in which the name falls on the map page.

Example: Norfolk Ct. Roth S65....................................115 E7 8

Norfolk Ct This is the full street name, which may have been abbreviated on the map.

Roth This is the abbreviation for the town, village or locality in which the street falls.

S65 This is the Post Office Postcode District for the street name.

115 This is the page number of the map on which the street name appears.

E7 The letter and figure indicate the square on the map in which the centre of the street falls. The square can be found at the junction of the vertical column carrying the appropriate letter and the horizontal row carrying the appropriate figure.

8 In congested areas numbers may have been used to indicate the location of a street. In certain circumstances, the number used to represent a street will follow the reference in the gazetteer entry.

ABBREVIATIONS USED IN THE INDEX
Road Names

Approach ... App	Corner ... Cnr	Heights ... Hts	Road ... Rd
Arcade ... Arc	Cottages ... Cotts	Industri al Estate ... Ind Est	Roundabout ... Rdbt
Avenue ... Ave	Court ... Ct	Interchange ... Intc	South ... S
Boulevard ... Bvd	Courtyard ... Ctyd	Junction ... Junc	Square ... Sq
Buildings ... Bldgs	Crescent ... Cres	Lane ... La	Stairs ... Strs
Business Park ... Bsns Pk	Drive ... Dr	North ... N	Steps ... Stps
Business Centre ... Bsns Ctr	Drove ... Dro	Orchard ... Orch	Street,Saint ... St
Bungalows ... Bglws	East ... E	Parade ... Par	Terrace ... Terr
Causeway ... Cswy	Embankment ... Emb	Park ... Pk	Trading Estate ... Trad Est
Centre ... Ctr	Esplanade ... Espl	Passage ... Pas	Walk ... Wlk
Circle ... Circ	Estate ... Est	Place ... Pl	West ... W
Circus ... Cir	Gardens ... Gdns	Precinct ... Prec	Yard ... Yd
Close ... Cl	Green ... Gn	Promenade ... Prom	
Common ... Comm	Grove ... Gr	Retail Park ... Ret Pk	

Key to abbreviations of Town, Village and Rural locality names used in the index of street names.

Adwick le Street ... Ad le S 40 A6	Dinnington ... Din 134 E1	Killamarsh ... Kill 156 E6	Sykehouse ... Syke 7 C6
Armthorpe ... Arm 64 A5	Dodworth ... Dod 53 F7	Kirk Bramwith ... K Bram 24 A4	Snaith ... Snaith 1 A8
Askern ... Askern 22 A7	Doncaster ... Don 62 E3	Kirk Smeaton ... K Smea 3 D5	South Anston ... S Anst 146 C4
Aston ... Aston 144 E6	Dronfield ... Dron 152 E2	Kirkburton ... Kirkb 28 B8	South Elmsall ... S Elm 19 A2
Auckley ... Auck 86 B7	Dunford Bridge ... Dun Br 48 D1	Langold ... Lan 136 E4	South Hiendley ... S Hie 16 D6
Austerfield ... Aust 105 C2	Eckington ... Eck 155 C4	Langsett ... Lang 71 C6	South Kirkby ... S Kirk 18 C1
Badsworth ... Bad 18 E8	Emley ... Emley 12 A6	Laughton en le Morthen Laugh 134 E5	Sprotbrough ... Sprot 61 C1
Balne Moor ... Bal M 5 F8	Epworth ... Epw 67 F6	Letwell ... Let 136 A3	Stainforth ... Stai 24 F3
Bamford ... Bam 124 B1	Everton ... Ever 123 F3	Maltby ... Maltby 119 C5	Stainton ... Ston 119 F8
Barlborough ... Barl 157 B2	Eyam ... Eyam 149 A2	Mapplewell ... Mapp 14 C1	Stocksbridge ... Stock 73 C2
Barnby Dun ... B Dun 42 F8	Fenwick ... Fenw 6 B5	Marr ... Marr 60 D7	Styrrup ... Styr 121 D1
Barnburgh ... Bnbur 59 D3	Finningley ... Finn 86 E2	Mattersey ... Matt 123 E1	Swinton ... Swint 79 C2
Barnsley ... Barn 33 C1	Firbeck ... Fir 136 A6	Mexborough ... Mex 80 B7	Thorne ... Thorne 26 C8
Bawtry ... Bawtry 123 B7	Fishlake ... Fish 25 C1	Midhopestones ... Midhop 72 A3	Thorpe in Balne ... T in B 23 B2
Belton ... Belton 46 F4	Gildingwells ... Gild 147 F7	Misson ... Misson 105 F2	Thorpe Salvin ... Th Sa 158 F6
Bentley ... Ben 62 B8	Glossop ... Glos 68 A1	Moss ... Moss 6 B1	Thurcroft ... Thurcr 133 D6
Bircotes ... Bir 122 D4	Goole Fields ... G Field 11 B8	Netherton ... Neth 12 A8	Thurgoland ... Thurgo 73 F7
Blaxton ... Blax 86 E6	Great Houghton ... Gt Hou 36 E2	New Edlington ... N Edl 82 C1	Tickhill ... Tick 121 B6
Bradfield ... Bfield 110 B5	Grimethorpe ... Grime 36 B7	North Anston ... N Anst 146 D6	Tintwistle ... Tint 68 A7
Braithwell ... Braith 101 A2	Grindleford ... Grin 149 C1	Norton ... Norton 4 C3	Todwick ... Tod 145 E6
Branton ... Bran 85 D8	Hallam Moors ... Hal M 137 E8	Notton ... Notton 14 F6	Treeton ... Treet 131 E4
Brierley ... Bri 17 A3	Hampole ... Ham 20 B1	Oldcotes ... Old 136 F6	Ulley ... Ulley 132 F3
Brinsworth ... Brin 131 C8	Harthill ... Hart 157 F6	Oughtibridge ... Ought 111 E7	Unstone ... Uns 153 E1
Brodsworth ... Brod 39 B4	Harworth ... Har 121 E4	Oxspring ... Oxspr 52 B1	Upton ... Upton 19 A8
Burghwallis ... Burg 21 B4	Hatfield ... Hat 44 C8	Penistone ... Pen 51 C3	Wadworth ... Wad 102 C7
Cadeby ... Cade 81 D5	Hathersage ... Hath 149 B7	Pilley ... Pilley 75 D5	Walden Stubbs ... W Stub 4 E6
Carlecotes ... Carl 49 B3	Hemsworth ... Hem 17 C8	Pollington ... Poll 6 C8	Wales ... Wales 145 B3
Carlton in Lindrick ... C in L 148 F5	Hickleton ... Hick 59 B7	Rawcliffe ... Rawcl 2 A8	Wath upon Dearne ... W up D 78 E7
Cawthorne ... Caw 31 D4	High Hoyland ... H Hoy 12 C1	Rawmarsh ... Rawm 97 C6	Wentworth ... Went 77 B1
Chapeltown ... Chap 95 B3	High Melton ... H Mel 81 C8	Rossington ... Ross 85 B1	West Bretton ... W Bret 12 E8
Clayton ... Clay 37 C4	High Peak ... H Pk 106 B1	Rotherham ... Roth 115 F6	Wharncliffe Side ... Wharn 93 B2
Clayton West ... Clay W 12 A3	Holme ... Holme 47 A8	Royston ... Roy 15 D3	Whitley Common ... Wh Com 49 E7
Clifton ... Clift 100 E5	Holmesfield ... Hol 151 E1	Ryhill ... Ryhill 16 B8	Whitwell ... Whit 158 C1
Conisbrough ... Con 81 B3	Holmfirth ... Holmfi 28 A5	Scrooby ... Scro 123 A2	Wombwell ... Wombw 56 D2
Crowle ... Crowle 11 F1	Hood Green ... Hd Gr 53 E2	Shafton ... Shaf 16 B3	Womersley ... Womer 4 B8
Cudworth ... Cud 35 C6	Hooton Pagnell ... H Pag 38 C5	Sheffield ... Shef 129 D3	Woodsetts ... Woods 147 F4
Darfield ... Dar 57 B5	Hooton Roberts ... H Rob 99 D7	Shepley ... Shep 28 F8	Woolley ... Wool 13 F7
Dearne ... Dearne 58 D5	Hoyland ... Hoy 76 C6	Shireoaks ... Shire 159 F1	Worksop ... Work 159 F1
Denby Dale ... D Dale 30 B6	Ingbirchworth ... Ingb 29 E1	Silkstone ... Silk 52 F8	Wortley ... Wort 74 D3
Derwent ... Derw 124 A5	Kexbrough ... Kex 32 C7	Skelmanthorpe ... Skel 30 A8	Wroot ... Wroot 67 B3

Beaumont Ave. Barn S70 33 B1
Beaumont Ave. S Elm WF9 18 F3
Beaumont Ave. Shef S2 130 B2
Beaumont Cl. Shef S2 130 B2
Beaumont Cres. Shef S2 130 B2
Beaumont Dr. Roth S65 116 B5
Beaumont Dr. W Bret S65 12 F6
Beaumont Mews. Shef S2 130 B1
Beaumont Rd. Kex S75 32 C8
Beaumont Rd N. Shef S2 130 B1
Beaumont St. Hoy S74 76 B5
Beaumont Way. Shef S2 130 A2
Beaver Ave. Shef S13 143 B8
Beaver Cl. Shef S13 143 B8
Beaver Dr. Shef S13 143 B8
Beaver Hill Comp Sch. Shef 143 B8
Beaver Hill Rd. Shef S13 143 B7
Beccles Way. Roth S66 117 E5
Beck Cl. Shef S5 113 F7
Beck Cl. Swint S64 79 D1
Beck Fst & Mid Sch. Shef 113 D7
Beck Rd. Shef S5 113 D7
Beck Rise. Hem WF9 17 D7
Beck View. Notton WF4 15 A6
Becket Cres. Roth S61 96 D2
Becket Cres. Shef S8 152 E6
Becket Rd. Shef S8 152 E6
Becket Wlk. Shef S8 152 E6
Beckett Ave. C in L S81 148 F7
Beckett Hospl Terr. Barn S70 54 F8 15
Beckett Rd. Don DN2 62 F5
Beckett St. Barn S71 33 F2
Beckfield Gr. Dearne S63 58 B3
Becknoll Rd. W up D S73 78 A8
Beckton Ave. Shef S19 143 E2
Beckton Ct. Shef S19 143 F2
Beckton Gr. Shef S19 143 E2
Beckwith Rd. Laugh S31 134 C2
Beckwith Rd. Roth S65 116 D7
Bedale Ct. Roth S60 115 F4
Bedale Rd. Ben DN5 61 D7
Bedale Rd. Shef S8 140 F6
Bedale Wlk. Shaf S72 16 C3
Bedding Edge Rd. Holmfi HD7 49 A7
Bedford Cl. N Anst S31 146 D7
Bedford Ct. Bawtry DN10 122 F7
Bedford Rd. Ought S30 111 D8
Bedford St. Barn S70 54 F7
Bedford St. Grime S72 36 A5
Bedford St. Maltby S66 119 B4
Bedford St. Shef S6 128 F5
Bedford Terr. Barn S71 34 A5
Bedgebury Cl. Shef S19 144 B1
Bedgrave Cl. Kill S31 156 F8
Beech Ave. Cud S72 35 B8
Beech Ave. Finn DN9 86 A4
Beech Ave. Rawm S62 98 B5
Beech Ave. Roth S65 116 E4
Beech Ave. Silk S75 53 A5
Beech Ave. Tick DN11 121 B7
Beech Cl. Bri S72 17 A3
Beech Cl. Hoy S73 77 D8
Beech Cl. Maltby S66 118 D5
Beech Cl. S Kirk WF9 18 B2
Beech Cres. Eck S31 155 B1
Beech Cres. Kill S31 156 D5
Beech Cres. Mex S64 79 E5
Beech Cres. Stai DN7 24 F4
Beech Dr. Bran DN3 64 E1
Beech Gr. Barn S70 54 D7
Beech Gr. Ben DN5 62 B8
Beech Gr. C in L S81 148 E7
Beech Gr. Con DN12 81 B1
Beech Gr. Din S31 146 F7
Beech Gr. Don DN4 82 C6
Beech Gr. Roth S66 117 C5
Beech Hill. Con DN12 81 C2
Beech Hill Rd. Shef S10 128 D2
Beech House Rd. Hoy S73 77 D7
Beech Rd. Ad le S DN6 21 A1
Beech Rd. Arm DN3 64 B7
Beech Rd. Har DN11 122 A5
Beech Rd. Maltby S66 118 D5
Beech Rd. Norton DN6 4 D1
Beech Rd. Ross DN11 104 A8
Beech Rd. Shaf S72 16 D2
Beech Rd. Upton WF9 19 B7
Beech Rd. W up D S63 79 A6
Beech St. Barn S70 54 F8
Beech St. S Elm WF9 18 E1
Beech Tree Ave. Thorne DN8 26 C6
Beech Tree Cl. Bran DN3 64 B1
Beech Way. Aston S31 144 C8
Beech Way. Dron S18 153 A3
Beecham Ct. Swint S64 79 C1
Beechcroft Dr. Don DN4 82 E5
Beeches Ave. Shef S2 141 C8
Beeches Dr. Shef S2 141 C8
Beeches Gr. Shef S19 144 A3
Beeches Rd. Wales S31 145 B3
Beeches The. Aston S31 144 D7
Beeches The. Don DN3 42 F4
Beeches The. Swint S64 79 C2
Beechfern Cl. Chap S30 94 D8
Beechfield Rd. Don DN1 62 D2
Beechfield Rd. Hat DN7 43 F7
Beechville Ave. Swint S64 79 C1
Beechwood Cl. Don DN3 43 A1
Beechwood Cl. Rawm S62 98 C7
Beechwood Cl. Swint S63 78 F3
Beechwood Cres. Hem WF9 17 C6
Beechwood Mount. Hem WF9 17 D6
Beechwood Rd. Chap S30 94 E6
Beechwood Rd. Dron S18 152 F1
Beechwood Rd. Roth S60 116 A4
Beechwood Rd. Shef S6 128 B8
Beechwood Rd. Stock S30 92 B8
Beechwood. Roth S65 115 F7
Beechwood Wlk. N Edl DN12 82 A1
Beehive Rd. Shef S10 128 D4
Beeley St. Shef S3 128 F1
Beeley Wood La. Shef S6 112 A4
Beeley Wood Rd. Shef S6 112 C3
Beeley Wood Senior Sch. Shef 112 C3
Beely Rd. Ought S30 111 E6
Beeston Cl. Dron S18 152 C2
Beeston Sq. Barn S71 33 F8
Beet St. Shef S3 128 F3
Beeton Gn. Shef S6 126 C5
Beeton Rd. Shef S8 140 F5
Beever La. Barn S75 33 A3
Beevers Rd. Roth S61 96 D2
Beeversleigh. Roth S65 115 E6 3
Beevor St. Barn S71 34 B1
Begonia Cl. S Anst S31 146 D4
Beighton Inf Sch. Shef 144 A3
Beighton Rd E. Shef S19 143 D3
Beighton Rd. Shef S12 143 C3
Beighton Rd. Shef S12, S13 143 D5
Beighton Rd. Swint S62 98 E8
Belcourt Rd. Roth S65 116 D4
Beldon Cl. Shef S2 141 D7
Beldon Pl. Shef S2 141 D7
Beldon Rd. Shef S2 141 D7
Belford Cl. Roth S66 117 C6
Belford Dr. Roth S66 117 C6
Belfry Gdns. Don DN4 85 A7
Belfry Way. Din S31 147 A7
Belgrave Ct. Bawtry DN10 122 F7
Belgrave Dr. Shef S10 127 D1
Belgrave Pl. Aston S31 144 D7
Belgrave Rd. Barn S71 34 A1
Belgrave Rd. Shef S10 127 E1
Belgrave Sq. Shef S2 141 A8 6
Belklane Dr. Kill S31 156 E7
Bell Bank View. Barn S70 54 F5
Bell Butts La. Auck DN9 85 F6
Bell Gn. Fish DN14 7 D4
Bell St. Aston S31 144 F7
Bell St. Upton WF9 19 E8
Bell's Cl. Finn DN9 86 E4
Bellbrooke Pl. Dar S73 56 F7
Belle Green Cl. Cud S72 35 C7
Belle Green Gdns. Cud S72 35 C7
Belle Green La. Cud S72 35 C7
Belle Vue Ave. Don DN4 63 A2
Belle Vue Rd. Mex S64 80 A5
Belle Vue Terr. Thorne DN8 26 B7
Bellefield St. Shef S3 128 E4
Bellerby Pl. Ad le S DN6 20 F2
Bellerby Rd. Ad le S DN6 20 F2
Bellfield Ave. Kex S75 32 C8
Bellhagg Rd. Shef S6 128 B6
Bellhouse Rd. Shef S5 113 E5
Bellis Ave. Don DN4 83 B8
Bellmont Cres. Hem WF9 17 E6
Bellows Rd. Rawm S62 97 F5
Bellrope Acre. Arm DN3 64 B5
Bells Sq. Shef S1 129 A3
Bellscroft Ave. Roth S65 98 E2
Bellwood Cres. Hoy S74 76 C5
Bellwood Cres. Thorne DN8 26 A8
Belmont Ave. Barn S71 34 A5
Belmont Ave. Chap S30 95 A5
Belmont Ave. Don DN4 83 C8
Belmont Cl. Bran DN3 85 E8
Belmont Cres. G Hou S72 57 E7
Belmont. Cud S72 35 C4
Belmont. Cud S72 35 C5
Belmont Dr. Stock S30 73 C1
Belmont St. Mex S64 79 F4
Belmont St. Roth S61 115 A6
Belmont Terr. Thorne DN8 26 B7
Belmont Terr. Thurgo S30 74 A7
Belmont Way. S Elm WF9 19 B3
Belmonte Gdns. Shef S2 129 C2
Belper Rd. Shef S7 140 F6 4
Belsize Rd. Shef S10 139 E7
Beltoft Way. Con DN12 81 E3
Belton Cl. Dron S18 152 C1
Belvedere Cl. Askern DN6 22 B8
Belvedere Cl. N Anst S31 146 F5
Belvedere Cl. Shaf S72 16 C2
Belvedere. Don DN4 82 F6
Belvedere Dr. Dar S73 56 F7
Belvedere Dr. Thorne DN8 9 C3
Belvedere Par. Roth S66 117 C6
Belvoir Ave. Bnbur DN5 59 C3
Ben Bank Rd. Dod S75 53 C6
Ben Cl. Shef S6 111 F1
Bence Cl. Kex S75 32 E7
Bence La. Kex S75 32 D7
Benita Ave. Mex S64 80 C4
Benmore Dr. Shef S19 144 B1
Bennett Cl. Rawm S62 98 B7
Bennett St. Roth S61 114 E6
Bennett St. Shef S2 140 F8 3
Bennetthorpe. Don DN2 62 F2
Benson Rd. Shef S2 129 E2
Bent Hills La. Wharn S30 92 E1
Bent La. Holmfi HD7 48 B8
Bent Lathes Ave. Roth S60 116 C3
Bent Rd. Holmfi HD7 48 D7
Bent St. Pen S30 51 C4
Bentfield Ave. Roth S60 116 C3
Bentham Dr. Barn S71 34 D4
Bentham Way. Mapp S75 14 A2
Bentinck Cl. Don DN1 62 D2
Bentinick St. Con DN12 81 D2
Bentley Ave. Don DN4 62 B2
Bentley Cl. Barn S71 34 E5
Bentley Common La. Ben DN5 62 D8
Bentley High Street Fst & Middle Schs. Ben 62 B7
Bentley Kirkby Ave Fst Sch. Ben 62 A6
Bentley Kirkby Ave Mid Sch. Ben 62 B6
Bentley Moor La. Ad l S DN6 40 E7
Bentley New Village Fst Sch. Ben 41 B2
Bentley RC Sch. Ben 41 B1
Bentley Rd. Ben DN5 62 B6
Bentley Rd. Chap S30 95 B3
Bentley Rd. Roth S66 117 E5
Bentley Rd. Shef S6 128 A5
Bentley St. Roth S60 115 D3
Bentley Sta. Ben 62 A8
Benton Terr. Swint S64 79 D1
Benton Way. Roth S61 114 F7
Bents Cl. Chap S30 95 A5
Bents Cl. Shef S11 139 E5
Bents Cres. Dron S18 153 C3
Bents Cres. Shef S11 139 F5
Bents Dr. Shef S11 139 E5
Bents Green Ave. Shef S11 139 E6
Bents Green Pl. Shef S11 139 E5
Bents Green Rd. Shef S11 139 F5
Bents Green Sch. Shef 139 E5
Bents La. Dron S18 153 C3
Bents La. Shef S6 126 D6
Bents Rd. Carl S30 49 D4
Bents Rd. Roth S61 96 F1
Bents Rd. Shef S11 139 F5
Bents Rd. Shef S17 151 C4
Bents View. Shef S11 139 E5
Benty La. Shef S10 127 F3
Beresford Rd. Maltby S66 119 B4
Beresford Rd. Ben DN5 41 C1
Berkeley Croft. Roy S71 15 B4
Berkeley Prec. Shef S11 140 D8
Berkley Cl. Barn S70 54 F5
Bernard Gdn. Shef S2 129 C4
Bernard Rd. N Edl DN12 82 C1
Bernard Rd. Shef S2, S4 129 D4
Bernard St. Rawm S62 98 B7
Bernard St. Roth S60 115 E5
Bernard St. Shef S2 129 C3
Berne Sq. Woods S81 147 D4
Berners Cl. Shef S2 141 E6
Berners Dr. Shef S2 141 E6
Berners Pl. Shef S2 141 E6
Berners Rd. Shef S2 141 E6
Berneslai Cl. Barn S70 33 E2
Berneslai Ct. Barn S70 33 E2 2
Bernshall Cres. Shef S5 113 B7
Berresford Rd. Shef S11 140 D8 8
Berrington Cl. Don DN4 83 A4
Berry Ave. Eck S31 155 C3
Berry Dr. Wales S31 145 F3
Berry Holme Cl. Chap S30 95 A5
Berry Holme Ct. Chap S30 95 A5
Berry Holme Dr. Chap S30 95 A5
Berry La. Wort S30 94 A8
Berry Moor Cotts. Thurgo S75 53 A3
Berrydale. Barn S70 55 B5
Berrywell Ave. Pen S30 51 E2
Bertram Rd. Ought S30 111 E6
Bessacarr Fst Sch. Don 84 C8
Bessacarr La. Don DN4 84 E5
Bessemer Pl. Shef S9 129 E5
Bessemer Rd. Shef S9 129 E6
Bessemer Terr. Stock S30 73 B2
Bessemer Way. Roth S60 115 A4
Bessingby Rd. Shef S6 128 C7
Bethel Rd. Roth S65 115 F8
Bethel St. Hoy S74 76 F6
Bethel Terr. Shire S81 159 E7
Bethel Wlk. Shef S1 129 A3 16
Betjeman Gdns. Shef S10 128 C1
Betony Cl. Kill S31 156 B5
Between Rivers La. Snaith DN14 1 C4
Beulah Rd. Shef S6 112 D1
Bevan Ave. Ross DN11 84 F1
Bevan Cl. Hoy S74 77 A6
Bevan Cres. Maltby S66 118 F6
Bevan Way. Chap S30 94 F4
Bever St. Dearne S63 58 F5
Bevercotes Rd. Shef S5 113 E3
Beverley Ave. Barn S70 54 F5
Beverley Cl. Aston S31 144 D7
Beverley Cl. Barn S71 33 E7
Beverley Gdns. Ben DN5 61 D5
Beverley Rd. Don DN2 63 A6
Beverley Rd. Har DN11 122 A4
Beverley St. Shef S9 130 A6 2
Beverley Wlk. C in L S81 148 E7
Beverleys Rd. Shef S8 141 A4
Bevin Pl. Rawm S62 98 B6
Bevre Rd. Arm DN3 64 B7
Bewdley Ct. Roy S71 15 D4
Bewicke Ave. Ben DN5 61 D6
Bib La. Thurcr S31 134 C7
Bickerton Rd. Shef S6 112 C2
Bierlow Cl. W up D S73 78 A8
Bigby Way. Roth S66 117 D7
Bignor Pl. Shef S6 112 D5
Bignor Rd. Shef S6 112 D4
Bilham La. H Pag DN5 38 D2
Bilham Rd. Clay W HD8 12 A2
Bilham Row. H Pag DN5 38 F3
Billam Pl. Roth S61 96 E1
Billam St. Eck S31 155 B3
Billingley Dr. Dearne S63 58 C7
Billingley Green La. G Hou S72 57 E5
Billingley La. G Hou S72 57 F8
Billingley View. Dearne S63 58 B3
Billy Wright's La. Wad DN11 102 F4
Bilston St. Shef S6 128 D7
Binders Rd. Roth S61 96 E1
Binfield Rd. Shef S8 140 F5
Bingham Ct. Shef S11 139 F8
Bingham Park Cres. Shef S11 140 A8
Bingham Park Rd. Shef S11 140 A8
Bingham Rd. Shef S8 140 F2
Bingley La. Shef S6 127 A4
Bingley St. Barn S75 33 D2
Binsted Ave. Shef S5 112 D3
Binsted Cl. Shef S5 112 D3
Binsted Cres. Shef S5 112 D3
Binsted Croft. Shef S5 112 D3
Binsted Dr. Shef S5 112 D3
Binsted Gdns. Shef S5 112 D3
Binsted Glade. Shef S5 112 D3
Binsted Gr. Shef S5 112 D3
Binsted Rd. Shef S5 112 D3
Binsted Way. Shef S5 112 D3
Birch Ave. Ad le S DN6 21 A1
Birch Ave. Chap S30 95 A5
Birch Ave. Finn DN9 86 A4
Birch Cl. Kill S31 156 C5
Birch Cres. Roth S66 117 C5
Birch Farm Ave. Shef S8 153 A8
Birch Gr. Con DN12 81 D2
Birch Gr. Ought S30 111 E6
Birch Green Cl. Maltby S66 118 D6
Birch House Ave. Ought S30 111 D6
Birch Park Ct. Roth S61 115 A6
Birch Rd. Barn S70 55 D7
Birch Rd. Don DN4 84 F8
Birch Rd. Shef S9 129 E6
Birch Tree Cl. B Dun DN3 43 A7
Birch Tree Rd. Stock S30 92 B7
Birchall Ave. Roth S60 116 B1
Birchdale Cl. Don DN3 42 F1
Birchen Cl. Don DN4 84 E5
Birchen Cl. Dron S18 152 D1
Birches Fold. Dron S18 153 C4
Birches La. Dron S18 153 C4
Birchfield Cres. Dod S75 54 A8
Birchfield Rd. Maltby S66 119 B5
Birchfield Wlk. Barn S75 33 B2
Birchitt Cl. Shef S17 152 C5
Birchitt Pl. Shef S17 152 C5
Birchitt Rd. Shef S17 152 C5
Birchitt View. Dron S18 153 A3
Birchlands Dr. Kill S31 156 D5
Birchtree Rd. Roth S61 95 F3
Birchvale Rd. Shef S12 142 D3
Birchwood Ave. Rawm S62 97 F7
Birchwood Cl. Maltby S66 118 D6
Birchwood Cl. Shef S19 155 E8 7
Birchwood Cl. Thorne DN8 9 B1
Birchwood Croft. Shef S19 155 E8
Birchwood Ct. Ross DN4 85 B5
Birchwood Dell. Ross DN4 85 C5
Birchwood Dr. Roth S65 117 D8
Birchwood Gdns. Shef S19 155 E8 6
Birchwood Gr. Shef S19 155 E8
Birchwood Rd. Eck S31 154 D3
Birchwood Rise. Shef S19 155 E8 5
Birchwood View. Shef S19 155 E8
Birchwood Way. Shef S19 155 E8 16
Bircotes Wlk. Ross DN11 85 B1
Bird Ave. Wombw S73 56 C2
Bird La. Thurgo S30 52 E2
Birds Edge La. D Dale HD8 28 F4
Birdsedge Farm Mews. D Dale HD8 29 A4
Birdsedge Fst Sch. D Dale 29 A4
Birdsnest La. Wh Com HD7 28 D2
Birdwell Prim Sch. Barn 75 F7
Birdwell Rd. Dod S75 54 B6
Birdwell Rd. Shef S4 113 F1
Birdwell Rd. Swint S64 79 D1
Birk Ave. Barn S70 55 C7
Birk Cres. Barn S70 55 C7
Birk Gn. Barn S70 55 D7
Birk Hill County Inf Sch. Eck 155 B2
Birk House La. Barn S70 55 D7
Birk House La. Shep HD8 29 B8
Birk Rd. Barn S70 55 C7
Birk Terr. Barn S70 55 C7
Birkbeck Ct. Chap S30 94 D8
Birkdale Ave. Din S31 147 A8
Birkdale Cl. Cud S72 35 C8
Birkdale Cl. Don DN4 85 B6
Birkdale Preparatory Sch. Shef 128 D1
Birkdale Rd. Roy S71 15 B5
Birkdale Rise. Swint S64 79 D2
Birkdale Sch. Shef 128 C2
Birkendale Rd. Shef S6 128 D5
Birkendale. Shef S6 128 D5
Birkendale View. Shef S6 128 D5
Birklands Ave. Shef S13 130 E1
Birklands Cl. Shef S13 130 E1
Birklands Dr. Shef S13 130 E1
Birks Ave. Pen S30 50 E3
Birks Ave. Shef S13 143 B6
Birks Cotts. Pen S30 50 E3
Birks Holt Dr. Maltby S66 119 C3
Birks La. Pen S30 50 E3
Birks Rd. Roth S61 96 E1
Birks Wood Dr. Ought S30 111 D6
Birkwood Ave. Cud S72 35 C4
Birkwood Terr. Braith S66 101 B1
Birley Cty Inf Sch. Shef 142 D3
Birley Cty Prim Sch. Shef 142 D3
Birley Cty Secondary Sch. Shef 142 D3
Birley Ct. Shef S6 112 C6
Birley La. Shef S12 142 D2
Birley Moor Ave. Shef S12 142 E3
Birley Moor Cl. Shef S12 142 E3
Birley Moor Cres. Shef S12 142 E2
Birley Moor Dr. Shef S12 142 E2
Birley Moor Pl. Shef S12 142 E2
Birley Moor Rd. Shef S12 142 E4
Birley Moor Way. Shef S12 142 E2
Birley Rise Cres. Shef S6 112 C4
Birley Rise Rd. Shef S6 112 C4
Birley Spa Jun & Inf Sch. Shef 142 F4
Birley Spa La. Shef S12 143 B4
Birley Vale Ave. Shef S12 142 C5
Birley Vale Cl. Shef S12 142 C4
Birley View. Ought S30 111 D5
Birley Wood Golf Course. Shef 142 E2
Birthwaite Rd. Kex S75 13 B1
Bisby Rd. Rawm S62 98 A6
Biscay Way. W up D S63 78 F6
Bishop Gdns. Shef S13 143 A6
Bishop Hill. Shef S13 143 A6
Bishop St. Shef S3 128 F2
Bishopdale Ct. Shef S19 143 A1
Bishopdale Dr. Shef S19 155 A8
Bishopdale Rise. Shef S19 143 A1
Bishops Ct. Shef S8 141 B5
Bishops Way. Barn S71 34 C3
Bishopscourt Rd. Shef S8 141 A5
Bishopsgate La. Ross DN11 104 A7
Bishopsholme Rd. Shef S5 113 B2
Bishopstoke Ct. Roth S65 116 A7 1
Bishopston Wlk. Maltby S66 118 E6
Bisley Cl. Roy S71 15 E4
Bismarck St. Barn S70 54 F7
Bitholmes Gate. Wharn S30 93 B3
Bittern View. Roth S61 96 A6
Black Bull Cotts. Hat DN8 27 B2
Black Carr Rd. Roth S66 117 A4
Black Hill Rd. Roth S65 116 D4
Black Horse Cl. Silk S75 53 A5
Black Horse Dr. Silk S75 53 A5
Black La. Chap S74 76 B2
Black La. Hoy S74 76 B2
Black La. Shef S6 127 A3
Black Swan Wlk. Shef S1 129 A3 11
Black Syke La. Fish DN14 8 C4
Blacka Moor Cres. Shef S17 151 C6
Blacka Moor Rd. Shef S17 151 C6
Blacka Moor View. Shef S17 151 C6
Blackamoor Rd. Swint S64 78 F1
Blackberry Flats. Shef S19 155 E7
Blackbird Ave. Brin S60 131 D8
Blackbrook Ave. Shef S10 127 A1
Blackbrook Dr. Shef S10 127 A1
Blackbrook Rd. Shef S10 139 A8
Blackburn Cres. Chap S30 94 F6
Blackburn Croft. Chap S30 94 F6
Blackburn Dr. Chap S30 94 E6
Blackburn Jun & Inf Sch. Roth 114 B6
Blackburn La. Barn S75 33 D2
Blackburn La. Barn S70 55 A5
Blackburn La. Roth S61 114 B6
Blackburn Rd. Shef S61 114 B5
Blackburn St. Barn S70 55 A5
Blackburne St. Shef S6 128 D7 1
Blackdown Ave. Shef S19 143 D2
Blackdown Cl. Shef S19 143 D2
Blacker Green La. Askern DN5 22 D4
Blacker La. Barn S70 55 B2
Blacker La. Shaf S72 16 C3
Blacker Rd. Mapp S75 33 C8
Blackergreen La. Silk S75 52 E5
Blackheath Cl. Barn S71 34 B7
Blackheath Rd. Barn S71 34 B7
Blackheath Wlk. Barn S71 34 B7
Blackmoor Cres. Brin S60 115 B1
Blackmore St. Shef S4 129 D5
Blacksmith La. Shef S30 112 C8
Blacksmith's La. Marr DN5 60 C7
Blackstock Cl. Shef S14 141 D2
Blackstock Cres. Shef S14 141 D2
Blackstock Dr. Shef S14 141 D2
Blackstock Rd. Shef S14 141 D4
Blackthorn Ave. Roth S66 117 C5
Blackthorn Cl. Chap S30 94 D8
Blackthorne Cl. N Edl DN12 82 A1
Blackwell Cl. Shef S2 129 C3 3
Blackwell Ct. Shef S2 129 C3 2
Blackwell Pl. Shef S2 129 C3
Blackwood Ave. Don DN4 82 F6
Blagden St. Shef S2 129 C2
Blair Athol Rd. Shef S11 140 B7
Blake Ave. Don DN2 62 F6
Blake Ave. W up D S63 78 C7
Blake Cl. Roth S66 117 E4
Blake Grove Rd. Shef S6 128 E5
Blake St. Shef S6 128 D5
Blakeley Cl. Barn S71 34 B7
Blakeney Rd. Shef S10 128 C3
Bland La. Shef S6 111 F1
Bland St. Shef S4 129 E8
Blast La. Shef S2, S4 129 C4
Blaxton Cl. Shef S19 143 A2
Blayton Rd. Shef S4 129 C8
Bleachcroft Way. Barn S73 55 E7
Bleak Ave. Shaf S72 16 C2
Bleakley Ave. Notton WF4 15 B6
Bleakley Cl. Shaf S72 16 C2
Bleakley La. Notton WF4 15 B6
Bleakley Terr. Notton WF4 15 B6
Bleasdale Gr. Barn S71 34 A4
Blenheim Ave. Barn S70 54 E8
Blenheim Cl. Din S31 146 E8
Blenheim Cl. Hat DN7 44 A6
Blenheim Cl. Roth S66 117 C7
Blenheim Cres. Mex S64 79 E5
Blenheim Ct. Roth S66 117 B6
Blenheim Gdns. Shef S11 140 A5
Blenheim Gr. Barn S70 54 D8
Blenheim Rd. Barn S70 54 E8
Blenheim Rd. Hat DN7 66 A8
Blenheim Rise. Bawtry DN10 122 F6
Blindside La. Bfield S6 109 C3
Bloemfontein Rd. Cud S72 35 A6
Bloemfontein St. Cud S72 35 B6
Blonk St. Shef S1 129 B4
Bloomfield Rd. Mapp S75 13 F1
Bloomfield Rise. Mapp S75 13 F1
Bloomhill Cl. Thorne DN8 9 D4
Bloomhill Ct. Thorne DN8 9 C4
Bloomhill Rd. Thorne DN8 9 B3
Bloomhouse La. Mapp S75 13 F1
Blossom Ave. Askern DN6 22 B7
Blossom Cres. Shef S12 142 B3
Blow Hall Cres. N Edl DN12 82 C2
Blucher St. Barn S70 33 E1
Blue Bell Ct. Blax DN9 86 E5
Blue Boy St. Shef S3 128 F4 12
Bluebell Ave. Pen S30 51 C2
Bluebell Cl. Shef S5 113 F3
Bluebell Rd. Shef S5 113 F3
Bluebell Rd. Wool S75 13 E3
Bluebird Hill. Aston S31 144 E6
Bluestone Cty Prim Sch. Shef 141 D8
Blundell Cl. Don DN4 84 E7
Blundell Ct. Barn S71 34 D5
Blundell St. S Elm WF9 18 E3
Bly Rd. Dar S73 56 F6
Blyde Rd. Shef S5 113 C1
Blyth Ave. Rawm S62 97 F5
Blyth Cl. Roth S60 116 D1
Blyth Gate La. Tick DN11 120 E3
Blyth Rd. Har DN11 121 F2
Blyth Rd. Maltby S66 119 A4
Blyth Rd. Old S81 136 F6
Blyth Rd. Styr DN11 121 F2
Blyth Rd. Tick DN11 121 E6
Blythe St. Wombw S73 56 D3
Boardman Ave. Rawm S62 97 C8
Boat La. Sprot DN5 82 B8
Boating Dyke Way. Thorne DN8 26 A7
Bochum Parkway. Shef S8 153 C8
Bocking Cl. Shef S8 140 D1
Bocking Hill. Stock S30 73 D1
Bocking La. Shef S8 140 D1
Bocking La. Shef S8 152 E8
Bocking Rise. Shef S8 152 E8
Boden La. Shef S1 128 F3
Boden Pl. Shef S9 130 C5
Bodmin Ct. Barn S71 34 B3
Bodmin St. Shef S9 129 F6
Boggard La. Ought S30 111 C6
Boggard La. Pen S30 51 C2
Boiley La. Kill S31 156 C4
Boland Rd. Shef S8 152 D5
Bold St. Shef S9 130 A8
Bole Cl. Dar S73 56 F4
Bole Hill Prim Sch. Shef 128 B6
Bole Hill Rd. Shef S6 128 A5
Bole Hill. Treet S60 131 F5
Bolehill La. Eck S31 154 F2
Bolehill La. Shef S10 128 B4
Bolsover Rd E. Shef S5 113 D1
Bolsover Rd. Shef S5 113 D2
Bolsover St. Shef S3 128 E3
Bolsterstone C of E Jun & Inf Sch. Stock 92 C6
Bolsterstone Rd. Bfield S30 92 C1
Bolton Hill Rd. Don DN4 84 E7
Bolton on Dearne Sta. Dearne 58 C2
Bolton Rd Managed Workshops. W up D S63 79 C7
Bolton Rd. W up D S63 79 C7
Bolton St. Con DN12 80 F3
Bolton St. Shef S3 128 F2

Cedar Cl. Finn DN9 86 A4
Cedar Cl. Kill S31 156 C5
Cedar Cl. Roy S71 15 A4
Cedar Cl. Stock S30 92 B8
Cedar Cres. Barn S70 55 B7
Cedar Dr. Maltby S66 118 D5
Cedar Dr. Roth S65 117 F8
Cedar Gr. Con DN12 100 A8
Cedar Rd. Arm DN3 64 C7
Cedar Rd. Don DN4 82 F6
Cedar Rd. Stock S30 92 B8
Cedar Rd. Thorne DN8 9 C1
Cedar Special Sch. Don 82 F6
Cedar Way. Chap S30 94 F4
Cedar Wlk. Norton DN6 21 C8
Cedars The. Shef S10 128 B2
Cedric Ave. Con DN12 81 A1
Cedric Cres. Thurcr S66 133 E6
Cedric Rd. Don DN3 43 A1
Celandine Ct. Shef S17 152 A5
Celandine Gdns. Shef S17 152 A5
Celandine Gr. Dar S73 57 A5
Celandine Rise. Swint S64 98 D8
Cemetery Rd. Ad I S DN6 40 B4
Cemetery Rd. Barn S70 55 A8
Cemetery Rd. Dearne S63 58 D1
Cemetery Rd. Grime S72 36 B6
Cemetery Rd. Hat DN7 44 E7
Cemetery Rd. Hem WF9 17 C8
Cemetery Rd. Hoy S74 77 B7
Cemetery Rd. Mex S64 80 A5
Cemetery Rd. Shef S11 128 F1
Cemetery Rd. W up D S63 78 E5
Cemetery Rd. Wombw S73 56 D3
Centenary Way. Roth S60 115 D4
Central Ave. Ad I S DN6 40 A4
Central Ave. Ben DN5 62 B8
Central Ave. Din S31 147 A8
Central Ave. Grime S72 36 A8
Central Ave. Roth S65 116 B6
Central Ave. Roth S66 117 B7
Central Ave. S Elm WF9 18 F2
Central Ave. Swint S64 79 C3
Central Bvd. Don DN2 63 B6
Central Dr. Bawtry DN10 123 A8
Central Dr. Rawm S62 97 C8
Central Dr. Ross DN11 103 E8
Central Dr. Roy S71 15 C3
Central Dr. Thurcr S66 133 E6
Central St. Dearne S63 58 E6
Central St. Hoy S74 76 B5
Central Terr. N Edl DN12 82 B2
Centre St. Hem WF9 17 D8
Centre St. S Elm WF9 19 A3
Century St. Shef S9 130 B6
Century View. Brin S60 131 A8
Chadbourne Cl. Arm DN3 64 A5
Chaddesden Cl. Dron S18 152 C1
Chaddesdon Wlk. Con DN12 81 A3
Chadwick Dr. Maltby S66 118 F6
Chadwick Rd. Ad I S DN6 40 A4
Chadwick Rd. Ben DN5 62 B5
Chadwick Rd. Shef S13 142 C7
Chadwick Rd. Thorne DN8 9 D4
Chaff Cl. Roth S60 116 B1
Chaff La. Roth S60 116 B1
Chaffinch Ave. Brin S60 131 D8
Challenger Cres. Dearne S63 37 D1
Challenger Dr. Ben DN5 61 E3
Challoner Gn. Shef S19 155 E8
Challoner Way. Shef S19 155 E8
Chalmers Dr. Don DN2 42 D1
Chamberlain Ave. Ben DN5 61 F6
Chamberlain Ct. Chap S30 94 F6
Chambers Ave. Con DN12 81 A2
Chambers La. Shef S4 113 F1
Chambers Rd. Hoy S74 76 D7
Chambers Rd. Roth S61 96 F1
Chamossaire. Ross DN11 103 E7
Champion Cl. Shef S5 113 D6
Champion Rd. Shef S5 113 D6
Chancel Way. Barn S71 34 C3
Chancery Pl. Don DN1 62 C3
Chancet Wood Cl. Shef S8 152 F8
Chancet Wood Dr. Shef S8 152 F8
Chancet Wood Rd. Shef S8 140 F1
Chancet Wood Rise. Shef S8 152 F8
Chancet Wood View. Shef S8 152 F8
Chandos Cres. Kill S31 156 D6
Chandos St. Shef S10 128 C2
Channing Gdns. Shef S6 128 D7
Channing St. Shef S6 128 D7
Chantrey Rd. Shef S8 140 F3
Chantry Cl. Don DN4 85 A7
Chantry Gr. Roy S71 15 C3
Chantry Pl. Wales S31 145 F3
Chapel Ave. W up D S73 78 A8
Chapel Baulk. Misson DN10 87 F2
Chapel Cl. Barn S70 75 E7
Chapel Cl. Chap S30 94 E5
Chapel Cl. Finn DN9 86 E3
Chapel Cl. Roth S61 97 A4
Chapel Cl. Shaf S72 16 C3
Chapel Cl. Shef S10 127 F1
Chapel Cl. Thurcr S66 133 F7
Chapel Ct. W up D S63 78 E5
Chapel Field La. Pen S30 51 C2
Chapel Hill. Askern DN6 22 A8
Chapel Hill. Clay DN5 37 C4
Chapel Hill. Hoy S74 55 D1
Chapel Hill. Roth S60 116 B1
Chapel Hill. Swint S64 79 C3
Chapel Hole La. Ston S66 101 C2
Chapel House. Rawm S62 97 F5
Chapel La. Bran DN3 85 E8
Chapel La. Con DN12 81 C1
Chapel La. Dearne S63 37 F1
Chapel La. Finn DN9 86 E3
Chapel La. G Hou S72 36 D1
Chapel La. G Hou S72 57 F6
Chapel La. K Smea WF8 3 E6
Chapel La. Midhop S30 72 B4
Chapel La. Pen S30 51 C2
Chapel La. Roth S60 115 D5
Chapel La. Roy S71 15 C1
Chapel La. S Elm WF9 19 B3
Chapel La. Scro DN10 123 A2
Chapel La. Shef S9 130 A6 4
Chapel La. Stock S30 73 E3
Chapel La. Syke DN14 7 B7
Chapel La. Thorne DN8 26 B7
Chapel La. Uns S18 154 A1
Chapel Pl. Barn S71 55 F8
Chapel Rd. Chap S30 94 E8
Chapel Rd. Chap S30 94 F4
Chapel Rd. Pilley S75 75 C6
Chapel Rise. N Anst S31 146 D5
Chapel St. Ad I S DN6 40 B8
Chapel St. Barn S71 55 F8
Chapel St. Barn S70 75 E7
Chapel St. Ben DN5 62 B8
Chapel St. Dearne S63 58 C2
Chapel St. Grime S72 36 A6
Chapel St. Hoy S74 76 B5
Chapel St. Mex S64 79 E5
Chapel St. Rawm S62 97 F5
Chapel St. Roth S61 97 B4
Chapel St. Shaf S72 16 C3
Chapel St. Shef S13 143 B6
Chapel St. Shef S19 155 C6
Chapel St. W up D S63 78 E6
Chapel Terr. Shef S10 127 F1
Chapel Way. Rawm S62 97 D7
Chapel Wlk. Rawm S62 97 D7
Chapel Wlk. Roth S60 115 C6
Chapel Wlk. Shef S1 129 B3
Chapel Yd. Dron S18 153 A2
Chapelfield Cres. Roth S61 95 F5
Chapelfield Dr. Roth S61 95 F5
Chapelfield La. Roth S61 95 F5
Chapelfield Mount. Roth S61 95 F5
Chapelfield Pl. Roth S61 95 F5
Chapelfield Rd. Went S61 95 F6
Chapelfield Way. Roth S61 95 F5
Chapelfields. S Kirk WF9 18 B1
Chapeltown Rd. Chap S30 95 B2
Chapeltown Sta. Chap 95 B5
Chapelwood Rd. Shef S9 130 B6
Chapman St. Dearne S63 58 E8
Chapman St. Shef S9 114 B4
Chappell Cl. Pen S30 51 F6
Chappell Dr. Don DN1 62 D4
Chappell Rd. Pen S30 51 F6
Chapter Way. Barn S71 34 C3
Chapter Way. Silk S75 32 A1
Charity St. Barn S71 34 F6
Charles Ashmore Rd. Shef S8 153 A8
Charles Clifford Dental Hospl The.
Shef 128 D3
Charles Cres. Arm DN3 63 F7
Charles Ct. Thorne DN8 9 C1
Charles La. Shef S1 129 A3 14
Charles La. Shef S1 129 B2
Charles Rd. W up D S63 79 A5
Charles Sq. Chap S30 94 D7
Charles St. Ad le S DN6 21 B1
Charles St. Barn S70 54 E8
Charles St. Barn S70 55 A4 6
Charles St. Cud S72 35 C8
Charles St. Dearne S63 58 E5
Charles St. Din S31 134 F2
Charles St. Don DN1 62 E5
Charles St. G Hou S72 57 E7
Charles St. Grime S72 36 A6
Charles St. Rawm S62 98 B7
Charles St. S Hie S72 16 E5
Charles St. Shef S1 129 A3
Charles St. Shef S1 129 B2
Charles St. Swint S64 79 D3
Charles St. Swint S62 98 E7
Charles St. Thurcr S66 133 E7
Charleville. S Elm WF9 18 E4
Charlotte La. Shef S1 128 F3 8
Charlotte Rd. Shef S1, S2 129 B1
Charlton Brook Cres. Chap S30 94 E5
Charlton Clough. Chap S30 94 D5
Charlton Dr. Chap S30 94 E6
Charlton & Linley Homes The.
Shef S7 140 B1
Charnell Rd. Maltby S66 119 A5
Charnley Ave. Shef S11 140 C5
Charnley Cl. Shef S11 140 B5
Charnley Dr. Shef S11 140 C5
Charnley Rise. Shef S11 140 C5
Charnock Ave. Shef S12 142 B2
Charnock Cres. Shef S12 142 A3
Charnock Dale Rd. Shef S12 142 B2
Charnock Dr. Ben DN5 61 F5
Charnock Dr. Shef S12 142 B3
Charnock Gr. Shef S12 142 B2
Charnock Hall Cty Prim Sch. Shef 142 B2
Charnock Hall Rd. Shef S12 142 A2
Charnock View Rd. Shef S12 142 B2
Charnock Wood Rd. Shef S12 142 B1
Charnwood Ct. Shef S19 144 A2 2
Charnwood Dr. Don DN4 82 F5
Charnwood Gr. Roth S61 114 F7
Charnwood St. Swint S64 79 D3
Charter Arc. Barn S70 33 F1 8
Charter Dr. Ben DN5 61 D8
Charter Row. Shef S1 129 A2
Charter Sq. Shef S1 129 A2 1
Chase Rd. Shef S6 111 D1
Chase The. Aston S31 144 E6
Chase The. Shef S10 128 D1
Chatfield Rd. Shef S8 140 E2
Chatham St. Roth S65 115 E6
Chatham St. Shef S3 129 A5
Chatsworth Ave. Mex S64 80 D5
Chatsworth Cl. Aston S31 144 F7
Chatsworth Cres. Ben DN5 61 F8
Chatsworth Ct. Har DN11 122 B5
Chatsworth Park Ave. Shef S12 142 A5
Chatsworth Park Dr. Shef S12 142 A5
Chatsworth Park Gr. Shef S12 142 A5
Chatsworth Park Rd. Shef S12 142 A5
Chatsworth Park Rise. Shef S12 142 A5
Chatsworth Pl. Dron S18 152 D2
Chatsworth Rd. Barn S71 34 A7
Chatsworth Rd. Roth S61 115 B6
Chatsworth Rd. Shef S17 151 F6
Chatsworth Rise. Brin S60 131 D8
Chatsworth Rise. Dod S75 53 F6
Chatterton Dr. Roth S65 116 B4
Chaucer Cl. Shef S5 112 D6
Chaucer House. Roth S65 116 B5
Chaucer Rd. Mex S64 80 C5
Chaucer Rd. Roth S65 116 B5
Chaucer Rd. Shef S5 112 E6
Chaucer Sch. Shef 112 E5
Cheadle St. Shef S6 128 C8 2
Cheapside. Barn S70 33 F1
Checkstone Ave. Don DN4 84 E5
Chedworth Cl. Kex S75 32 E7
Cheese Gate Nab Side. Holmfi HD7 28 A2
Cheetham Dr. Maltby S66 119 A6
Chelmsford Ave. Aston S31 144 E8
Chelmsford Dr. Don DN2 62 F6
Chelsea Ct. Shef S11 140 C7
Chelsea Rd. Shef S11 140 C6
Chelsea Rise. Shef S11 140 C7
Cheltenham Rd. Don DN2 63 D5
Cheltenham Rise. Ben DN5 61 D5
Chemist La. Roth S60 115 C7 2
Chemistry La. Wort S30 93 C8
Cheney Row. Shef S1 129 A3 12
Chepstow Dr. Mex S64 80 B6
Chepstow Gdns. Ben DN5 61 D5
Chequer Ave. Don DN4 62 E1
Chequer La. K Bram DN7 23 F3
Chequer Rd. Don DN1 62 E2
Cheriton Ave. Ad I S DN6 40 A5
Cherry Bank Rd. Shef S8 141 A3
Cherry Cl. Cud S72 35 B8
Cherry Cl. Roy S71 15 A4
Cherry Garth. Ben DN5 41 B3
Cherry Garth. Hem WF9 17 C6
Cherry Garth. Norton DN6 21 C8
Cherry Gr. Con DN12 100 A8
Cherry Gr. Ross DN11 104 A8
Cherry Hills. Mapp S75 14 A1
Cherry La. Don DN5 62 B4
Cherry St S. Shef S2 141 A8
Cherry St. Shef S2 141 A8
Cherry Tree Ave. Shire S81 159 F7
Cherry Tree Cl. Brin S60 131 D8
Cherry Tree Cl. Mapp S75 14 C1
Cherry Tree Cl. Shef S11 140 D7
Cherry Tree Cotts. Wort S30 74 B3
Cherry Tree Cres. Roth S66 117 C5
Cherry Tree Dell. Shef S11 140 D7
Cherry Tree Dr. Hat DN7 25 A1
Cherry Tree Dr. Kill S31 156 D5
Cherry Tree Dr. Shef S11 140 D7
Cherry Tree Dr. Thorne DN8 9 B1
Cherry Tree Gr. Hat DN7 25 A1
Cherry Tree Pl. W up D S63 78 F5
Cherry Tree Rd. Arm DN3 64 B6
Cherry Tree Rd. Don DN4 62 B2
Cherry Tree Rd. Maltby S66 118 D5
Cherry Tree Rd. Shef S11 140 D7
Cherry Tree Rd. Wales S31 145 A2
Cherry Tree St. Hoy S74 76 F6
Cherry Wlk. Chap S30 95 A4
Cherrys Rd. Barn S71 34 D2
Chesham Rd. Barn S70 33 D1
Cheshire Rd. Don DN1 62 E5
Chessel Cl. Shef S8 141 A4
Chester La. Shef S1 128 F2
Chester Rd. Don DN2 62 F6
Chester St. Shef S1 128 F3 12
Chesterfield Rd. Aston S31 144 B6
Chesterfield Rd. Dron S18 153 B1
Chesterfield Rd. Eck S31 155 B2
Chesterfield Rd S. Shef S8 153 A6
Chesterfield Rd. Shef S8 140 F4
Chesterfield Rd. Uns S31 155 B2
Chesterhill Ave. Roth S65 98 E1
Chesterton Rd. Don DN4 83 C6
Chesterton Rd. Roth S65 98 A1
Chesterton Way. Roth S65 98 B1
Chesterwood Dr. Shef S10 128 B2
Chestnut Ave. Ad le S DN6 21 B1
Chestnut Ave. Arm DN3 64 B7
Chestnut Ave. Bri S72 16 F2
Chestnut Ave. Don DN2 63 B7
Chestnut Ave. Eck S31 155 B2
Chestnut Ave. Kill S31 156 C5
Chestnut Ave. Ross DN11 104 A8
Chestnut Ave. Roth S65 116 B7
Chestnut Ave. Shef S9 130 E3
Chestnut Ave. Shef S19 143 F5
Chestnut Ave. Stai DN7 25 A4
Chestnut Ave. Stock S30 92 B8
Chestnut Ave. Thorne DN8 26 C6
Chestnut Ave. W up D S63 79 A4
Chestnut Ave. Wales S31 145 C3
Chestnut Cl. Roth S66 117 B6
Chestnut Cres. Barn S70 55 B7
Chestnut Ct. Barn S70 54 F7 4
Chestnut Ct. Ben DN5 41 A2
Chestnut Dr. Bawtry DN10 122 F7
Chestnut Dr. Chap S30 94 F4
Chestnut Dr. Finn DN9 86 A4
Chestnut Dr. S Hie S72 16 D5
Chestnut Gr. Con DN12 81 A1
Chestnut Gr. Dearne S63 58 D7
Chestnut Gr. Din S31 134 F2
Chestnut Gr. Hem WF9 17 F6
Chestnut Gr. Maltby S66 118 D5
Chestnut Gr. Mex S64 79 F6
Chestnut Gr. Sprot DN5 82 B8
Chestnut Rd. Aston S31 144 B8
Chestnut Rd. Lan S81 136 F4
Chestnut St. Grime S72 36 B5
Chestnut St. S Elm WF9 18 F1
Chestnut Wlk. Maltby S66 118 E4
Chevet La. Notton WF4 15 B8
Chevet Rise. Roy S71 15 B4
Chevet View. Roy S71 15 A4
Cheviot Cl. Hem WF9 17 F7
Cheviot Cl. Thorne DN8 26 A6
Cheviot Ct. C in L S81 148 E7
Cheviot Dr. Ben DN5 61 F7
Cheviot Wlk. Barn S75 33 B2 3
Chevril Ct. Roth S66 117 A4
Cheyne Wlk. Bawtry DN10 122 F7
Chichester Rd. Shef S10 128 B4
Chichester Wlk. C in L S81 148 E7
Childers Dr. Auck DN9 86 A7
Childers St. Don DN4 62 E1
Chiltern Cres. Sprot DN5 61 A1
Chiltern Ct. Hem WF9 17 F7
Chiltern Rd. Ben DN5 61 F7
Chiltern Rd. Shef S6 128 B8
Chiltern Rise. Brin S60 131 D7
Chiltern Way. C in L S81 148 E7
Chiltern Wlk. Barn S75 33 B2 2
Chilton St. Barn S70 55 A8
Chilwell Cl. Barn S71 14 F1
Chilwell Gdns. Barn S71 14 F1
Chilwell Mews. Barn S71 14 F1
Chilwell Rd. Barn S71 14 F1
Chinley St. Shef S9 130 A5 2
Chippingham Pl. Shef S9 129 F6
Chippingham St. Shef S9 130 A6
Chippinghouse Rd. Shef S7, S8 140 F7
Chiverton Cl. Dron S18 153 A2
Chorley Ave. Shef S10 139 C8
Chorley Dr. Shef S10 139 C8
Chorley Pl. Shef S10 139 C7
Chorley Rd. Shef S10 139 D8
Christ Church Rd. Don DN1 62 D4
Christ Church Rd. Shef S3 129 B7
Christchurch Ave. Aston S31 144 E8
Christchurch Rd. W up D S63 78 C7
Church Ave. Rawm S62 97 E4
Church Ave. S Kirk WF9 18 C2
Church Balk. Don DN3 42 F2
Church Balk Gdns. Don DN3 42 F3
Church Balk La. Don DN3 42 F2
Church Balk. Thorne DN8 26 C7
Church Bank. Hath S30 149 A8
Church Cl. Hem WF9 17 D7
Church Cl. Maltby S66 118 F4
Church Cl. Mapp S75 13 E1
Church Cl. Ought S30 111 D7
Church Cl. Roth S65 99 C3
Church Cl. Shep HD8 28 E8
Church Cl. Swint S64 79 C3
Church Cl. Thorne DN8 26 C7
Church Cl. Wales S31 145 B2
Church Cnr. Laugh S31 134 D5
Church Cottage Mews. Don DN4 82 E7
Church Croft. Don DN3 42 E3
Church Croft. Rawm S62 97 E4
Church Ct. Don DN4 84 F7
Church Ct. S Anst S31 146 E4
Church Dr. Bri S72 16 F3
Church Dr. S Kirk WF9 18 C2
Church Field Dr. Roth S66 117 B3
Church Field La. Went S73 77 A1
Church Field Rd. Askern DN6 21 E8
Church Field Rd. Clay DN5 37 E4
Church Field Rd. Norton DN6 4 D1
Church Fields Rd. Ross DN11 85 B2
Church Fields. Roth S61 114 E7
Church Gn. W up D S63 78 E6
Church Gr. Barn S71 34 C4
Church Gr. Brath S66 101 A2
Church Gr. S Kirk WF9 18 C2
Church Hill. Roy S71 15 D3
Church La. Ad I S DN6 40 C6
Church La. Aston S31 144 E6
Church La. Aston S31 144 F7
Church La. B Dun DN3 42 E8
Church La. Barn S70 33 E2 3
Church La. Bnbur DN5 59 C2
Church La. C in L S81 148 F4
Church La. Caw S75 31 F4
Church La. Chap S75 75 E3
Church La. Clift S66 100 D5
Church La. Din S31 134 D1
Church La. Don DN4 82 D7
Church La. Don DN4 84 F7
Church La. Finn DN9 86 E3
Church La. Fish DN7 25 B7
Church La. H Hoy S75 12 C1
Church La. Har DN11 121 E4
Church La. Kill S31 156 E6
Church La. Let S81 135 E3
Church La. Maltby S66 118 F4
Church La. Marr DN5 60 C7
Church La. Roth S66 117 B4
Church La. Roth S66 117 D5
Church La. Roth S65 99 D3
Church La. Ryhill S71 15 F7
Church La. Scro DN10 123 A2
Church La. Shef S9 130 E4
Church La. Shef S13 143 C6
Church La. Shef S19 144 A3
Church La. Shef S17 151 D6
Church La. Shep HD8 28 E8
Church La. Tick DN11 121 A7
Church La. Treet S60 131 C6
Church La. Treet S60 131 E4
Church La. W up D S63 78 E6
Church La. Wad DN11 102 B7
Church Lane Mews. Roth S66 117 D5
Church Lea. Hoy S74 76 E4
Church Meadow Rd. Ross DN11 85 B1
Church Mews. Ben DN5 62 A8
Church Mews. Kill S31 156 E7
Church Mews. Mex S64 80 C4
Church Mews. Shef S19 155 D7
Church Mount. S Kirk WF9 18 C2
Church Rd. B Dun DN3 42 F8
Church Rd. Bir DN11 122 C4
Church Rd. Caw S75 31 E4
Church Rd. Con DN12 81 A4
Church Rd. Don DN3 42 F4
Church Rd. N Edl DN12 82 B3
Church Rd. Stai DN7 24 E3
Church Rd. Wad DN11 102 B6
Church Rd. Wad DN11 102 B7
Church Rein Cl. Don DN4 82 C6
Church St. Arm DN3 64 B6
Church St. Barn S75 33 A3
Church St. Barn S70 33 E2
Church St. Bawtry DN10 123 A6
Church St. Ben DN5 41 B3
Church St. Caw S75 31 F4
Church St. Con DN12 81 C2
Church St. Cud S72 35 B6
Church St. Dar S73 57 B5
Church St. Dearne S63 58 C8
Church St. Dearne S63 58 D1
Church St. Don DN1 62 C4
Church St. Dron S18 153 A1
Church St. Eck S31 155 E4
Church St. Fish DN7 25 B7
Church St. G Hou S72 36 E2
Church St. Hoy S74 76 F7
Church St. Hoy S74 77 A5
Church St. Lan S81 136 F2
Church St. Mapp S75 13 E1
Church St. Mapp S75 14 C1
Church St. Mex S64 80 C4
Church St. Ought S30 111 C7
Church St. Pen S30 51 D3
Church St. Rawm S62 97 E4
Church St. Roth S61 114 E7
Church St. Roth S60 115 D6
Church St. Roth S61 97 B4
Church St. Roy S71 15 C3
Church St. Roy S71 15 D1
Church St. S Elm WF9 19 A2
Church St. Shef S6 127 C5
Church St. Shef S1 129 A3
Church St. Shef S30 95 A1
Church St. Swint S64 79 C3
Church St. Thorne DN8 26 B7
Church St. Thurcr S66 133 F6
Church St. W up D S63 78 E6
Church St. Wales S31 145 B2
Church St. Wombw S73 56 D2
Church St. Wool WF4 13 F7
Church Street Cl. Dearne S63 58 C8
Church Top. S Kirk WF9 18 C2
Church View. Aston S31 144 F7
Church View. Barn S75 33 D3
Church View. Bnbur DN5 59 C3
Church View Cres. Pen S30 51 D3
Church View. Cud S72 35 B6
Church View. Dar S73 57 C5
Church View. Don DN1 62 C4
Church View. Hoy S74 76 B5
Church View. Kill S31 156 E7
Church View. N Edl DN12 82 A1
Church View. Norton DN6 4 C1
Church View Rd. Pen S30 51 D3
Church View. Roth S66 117 B3
Church View. Roth S65 98 F3
Church View. S Kirk WF9 18 C2
Church View. Scro DN10 123 A2
Church View. Shef S13 143 C6
Church View. Swint S64 79 C3
Church View. Tod S31 145 F5
Church View. Wad DN11 102 B6
Church Villas. S Kirk WF9 18 C2
Church Way. Don DN1 62 D4
Church Wlk. Bawtry DN10 123 A7
Church Wlk. Con DN12 81 A4
Church Wlk. Dearne S63 58 C8
Church Wlk. Har DN11 121 E4
Church Wlk. Hat DN7 44 C8
Churchdale Rd. Shef S12 142 D4
Churchfield Ave. Cud S72 35 B6
Churchfield Ave. Kex S75 32 C8
Churchfield. Barn S70 33 E2
Churchfield Cl. Ben DN5 62 A8
Churchfield Cl. Kex S75 32 B8
Churchfield Cres. Cud S72 35 B6
Churchfield Ct. Kex S75 32 D8
Churchfield La. K Smea WF8 3 F7
Churchfield La. Kex S75 32 C8
Churchfield La. Womer WF8 4 A8
Churchfield Terr. Cud S72 35 B6
Churchfields. Thurgo S30 73 F7
Churchill Ave. Ben DN5 62 A6
Churchill Ave. Hat DN7 44 E7
Churchill Ave. Maltby S66 119 A6
Churchill Rd. Don DN1 62 E6
Churchill Rd. Shef S10 128 C3
Churchill Rd. Stock S30 72 F2
Cinder Bridge Rd. Roth S62 97 D4
Cinder Hills Way. Dod S75 54 A7
Cinder La. Kill S31 156 F7
Cinderhill La. Shef S8 153 C8
Cinderhill Rd. Roth S61 96 E2
Circle Cl. Shef S2 130 B1
Circle The. Chap S30 94 F7
Circle The. Ross DN11 84 E1
Circle The. Shef S2 130 A1
Circle The. Thorne DN8 9 D3
Circuit The. Ad le S DN6 39 F5
City Rd. Shef S12, S2 141 F8
City Sch. Shef 142 F6
Claire Ct. Roth S60 115 D7
Clanricarde St. Barn S71 33 F4
Claphouse Fold. W Bret S75 13 A5
Clara Pl. Roth S61 114 F6
Clarehurst Rd. Dar S73 57 A6
Clarel Cl. Pen S30 51 C2
Clarel St. Pen S30 51 C2
Clarell Gdns. Don DN4 63 E1
Claremont Cres. Shef S10 128 D3
Claremont Pl. Shef S10 128 D3
Claremont St. Roth S61 114 F6
Clarence Ave. Don DN4 83 B8
Clarence La. Shef S3 128 F1
Clarence Pl. Maltby S66 119 A6
Clarence Rd. Barn S71 34 B4
Clarence Rd. Shef S6 128 B8
Clarence Sq. Din S31 135 A1
Clarence St. Din S31 135 A1
Clarence St. W up D S63 78 D7
Clarence Terr. Dearne S63 58 E8
Clarendon Ct. Shef S10 139 E8
Clarendon Rd. Roth S65 115 F7
Clarendon Rd. Shef S10 139 E7
Clarendon St. Barn S70 54 D8
Clark Ave. Don DN4 62 E2
Clark Gr. Shef S6 127 D6
Clark St. Hoy S74 76 D7
Clarke Ave. Thurcr S66 134 A6
Clarke Dell. Shef S10 128 D1
Clarke Dr. Shef S10 128 D1
Clarke Sq. Shef S11 140 F8 6
Clarke St. Barn S75 33 D3
Clarke St. Dearne S63 58 E8
Clarke St. Shef S10 128 E2
Clarkegrove Rd. Shef S10 128 D1
Clarkehouse Rd. Shef S10 128 D2
Clarks Ct. Ad I S DN6 40 B6
Clarkson St. Barn S70 55 C5
Clarkson St. Shef S10 128 E3
Clarney Ave. Dar S73 56 F6
Clarney Pl. Dar S73 57 A6
Clay Bank Rd. Thorne DN8 26 F4
Clay Bank. T in B DN6 23 A5
Clay Flat La. Ross DN11 104 A8
Clay La. Don DN2 42 C2
Clay La. Don DN2 42 D1
Clay La. Shef S1 129 A2
Clay La W. Don DN2 42 C1
Clay Pit La. Rawm S62 98 B6
Clay Pits La. Stock S30 72 D2
Clay St. Shef S9 130 A7
Clay Wheels La. Shef S6 112 B3
Claycliffe Ave. Barn S75 32 F4

Fitzhubert Rd. Shef S2 142 A7
Fitzmaurice Rd. Shef S9 130 B6
Fitzroy Rd. Shef S2 141 B6
Fitzwalter Rd. Shef S2 129 D2
Fitzwilliam Ave. Con DN12 81 A2
Fitzwilliam Ave. W up D S63 78 E5
Fitzwilliam Cty Prim Sch. Swint 79 B2
Fitzwilliam Cty Prim Sch. Swint 79 C3
Fitzwilliam Dr. Bnbur DN5 59 C1
Fitzwilliam Gate. Shef S1 129 A2 7
Fitzwilliam Rd. Dar S73 57 D6
Fitzwilliam Rd. Roth S65 116 A8
Fitzwilliam Sq. Roth S61 97 B4
Fitzwilliam St. Barn S70 33 E1
Fitzwilliam St. Hoy S74 76 B5
Fitzwilliam St. Hoy S74 77 A5
Fitzwilliam St. Hoy S74 77 B7
Fitzwilliam St. Rawm S62 97 F3
Fitzwilliam St. Shef S1 128 F2
Fitzwilliam St. Swint S64 79 D2
Fitzwilliam St. W up D S63 78 E6
Five Acres. Caw S75 31 F5
Five Lane Ends. Ad le S DN6 20 E1
Five Oaks. Ben DN5 41 E3
Five Trees Ave. Shef S17 152 A6
Five Trees Cl. Shef S17 152 A6
Five Trees Dr. Shef S17 152 A6
Five Weirs Wlk. Shef S9 129 F6
Flanders Ct. Roth S61 95 F5
Flanderwell Ave. Roth S66 117 D5
Flanderwell Ct. Roth S66 117 C6
Flanderwell Gdns. Roth S66 117 C6
Flanderwell Jun & Inf Sch. Roth 117 B6
Flanderwell La. Roth S66 117 C6
Flash La. Roth S66 117 E4
Flash La. Shef S6 126 E4
Flashley Carr La. K Bram DN6 6 F2
Flask View. Shef S6 127 C7
Flat La. Fir S66 135 E8
Flat La. Fir S81 136 A6
Flat La. G Hou S72 57 F5
Flat La. Roth S60 116 B1
Flat St. Shef S1 129 B3
Flats The. Wombw S73 56 C2
Flats The. Wort S30 74 E3
Flatts Cl. Treet S60 131 E5
Flatts La. Treet S60 131 E5
Flatts La. W up D S63 78 D6
Flavell Cl. S Kirk WF9 18 B1
Flax Lea. Barn S70 55 A5
Flaxby Rd. Shef S9 130 B5
Flea La. Norton WF8 3 E4
Fleet Cl. W up D S63 78 B7
Fleet Hill Cres. Barn S71 34 A5
Fleet La. Stai DN7 24 E5
Fleet St. Shef S9 129 F7
Fleets Cl. Stai DN7 24 E5
Fleetwood Ave. Barn S71 34 C5
Fleming Pl. Barn S70 54 E8 5
Fleming Sq. W up D S63 78 E6
Fleming Way. Roth S66 117 B6
Fletcher Ave. Dron S18 153 A1
Fletcher House. Roth S65 115 E7 2
Fleury Cl. Shef S14 141 E4
Fleury Cres. Shef S14 141 E4
Fleury Pl. Shef S14 141 E4
Fleury Rd. Shef S14 141 E4
Fleury Rise. Shef S14 141 E4
Flight Hill. Dun Br HD7 48 C5
Flint La. Carl S30,HD7 49 A5
Flint Rd. Don DN2 63 C6
Flintway. Swint S63 78 F3
Flockton Ave. Shef S13 143 C8
Flockton Cres. Shef S13 143 C8
Flockton Ct. Shef S1 128 F3 10
Flockton Dr. Shef S13 143 C8
Flockton House. Shef S1 128 F3 9
Flockton Rd. Shef S13 143 C8
Flodden St. Shef S10 128 B4 1
Floodgate Dr. Shef S30 113 B8
Flora St. Shef S6 128 E6
Florence Ave. Aston S31 144 D7
Florence Ave. Don DN4 83 A8
Florence Rd. Roth S61 115 B6
Florence Rd. Shef S8 140 E2
Florence Rise. Dar S73 56 F5
Flower St. Dearne S63 58 F5
Flowitt St. Don DN4 62 B2
Flowitt St. Mex S64 79 F5
Fold The. Roth S65 116 D8
Folder La. Sprot DN5 61 A1
Folderings La. Stock S30 92 C6
Folds Cres. Shef S8 140 D1
Folds Dr. Shef S8 140 C1
Folds La. Shef S8 140 C1
Folds La. Tick DN11 120 D3
Foley Ave. Wombw S73 56 C2
Foley St. Shef S4 129 D5
Foljambe Cty Prim Sch. Roth 98 E1
Foljambe Cres. Ross DN11 84 E1
Foljambe Dr. Roth S65 98 E1
Foljambe Rd. Roth S65 116 B8
Foljambe St. Rawm S62 97 F4
Follett Rd. Shef S5 113 C5
Folly La. Pen S30 50 F5
Fonteyn House. Don DN2 62 F6
Fontwell Dr. Mex S64 80 B6
Footgate Cl. Ought S30 111 D6
Forbes Rd. Shef S6 128 C8
Ford Cl. Dron S18 152 F1
Ford La. Eck S12 154 E5
Ford La. Stock S30 73 C2
Ford Rd. Eck S31 154 E4
Ford Rd. Shef S11 140 B6
Fordoles Head La. Braith S66 100 C1
Fordoles Head La. Maltby S66 118 C7
Fore Hill Ave. Don DN4 84 D6
Fore's Rd. Arm DN3 64 C5
Foremark Rd. Shef S5 113 D4
Forest Rd. Barn S71 33 F8
Forest Rise. Don DN4 82 F5
Forge Hill. Ought S30 111 D7
Forge La. Hoy S74 77 B4
Forge La. Kill S31 156 B7
Forge La. Ought S30 111 D7
Forge La. Roth S60 115 D6
Forge La. Shef S3 129 A1
Forge La. Wort S30 74 A3
Forge Rd. Wales S31 145 C3
Formby Ct. Barn S71 34 D6
Forncett St. Shef S4 129 D6
Forncett St. Shef S4 129 D7
Fornham St. Shef S2 129 B2
Forres Ave. Shef S10 128 A3
Forres Rd. Shef S10 128 B3
Forrester Cl. Roth S66 117 B6
Forrester's Cl. Norton DN6 4 C3
Forrester's La. Dron S18 153 C4
Forstead La. B Dun DN3 42 D7
Forster Rd. Don DN4 83 B6
Fort Hill Rd. Shef S9 114 A3
Forth Ave. Dron S18 152 D2
Fortway Rd. Brin S60 115 C2
Fossard Cl. Don DN2 63 A7
Fossard Way. Ben DN5 40 F1
Fossdale Rd. Shef S7 140 D5
Foster Place La. Holmfi HD7 28 A2
Foster Rd. Roth S66 117 B5
Foster Rd. Thorne DN8 26 A8
Foster St. Barn S70 55 D8
Foster Way. Chap S30 94 D7
Foster's Cl. Swint S64 79 C3
Fosters The. Chap S30 94 D7
Foulstone Row. Wombw S73 56 E2
Foundry Ct. Shef S3 129 B7
Foundry La. Thorne DN8 26 A7
Foundry Rd. Don DN4 62 B1
Foundry St. Barn S70 54 E8 2
Foundry St. Hoy S74 77 A5
Foundry St. Rawm S62 97 F3
Fountain Cl. Mapp S75 13 E1
Fountain Ct. Barn S71 14 E1
Fountain Prec. Shef 129 A3 18
Fountain Sq. Mapp S75 13 E1
Fountains Way. Barn S71 34 D3
Fountside. Shef S7 140 D6
Four Lane Ends. Maltby S66 136 B7
Four Lane Ends. Wad DN11 103 A4
Four Lane Ends. Wort S30 74 D3
Four Row. D Dale HD8 29 A4
Four Wells Dr. Shef S12 143 B4
Fourth Ave. Ad l S DN6 40 C3
Fourth Sq. Stai DN7 24 E4
Fowler Bridge Rd. Ben DN5 62 C7
Fowler Cres. Ross DN11 84 E1
Fox Cl. Roth S61 96 D2
Fox Covert Cl. Dearne S63 58 C4
Fox Covert Road or Whin Covert La. Norton WF8 3 E2
Fox Ct. Swint S64 79 D1
Fox Glen Rd. Stock S30 92 D8
Fox Gr. Don DN4 82 C6
Fox Hill Ave. Shef S6 112 C5
Fox Hill Cl. Shef S6 112 C5
Fox Hill Cres. Shef S6 112 C5
Fox Hill Dr. Shef S6 112 C5
Fox Hill Pl. Shef S6 112 C6
Fox Hill Rd. Shef S6 112 C5
Fox Hill. Shef S3 129 A6
Fox Hill Way. Shef S6 112 C6
Fox Hole La. Tick DN11 102 D1
Fox La. Bnbur DN5 59 D3
Fox La. Shef S12 142 C3
Fox La. Shef S17 152 D6
Fox Rd. Shef S6 128 E6
Fox Royd. Shep HD8 28 E8
Fox St. Roth S61 114 E6
Fox St. Shef S3 129 B6
Fox Wlk. Shef S6 128 D6
Foxcote Lea. Roth S65 99 A2
Foxcroft Chase. Kill S31 156 C6
Foxcroft Dr. Kill S31 156 C5
Foxcroft Gr. Kill S31 156 C6
Foxdale Ave. Shef S12 142 B5
Foxfield Wlk. Barn S70 55 D6
Foxglove Cl. Blax DN9 86 F6
Foxglove Rd. Shef S5 113 E4
Foxhall La. Shef S10 139 A6
Foxhill Jun & Inf Sch. Shef 112 D6
Foxhill Rd. Thorne DN8 26 C6
Foxland Ave. Swint S64 79 A3
Foxroyd Cl. Barn S71 55 F8
Foxwood Ave. Shef S12 142 B6
Foxwood Dr. Shef S12 142 B5
Foxwood Gr. Shef S12 142 B5
Foxwood Rd. Shef S12 142 B6
Framlingham Pl. Shef S2 141 D7
Framlingham Rd. Shef S2 141 D7
France Rd. Shef S6 111 D1
France St. Rawm S62 97 F3
Frances St. Don DN1 62 D3
Frances St. Roth S60 115 E5
Francis Cres N. Roth S60 116 D3
Francis Cres S. Roth S60 116 D3
Francis Dr. Roth S60 116 D4
Francis Gr. Chap S30 94 D7
Frank Hillock Field. Stock S30 73 E1
Frank Pl. Shef S9 130 A7
Frank Rd. Ben DN5 62 B6
Franklin Cres. Don DN2 62 F3
Fraser Cl. Shef S8 140 E3
Fraser Cres. Shef S8 140 F3
Fraser Dr. Shef S8 140 F3
Fraser Rd. Roth S60 115 F5
Fraser Rd. Shef S8 140 E3
Fraser Wlk. Shef S8 140 F2
Frecheville Inf Sch. Shef 142 C4
Frecheville Sch. Shef 142 C4
Frederic Pl. Barn S70 54 F7 8
Frederick Ave. Barn S70 54 D8
Frederick Dr. Shef S30 94 B1
Frederick Rd. Shef S7 140 F7 10
Frederick St. Dearne S63 58 E5
Frederick St. Mex S64 79 F5
Frederick St. Roth S60 115 D7
Frederick St. Shef S9 130 B4
Frederick St. Treet S60 131 C5
Frederick St. W up D S63 78 D7
Frederick St. Wombw S73 56 C3
Freedom Ct. Shef S6 128 D7
Freedom Rd. Shef S6 128 C6
Freeman Gdns. Chap S30 94 D6
Freeman Rd. Roth S66 117 B5
Freeman St. Barn S70 54 F8
Freemans Yd. Barn S70 33 F1
Freesia Cl. S Anst S31 146 C4
Freeston Pl. Shef S9 130 A7
French Gate Ctr. Don 62 C3
French Gate. Don DN1 62 C3
French St. Ad le S DN6 21 A1
French St. Ben DN5 41 B2
Fretson Rd. Shef S2 142 A8
Fretwell Cl. Maltby S66 118 E6
Fretwell Rd. Roth S65 116 C8
Friar Cl. Shef S6 127 D6
Friar's Rd. Barn S71 34 F3
Friars Croft. Went S73 77 B1
Friars Gate. Don DN1 62 C4
Frickley Bridge La. Bri S72 16 F4
Frickley La. Clay WF9 38 A8
Frickley La. S Elm WF9 38 A8
Frickley Rd. Shef S11 139 F8
Frith Cl. Shef S12 142 B5
Frith Rd. Shef S12 142 B5
Frithbeck Cl. Arm DN3 64 B6
Frobisher Gr. Maltby S66 118 E6
Froggatt La. Shef S1 129 A2
Frogmore Cl. Roth S66 117 D6
Front St. Treet S60 131 E4
Frostings Cl. Shef S30 94 C1
Frostings The. Shef S30 94 C1
Fulford Cl. Mapp S75 14 A1
Fulford Cl. Shef S9 130 C5
Fulford Pl. Shef S9 130 C5
Fulford Way. Con DN12 81 E3
Fuller Gr. Swint S64 79 D1
Fullerton Ave. Con DN12 81 A2
Fullerton C of E Aided Prim Sch The. Roth 98 F3
Fullerton Cl. Ad le S DN6 20 F2
Fullerton Cres. Roth S65 98 E3
Fullerton Dr. Brin S60 131 B8
Fullerton Hospl. Con 80 F3
Fullerton Rd. Roth S60 115 C4
Fullshaw La. Lang S30 71 B7
Fulmar Way. Roth S61 96 A6
Fulmer Cl. Barn S71 34 B6
Fulmer Rd. Shef S11 140 C7
Fulmere Cres. Shef S5 112 E6
Fulmere Rd. Shef S5 112 E6
Fulney Rd. Shef S11 139 F8
Fulstone Hall La. Holmfi HD7 28 A7
Fulstone Rd. Kirkb HD4 28 B8
Fulton Rd. Shef S6 128 D5
Fulwood Dr. Don DN4 83 B4
Fulwood Head Rd. Shef S10 138 D7
Fulwood La. Shef S10, S11 138 E5
Fulwood Rd. Shef S10 128 B2
Furlong Rd. Bnbur S63 59 B1
Furlong Rd. Dearne S63 58 D3
Furlong View. Bnbur DN5 59 B2
Furnace Cotts. Wh Com S30 49 D6
Furnace Hill. Shef S3 129 A4
Furnace La. Shef S13 143 E7
Furnace Yd. Barn S70 55 A3
Furness Cl. Din S31 146 F7
Furness Cl. Shef S6 127 D7
Furness Dene. Barn S71 34 D5
Furness Rd. Chap S30 94 C7
Furniss Ave. Shef S17 151 D6
Furnival Cl. Tod S31 145 E5
Furnival Gate. Shef S1 129 A2
Furnival Rd. Shef S4 129 C4
Furnival Rd. Tod S31 145 E5
Furnival Sq. Shef S1 129 A2 5
Furnival St. Shef S1 129 A2
Furnival Way. Roth S60 116 D1
Furnivall Rd. Don DN4 83 A7
Fylde Cl. Barn S71 34 D6
Gables Sch The. Wombw 56 D2
Gadding Moor Rd. Caw S30 30 F1
Gainford Rd. Thorne DN8 9 D4
Gainford Sq. Thorne DN8 9 D4
Gainsborough Cl. Roth S66 117 B5
Gainsborough Rd. Bawtry DN10 123 A6
Gainsborough Rd. Dron S18 152 E1
Gainsborough Rd. Shef S11 140 D7
Gainsborough Way. Barn S71 34 B4
Gainsford Rd. Shef S9 130 C4
Gaitskell Cl. Dearne S63 58 D3
Gaitskell Cl. Maltby S66 119 B4
Gallery The. Shef S3 129 B4 5
Galley Dr. Shef S19 143 D1
Gallon Croft. S Elm WF9 18 E3
Gallow Tree Rd. Roth S65 116 D4
Gallows La. Wool WF4 13 F8
Galsworthy Ave. Shef S5 112 F3
Galsworthy Cl. Don DN4 82 F5
Galsworthy Rd. Shef S5 112 F3
Galway Ave. Bir DN11 122 D5
Galway Cl. Rawm S62 98 A6
Galway Dr. Bir DN11 122 D5
Galway Rd. Bir DN11 122 D5
Game La. Shef S6 126 D6
Gamston Rd. Shef S8 140 F7 5
Gannow Cl. Kill S31 156 F7
Ganton Pl. Barn S71 33 E7
Ganton Rd. Shef S6 112 B2
Garbroads Cres. Roth S65 98 E2
Garbutt St. Dearne S63 58 D1
Garden Cres. Roth S60 116 A2
Garden Dr. W up D S73 78 A8
Garden Gr. Hoy S73 77 C8
Garden House Cl. Barn S71 34 C5
Garden House Dr. Wales S31 145 F3
Garden La. Cade DN5 81 D5
Garden La. Roth S60 115 C7 3
Garden La. Roth S65 99 D3
Garden St. Barn S70 54 F8 16
Garden St. Dar S73 57 A5
Garden St. Dearne S63 58 D8
Garden St. Dearne S63 58 F5
Garden St. Mex S64 80 A4
Garden St. Roth S61 115 B7
Garden St. Shef S1 128 F4
Garden St. W up D S63 78 D7
Garden Terr. Ben DN5 62 B8
Garden Terr. D Dale HD8 29 F5
Garden Wlk. Roth S60 116 A2
Garden Wlk. Shef S19 144 A3
Gardenia Rd. Don DN3 42 E3
Gardens La. Con DN12 81 B2
Gardom Cl. Dron S18 152 D1
Garfield Mount. Roth S65 115 F5
Gargrave Cl. Askern DN6 22 C8
Gargrave Cres. Hem WF9 17 C6
Gargrave Pl. Hem WF9 17 C6
Garland Cl. Shef S19 155 E7
Garland Croft. Shef S19 155 E7
Garland Dr. Shef S6 111 E1
Garland Mount. Shef S19 155 E8 15
Garland Way. Shef S19 155 E7
Garraby Cl. G Hou S72 36 E2
Garry Rd. Shef S6 112 B1
Garter St. Shef S4 129 D7
Garth Cl. Shef S9 130 A5 3
Garth Way Cl. Dron S18 152 F1
Garth Way. Dron S18 152 F1
Gartrice Gdns. Kill S19 156 A5
Gashouse La. Eck S19, S31 155 D5
Gashouse La. Shef S19, S31 155 D5
Gate Cres. Dod S75 53 F8
Gate Foot La. Holmfi HD8 28 C5
Gate Head La. Holmfi HD7 49 A8
Gate House La. Blax DN9 86 B5
Gatebeck Cl. Bran DN3 64 E2
Gatefield Rd. Shef S7 140 E6
Gateford Rd. Work S81 148 A1
Gatesbridge Pk. Finn DN9 86 F4
Gateway Cl. Roth S62 97 E2
Gateway Ct. Roth S62 97 E2
Gateway The. Roth S62 97 E2
Gatewood La. Hat DN7 44 D2
Gatewood La. Hat DN7 44 D4
Gateworth Gr. Askern DN6 22 B8
Gattison La. Ross DN11 103 F8
Gatty Rd. Shef S5 113 D7
Gaunt Cl. Roth S66 117 E6
Gaunt Cl. Shef S14 141 D3
Gaunt Dr. Roth S66 117 D6
Gaunt Dr. Shef S14 141 D3
Gaunt Pl. Shef S14 141 D4
Gaunt Rd. Roth S66 117 D6
Gaunt Rd. Shef S14 141 D3
Gaunt Way. Shef S14 141 D3
Gawber Jun & Inf Sch. Barn 33 A3
Gawber Rd. Barn S75 33 C3
Gawtress Row. W up D S63 78 E6
Gayle Ct. Barn S70 33 D2 6
Gayton Cl. Don DN4 83 A5
Gayton Ct. Don DN4 83 A5
Gayton Rd. Shef S4 129 C8
Geer La. Eck S12 154 D5
Geeseness La. Fish DN7 8 B3
Gell St. Shef S3 128 E3
Geneva Sq. Thorne DN8 9 D3
Genn La. Barn S70 54 E5
Genoa Cl. Dar S73 56 E6
Genoa St. Mex S64 80 B5
Gentre The. Roth S66 117 D5
George Buckley Ct. S Kirk WF9 18 A2
George La. Notton WF4 14 E6
George Pl. Mex S64 80 C4
George Pl. Rawm S62 98 A5
George Sq. Barn S70 33 E1
George St. Ad le S DN6 21 B1
George St. Arm DN3 63 F7
George St. Barn S70 33 E1
George St. Barn S70 55 A4
George St. Barn S70 55 C4
George St. Ben DN5 41 B2
George St. Cud S72 35 C8
George St. Dar S73 56 F4
George St. Dearne S63 58 C5
George St. Dearne S63 58 F8
George St. G Hou S72 57 D7
George St. Hem WF9 17 E6
George St. Hoy S74 76 E5
George St. Mapp S75 14 B1
George St. Roth S60 115 D7 2
George St. S Hie S72 16 D6
George St. Shef S1 129 B3
George St. Wombw S73 56 D2
George Woodfindin Almshouses. Shef S11 140 C8 3
George Yd. Barn S70 33 E1
Gerald Cl. Barn S70 55 C7
Gerald Cres. Barn S70 55 D8
Gerald Pl. Barn S70 55 C7
Gerald Rd. Barn S70 55 C7
Gerald St. Shef S9 130 A7
Gerald Wlk. Barn S70 55 C7
Gerard Ave. Roth S65 99 A2
Gerard Cl. Shef S8 141 B6
Gerard Rd. Roth S60 115 E5
Gerard St. Shef S8 141 B6
Gertrude St. Shef S6 128 E6
Gervase Ave. Shef S8 152 E6
Gervase Dr. Shef S8 152 E6
Gervase Pl. Shef S8 152 E6
Gervase Rd. Shef S8 152 E6
Gervase Wlk. Shef S8 152 E6 2
Ghest Villas. C in L S81 136 F1
Gibbet Hill La. Scro DN10 122 F4
Gibbing Greaves Rd. Roth S65 116 E4
Gibbons Dr. Shef S14 141 E2
Gibbons Way. Shef S14 141 E2
Gibbons Wlk. Shef S14 141 E2
Gibraltar St. Shef S3 129 A4
Gibson Rd. Hat DN7 66 A8
Gibson Wlk. Swint S64 79 D1
Gifford Dr. Don DN4 82 D6
Gifford Rd. Shef S8 141 A7
Gig La. Barn S74 76 B8
Gilbert Ct. Shef S2 129 C2 6
Gilbert Gr. Barn S70 55 D8
Gilbert Hill. Lang S30 71 B6
Gilbert Rd. Bir DN11 122 B4
Gilbert Row. Shef S2 129 C3 8
Gilbert St. Shef S1 129 B3
Gilberthorpe Dr. Roth S65 116 A6 2
Gilberthorpe Rd. Don DN4 82 F7
Gilberthorpe St. Roth S65 115 F6
Gildingwells Rd. Let S81 135 F2
Gildingwells Rd. Woods S81 147 E5
Giles Ave. W up D S63 78 C6
Gill Cl. Roth S66 117 C3
Gill Croft. Shef S6 127 C6
Gill Meadows. Shef S6 127 C6
Gill Royd La. Midhop S30 71 F2
Gill St. Don DN1 62 D2
Gill St. Hoy S74 76 F5
Gilleyfield Ave. Shef S17 151 E7
Gillot Ind Est. Barn S70 33 D2
Gillott La. Roth S66 117 B3
Gillott Rd. Shef S6 112 D4
Gilpin La. Shef S6 128 E6
Gilpin St. Shef S6 128 E6
Gilroyd La. Dod S75 54 B5
Gilthwaites Cres. D Dale HD8 30 A7
Gilthwaites Fst Sch. D Dale 30 A7
Gilthwaites Gr. D Dale HD8 30 A6
Gilthwaites La. D Dale HD8 30 A7
Gilthwaites Top. D Dale HD8 30 A7
Ginhouse La. Roth S61 115 C8
Gipsy Green La. W up D S63 78 F4
Gipsy La. Maltby S66 119 C1
Gipsy La. Uns S18 154 A1
Gipsy La. Wool WF4 13 F6
Gipsyhill La. Whit S80 158 C1
Gisborne Rd. Shef S11 140 B6
Glade Croft. Shef S12 142 A4
Glade Lea. Shef S12 142 A4
Glade The. Shef S10 128 B1
Glade View. Don DN3 42 F4
Gladstone Mews. Shef S10 127 E1
Gladstone Rd. Don DN4 62 A1
Gladstone Rd. Maltby S66 118 E6
Gladstone Rd. Shef S10 127 F1
Gladys Buxton Community Ed Ctr. Dron 153 C2
Gladys St. Roth S65 116 A6
Glaisdale Cl. Laugh S31 134 C3
Glamis Rd. C in L S81 148 E6
Glamis Rd. Don DN2 63 A3
Glasshouse La. Swint S62 98 E7
Glasshouse St. Roth S60 115 D7
Glastonbury Gate. Ben DN5 61 D5
Gleadless Ave. Shef S12 142 A4
Gleadless Bank. Shef S12 141 F4
Gleadless Comm. Shef S12 142 A5
Gleadless Cres. Shef S12 141 F5
Gleadless Ct. Shef S2 141 B6
Gleadless Dr. Shef S12 141 F4
Gleadless Fst Sch. Shef 142 B5
Gleadless Mid Sch. Shef 142 B5
Gleadless Mount. Shef S12 142 A3
Gleadless Rd. Shef S14 141 D5
Gleadless Valley Sch. Shef 141 C1
Glebe Ave. Hart S31 157 E7
Glebe Cl. Swint S64 79 C1
Glebe Cres. Roth S65 98 E1
Glebe Farm Cl. Arm DN3 64 A7
Glebe Farm Cl. Hart S31 157 E7
Glebe Rd. Norton DN6 4 D1
Glebe Rd. Shef S10 128 C3
Glebe Rd. Swint S64 79 C1
Glebe Rd. Thorne DN8 26 C7
Glebe St. Don DN4 82 D6
Glebeland Cl. Rawm S62 97 E7
Glebelands Rd. Stock S30 92 C8
Gledhill Ave. Pen S30 51 C1
Gledhill Cl. Dron S18 153 A1
Glen Field Ave. Don DN4 62 A1
Glen Rd. Bran DN3 85 E8
Glen Rd. Shef S7 140 E6
Glen The. Shef S10 128 B1
Glen View Rd. Shef S8 152 E8
Glen View. Shef S11 139 F8
Glenalmond Rd. Shef S11 140 B6
Glencoe Cl. Hat DN7 44 A8
Glencoe Dr. Shef S2 129 C2 2
Glencoe Pl. Shef S2 129 C2 1
Glencoe Rd. Shef S2 129 C2
Glendale Cl. Barn S75 33 B2
Glendale Rd. Sprot DN5 61 B1
Gleneagles Dr. Don DN4 85 B6
Gleneagles Rd. Din S31 146 F8
Gleneagles Rise. Swint S64 79 D2
Glenholme Dr. Shef S13 142 E7
Glenholme Pl. Shef S13 142 F7
Glenholme Rd. Shef S13 142 F7
Glenholme Way. Shef S13 142 E8
Glenmoor Ave. Barn S70 54 B8
Glenmore Croft. Shef S12 142 C6
Glenmore Rise. Wombw S73 56 E1
Glenorchy Rd. Shef S7 140 D5
Glenthorn Cl. Shire S81 159 F7
Glentilt Rd. Shef S7 140 D5
Glenville Cl. Hoy S74 76 D5
Glenwood Cres. Chap S30 95 B4
Gliwice Way. Don DN4 63 B2
Glossop La. Shef S10 128 E3
Glossop Rd. Shef S10 128 D2
Glossop Row. Ought S30 111 D7
Gloucester Cres. Shef S10 128 E2
Gloucester Rd. Don DN2 63 A6
Gloucester Rd. Roth S61 96 F1
Gloucester St. Shef S10 128 E2
Glover Rd. Shef S8 141 A7
Glover Rd. Shef S17 151 F5
Glyn Ave. Don DN1 62 E4
Goathead La. Snaith DN14 1 D7
Goathland Cl. Shef S13 143 D7
Goathland Dr. Shef S13 143 D7
Goathland Pl. Shef S13 143 D7
Goathland Rd. Shef S13 143 D7
Goddard Ave. Stock S30 72 F2
Goddard Hall Rd. Shef S5 113 C1
Godfrey Rd. Thorne DN8 26 A7
Godfrey's Cotts. Thorne DN8 9 B8
Godley Cl. Roy S71 15 D4
Godley St. Roy S71 15 D4
Godric Dr. Brin S60 115 B1
Godric Gn. Brin S60 115 B1
Godric Rd. Shef S5 113 C7
Godstone Rd. Roth S60 115 E5
Gold Croft. Barn S70 55 A8 5
Gold St. Barn S70 55 A8
Goldcrest Wlk. Roth S61 96 A5
Golden Oak Dell. Shef S6 127 C7
Golden Smithies La. Swint S64 79 C4
Golden Smithies La. W up D S64 79 C4
Goldsborough Rd. Don DN2 63 A3
Goldsmith Dr. Roth S65 116 B6
Goldsmith Rd. Don DN4 83 A6
Goldsmith Rd. Roth S65 116 B6
Goldthorpe Ave. Lan S81 136 F3
Goldthorpe Cl. Lan S81 136 F3
Goldthorpe Gn. Dearne S63 58 D4
Goldthorpe Ind Est. Dearne 58 C3
Goldthorpe Rd. Dearne S63 58 E4
Goldthorpe Sta. Dearne 58 D5
Gomersal La. Dron S18 153 A1
Gomersall Ave. Con DN12 80 F2
Gooder Ave. Roy S71 15 C3
Goodison Bvd. Don DN4 85 A7
Goodison Cres. Shef S6 127 F6
Goodison Rise. Shef S6 127 F6

Hall Farm Dr. Dearne S63 58 D7
Hall Farm Gr. Pen S30 52 A6
Hall Farm Rise. Dearne S63 58 D7
Hall Field La. Ryhill S72 16 A7
Hall Flat La. Don DN4 83 A7
Hall Gate. Don DN1 62 D3
Hall Gate. Mex S64 80 C5
Hall Gate. Pen S30 51 D4
Hall Gr. Mapp S75 14 C1
Hall Gr. Roth S60 115 E5
Hall La. Bfield S6 109 B4
Hall La. K Bram DN7 24 B3
Hall La. S Elm WF9 19 B6
Hall Park Head. Shef S6 127 E5
Hall Park Hill. Shef S6 127 E5
Hall Park Mount. Shef S6 127 E5
Hall Pl. Barn S71 34 C4
Hall Rd. Aston S31 132 D1
Hall Rd. Roth S60 115 E5
Hall Rd. Shef S13, S9 130 E3
Hall Rd. Shef S13, S31, S9 130 F2
Hall Royd La. Silk S75 53 B6
Hall Royd Wlk. Silk S75 53 A5
Hall St. Bnbur DN5 59 D3
Hall St. Dearne S63 58 E5
Hall St. Hoy S74 76 E6
Hall St. Roth S60 115 C6
Hall St. Wombw S73 56 E2
Hall View Rd. Ross DN11 104 A7
Hall Villa La. Ben DN5 41 B6
Hall Wood Rd. Chap S30 94 C5
Hallam Chase. Shef S10 127 D2
Hallam Chase. Shef S10 128 B1
Hallam Cl. Aston S31 132 C1
Hallam Cl. Don DN4 84 C7
Hallam Ct. Shef S10 128 D1
Hallam Dale Ct. Rawm S62 98 A7
Hallam Grange Cl. Shef S10 139 C8
Hallam Grange Cres. Shef S10 127 C1
Hallam Grange Croft. Shef S10 127 C1
Hallam Grange Rd. Shef S10 127 C1
Hallam Grange Rise. Shef S10 127 C1
Hallam La. Shef S1 129 A2 6
Hallam Pl. Rawm S62 98 A5
Hallam Primary Schs. Shef 127 C1
Hallam Rd. Roth S60 116 A1
Hallam Rock. Shef S5 113 B1
Hallam Way. Shef S30 113 B8
Hallamgate Rd. Shef S10 128 B3
Hallamshire Cl. Shef S10 139 B8
Hallamshire Dr. Shef S10 139 C8
Hallamshire Rd. Shef S10 139 B8
Hallcar St. Shef S4 129 C5
Hallcroft Dr. Arm DN3 64 C4
Hallcroft Rise. Roy S71 15 B3
Hallgate. Dearne S63 58 D7
Hallgate Rd. Shef S10 128 A3
Halliwell Cl. Shef S5 112 D3
Halliwell Cres. Shef S5 112 E4
Hallowes Ct. Dron S18 153 B1
Hallowes La. Dron S18 153 B1
Hallowmoor Rd. Shef S6 128 A8
Hallsworth Ave. Hoy S73 77 B7
Hallwood Rd. Chap S30 94 C5
Hallworth Wlk. Eck S31 154 E2
Hallyburton Cl. Shef S2 141 C6
Hallyburton Dr. Shef S2 141 C6
Hallyburton Rd. Shef S2 141 C6
Halmshaw Terr. Ben DN5 62 A8
Halsall Ave. Shef S9 130 C3
Halsall Dr. Shef S9 130 C3
Halsall Rd. Shef S9 130 C3
Halsbury Rd. Roth S65 116 A8
Halstead Gr. Mapp S75 14 A2
Halton Ct. Shef S12 143 C3
Hamble Ct. Mapp S75 33 C8
Hambleton Cl. Barn S75 33 B2
Hambleton Cl. Hoy S74 77 B6
Hambleton Ct. C in L S81 148 E7
Hamel Rise. Hem WF9 17 D6
Hameline Rd. Con DN12 81 B1
Hamer Wlk. Roth S65 116 C7
Hamilton Cl. Don DN4 62 F1
Hamilton Cl. Mex S64 80 C6
Hamilton Park Rd. Ben DN5 61 D6
Hamilton Rd. Dearne S63 58 F6
Hamilton Rd. Don DN4 62 F2
Hamilton Rd. Maltby S66 119 B4
Hamilton Rd. Shef S5 113 D2
Hammerton Cl. Shef S6 128 C7
Hammerton Rd. Shef S6 128 C7
Hammerton St. Wombw S73 56 C4
Hammond St. Shef S3 128 E4
Hampden Cres. Hat DN7 66 A8
Hampden Rd. Mex S64 80 B4
Hamper La. Pen S30 51 F6
Hampole Balk. Ad le S DN6 20 E1
Hampole Field La. Ham DN6 19 F1
Hampton Rd. Don DN2 62 F4
Hampton Rd. Hat DN7 43 F8
Hampton Rd. Shef S5 113 C1
Hanbury Cl. Barn S71 34 D4
Hanbury Cl. Don DN4 83 A4
Hanbury Cl. Dron S18 152 F1
Hand La. Thurgo S30 74 C8
Handley St. Shef S3 129 B5
Hands Rd. Shef S10 128 C4
Handsworth Ave. Shef S9 130 D3
Handsworth Cres. Shef S9 130 D3
Handsworth Fst Sch. Shef 130 F1
Handsworth Gdns. Arm DN3 64 C6
Handsworth Grange Cl. Shef S13 131 A1
Handsworth Grange Cres.
Shef S13 131 B1
Handsworth Grange Dr. Shef S13 131 B1
Handsworth Grange Rd. Shef S13 131 A1
Handsworth Grange Way.
Shef S13 131 B1
Handsworth Rd. Shef S13, S9 130 F2
Handsworth Rd. Shef S13 143 C8
Handsworth St Joseph's R C
Jun & Inf Sch. Shef 130 F1
Hanging Water Cl. Shef S10 139 F8
Hangingwater Cotts. Shef S11 139 F7
Hangingwater Rd. Shef S11 139 F8
Hangman Stone La. H Mel DN5 60 B2
Hangman Stone Rd. Bnbur DN5 59 F2
Hangman Stone Rd. Marr DN5 60 A5
Hangram La. Shef S11 139 B5
Hangsman La. Laugh S31 134 C3
Hangthwaite La. Ad l S DN6 40 D3
Hangthwaite Rd. Ad l S DN6 40 D7
Hanley Cl. Shef S12 143 B3
Hanmoor Rd. Shef S6 127 C6
Hannah Rd. Shef S13 143 D7
Hannas Royd. Dod S75 54 A7
Hanover Ct. Barn S70 55 A5 3
Hanover Ct. Shef S3 128 E2 3
Hanover Sq. Dearne S63 58 E8
Hanover Sq. Shef S3 128 F2
Hanover St. Dearne S63 37 E1
Hanover St. Shef S3 128 F2
Hanover Way. Shef S3 128 F2
Hanson Rd. Shef S6 127 D8
Hanson St. Barn S70 33 F1
Harbord Rd. Shef S8 140 E2
Harborough Ave. Shef S2 130 A1
Harborough Cl. Shef S2 130 A2
Harborough Dr. Shef S2 130 A2
Harborough Hill Rd. Barn S71 33 F2
Harborough Rd. Shef S2 130 A2
Harborough Rise. Shef S2 130 A2
Harborough Way. Shef S2 130 A1
Harbury St. Shef S13 143 E8
Harcourt Cl. Don DN4 84 C7
Harcourt Cres. Shef S10 128 D3
Harcourt Rd. Shef S10 128 D4
Harcourt Rise. Chap S30 95 B4
Harcourt Terr. Roth S65 115 F6 3
Hard La. Hart S31 145 F1
Hardcastle Dr. Shef S13 143 A7
Hardcastle Gdns. Shef S13 143 A7
Hardcastle Rd. Shef S13 143 A7
Harden Cl. Barn S75 33 A2
Harden Cl. Pen S30 51 D2
Hardie Cl. Maltby S66 119 B4
Hardie Pl. Rawm S62 97 F6
Hardie St. Eck S31 155 D3
Harding Ave. Rawm S62 97 D8
Harding Cl. Rawm S62 97 D7
Harding St. Shef S9 130 B6
Hardwick Cl. Aston S31 144 F7
Hardwick Cl. Barn S70 55 A4 7
Hardwick Cl. Dron S18 153 C2
Hardwick Cres. Barn S71 34 B7
Hardwick Cres. Shef S11 140 C8
Hardwick Ct. Har DN11 122 B5
Hardwick Gr. Dod S75 53 F6
Hardwick La. Tod S31 145 C8
Hardwick St. Roth S65 116 D8
Hardwicke Rd. Roth S65 115 E8
Hardy Pl. Shef S6 128 D5
Hardy Rd. Don DN2 62 E6
Hardy St. Roth S60 115 C7
Haredon Cl. Mapp S75 14 A2
Harefield Rd. Shef S11 140 D8 3
Harehills Rd. Roth S60 115 E5
Harewood Ave. Ad le S DN6 39 F5
Harewood Ave. Barn S70 33 B1
Harewood Ave. Don DN3 43 A4
Harewood Ct. Har DN11 122 B5
Harewood Gr. Roth S66 117 D6
Harewood La. Upton WF9 19 D8
Harewood Lane Fst Sch. Upton 19 E8
Harewood Rd. Don DN2 63 A3
Harewood Way. Shef S11 140 A2
Hargrave Pl. Roth S65 98 F2
Harland Rd. Shef S11 128 E1
Harlech Cl. Chap S30 94 F6
Harleston St. Shef S4 129 D6
Harley Rd. Shef S11 139 F5
Harley Rd. Went S62 76 D1
Harlington Ct. Con DN12 81 A3
Harlington Rd. Mex S64 79 F8
Harlington Rd. Mex S64 80 B6
Harmby Cl. Ad le S DN6 20 F2
Harmer La. Shef S1 129 B3
Harmony Way. Treet S60 131 C6
Harney Cl. Shef S9 130 C5
Harold Ave. Ad l S DN6 40 A5
Harold Ave. Barn S71 34 E4
Harold Croft. Roth S61 97 C4
Harold St. Shef S6 128 D6
Harpenden Cl. Hat DN7 44 A6
Harpendon Dr. Hat DN7 44 A6
Harriet Cl. Barn S70 55 A7
Harrington Ct. Barn S71 34 E4
Harrington Rd. Shef S2 141 A8 10
Harrington St. Don DN1 62 D4
Harris Rd. Shef S6 112 B2
Harrison Dr. Lan S81 136 F3
Harrison La. Shef S10 139 A7
Harrison Rd. Shef S6 128 B7
Harrison St. Roth S61 115 A6
Harrogate Dr. Con DN12 80 E2
Harrogate Rd. Aston S31 144 C6
Harrop Dr. Swint S64 79 C1
Harrop La. Shef S10 138 F6
Harrow Rd. Arm DN3 64 C7
Harrow St. S Elm WF9 18 E3
Harrow St. Shef S11 128 F1
Harrowden Ct. Shef S9 114 E2
Harrowden Rd. Don DN2 62 F6
Harrowden Rd. Shef S9 114 E2
Harry Firth Cl. Shef S9 130 A5 7
Harry Rd. Barn S75 33 B3
Hart Hill. Rawm S62 97 D8
Hartcliff Ave. Pen S30 51 C3
Hartcliff Hill Rd. Lang S30 72 A7
Hartcliff Nick. Pen S30 71 E8
Hartcliff Rd. Pen S30 51 B1
Hartcliff Rd. Pen S30 71 D8
Hartcliffe La. Pen S30 50 E1
Hartcliffe View. Thurgo S30 73 F7
Hartford Cl. Shef S8 141 A3
Hartford Rd. Shef S8 141 A3
Harthill Field Rd. Hart S31 158 A3
Harthill Jun & Inf Sch. Hart 157 E5
Harthill La. Barl S31 157 E1
Harthill Rd. Con DN12 81 A1
Harthill Rd. Shef S13 142 B7
Harthill Rd. Th Sa S80 158 D7
Hartington Ave. Shef S7 140 C3
Hartington Cl. Roth S61 115 A6
Hartington Ct. Dron S18 153 B2
Hartington Dr. Barn S71 33 F4
Hartington Rd. Dron S18 153 B2
Hartington Rd. Roth S61 115 A6
Hartington Rd. Shef S7 140 C3
Hartland Ave. Shef S19 144 A2
Hartland Cres. Don DN3 42 F2
Hartland Ct. Shef S19 144 A2 6
Hartland Dr. Shef S19 144 A2
Hartley Brook Ave. Shef S5 113 C6
Hartley Brook Fst Sch. Shef 113 C6
Hartley Brook Mid Sch. Shef 113 C6
Hartley Brook Rd. Shef S5 113 C6
Hartley Cl. S Elm WF9 19 A4
Hartley La. Roth S61 115 C7
Hartley St. Mex S64 79 F4
Hartley St. Shef S2 141 A7
Hartopp Ave. Shef S2 141 D6
Hartopp Cl. Shef S2 141 C6
Hartopp Dr. Shef S2 141 D6
Hartopp Rd. Shef S2 141 D6
Harts Head. Shef S1 129 B4
Harvest Cl. Barn S70 55 A4
Harvest Cl. Don DN3 43 A3
Harvest La. Shef S3 129 A5
Harvest Rd. Roth S66 117 B5
Harvest Way. Rawcl DN14 2 D7
Harvey Cl. Finn DN9 86 F4
Harvey Close Mews. Shef S8 141 B3
Harvey Clough Rd. Shef S8 141 B3
Harvey Rd. Chap S30 95 A5
Harvey St. Barn S70 54 D8
Harvey St. Stock S30 73 D1
Harwell Rd. Shef S8 140 F7
Harwich Rd. Shef S2 129 F1
Harwood Cl. Shef S2 141 A8
Harwood Dr. Shef S19 143 D1
Harwood Gdns. Shef S19 143 E1
Harwood St. Shef S2 141 A8 2
Harwood Terr. Barn S71 34 E2
Harworth C of E Prim Sch. Har 122 A4
Haslam Cres. Shef S8 152 E6
Haslam Pl. Maltby S66 119 B6
Haslam Rd. Ross DN11 84 F1
Haslehurst Rd. Shef S2 129 E2
Haslemere Gr. Ben DN5 62 B6
Hastilar Cl. Shef S2 142 B8
Hastilar Rd S. Shef S13 142 C7
Hastilar Rd. Shef S2 142 B8
Hastings Mount. Shef S7 140 C4
Hastings Rd. Shef S7 140 C4
Hastings St. Grime S72 36 A7
Hatchell Dr. Don DN4 85 A5
Hatchellwood View. Don DN4 85 B5
Hatfield Ash Hill Mid Sch. Hat 44 B7
Hatfield Cl. Barn S71 33 E7
Hatfield Cres. Laugh S31 134 C2
Hatfield Dunsville Cty Prim Sch.
Hat 44 A5
Hatfield Fst Sch. Hat DN7 44 A8
Hatfield Gdns. Roy S71 15 B4
Hatfield High Sch. Hat DN7 44 B7
Hatfield House Croft. Shef S5 113 D5
Hatfield House Ct. Shef S5 113 D5
Hatfield House. Don DN1 62 C2 3
Hatfield House La. Shef S5 113 D5
Hatfield House Lane Fst &
Mid Sch. Shef 113 D5
Hatfield La. Arm DN3 64 C7
Hatfield La. B Dun DN3 43 B6
Hatfield La. Don DN3 43 C1
Hatfield Levels Cty Prim Sch. Hat 27 B2
Hatfield Manor Mid Sch. Hat 44 C8
Hatfield Rd. Thorne DN8 25 F3
Hatfield Sheep Dip Lane Fst Sch.
Hat DN7 44 A7
Hatfield Woodhouse Fst Sch. Hat 45 A6
Hatherley Rd. Roth S65 115 E8
Hatherley Rd. Shef S9 114 E2
Hatherley Rd. Swint S64 79 D5
Hathersage Rd. Shef S17 150 D6
Hathersage Rd. Shef S17, S30 151 B8
Hathersage Sta. Hath 149 A7
Hatton Rd. Shef S6 128 D7
Haugh La. Shef S11 139 F5
Haugh Rd. Rawm S62 97 D7
Haughton Rd. Shef S8 140 F2
Havelock Cl. Ad le S DN6 20 F2
Havelock Rd. Don DN4 62 C1
Havelock St. Barn S73 54 D8
Havelock St. Dar S73 57 A5
Havelock St. Shef S10 128 E2
Haven Hill. Maltby S81 136 D6
Havercroft Cty Inf Sch. Ryhill 16 B8
Havercroft Rd. Roth S60 116 C3
Havercroft Rd. Shef S8 140 E3
Havercroft Rise. S Hie S72 16 E6
Havercroft Terr. Kill S31 156 B7
Haverdale Rise. Barn S75 33 D3
Haverlands La. Barn S70 54 E4
Haverlands Ridge. Barn S70 54 F4
Haw Ct. Silk S75 52 F8
Hawes Cl. Mex S64 80 C6
Hawfield Cl. Don DN4 62 A1
Hawk Hill La. Thurcr S66 133 E4
Hawke Cl. Rawm S62 97 C7
Hawke Rd. Don DN2 62 F6
Hawke St. Shef S9 130 A8
Hawkhouse Green La. Moss DN3 23 D7
Hawkhurst Ridge. Roth S65 116 B8 12
Hawkins Ave. Chap S30 94 E5
Hawkshead Ave. Dron S18 152 E1
Hawkshead Cres. N Anst S31 146 F6
Hawkshead Rd. Shef S4 113 F1
Hawksley Ave. Shef S6 128 C8
Hawksley Mews. Shef S6 128 C8
Hawksley Rd. Shef S6 128 C8
Hawksley Rise. Ought S30 111 D6
Hawksway. Eck S31 155 B3
Hawksworth Cl. Roth S65 116 C7
Hawksworth Rd. Roth S65 116 D8
Hawksworth Rd. Shef S6 128 D6
Hawley St. Rawm S62 97 F5
Hawley St. Shef S1 129 A4
Hawley St. Uns S18 154 A1
Haworth Bank. Roth S60 115 F1
Haworth Cl. Barn S71 34 B3
Haworth Cres. Roth S60 115 F1
Hawshaw La. Hoy S74 76 C6
Hawson St. Wombw S73 56 E2
Hawthorn Ave. Arm DN3 64 B7
Hawthorn Ave. Maltby S66 118 E5
Hawthorn Ave. Shef S19 143 D1
Hawthorn Ct. Roth S65 116 B7
Hawthorn Gr. Con DN12 100 A8
Hawthorn Gr. Silk S75 31 F1
Hawthorn Prim Schs. Don 63 E1
Hawthorn Rd. Chap S30 94 E7
Hawthorn Rd. Eck S31 155 B2
Hawthorn Rd. Shef S6 128 B8
Hawthorn Way. C in L S81 148 E7
Hawthorne Ave. Dron S18 153 A3
Hawthorne Ave. Hat DN7 43 E4
Hawthorne Ave. Hem WF9 17 D6
Hawthorne Ave. Norton DN6 4 F3
Hawthorne Ave. Rawm S62 98 A5
Hawthorne Ave. S Anst S31 146 E3
Hawthorne Ave. Stock S30 72 F2
Hawthorne Ave. Thorne DN8 9 B1
Hawthorne Cl. Kill S31 156 D5
Hawthorne Cres. Ad le S DN6 21 A1
Hawthorne Cres. Dod S75 53 E8
Hawthorne Cres. Hem WF9 17 C6
Hawthorne Cres. Mex S64 79 E5
Hawthorne Flats. Dearne S63 37 D1
Hawthorne Gr. Ben DN5 41 B2
Hawthorne Gr. Thorne DN8 9 B1
Hawthorne Rd. Finn DN9 86 A4
Hawthorne Rd. Thorne DN8 9 B1
Hawthorne Rd. W up D S63 79 A5
Hawthorne St. Barn S70 54 E8
Hawthorne St. Shaf S72 16 C3
Hawthorne St. Shef S6 128 B6
Hawthorne Way. Shaf S72 16 C3
Hawthornes The. Shef S19 143 F4
Hawthorns The. Braith S66 119 A8
Hawtop La. Wool WF4 13 F5
Haxby Cl. Shef S13 142 E6
Haxby Pl. Shef S13 142 E6
Haxby St. Shef S13 142 E6
Hay Green La. Barn S70 75 F7
Haybrook Ct. Shef S17 151 E5
Haydn Rd. Maltby S66 119 B4
Haydock Cl. Mex S64 80 B6
Haydon Gr. Roth S66 117 B6
Hayes Croft. Barn S70 33 F1 10
Hayes Ct. Shef S19 155 E6
Hayes Dr. Shef S19 155 E6
Hayes La. Fish DN7 8 B2
Hayfield Cl. B Dun DN3 43 A7
Hayfield Cl. Dod S75 53 E7
Hayfield Cl. Dron S18 152 D1
Hayfield Comp Sch. Finn 85 F5
Hayfield Cres. Shef S12 142 D3
Hayfield Dr. Shef S12 142 D3
Hayfield La. Finn DN9 85 D4
Hayfield Pl. Shef S12 142 D3
Hayfield View. Eck S31 155 C3
Hayfield Wlk. Roth S61 96 E1
Hayhurst Cres. Maltby S66 119 A4
Hayland St. Shef S9 114 B2
Haylock Cl. Barn S75 32 E3
Haymarket. Shef S1 129 B4
Haynes Cl. Thorne DN8 26 C6
Haynes Cl. Thorne DN8 26 C7
Haynes Gdns. Thorne DN8 26 C7
Haynes Gr. Thorne DN8 26 C6
Haynes Rd. Thorne DN8 26 C7
Haythorne Way. Swint S64 79 D1
Haywood Ave. Stock S30 73 D1
Haywood Cl. Roth S65 116 C7
Haywood La. Askern DN5 22 E5
Haywood La. Stock S30 73 D1
Haywood La. Stock S30 73 E1
Hazel Ave. Finn DN9 86 A4
Hazel Ave. Kill S31 156 C5
Hazel Gr. Arm DN3 64 C7
Hazel Gr. Chap S30 95 A4
Hazel Gr. Con DN12 81 B1
Hazel Gr. Ross DN11 103 F8
Hazel Gr. Roth S66 117 C5
Hazel La. Ham DN6 20 A2
Hazel Rd. Eck S31 155 C2
Hazel Rd. Hat DN7 24 F1
Hazel Rd. Maltby S66 118 D5
Hazel Rd. N Edl DN12 82 B2
Hazelbadge Cres. Shef S12 142 E3
Hazelshaw. Dod S75 54 A6
Hazelshaw Gdns. Chap S30 94 D7
Hazelwood Cl. Dron S18 152 C1 5
Hazelwood Dr. Swint S64 98 D8
Hazlebarrow Cl. Shef S8 153 C6
Hazlebarrow Cres. Shef S8 153 C7
Hazlebarrow Ct. Shef S8 153 B7
Hazlebarrow Dr. Shef S8 153 B7
Hazlebarrow Gr. Shef S8 153 C7
Hazlebarrow Prim Schs. Shef 153 C6
Hazlebarrow Rd. Shef S8 153 B7
Hazledene Cres. Shaf S72 16 D1
Hazledene Rd. Shaf S72 16 D1
Hazlehurst La. Eck S8 153 F8
Headford Gdns. Shef S3 128 F2
Headford Gr. Shef S3 128 F2
Headford St. Shef S3 128 F2
Headingley Rd. Norton DN6 4 D3
Headingley Way. N Edl DN12 82 C3
Headland Dr. Shef S10 128 A3
Headland Rd. Shef S10 128 A3
Headlands Rd. Hoy S74 76 D6
Heads La. Stock S30 92 B6
Heath Ave. Kill S31 156 D5
Heath Bank Rd. Don DN2 63 C7
Heath Gr. Dearne S63 58 B1
Heath Rd. Shef S6 112 D4
Heath Rd. Stock S30 92 D8
Heathcote St. Shef S4 113 D1
Heather Cl. Roth S60 115 E4
Heather Cl. S Kirk WF9 18 D3
Heather Cl. Tick DN11 121 B8
Heather Ct. Dearne S63 58 B3
Heather Ct. Roth S66 117 D4
Heather Garth Jun & Inf Sch.
Dearne 58 B3
Heather Knowle. Dod S75 54 A7
Heather Lea Ave. Shef S17 151 C7
Heather Lea Pl. Shef S17 151 C7
Heather Rd. Shef S5 113 E3
Heather Wlk. Dearne S63 58 B3
Heatherbank Rd. Don DN4 84 E7
Heatherdale Rd. Maltby S66 119 B5
Heathfield Cl. B Dun DN3 43 A6
Heathfield Cl. Dron S18 152 F1 2
Heathfield Rd. Shef S12 142 D4
Heathy La. Derw S6 125 A5
Heaton Cl. Dron S18 152 D1
Heatons Bank. Rawm S62 98 A6
Heator La. D Dale HD8 29 A7
Heavygate Ave. Shef S10 128 B6
Heavygate Rd. Shef S10 128 C5
Hedge Hill Rd. Pen S30 51 A3
Hedge La. Kex S75 32 D7
Hedge La. Kex S75 32 D8
Heeley Bank Inf Sch. Shef 141 B7
Heeley Bank Jun Sch. Shef 141 B7
Heeley Bank Rd. Shef S2 141 B7
Heeley Gn. Shef S2 141 B6
Heelis St. Barn S70 54 F8
Heighton View. Aston S31 132 D1
Heights View. Thurgo S30 74 A6
Hekeward Ct. Con DN12 81 E2
Helena Cl. Barn S70 54 D8
Helena St. Mex S64 80 A5
Helensburgh Cl. Barn S75 33 C2
Hellaby Hall Rd. Maltby S66 118 B4
Hellaby Ind Est. Maltby 118 A6
Hellaby La. Maltby S66 118 B5
Hellaby La. Maltby S66 118 B7
Hellaby View. Roth S65 117 D7
Helliwell Ct. Stock S30 92 E7
Helliwell La. Stock S30 92 E8
Helmsley Ave. Shef S19 155 E7
Helmsley Cl. Aston S31 144 C6
Helmton Dr. Shef S8 141 A2
Helmton Rd. Shef S8 140 F2
Helston Cres. Barn S71 34 B3
Helston Rise. Shef S7 140 C4
Hemingfield Rd. Hoy S73 77 C8
Hemp Pits Rd. Ben DN5 41 D1
Hemper Gr. Shef S8 152 D7
Hemper La. Shef S8 152 D7
Hemsworth Archbishop Holgate
C of E Fst Sch. Hem 17 D8
Hemsworth Grove Lea Fst Sch.
Hem 17 E7
Hemsworth High Sch. Hem 17 E7
Hemsworth Hollygarth Sch. Hem 17 D7
Hemsworth Prim Sch. Shef 141 D2
Hemsworth Rd. S Kirk WF9 17 F4
Hemsworth Rd. Shef S8, S14 141 C2
Hemsworth St Helens C of E
(aided) Mid Sch. Hem 17 C6
Hemsworth West End Mid Sch.
Hem 17 C7
Henderson Glen. Roy S71 15 A3
Hendon St. Shef S13 130 F1
Hengist Rd. Ben DN5 61 F2
Henley Ave. Shef S8 153 C8
Henley Grove Rd. Roth S61 115 B7
Henley Rd. Don DN2 63 C5
Henley Rise. Roth S61 115 B7
Henley Way. Roth S61 115 A7
Hennings Cl. Don DN4 84 B7
Henry Ave. Ryhill WF4 16 C8
Henry Cl. Shaf S72 16 C3
Henry Ct. Roth S60 115 D7 4
Henry Ct. Thorne DN8 9 C1
Henry Fanshawe Sch. Dron 153 B2
Henry La. Ross DN11 84 D1
Henry Pl. Mex S64 80 C5
Henry Rd. W up D S63 79 A6
Henry St. Chap S30 94 C7
Henry St. Dar S73 56 F4
Henry St. Eck S31 155 D3
Henry St. Rawm S62 97 E3
Henry St. Roth S65 115 E7
Henry St. Shef S3 128 F5
Henshall St. Barn S70 55 A8 8
Henson St. Shef S9 130 B6
Heppenstall La. Shef S9 129 F6
Heptinstall St. Barn S70 55 B5
Hepworth Dr. Aston S31 144 D7
Hepworth Rd. Don DN4 82 F7
Herbert Cl. Ben DN5 62 A5
Herbert Rd. Ben DN5 62 A5
Herbert Rd. Shef S7 140 E6
Herbert St. Mex S64 80 C5
Herbert St. Roth S61 114 E7
Herdings Ct. Shef S12 142 A3
Herdings Prim Sch. Shef 141 F2
Herdings Rd. Shef S12 142 A3
Herdings View. Shef S12 142 A3
Hereford Cl. Hem WF9 17 D8
Hereford Rd. Don DN2 63 B7
Hereford St. Shef S1 129 A1
Hereward Rd. Shef S5 113 C4
Hereward's Rd. Shef S14 141 D1
Hermes Cl. Bawtry DN10 122 F8
Hermit Hill La. Wort S30 74 E4
Hermit Hill. Wort S30 74 F6
Hermit La. Barn S75 32 F3
Hermitage St. Shef S3, S11 128 F1
Hermitage The. Thorne DN8 9 D3
Heron Hill. Aston S31 144 E6
Heron Mount. Shef S2 129 E2
Herons Way. Barn S70 75 F8
Herrick Gdns. Don DN4 83 C6
Herrick Rd. B Dun DN3 42 F8
Herries Ave. Shef S5 113 A3
Herries Dr. Shef S5 113 B2
Herries Pl. Shef S5 113 A2
Herries Rd S. Shef S6 112 D2
Herries Rd. Shef S5, S6 112 D2
Herries Sch. Shef 112 E2
Herril Ings. Tick DN11 121 B8
Herringthorpe Ave. Roth S65 116 B4
Herringthorpe Cl. Roth S65 116 B5
Herringthorpe Gr. Roth S65 116 C4
Herringthorpe Jun & Inf Sch.
Roth 116 B4
Herringthorpe La. Roth S65 116 C5
Herringthorpe Valley Rd.
Roth S60, S65 116 C6
Herriot Gr. Bir DN11 122 A4
Herschell Rd. Shef S7 140 F7
Hesketh Dr. Don DN3 43 A4
Hesley Bar. Roth S61 95 E4
Hesley Ct. Con DN12 80 F3 1
Hesley Gr. Chap S30 95 C4
Hesley Grange. Roth S61 96 C2
Hesley Hall Sch. Tick 103 F4
Hesley La. Roth S61 95 E4
Hesley Rd. Ross DN11 103 F8
Hesley Rd. Shef S5 113 D7
Hesley Terr. Shef S5 113 E7
Heslow Gr. Roth S61 95 E5
Hessey St. Shef S13 142 F6
Hessle Rd. Shef S6 112 B2

Hethersett Way. Ross DN11 103 E7
Hewitt Pl. Hart S31 157 E5
Hewitt St. Mex S64 80 D5
Hexthorpe Fst Sch. Don 62 A2
Hexthorpe Mid Sch. Don 62 A1
Hexthorpe Rd. Don DN4 62 B2
Hey Slack La. Wh Com HD7 28 C2
Heyhouse Dr. Chap S30 94 F7
Heyhouse Way. Chap S30 94 F7
Heysham Gn. Barn S71 34 D6
Heyworth La. Moss DN6 22 E8
Hibberd Pl. Shef S6 128 A8
Hibberd Rd. Shef S6 128 B8
Hibbert Terr. Barn S70 54 F7 3
Hickleton Ct. Dearne S63 58 C7
Hickleton Rd. Bnbur DN5 59 C4
Hickleton St. Con DN12 80 F3
Hickleton Terr. Dearne S63 58 E7
Hickmott Rd. Shef S11 140 D8
Hicks La. Shef S3 129 A4 5
Hicks St. Shef S3 129 A6
Hickson Dr. Barn S71 34 E4
Hides St. Shef S9 130 B8
High Alder Rd. Don DN4 84 C8
High Ash Ave. Clay W HD8 12 A2
High Ash Cl. Notton WF4 14 F7
High Ash Dr. S Anst S31 146 D3
High Bank La. Pen S30 50 E4
High Bridge Rd. Thorne DN8 26 F5
High Cl. Kex S75 13 D1
High Common La. Aust DN10 105 B6
High Common La. Tick DN11 121 F8
High Croft. Hoy S74 76 E5
High Ct. Shef S1 129 B4 4
High Field La. Aust DN10 105 B3
High Fisher Gate. Don DN1 62 D4
High Greave Ave. Shef S5 113 C7
High Greave Pl. Roth S65 116 C7
High Greave Rd. Roth S65 116 C8
High Greave Road Prim Sch. Roth 116 C8
High Green Jun & Inf Sch. Chap 94 D8
High Green Sch. Chap 94 E8
High Hazel Cres. Treet S60 131 C6
High Hazel Rd. Thorne DN8 9 D3
High Hazels Cl. Shef S9 130 D4
High Hazels Mead. Shef S9 130 D4
High Hooton Rd. Maltby S66 118 E1
High House Farm Ct. Wales S31 145 B2
High House Terr. Shef S6 128 D7
High Hoyland La. H Hoy S75 31 B8
High La. Eck S12 142 E1
High La. Ingb S30 50 E7
High La. Shef S12 154 F8
High La. Ulley S31 133 C3
High Lee La. Pen S30 52 A4
High Levels Bank. Thorne DN8 27 C1
High Matlock Ave. Shef S6 127 D6
High Matlock Rd. Shef S6 127 D6
High Meadow. Bawtry DN10 122 F7
High Nook Rd. Din S31 147 A8
High Pavement Row. Shef S2 129 C4
High Rd. Don DN4 82 C6
High Rd. Don DN4 83 A7
High Rd. N Edl DN12 82 B1
High Ridge. Barn S70 54 F5
High Royd Ave. Cud S72 35 B6
High Royd La. Pen S30 52 A5
High St. Ad l S DN6 40 C8
High St. Askern DN6 22 A7
High St. Aston S31 144 C7
High St. B Dun DN3 42 F7
High St. Barn S70 33 E1
High St. Barn S71 34 C4
High St. Barn S70 55 B5
High St. Bawtry DN10 123 A6
High St. Ben DN5 41 D2
High St. Ben DN5 62 B8
High St. Bnbur DN5 59 D3
High St. Braith S66 101 A2
High St. Clay W HD8 12 A1
High St. Con DN12 81 C2
High St. Dearne S63 58 C2
High St. Dearne S63 58 C7
High St. Dearne S63 58 E5
High St. Dod S75 53 F7
High St. Don DN1 62 D3
High St. Dron S18 153 A1
High St. Eck S31 155 D3
High St. G Hou S72 36 D2
High St. G Hou S72 57 F6
High St. Grime S72 36 A6
High St. Hat DN7 43 E4
High St. Hat DN7 44 D8
High St. Hoy S74 76 E6
High St. Kill S31 156 D6
High St. Laugh S31 134 D5
High St. Maltby S66 119 A5
High St. Mapp S75 14 A2
High St. Mex S64 80 A4
High St. Norton DN6 4 D3
High St. Norton DN6 21 C8
High St. Pen S30 51 D2
High St. Rawm S62 97 F5
High St. Roth S61 114 E7
High St. Roth S60 115 D6
High St. Roth S60 116 B1
High St. Roy S71 15 B3
High St. S Anst S31 146 D4
High St. S Elm WF9 19 A3
High St. S Hie S72 16 E5
High St. Shaf S72 16 C2
High St. Shef S3 129 B3
High St. Shef S19 144 A4
High St. Shef S17 151 D7
High St. Shef S19 155 D7
High St. Shef S30 113 B8
High St. Silk S75 53 A8
High St. Snaith DN14 1 A7
High St. Snaith DN14 1 C7
High St. Uns S18 154 A1
High St. Upton WF9 19 B7
High St. W up D S63 78 F6
High St. Wad DN11 102 B7
High St. Wombw S73 56 D3
High St. Wool WF4 14 A7
High St. Wroot DN9 67 A3
High Storrs Cl. Shef S11 140 A6
High Storrs Cres. Shef S11 140 A7
High Storrs Dr. Shef S11 140 A7
High Storrs Rd. Shef S11 139 F6
High Storrs Rise. Shef S11 140 A7
High Storrs Sch. Shef 139 F6
High Street La. Shef S2 129 C3 1
High Thorns. Silk S75 52 F8
High Trees. Roth S60 116 B3
High Trees. Shef S17 151 D7
High View Cl. Dar S73 57 B6
High View. Roy S71 15 B3
High Well Hill La. S Hie S72 16 C7
High Wray Cl. Shef S11 140 B4
Higham Common Rd. Barn S75 32 E3
Higham La. Dod S75 32 E1
Higham View. Kex S75 32 D7
Highbury Ave. Don DN4 84 E8
Highbury Cres. Don DN4 84 E8
Highbury Vale. N Edl DN12 82 A1
Highcliffe Ct. Swint S64 79 E3
Highcliffe Dr. Ought S30 111 D6
Highcliffe Dr. Shef S11 139 F7
Highcliffe Dr. Swint S64 79 D3
Highcliffe Pl. Shef S11 139 F6
Highcliffe Rd. Shef S11 139 F6
Highfield Ave. BarnS71 34 A6
Highfield Ave. Barn S70 54 F6
Highfield Ave. D Dale HD8 29 A4
Highfield Ave. Dearne S63 58 D5
Highfield Ave. Wales S31 145 E3
Highfield Bglws. W up D S63 78 F6
Highfield Ct. Shep HD8 28 E6
Highfield Ct. Swint S64 79 C3
Highfield Ctr. Hem WF9 17 D6
Highfield Gr. W up D S63 78 A7
Highfield La. T in B DN6 23 B4
Highfield La. Treet S13, S60 131 C3
Highfield Pk. Maltby S66 119 B6
Highfield Pl. Hem WF9 17 C6
Highfield Pl. Shef S2 141 A8
Highfield Range. Dar S73 57 A7
Highfield Rd. Askern DN6 22 B8
Highfield Rd. Bawtry DN10 123 B8
Highfield Rd. Con DN12 81 D2
Highfield Rd. Dar S73 57 A6
Highfield Rd. Don DN1 62 E4
Highfield Rd. Hem WF9 17 D6
Highfield Rd. Roth S61 97 C3
Highfield Rd. Swint S64 79 B3
Highfield Rise. Shef S6 127 C6
Highfield Sch. Shef 140 F8
Highfield View. Treet S60 131 C6
Highfield Villas. C in L S81 148 F8
Highfields Fst/Mid Sch. Ad le S 40 B2
Highfields. Pen S30 51 F6
Highfields Rd. Kex S75 32 B8
Highgate Cl. Ross DN11 104 A7
Highgate Ct. Dearne S63 58 C4
Highgate. Dar S73 57 B2
Highgate Greyhound Stad. Dearne 58 D6
Highgate Jun Mix & Inf Sch. Dearne 58 C5
Highgate La. Dearne S63 58 C4
Highgate. Shef S9 114 E2
Highgreave. Shef S5 113 C6
Highgrove Ct. Don DN4 85 A6
Highlow View. Brin S60 115 C1
Highmill Ave. Swint S64 79 B3
Highmoor Ave. Wales S31 145 C2
Highnam Crescent Rd. Shef S10 128 C3
Highroyds. Barn S70 54 F6
Highstone Ave. Barn S70 54 F7
Highstone Cres. Barn S70 54 E7
Highstone La. Barn S70 54 F6
Highstone Rd. Barn S70 54 F7
Highstone Vale. Barn S70 54 E7
Highthorn Rd. Swint S62 98 E8
Highton St. Shef S6 128 C6
Highwood Cl. Kex S75 32 C8
Highwood Pl. Eck S31 155 C3
Highwoods Cres. Mex S64 79 E5
Highwoods Inf Sch. Swint 79 E6
Highwoods Rd. Mex S64 79 E6
Hilary Way. Aston S31 144 D7
Hild Ave. Cud S72 35 D4
Hill Cl. Roth S65 116 E4
Hill Cl. Shef S6 127 C6
Hill Crest. Ad le S DN6 20 E1
Hill Crest. Hoy S74 76 C5
Hill Crest Rd. Chap S65 94 F5
Hill Crest Rd. Roth S65 116 B7
Hill End Rd. Mapp S75 33 C7
Hill Estate. Upton WF9 19 B7
Hill Farm Cl. Dearne S63 58 B7
Hill House Sch. Don 62 E4
Hill Park Gr. Dod S75 53 F8
Hill Rd. Har DN11 121 F4
Hill Side La. Pen S30 50 F2
Hill Side. Roth S60 116 C1
Hill St. Barn S71 55 E8
Hill St. Dar S73 57 A5
Hill St. Hoy S74 77 A5
Hill St. Shef S2 129 A1
Hill Top Ave. Barn S71 14 E1
Hill Top. Barn S71 33 F6
Hill Top. Caw S75 31 E5
Hill Top Cl. Brin S60 115 B1
Hill Top Cl. Roth S61 114 D6
Hill Top Cres. Don DN2 63 C7
Hill Top Cres. N Edl DN12 101 B8
Hill Top Cres. Shef S19 143 D2
Hill Top Ct. Har DN11 122 A4
Hill Top La. Barn S75 33 B3
Hill Top La. Roth S61 114 D6
Hill Top La. Roth S65 117 A6
Hill Top La. Shef S30 112 B8
Hill Top La. Stock S30 73 D3
Hill Top Rd. Barn S70 75 F8
Hill Top Rd. Con DN12 80 E2
Hill Top Rd. Shef S6 126 E7
Hill Top Rd. Shef S30 112 D8
Hill Top Rise. Shef S30 112 D8
Hill Top Sch. Maltby 118 D6
Hill Turrets Cl. Shef S11 139 F4
Hill View E. Roth S61 114 D8
Hill View Rd. Roth S61 114 D8
Hillary House. Don DN2 62 F6
Hillcote Cl. Shef S10 127 D1
Hillcote Dr. Shef S10 127 D1
Hillcote Mews. Shef S10 127 D1
Hillcote Rise. Shef S10 127 D1
Hillcrest. Dearne S63 58 C7
Hillcrest Dr. Ought S30 111 C6
Hillcrest Dr. S Anst S31 146 D4
Hillcrest Rd. Don DN2 63 A6
Hillcrest Rd. Stock S30 92 F8
Hillcrest Rise. Stock S30 92 F8
Hillfold. S Elm WF9 19 B3
Hillfoot Rd. Shef S3 128 E6
Hillfoot Rd. Shef S17 151 D5
Hills Cl. Ben DN5 61 E2
Hills Rd. Stock S30 73 D1
Hillsborough Barracks Bsns & Sh Ctr. Shef 128 D8
Hillsborough Ctr Sh Arcade. Shef 128 C8
Hillsborough Fst & Mid Schs. Shef 112 C2
Hillsborough Football Gd. Shef 112 C2
Hillsborough Golf Course. Shef 111 D3
Hillsborough Hall (Public Liby). Shef 112 C1
Hillsborough Pl. Shef S6 128 C8
Hillsborough Rd. Don DN4 84 E8
Hillsborough Rd. Shef S6 128 C8
Hillsborough Sacred Heart Prim Sch. Shef 128 C7
Hillscroft Rd. Blax DN9 86 E5
Hillside Ave. Dron S18 153 A1
Hillside Ave. ShefS5 113 B6
Hillside. Barn S71 56 A8
Hillside Cl. Pen S30 51 F6
Hillside Cres. Bri S72 17 A2
Hillside Ct. Roth S61 97 D1
Hillside Ct. S Elm WF9 19 A4
Hillside Ct. Sprot DN5 82 B8
Hillside. D Dale HD8 30 A6
Hillside Dr. Hoy S74 76 F5
Hillside Dr. N Edl DN12 82 A1
Hillside Gr. Bri S72 17 A2
Hillside Mount. Bri S72 17 A2
Hillside. N Anst S31 146 D6
Hillside Rd. Don DN2 63 C7
Hillside. Shef S19 155 C7
Hillside Way. Wort S30 74 D4
Hilltop. Bri S72 16 F3
Hilltop Cl. Maltby S66 118 D6
Hilltop Dr. Wharn S30 111 B8
Hilltop Est. S Kirk WF9 17 F1
Hilmian Way. Hem WF9 17 F5
Hilton Dr. Shef S30 113 B8
Hilton St. Askern DN6 22 A8
Hilton St. Barn S75 33 D2
Hind Rd. Roth S60 116 C2
Hindburn Cl. Don DN4 84 C7
Hinde House Comp Sch. Shef 113 F4
Hinde House Cres. Shef S4 113 E2
Hinde House Croft. Shef S4 113 E2
Hinde House La. Shef S4 113 E2
Hinde St. Shef S4 113 E1
Hindewood Cl. Shef S4 113 E2
Hindle St. Barn S70 33 D1
Hinds Cres. S Elm WF9 18 F3
Hirst Common La. Shef S6 112 B6
Hirst Dr. Roth S65 116 D7
Hirst Gate. Mex S64 80 C5
Hirst La. Holmfi HD7 28 B5
Hirst La. Ston S66 101 E1
HM Young Offender Inst. Hat 25 F1
Hoads Ave. Woods S81 147 E4
Hoar Stones Rd. Bfield S6 109 D3
Hob La. Wharn S30 92 E2
Hobart St. Shef S11 140 F8
Hobcroft Terr. Ad le S DN6 21 B1
Hobson Ave. Shef S6 128 E7
Hobson Pl. Shef S6 128 E7
Hodder Ct. Chap S30 94 F6
Hoddesdon Cres. Hat DN7 44 A5
Hodge La. K Smea WF8 3 E6
Hodgkinson Ave. Pen S30 51 D3
Hodgson St. Shef S3 128 F2
Hodroyd Cl. Shaf S72 16 D1
Hodroyd Cotts. Bri S72 16 F2
Hodster La. G Hou S72 36 D4
Hog Close La. Wh Com HD7 49 C8
Hoggarth Rise. Dron S18 152 F1 1
Holberry Cl. Shef S10 128 E2
Holberry Gdns. Shef S10 128 E2
Holbourne Gr. Chap S30 94 D8
Holbrook Ave. Shef S19 156 A8
Holbrook Dr. Shef S13 142 B6
Holbrook Gn. Shef S19 156 A8
Holbrook Rd. Shef S13 142 B7
Holbrook Rise. Shef S19 144 A1
Holburn Ave. Dron S18 153 A2
Holderness Cl. Har DN11 122 A4
Holderness Dr. Aston S31 144 D8
Holdings Rd. Shef S2 129 D1
Holdroyd's Yd. Dod S75 53 F6
Holdworth La. Shef S6 110 F4
Hole House La. Stock S30 73 B1
Holgate Ave. Shef S5 112 F6
Holgate Cl. Shef S5 112 F6
Holgate Cres. Hem WF9 17 C7
Holgate Cres. Shef S5 113 A6
Holgate Dr. Shef S5 113 A6
Holgate Gdns. Hem WF9 17 C7
Holgate Hospl. Hem 17 A6
Holgate Mount. Barn S70 54 F6
Holgate Rd. Shef S5 113 A6
Holgate Sch. Barn 33 D1
Holgate View. Bri S72 17 B3
Holgate. Wombw S73 56 B5
Holiwell Cl. Maltby S66 119 B6
Holkham Rise. Shef S11 139 F2
Holland Cl. Rawm S62 97 F7
Holland Pl. Shef S2 141 A8 8
Holland Rd. Chap S30 94 D7
Holland Rd. Shef S2 141 A8
Holland St. Shef S1 128 F3
Hollin Bridge La. Hat DN7 45 A5
Hollin Busk La. Stock S30 92 C7
Hollin Busk Rd. Stock S30 92 C8
Hollin Cl. Ross DN11 85 B2
Hollin Croft. Dod S75 54 A8
Hollin Edge. D Dale HD8 30 A6
Hollin Edge La. Stock S30 92 F5
Hollin Hill La. Roth S66 116 F4
Hollin House La. Clay W HD8 31 A8
Hollin House La. Holmfi HD7 28 A5
Hollin House La. Shef S6 110 F3
Hollin La. Wh Con S30 50 A4
Hollin Moor La. Roth S66 117 A4
Hollin Moor La. Thurgo S30 53 B1
Hollin Rd. Ought S30 111 C6
Hollinberry La. Wort S30 75 B1
Hollindale Dr. Shef S12 142 C5
Holling Croft. Stock S30 73 E1
Holling's La. Roth S65 117 C8
Hollins Cl. Shef S6 127 F5
Hollins Ct. Shef S6 127 F6
Hollins Dr. Shef S6 128 A5
Hollins La. Shef S6 128 A6
Hollins Mount. Hem WF9 17 C7
Hollins The. Dod S75 54 A6
Hollinsend Ave. Shef S12 142 C5
Hollinsend Pl. Shef S12 142 C5
Hollinsend Rd. Shef S12 142 B5
Hollis Cl. Rawm S62 97 D8
Hollis Croft. Shef S1 128 F4
Hollis Croft. Shef S13 143 A6
Hollis Hospl. Shef 139 E2
Hollow Gate. Cade DN5 81 C5
Hollow Gate. Chap S30 94 D5
Hollow Gate. Roth S60 116 B1 2
Hollow La. Shef S19 155 D6
Hollow La. Shef S19 155 E6
Hollowdene. Barn S75 33 C3
Hollowgate Ave. W up D S63 78 C8
Hollowgate. Bnbur DN5 59 C2
Hollowgate. Roth S60 115 E5
Hollows The. Auck DN9 86 A6
Hollows The. Don DN4 84 E6
Holly Ave. Ben DN5 62 A7
Holly Cl. Chap S30 94 F4
Holly Cl. Kill S31 156 C5
Holly Cres. Roth S66 117 C6
Holly Croft Gr. Tick DN11 121 B7
Holly Ct. Har DN11 121 E4
Holly Dene. Arm DN3 64 B8
Holly Dr. Ben DN5 41 B2
Holly Gdns. Shef S12 142 C6
Holly Gr. Bri S72 17 A3
Holly Gr. Ross DN11 85 A2
Holly Gr. W up D S63 78 F4
Holly Hall La. Stock S30 74 A3
Holly La. Shef S1 129 A3 4
Holly Mount. Roth S66 117 C4
Holly Rd. Finn DN9 86 A4
Holly Rd. Thorne DN8 9 C2
Holly St. Don DN1 62 C1
Holly St. Hem WF9 17 D7
Holly St. Shef S1 129 A3
Holly Terr. Aston S31 144 C8
Holly Terr. Don DN4 82 F7
Holly Wlk. Thorne DN8 9 C2
Holly's House Rd. Roth S65 99 F1
Hollybank Ave. D Dale HD8 29 C6
Hollybank Ave. Shef S12 142 C6
Hollybank Cl. Shef S12 142 D6
Hollybank Cres. Shef S12 142 C6
Hollybank Dr. Shef S12 142 D6
Hollybank Rd. Shef S12 142 C6
Hollybank Way. Shef S12 142 D6
Hollybush St. Rawm S62 97 F3
Hollycroft Ave. Roy S71 15 B3
Hollygate. Barn S70 55 B5
Hollythorpe Cres. Shef S8 141 A4
Hollythorpe Rd. Shef S8 141 B4
Hollytree Ave. Maltby S66 118 D6
Hollywell Cl. Rawm S62 98 B7
Holm Cl. Dron S18 152 D2
Holm Flatt St. Rawm S62 97 E3
Holme Cl. Shef S6 128 C8
Holme Ct. Dearne S63 58 C4
Holme Fleet La. K Bram DN3 23 D2
Holme Gdns. Stai DN7 24 F5
Holme Hall La. Ston S66 119 E8
Holme La. Askern DN5 22 B2
Holme La. Shef S6 128 B7
Holme La. Shef S6 112 D7
Holme Oak Way. Shef S6 127 C7
Holme Styes La. Holme HD7 48 A8
Holme View Rd. Kex S75 32 B8
Holme Way. Shef S6 128 B7
Holme Wood Gdns. Don DN4 84 E7
Holme Wood La. Arm DN3 64 E6
Holmefield Cl. Arm DN3 64 C5
Holmefield Croft. Scro DN10 123 A2
Holmeroyd Rd. Ad l S DN6 40 E7
Holmes Carr Cres. Ross DN11 84 D1
Holmes Carr Rd. Don DN4 84 D6
Holmes Carr Rd. Ross DN11 84 D1
Holmes Cres. Treet S60 131 E4
Holmes La. H Rob S65 99 C7
Holmes La. Roth S61 115 B6
Holmes Market The. Don DN1 62 D4
Holmes Rd. Roth S66 117 D4
Holmes The. Don DN1 62 D4
Holmesdale Cl. Dron S18 153 C3
Holmesdale Inf Sch. Dron 153 C2
Holmesdale Rd. Dron S18 153 C3
Holmesfield Rd. Dron S18 152 B1
Holmesfield Rd. Ought S30 111 D7
Holmhirst Cl. Shef S8 140 E2
Holmhirst Dr. Shef S8 140 E3
Holmhirst Rd. Shef S8 140 F2
Holmhirst Way. Shef S8 140 E3
Holmley Bank. Dron S18 153 A3
Holmley La. Dron S18 152 F3
Holmley La. Dron S18 153 A3
Holmoak Cl. Swint S64 79 D1
Holmshaw Dr. Shef S13 142 E8
Holmshaw Gr. Shef S13 142 E8
Holmsley Ave. S Kirk WF9 18 A2
Holmsley Gr. S Kirk WF9 18 A2
Holmsley La. S Kirk WF9 17 F2
Holmsley Mount. S Kirk WF9 18 A2
Holt House Inf Sch. Shef 140 D4
Holtwood Rd. Shef S4 129 B7
Holwick Cl. Silk S75 52 F8
Holwick Ct. Barn S70 33 E1 2
Holy Cross Deanery C of E Prim Sch. Barn 34 B6
Holy Family Prim Sch. Stai 24 F5
Holy Rood RC Prim Sch. Barn 33 D1
Holyoake Ave. Shef S13 142 E8
Holyrood Rd. Don DN2 63 A3
Holyrood Rise. Roth S66 117 D6
Holywell Cres. Braith S66 101 A1
Holywell La. Braith S66 101 A1
Holywell La. Con DN12 81 C1
Holywell Pl. Roth S65 115 E7 7
Holywell Rd. Shef S4, S9 114 A2
Holywell Rd. Swint S64 79 D1
Home Farm Ct. H Pag DN5 38 D5
Home Farm Ct. Hick DN5 59 C7
Home Farm Ct. Wort S30 74 D4
Home Meadows. Tick DN11 121 A6
Homecroft Rd. Dearne S63 58 D5
Homefield Cres. Ben DN5 61 E8
Homestead Cl. Shef S5 113 D5
Homestead Dr. Brin S60 115 B1
Homestead Dr. Rawm S62 97 F7
Homestead Garth. Hat DN7 44 B8
Homestead Rd. Shef S5 113 D5
Homestead The. Ben DN5 41 B1
Honey Lands La. Askern DN5 22 D2
Honeysuckle Ct. Finn DN9 86 E3
Honeysuckle Rd. Shef S5 113 F3
Honeywell Cl. Barn S71 33 F3
Honeywell Gr. Barn S71 33 F4
Honeywell La. Barn S71, S75 33 E3
Honeywell Pl. Barn S71 33 F3
Honeywell St. Barn S71 33 F3
Honister Cl. W up D S63 78 A7
Hoober Ave. Shef S11 140 A5
Hoober Ct. Rawm S62 97 D8
Hoober Field. W up D S62 78 B2
Hoober Hall La. W up D S62 78 B3
Hoober La. Went S62 78 B1
Hoober Rd. Shef S11 140 A5
Hoober St. W up D S63 78 B7
Hoober View. Rawm S62 97 D8
Hoober View. Wombw S73 56 F1
Hood Green Rd. Hd Gr S75 53 E2
Hood St. S Elm WF9 18 E1
Hoole La. Shef S10 128 C2
Hoole Rd. Shef S10 128 C3
Hoole St. Shef S6 128 D6
Hooton Cl. Laugh S31 134 E5
Hooton La. Laugh S31 134 E6
Hooton La. Maltby S66 118 E4
Hooton La. Roth S65 99 C3
Hooton Pagnell C of E Fst & Mid Sch. H Pag 38 C5
Hooton Rd. Swint S62 98 F7
Hop Hills. Hat DN7 25 A1
Hop Hills La. Hat DN7 25 A1
Hop Inge The. Hart S31 157 F5
Hope Ave. Dearne S63 58 D5
Hope Rd. Ought S30 111 E6
Hope St. Barn S75 33 D2
Hope St. Barn S71 34 F6
Hope St. Dar S73 56 F4
Hope St. Mapp S75 33 C8
Hope St. Mex S64 80 A4
Hope St. Roth S60 115 C7
Hope St. Ryhill WF4 16 C8
Hope St. Shef S3 128 E4
Hope St. Stock S30 73 C1
Hope St. Wombw S73 56 E2
Hope Street Extension. Roth S60 115 C7
Hopedale Rd. Shef S12 142 D4
Hopefield Ave. Shef S12 142 D4
Hopewell St. Barn S70 55 D8
Hopping La. Thurgo S30 52 F1
Hopwood La. Shef S6 127 B4
Hopwood St. Barn S70 33 E2
Hopyard La. Tick DN11 103 C1
Horace St. Roth S60 115 E5
Horbiry End. Tod S31 145 E5
Horbury La. Chap S30 94 E4
Horbury Rd. Cud S72 35 B8
Hordron Rd. Lang S30 70 C5
Horn Cote La. Holmfi HD7 28 A6
Horn Croft. Caw S75 31 F5
Horn La. Holmfi HD7 28 A6
Horn La. Ingb S30 29 B1
Hornbeam Cl. Chap S30 94 F4
Hornbeam Rd. Roth S66 117 B6
Hornby Ct. Shef S11 140 A7
Hornby St. Barn S70 55 A7
Horndean Rd. Shef S5 113 D1
Horner Cl. Stock S30 73 B2
Horner Rd. Shef S7 141 A7 1
Hornes La. Mapp S75 14 C1
Horninglow Cl. Don DN4 85 A7
Horninglow Cl. Shef S5 113 C3
Horninglow Rd. Shef S5 113 D3
Hornsby Rd. Arm DN3 64 C5
Hornthorpe Rd. Eck S31 155 C2
Hornthwaite Hill Rd. Pen S30 51 A3
Horse Carr View. Barn S71 56 A8
Horse Croft La. Wharn S30 111 B8
Horse Fair Gn. Thorne DN8 26 B7
Horsehills La. Arm DN3 64 A5
Horsemoor Rd. Dearne S63 58 B8
Horseshoe Cl. Wales S31 145 C3
Horsewood Cl. Barn S70 54 B8
Horsewood Rd. Shef S13 143 D8
Horton Cl. Shef S19 155 E7
Horton Dr. Shef S19 155 E7
Hough La. Wombw S73 56 C2
Houghton Rd. Dearne S63 58 B8
Houghton Rd. N Anst S31 146 B8
Hound Hill La. Barn S75,S70 54 D5
Hound Hill La. Mex S63 79 D8
Houndkirk Rd. Shef S11 138 F2
Hounsfield Cres. Roth S65 116 D7
Hounsfield La. Shef S10 128 E3
Hounsfield Rd. Roth S65 116 D7
Hounsfield Rd. Shef S3 128 E3
Houps Rd. Thorne DN8 26 C7
House Carr La. Hd Gr S75 53 C4
Housley La. Chap S30 94 F5
Housley Pk. Chap S30 95 A6
Houstead Rd. Shef S9 130 D3
Howard La. Shef S2 129 B2
Howard Rd. Bir DN11 122 C4
Howard Rd. Maltby S66 119 B5
Howard Rd. Roth S66 117 E6
Howard Rd. Shef S6 128 D5
Howard St. Barn S70 54 F7 7
Howard St. Dar S73 57 C5
Howard St. Din S31 135 A1
Howard St. Roth S60, S65 115 E6
Howard St. Shef S1 129 B2
Howards Cl. Thurcr S66 134 A6
Howarth Rd. Brin S60 131 D7
Howbeck Dr. N Edl DN12 82 A1
Howbrook Cl. Chap S30 94 C8
Howden Ave. Ad le S DN6 20 E1
Howden Cl. Don DN4 84 C6

Howden Cl. Mapp S75 13 F1
Howden Rd. Shef S9 130 A7
Howdike La. H Rob DN12 99 B7
Howe La. Thurcr S31 134 E8
Howell La. G Hou S72 36 F5
Howell Wood Ctry Pk. G Hou 36 F7
Howell Wood Ctry Pk. S Kirk 37 A7
Howlett Cl. Roth S60 116 D1
Howlett Dr. Brin S60 131 C7
Howse St. Hoy S74 77 B6
Howson Cl. Roth S65 117 E8
Howson Rd. Stock S30 73 D1
Howville Ave. Hat DN7 44 E6
Howville Rd. Hat DN7 44 E6
Hoylake Dr. Swint S64 79 D2
Hoyland Cl. Pen S30 50 D3
Hoyland Common Inf Sch. Hoy 76 B5
Hoyland Common Jun Sch. Hoy 76 A5
Hoyland Greenfield Prim Sch. Hoy 76 F6
Hoyland Market St Jun & Inf Sch. Hoy 76 E7
Hoyland Rd. Hoy S74 76 B5
Hoyland Rd. Shef S3 128 E7
Hoyland St. Maltby S66 119 B4
Hoyland St. Wombw S73 56 D2
Hoyland Terr. S Kirk WF9 18 A2
Hoylandswaine Prim Sch. Pen 52 A7
Hoyle Croft La. Braith S66 100 F1
Hoyle Mill Rd. Barn S70 55 D8
Hoyle St. Shef S3 128 F5
Hucklow Dr. Shef S5 113 D3
Hucklow Fst & Mid Sch. Shef 113 C2
Hucklow Rd. Shef S5 113 D3
Huddersfield Rd. Barn S70, S75 33 D3
Huddersfield Rd. Ingb S30 50 F8
Huddersfield Rd. Pen S30 51 C5
Huddersfield Rd. W Bret WF4 13 A6
Hudson Ave. Notton WF4 15 B6
Hudson Cl. Hart S31 157 E7
Hudson Rd. Roth S61 96 E2
Hudson Rd. Shef S13 143 E8
Huggin Carr Rd. Hat DN7 44 F1
Hugh Hill La. Stai DN7 25 B4
Humber Cl. Ad le S DN6 21 A1
Humberside Way. Barn S71 34 D6
Humphrey Rd. Shef S8 152 E8
Humphries Ave. Rawm S62 97 D7
Hund Oak Dr. Hat DN7 44 B8
Hunger Hill La. Roth S60 116 C1
Hunger Hill Rd. Roth S60 116 C1
Hungerhill Cl. Roth S61 114 D8
Hungerhill La. Don DN3 42 E2
Hungerhill Rd. Roth S61 96 D1
Hungerhill Sch. Don 42 E2
Hungry La. Hath S30 149 B8
Hunningley Cl. Barn S70 55 E7
Hunningley Jun Sch. Barn 55 D7
Hunningley La. Barn S70 55 E7
Hunsdon Rd. Eck S31 155 C3
Hunshelf Hall La. Stock S30 73 B4
Hunshelf La. Chap S30 95 B2
Hunshelf Pk. Stock S30 73 C2
Hunshelf Rd. Chap S30 95 A5
Hunshelf Rd. Stock S30 73 A3
Hunshelf Rd. Stock S30 73 C2
Hunsley St. Shef S4 129 E8
Hunster Cl. Don DN4 84 F7
Hunster Gr. Ross DN11 103 F8
Hunstone Ave. Shef S8 153 A7
Hunt Cl. Barn S71 34 C4
Hunt La. Ben DN5 62 B5
Hunt St. Hoy S74 76 B5
Hunter Ct. Shef S11 140 B7
Hunter Hill Rd. Shef S11 140 C8
Hunter House Rd. Shef S11 140 C8
Hunter Rd. Shef S6 128 B8
Hunter's Ave. Barn S70 54 A8
Hunter's Bar. Shef S11 140 C8 4
Hunter's La. Shef S13 142 C6
Hunters Bar First & Middle Schs. Shef 140 C8
Hunters Chase. Din S31 134 F3
Hunters Cl. Din S31 134 F3
Hunters Ct. Din S31 134 F3
Hunters Dr. Din S31 134 F3
Hunters Gdns. Din S31 134 F3
Hunters Gdns. Shef S6 111 D1
Hunters Gn. Din S31 134 F3
Hunters Pk. Din S31 134 F3
Hunters Rise. Barn S75 33 B1
Hunters Way. Din S31 134 F3
Huntingdon Cres. Shef S11 140 E8
Huntingdon Rd. Don DN2 63 C6
Huntington St. Ben DN5 41 B2
Huntington Way. Maltby S66 118 E7
Huntingtower Rd. Shef S11 140 B7
Huntley Gr. Shef S11 139 F6
Huntley Rd. Shef S11 140 A6
Huntsman Rd. Shef S9 130 D4
Hurl Dr. Shef S12 141 F5
Hurley Croft. W up D S63 78 A7
Hurlfield Campus. Shef 141 F6
Hurlfield Ct. Shef S12 142 A6
Hurlfield Dr. Roth S65 117 D7
Hurlfield Dr. Shef S12 141 F6
Hurlfield Rd. Shef S12 141 F5
Hurlingham Cl. Shef S11 140 C5
Hursley Cl. Shef S19 144 A1 4
Hursley Dr. Shef S19 144 A1
Hurst Gn. Chap S30 94 D7
Hurst La. Auck DN9 86 A5
Hurst La. Finn DN9 85 F3
Hushells La. Fish DN7 7 F3
Huskar Cl. Silk S75 52 F8
Hut La. Kill S31 156 F4
Hutchinson La. Shef S7 140 D3
Hutchinson Rd. Rawm S62 98 A6
Hutchinson Rd. Shef S7 140 D3
Hutcliffe Dr. Shef S8 140 D2
Hutcliffe Wood Rd. Shef S8 140 D2
Huthwaite La. Thurgo S30 73 F5
Hutton Croft. Shef S12 143 B3
Hutton Dr. S Elm WF9 19 A4
Hutton Rd. Roth S61 96 F1
Hyacinth Cl. Shef S5 113 F3
Hyacinth Rd. Shef S5 113 F3
Hyde Park Fst Sch. Don 63 A1
Hyde Park Terr. Shef S2 129 C3
Hyde Park Wlk. Shef S2 129 C3
Hyland Cres. Don DN4 82 D6
Hyman Cl. Don DN4 82 D7
Hyman Walk. S Elm WF9 19 A4
Hyperion Way. Ross DN11 103 E8

Ibberson Ave. Mapp S75 33 B8
Ibbotson Rd. Shef S6 128 C6
Ibsen Cres. B Dun DN3 42 F8
Ickles Way. Brin S60 115 B3
Icknield Way. Brin S60 131 C8
Ida's Rd. Eck S31 155 D4
Idle Bank. Epw DN9 67 E4
Idle Bank. Wroot DN9 67 E4
Idle Ct. Bawtry DN10 123 A7
Idsworth Rd. Shef S5 113 D2
Ilkley Cres. Aston S31 144 C6
Ilkley Rd. Shef S5 113 D4
Illsley Rd. Dar S73 57 A6
Immaculate Conception Prim Sch. Eck 156 C2
Imperial Bldgs. Roth S60 115 D6
Imperial Cres. Don DN2 62 F4
Industry Rd. Roy S71 34 C7
Industry Rd. Shef S9 130 C5
Industry St. Shef S6 128 D6
Infield La. Shef S9 130 D4
Infirmary Rd. Rawm S62 98 A3
Infirmary Rd. Shef S6 128 E5
Ingbirchworth La. Ingb S30 50 E7
Ingbirchworth Rd. Pen S30 51 A4
Ingelow Ave. Shef S5 113 B5
Ingfield Ave. Shef S9 114 E2
Ingham Bglws. C in L S81 148 F8
Ingham Rd. Bawtry DN10 122 F8
Ingle Gr. Ben DN5 61 E2
Ingleborough Croft. Chap S30 94 F6
Ingleborough Dr. Ben DN5 61 E2
Ingleby Cl. Dron S18 152 C1
Ingledene Mews. B Dun DN3 42 F7
Inglenook Dr. Thorne DN8 26 C8
Ingleton Wlk. Barn S70 33 D2 4
Inglewood Ave. Shef S19 144 A1
Inglewood Ct. Shef S19 144 A1 5
Inglewood Dell. Shef S19 144 A1 6
Inglewood. Mapp S75 14 A1
Ingram Cres. Hat DN7 43 F7
Ingram Ct. Shef S2 129 D2
Ingram Gr. Hat DN7 43 F7
Ingram Rd. Hat DN7 43 F6
Ingram Rd. Shef S2 129 D2
Ings Cl. S Kirk WF9 18 D3
Ings Holt. S Kirk WF9 18 D4
Ings La. Ad l S DN6 40 A8
Ings La. Ben DN5 42 A2
Ings La. Ben DN5 42 A2
Ings La. Ben DN5 61 E1
Ings La. G Hou S72 57 C8
Ings La. K Bram DN7 24 E6
Ings Rd. Ben DN5 62 C6
Ings Rd. Cade DN5 81 D6
Ings Rd. Dar S73 57 B3
Ings Way. Ben DN5 41 D2
Ings Way. Ingb S30 29 D1
Ings Wlk. S Kirk WF9 18 D3
Ingsfield La. Dearne S63 58 B2
Ingshead Ave. Rawm S62 98 A5
Ingshead House. Rawm S62 97 F5
Ingswell Ave. Notton WF4 15 A7
Ingswell Dr. Notton WF4 14 F7
Inkerman Ct. D Dale HD8 30 A6
Inkerman Rd. Dar S73 57 A5
Inkerman Way. D Dale HD8 29 F5
Inkersall Dr. Shef S19 155 E8
Innovation Way. Barn S75 33 C4
Insley Gdns. Don DN4 84 E7
Instone Terr. Askern DN6 21 F7
Intake Cres. Dod S75 53 F5
Intake First & Mid Sch. Shef 142 C6
Intake La. Barn S75 33 B2
Intake La. Cud S72 35 B8
Intake La. Wool WF4 13 E8
Intake Prim Sch. Don 63 B4
Inverness Rd. Hat DN7 44 A8
Ironside Cl. Shef S14 141 D3
Ironside Pl. Shef S14 141 E3
Ironside Rd. Shef S14 141 E3
Ironside Wlk. Shef S14 141 D2
Irving St. Shef S9 130 C4
Irwell Gdns. Don DN4 63 D2
Islay St. Shef S10 128 B3
Issott St. Barn S71 33 F3
Ivan Brook Cl. Dron S18 152 C1 4
Ivanhoe Ave. Wales S31 145 E3
Ivanhoe Cl. Ben DN5 61 F4
Ivanhoe Mews. Aston S31 144 C8
Ivanhoe Rd. Con DN12 81 B2
Ivanhoe Rd. Don DN3 42 F1
Ivanhoe Rd. Don DN4 82 E6
Ivanhoe Rd. N Edl DN12 82 B1
Ivanhoe Rd. Shef S6 128 A6
Ivanhoe Rd. Thurcr S66 133 E5
Ivanhoe Way. Ben DN5 61 F4
Ivatt Cl. Bawtry DN10 123 A8
Ivor Gr. Don DN4 83 A8
Ivy Cl. Hat DN7 44 C8
Ivy Cl. Ross DN11 85 A2
Ivy Cottage La. Shef S10, S11 139 D6
Ivy Cotts. Roy S71 15 D4
Ivy Cotts. Shef S11 139 E7
Ivy Ct. Shef S8 141 C2
Ivy Farm Cl. Roy S71 15 D1
Ivy Farm Croft. Roth S65 98 D1
Ivy Gr. Shef S10 128 D4
Ivy Hall Rd. Shef S5 113 E7
Ivy House Ct. Auck DN9 85 F7
Ivy La. Shef S19 144 A4
Ivy La. Snaith DN14 1 A7
Ivy Lodge La. Let S81 136 B3
Ivy Park Ct. Shef S10 127 E2
Ivy Park Rd. Shef S10 127 E1
Ivy Rd. Thorne DN8 9 B1
Ivy Terr. Barn S70 55 A8 4
Ivy Terr. S Elm WF9 19 A3
Ivyside Cl. Kill S31 156 D6
Ivyside Gdns. Kill S31 156 D6

Jack Close Orch. Roy S71 15 C4
Jack La. Wharn S30 92 C4
Jack Row La. K Bram DN7 24 C7
Jackey La. Ought S30 111 B7
Jackson Cres. Rawm S62 97 E7
Jackson House. Hem WF9 17 D6
Jackson St. Cud S72 35 A6
Jackson St. Dearne S63 58 E5
Jackys La. Hart S31 157 E6
Jacobs Cl. Shef S5 113 E4
Jacobs Dr. Shef S5 113 F4
Jacobs Hall Ct. Kex S75 32 C8
Jacques Pl. Barn S71 34 D2
Jamaica St. Shef S4 129 C7
James Andrew Cl. Shef S8 152 F7
James Andrew Cres. Shef S8 152 E7
James Andrew Croft. Shef S8 152 F7
James Ct. Thorne DN8 9 C1
James St. Barn S71 33 F2
James St. Barn S70 55 C5
James St. Mex S64 80 D5
James St. Roth S60 115 C7
James St. S Hie S72 16 F6
James St. Shef S9 130 C3
Janet's Wlk. Wombw S73 56 B4
Janson St. Shef S9 130 A8
Jardine Cl. Shef S9 114 B4
Jardine St. Shef S9 114 B4
Jardine St. Wombw S73 56 D2
Jarratt St. Don DN1 62 D2
Jarrow Rd. Shef S11 140 D8
Jasmine Ave. Shef S19 143 F3
Jasmine Cl. Con DN12 81 D1
Jaunty Ave. Shef S12 142 C4
Jaunty Cl. Shef S12 142 B3
Jaunty Cres. Shef S12 142 C4
Jaunty Dr. Shef S12 142 B3
Jaunty La. Shef S12 142 B4
Jaunty Mount. Shef S12 142 C3
Jaunty Pl. Shef S12 142 B3
Jaunty Rd. Shef S12 142 C3
Jaunty View. Shef S12 142 C3
Jaunty Way. Shef S12 142 B4
Jay La. Aston S31 144 E6
Jebb La. Caw S75 12 E3
Jebb La. H Hoy S75 12 F3
Jedburgh Dr. Shef S9 114 A4
Jedburgh St. Shef S9 114 B4
Jeffcock Rd. Chap S30 94 E7
Jeffcock Rd. Shef S9 130 C4
Jefferson Ave. Don DN2 42 D1
Jeffery Cres. Stock S30 92 D8
Jeffery St. Shef S2 141 B6 4
Jenkin Ave. Shef S9 114 A2
Jenkin Cl. Shef S9 114 A3
Jenkin Dr. Shef S9 114 A2
Jenkin Rd. Shef S5, S9 114 A3
Jenkyn La. Shep HD8 28 D8
Jepson Rd. Shef S5 113 F4
Jericho St. Shef S3 128 F4
Jermyn Ave. Shef S12 142 F4
Jermyn Cl. Shef S12 142 F3
Jermyn Cres. Shef S12 142 F4
Jermyn Croft. Dod S75 53 F7
Jermyn Dr. Shef S12 142 F3
Jermyn Way. Shef S12 142 F3
Jersey Rd. Shef S2 141 A7
Jesmond Ave. Roy S71 15 C3
Jessamine Rd. Shef S5 113 E4
Jessell St. Shef S9 129 F5
Jessop Hospl. Shef 128 F3
Jessop St. Shef S1 129 A2
Jewitt Rd. Roth S61 96 E2
Joan Croft La. Ad le S DN5 22 E1
Joan La. Maltby S66 118 E4
Joan Royd La. Pen S30 72 C8
Joan's Wlk. Hoy S74 76 F7
Jobson Pl. Shef S3 128 F5 4
Jobson Rd. Shef S3 128 F5
Jockel Dr. Rawm S62 97 F5
Jockey Rd. Oxspr S30 52 C2
John Calvert Rd. Shef S13 143 D6
John Eaton's Almshouses. Shef S8 141 B2
John La. Ross DN11 84 E1
John St. Ad l S DN6 40 C6
John St. Barn S70 54 F8
John St. Barn S70 55 A4
John St. Dearne S63 58 D8
John St. Eck S31 155 D3
John St. G Hou S72 36 F1
John St. G Hou S72 57 E7
John St. Mex S64 80 A4
John St. Roth S60 115 C6
John St. S Elm WF9 18 F2
John St. Shef S2 129 A1
John St. Thurcr S66 133 E7
John St. Wombw S73 56 C3
John Trickett House. Chap S30 94 F5
John Ward St. Shef S13 143 D7
John West St. Stock S30 92 B8
Johnny Moor Long La. Rawcl DN8 2 C4
Johnson Ct. N Edl DN12 82 C3
Johnson Ct. Roth S65 115 F5
Johnson La. Shef S3 129 B5
Johnson La. Shef S30 95 B1
Johnson St. Barn S75 33 D2
Johnson St. Shef S3 129 B5
Johnson St. Stock S30 73 B1
Johnston's Rd. Stai DN8 25 C5
Joiner St. Shef S3 129 B4 7
Jones Ave. Wombw S73 56 B3
Jons Ave. S Kirk WF9 18 A2
Jordan Cres. Roth S61 114 E5
Jordanthorpe Gn. Shef S8 153 C6
Jordanthorpe Parkway. Dron S8 153 A5
Jordanthorpe Parkway. Shef S8 153 C6
Jordanthorpe Sch. Shef 153 B6
Jordanthorpe Sch. Shef 153 A7
Jos La. Shep HD8 28 E8
Jos Way. Shep HD8 28 E8
Joseph Ct. Barn S70 54 F8 12
Joseph La. Midhop S30 71 C4
Joseph Rd. Shef S6 128 C5
Joseph St. Barn S70 54 F8
Joseph St. Eck S31 155 D3
Joseph St. Grime S72 36 A6
Joseph St. Roth S60 115 C7
Josephine Rd. Roth S61 115 A6
Joshua Rd. Shef S7 140 E6
Josselin Ct. Chap S30 94 F5
Jossey La. Ben DN5 40 E1
Jowett House La. Caw S75 31 B4
Jowitt Cl. Maltby S66 119 B4
Jowitt Rd. Shef S11 140 C6
Jubb Cl. Roth S65 116 D4
Jubilee Cl. Hem WF9 17 F6
Jubilee Cotts. Brin S60 115 B1
Jubilee Cotts. Hoy S74 76 A5
Jubilee Cres. Kill S31 156 E7
Jubilee Ct. Don DN2 63 C6
Jubilee Rd. Don DN1 62 E5
Jubilee Rd. Shef S9 130 C6
Jubilee St. Roth S60 115 D4
Jubilee Terr. Barn S70 55 B8 1
Judd Field La. Lang S30 72 B6
Judith Rd. Aston S31 144 D6
Judy Row. Barn S71 34 C4
Judy St. Stock S30 92 C6
Julian Rd. Shef S9 114 B3
Julian Way. Shef S9 114 B3
Jumble La. Shef S30 95 E2
Jumble Rd. Shef S11 138 F1
Junction Cl. Wombw S73 57 A1
Junction Rd. Ross DN11 103 E8
Junction Rd. Shef S11 140 C8
Junction Rd. Shef S13 143 E7
Junction Rd. Stai DN7 24 E4
Junction St. Barn S70 55 B8
Junction St. Wombw S73 56 F1
Junction Terr. Barn S70 55 B8 4
June Rd. Shef S13 143 D7
Juniper Rise. Kill S31 156 C5

Kashmir Gdns. Shef S9 130 B5
Katherine Rd. Thurcr S66 133 E7
Katherine St. Thurcr S66 133 F6
Kathleen Gr. Dearne S63 58 F6
Kathleen St. Dearne S63 58 F6
Kay Cres. Rawm S62 97 C8
Kay St. Hoy S74 76 B5
Kay's Terr. Barn S70 55 E7
Kaye Pl. Shef S6 128 D4
Kaye St. Barn S71 33 F2 1
Kearsley La. Con DN12 100 C8
Kearsley Rd. Shef S2 141 A8
Keats Dr. Din S31 147 B8
Keats Gr. Pen S30 51 D4
Keats Rd. Don DN4 83 B6
Keats Rd. Shef S6 112 D6
Keble Martin Way. W up D S63 78 D6
Keenan Ave. S Elm WF9 18 E1
Keeper La. Notton WF4 14 D5
Keepers Cl. Ross DN11 85 B1
Keeton Hall Rd. Wales S31 145 F3
Keeton's Hill. Shef S2 140 F8 1
Keir Pl. Rawm S62 98 B6
Keir St. Barn S70 33 D2
Keir St Jun Sch. Barn 33 D2
Keir Terr. Barn S70 33 D2
Kelford Sch. Roth 114 F6
Kelham Island. Shef S3 129 A5
Kelham St. Don DN1 62 C1
Kelly St. Dearne S63 58 E5
Kelsey Gdns. Don DN4 84 E5
Kelsey Terr. Barn S70 54 F7 2
Kelso Dr. Don DN4 82 D7
Kelvin Gr. Wombw S73 56 E2
Kelvin St. Mex S64 80 A5
Kelvin St. Roth S65 98 D1
Kelvin Wlk. Shef S6 128 E6 4
Kempton Gdns. Mex S64 80 C6
Kempton Park Rd. Ben DN5 61 D5
Kempton St. Don DN4 63 D2
Kempwell Dr. Rawm S62 97 F8
Kenbourne Gr. Shef S7 140 E7
Kenbourne Rd. Shef S7 140 E7
Kendal Ave. N Anst S31 146 F6
Kendal Cl. Sprot DN5 61 A1
Kendal Cres. Barn S70 55 A3
Kendal Cres. Con DN12 81 D2
Kendal Dr. Dearne S63 58 C1
Kendal Dr. Dron S18 152 E1
Kendal Gr. Barn S71 56 A8
Kendal Green Rd. Barn S70 54 E4
Kendal Rd. Ben DN5 62 A7
Kendal Rd. Shef S6 128 B8
Kendon Gdns. Thorne DN8 26 C8
Kendray Hospl. Barn 55 C8
Kendray Inf Sch. Barn 55 B7
Kendray Jun Sch. Barn 55 C7
Kendray St. Barn S70 33 F1
Kenilworth Cl. Ben DN5 61 D6
Kenilworth Ct. Shef S11 139 F4
Kenilworth Dr. C in L S81 148 F6
Kenilworth Pl. Shef S11 140 C8
Kenilworth Rd. Don DN4 82 E7
Kenmare Cres. Don DN2 63 B5
Kennedy Cl. Pen S30 50 E3
Kennedy Ct. Shef S10 128 B3
Kennedy Dr. Dearne S63 58 D3
Kennedy Rd. Shef S8 140 E2
Kenneth Ave. Hat DN7 43 F4
Kenneth Ave. Stai DN7 24 F4
Kenneth St. Roth S65 115 E7
Kenninghall Cl. Shef S2 141 D7
Kenninghall Dr. Shef S2 141 D7
Kenninghall Mount. Shef S2 141 D7
Kenninghall Pl. Shef S2 141 D7
Kenninghall Rd. Shef S2 141 D7
Kennington Ave. Ad le S DN6 39 F5
Kenrock Cl. Ben DN5 41 E1
Kensington Ave. Pen S30 51 A4
Kensington Rd. Barn S75 33 D3
Kent Ave. Rawm S62 97 E7
Kent House Cl. Eck S12 154 E8
Kent Rd. Don DN4 83 B7
Kent Rd. Roth S61 96 E1
Kent Rd. Shef S8 141 B6
Kentmere Cl. Dron S18 152 E1
Kents Gdns. Thorne DN8 9 D3
Kenwell Dr. Shef S17 152 B5
Kenwood Ave. Shef S7 140 E7
Kenwood Bank. Shef S7 140 E8
Kenwood Chase. Shef S7 140 F8 12
Kenwood Cl. Barn S70 55 D8
Kenwood Park Rd. Shef S7 140 E7
Kenwood Rd. Shef S7 140 E7
Kenwood Rise. Roth S66 117 C6
Kenworthy Rd. Barn S70 54 F7
Kenworthy Rd. Stock S30 92 B8
Kenyon St. S Elm WF9 19 A3
Kenyon St. Shef S3 128 F4 10
Keppel Dr. Roth S61 96 B2
Keppel Pl. Shef S5 113 E6
Keppel Rd. Roth S61 96 E6
Keppel Rd. Shef S5 113 F7
Keppel View Rd. Roth S61 114 D8
Kepple Cl. Ross DN11 103 F7
Keresforth Cl. Barn S70 54 C8
Keresforth Hall Rd. Barn S70 54 D7
Keresforth Hill Rd. Barn S70 54 C7
Keresforth Rd. Dod S75 54 A6
Kerwin Cl. Shef S17 151 C8
Kerwin Dr. Shef S17 151 C8
Kerwin Rd. Shef S17 151 C8
Kestrel Ave. Roth S61 96 A5
Kestrel Cl. Kill S31 156 B7
Kestrel Dr. Eck S31 155 B3
Kestrel Dr. Ross DN11 85 A1
Kestrel Gn. Shef S2 129 E2
Kestrel Rise. Barn S70 75 F8
Keswick Cl. Ben DN5 62 A8
Keswick Cl. Shef S6 127 E8
Keswick Cres. Brin S60 131 B7
Keswick Pl. Dron S18 152 D1
Keswick Rd. Mapp S75 14 A3
Keswick Way. N Anst S31 146 F6
Keswick Wlk. Barn S71 56 A8
Kettlebridge Fst Sch. Shef 130 A5
Kettlebridge Rd. Shef S9 130 A4
Ketton Ave. Shef S8 141 B3
Ketton Wlk. Barn S75 33 C3
Kevin Gr. Maltby S66 118 B4
Kew Cres. Shef S12 142 A2
Kexbrough Dr. Kex S75 32 D8
Kexbrough Jun Sch. Kex 32 B8
Key Ave. Hoy S74 76 F6
Key Hill La. Bri S72 16 F3
Keyworth Cl. Askern DN6 22 B8
Keyworth Pl. Shef S13 143 A6
Keyworth Rd. Shef S6 112 C1
Khartoum Rd. Shef S11 128 D1
Kibroyd Dr. Kex S75 32 D7
Kid La. Fir S81 136 A5
Kier Hardie Ave. Ross DN11 104 A8
Kilburn Rd. Dron S18 152 C1
Kildale Gdns. Shef S19 155 D7
Kildonan Gr. Shef S12 142 C3
Kilham La. Bran DN3 64 F1
Killamarsh Inf Sch. Kill 156 E7
Killamarsh Jun Sch. Kill 156 E7
Killamarsh La. Hart S31 157 B6
Killamarsh St Giles C of E Aided Sch. Kill 156 C6
Kiln Bent Rd. Holme HD7 47 A6
Kiln La. Emley HD8 12 A4
Kiln Rd. Roth S61 114 F8
Kilner Way. Shef S6 112 D3
Kilnhurst Cty Prim Sch. Swint 98 F7
Kilnhurst Rd. H Rob S65 99 B7
Kilnhurst Rd. Rawm S62 98 C6
Kilnhurst St Thomas CE Controlled Sch. Swint 98 D8
Kilnsea Wlk. Barn S70 33 E1 1
Kilton Hill. Shef S3 129 B6
Kilton Pl. Shef S3 129 B6
Kilvington Ave. Shef S13 142 B7
Kilvington Cres. Shef S13 142 B7
Kilvington Rd. Shef S13 142 B7
Kimberley St. Shef S9 129 F6
Kimberworth Inf Sch. Roth 114 F7
Kimberworth Park Rd. Roth S61 96 E1
Kimberworth Rd. Roth S61 115 A6
Kimberworth Secondary Sch. Roth 114 F7
Kine Moor La. Silk S75 52 D6
King Ave. Maltby S66 119 B4
King Ave. Ross DN11 84 E1
King Ecgbert Lower Sch. Shef 151 D6
King Ecgbert Rd. Shef S17 151 E5
King Ecgbert Upper Sch. Shef 151 E6
King Edward Cres. Thorne DN8 9 B1
King Edward Rd. Don DN4 83 B8
King Edward St. Barn S71 34 D6
King Edward St. Hem WF9 17 E6
King Edward VII Orthopaedic Hospl. Shef 127 B4
King Edward VII Sch. Shef 127 F2
King Edward VII Sch (upper). Shef 128 D2
King Edward's Gdns. Barn S70 54 E8 9
King Edwards Rd. Tick DN11 120 F7
King George Sq. Don DN3 42 F5
King George Terr. Barn S70 55 B8 5
King George's Rd. Ross DN11 84 D1
King Georges Ct. Stai DN7 24 E2
King James St. Shef S6 128 D6
King St. Arm DN3 63 F7
King St. Aston S31 144 C8
King St. Barn S70 54 F8
King St. Chap S30 95 A6
King St. Dearne S63 58 E5
King St. Dearne S63 58 E7
King St. Don DN1 62 D3
King St. Hoy S74 76 F6
King St. Shef S3 129 B4
King St. Swint S64 79 D3
King St. Thorne DN8 26 B7
King's Cl. Hat DN7 44 B8
King's Cres. N Edl DN12 82 B3
King's Rd. Askern DN6 22 B8
King's Rd. Cud S72 16 C1
King's Rd. Don DN1 62 E4
King's Rd. Mex S64 80 B5
King's St. Grime S72 36 A6
King's Terr. Askern DN6 22 B8
Kingfield Rd. Shef S11 140 D7
Kingfisher Cl. Don DN2 63 B7
Kingfisher Ct. Ross DN11 85 A1
Kingfisher Primary Schs. Don 63 B7
Kingfisher Rd. Ad l S DN6 40 B6
Kingfisher Rise. Roth S61 96 A6
Kings Coppice. Shef S17 151 D6
Kings Croft. S Kirk WF9 18 B3
Kings Ct. Barn S70 55 C5
Kings Mews. Don DN1 62 D3
Kings Mews. Eck S31 155 E3
Kings Rd. Wombw S73 56 E2
Kings Road Ct. Thorne DN8 9 C1
Kings Way. Roth S60 116 A2
Kings Wood Cl. Bawtry DN10 123 A8
Kings Wood La. Laugh S31 135 C6
Kingscroft Cl. Shef S17 151 E8
Kingsforth La. Thurcr S66 117 F2
Kingsforth Rd. Thurcr S66 133 E8

Kingsgate. Don DN1 62 D3
Kingsland Ct. Roy S71 15 D4
Kingsley Ave. Ben DN5 61 F4
Kingsley Cl. Barn S71 34 A6
Kingsley Cres. Arm DN3 64 C6
Kingsley Park Ave. Shef S7 140 B4
Kingsley Park Gr. Shef S11 140 B4
Kingsley Rd. Ad I S DN6 40 A5
Kingsmead Dr. Bran DN3 85 D8
Kingston Cl. Bran DN3 64 E1
Kingston Jun Sch. C in L 148 F6
Kingston Rd. C in L S81 148 E6
Kingston Rd. Don DN2 63 B4
Kingston St. Shef S4 129 D7
Kingstone Pl. Barn S70 54 D7
Kingstone Sch The. Barn 54 C8
Kingsway Cl. Ross DN11 104 A7
Kingsway. Dearne S63 58 C8
Kingsway Gr. Dearne S63 58 C8
Kingsway. Mapp S75 14 A1
Kingsway. Stai DN7 24 E3
Kingsway. Wombw S73 56 D2
Kingswood Ave. Laugh S31 134 E4
Kingswood Ave. Shef S19 143 A2
Kingswood Cl. Fir S81 136 A6
Kingswood Cl. Shef S19 143 A2 6
Kingswood Cres. Hoy S74 76 E7
Kingswood Croft. Shef S19 143 A2 9
Kingswood Gr. Shef S19 143 A2 10
Kingwell Cres. Barn S70 54 F6
Kingwell Croft. Barn S70 55 A5
Kingwell Mews. Barn S70 55 A5 1
Kingwell Rd. Barn S70 55 A5
Kinharvie Rd. Shef S5 112 F3
Kinnaird Ave. Shef S5 113 C5
Kinnaird Pl. Shef S5 113 C5
Kinnaird Rd. Shef S5 113 C5
Kinsbourne Gn. Hat DN7 44 A7
Kinsey Rd. Chap S30 94 C7
Kipling Ave. Don DN4 82 F6
Kipling Rd. B Dun DN3 42 F8
Kipling Rd. Shef S6 128 C8
Kirby Cl. Shef S9 130 C4
Kirby La. Went S30 95 D7
Kirby St. Mex S64 80 A5
Kirk Balk. Hoy S74 76 D6
Kirk Balk Sch. Hoy 76 C6
Kirk Cross Cres. Roy S71 15 C2
Kirk Edge Ave. Ought S30 111 D4
Kirk Edge Dr. Ought S30 111 C4
Kirk Edge Rd. Bfield S30 110 D5
Kirk Edge Rd. Ought S30 111 B5
Kirk La. Syke DN14 7 E6
Kirk Sandall Fst Sch. Don 42 F3
Kirk Sandall Ind Est. Don 42 E4
Kirk Sandall Mid Sch. Don 42 F3
Kirk Sandall Sta. Don 42 E4
Kirk Smeaton C of E (Con) Sch.
K Smea 3 D6
Kirk St. Don DN4 62 B2
Kirk St. Shef S4 129 C6
Kirk View. Hoy S74 76 D6
Kirk Way. Barn S71 34 D3
Kirkbridge Way. S Elm WF9 18 F3
Kirkby Ave. Barn S71 34 A8
Kirkby Ave. Ben DN5 62 B6
Kirkby Ave. Shef S12 142 A4
Kirkby Cl. S Kirk WF9 18 C3
Kirkby Dr. Shef S12 142 A4
Kirkby Rd. Hem WF9 17 E6
Kirkby Rd. Shef S12 142 A4
Kirkby View. Shef S12 142 A4
Kirkby Way. Shef S12 142 A3
Kirkbygate. Hem WF9 17 E5
Kirkcroft Ave. Kill S31 156 D7
Kirkcroft Ave. Roth S61 96 A5
Kirkcroft Cl. Roth S61 95 F5
Kirkcroft Dr. Kill S31 156 D6
Kirkcroft La. Kill S31 156 D6
Kirkdale Cres. Shef S13 131 B1
Kirkdale Dr. Shef S13 131 B1
Kirkfield Cl. Caw S75 31 F4
Kirkfield Way. Roy S71 15 C2
Kirkgate La. S Hie S72 16 C6
Kirkhall Cl. Arm DN3 64 C5
Kirkham Cl. Barn S71 34 C3
Kirkham Pl. Barn S71 34 D7
Kirkhill Sch. Shef 141 C8
Kirkhouse Green Rd. K Bram DN7 24 A8
Kirklands Dr. Rawm S62 97 E6
Kirkstall Cl. Ben DN5 61 D5
Kirkstall Cl. Brin S60 115 A1
Kirkstall Cl. S Anst S31 146 D3
Kirkstall Rd. Barn S71 33 E7
Kirkstall Rd. Shef S11 140 C8
Kirkstead Abbey Mews. Roth S61 96 A3
Kirkstead Rd. Roth S61 114 A6
Kirkstone Cl. Ben DN5 62 A7
Kirkstone Rd. Shef S6 128 C7
Kirton La. Hat DN8 25 D4
Kirton Rd. Shef S4 129 C8
Kitchin Rd. Wombw S73 56 B3
Kitson Dr. Barn S71 34 D3
Kiveton Bridge Sta. Wales 145 D2
Kiveton Gdns. Wales S31 145 F3
Kiveton La. Tod S31 145 F5
Kiveton La. Wales S31 145 F5
Kiveton Park Inf Sch. Wales 145 D3
Kiveton Park Meadows
Jun Mix Sch. Wales 145 C3
Kiveton Park Sta. Hart 146 B1
Knab Cl. Shef S7 140 C5
Knab Croft. Shef S7 140 C5
Knab Rd. Shef S7 140 C5
Knab Rise. Shef S7 140 C5
Knabbs La. Silk S75 52 F5
Knapton Ave. Rawm S62 97 E6
Knaresboro Rd. Shef S7 140 C3
Knaresborough Cl. Aston S31 144 C7
Knaresborough Rd. Con DN12 80 F1
Knaton Rd. C in L S81 148 E7
Knavesmire Gdns. Don DN4 63 D2
Knightscroft Par. S Elm WF9 19 A2
Knightwood Pl. Roth S65 116 B8 7
Knoll Beck Cl. Dearne S63 58 C4
Knoll Beck Cres. W up D S73 78 A8
Knoll Cl. Stock S30 73 C1
Knoll The. Dron S18 153 D3
Knollbeck Ave. W up D S73 78 A8
Knollbeck La. W up D S73 78 A8
Knott End. Lan S81 136 E3
Knowle Cl. Shef S6 127 C6
Knowle Croft. Shef S11 140 A5
Knowle Ct. Shef S11 140 B5
Knowle La. Shef S11 139 F5
Knowle Park Ave. Shep HD8 28 F8
Knowle Rd. Barn S70 55 B6
Knowle Rd. Shef S5 113 B6
Knowle The. Shep HD8 28 F8
Knowle Top. Shef S19 155 E7
Knowles Ave. Stock S30 92 D8
Knowles St. Pen S30 51 F2
Knowsley St. Barn S70 33 D1
Knutton Cres. Shef S5 112 E7
Knutton Rd. Shef S5 112 F6
Knutton Rise. Shef S5 112 E7
Kye La. Hart S31 157 E6
Kyle Cl. Shef S5 112 F4
Kyle Cres. Shef S5 112 F4
Kynance Cres. Brin S60 131 C7

Laburnam Gr. Barn S70 55 C4
Laburnum Ave. Roth S66 117 B6
Laburnum Ave. Thorne DN8 9 C3
Laburnum Cl. Chap S30 95 A4
Laburnum Cl. S Anst S31 146 D4
Laburnum Dr. Arm DN3 64 C7
Laburnum Gr. Con DN12 81 A1
Laburnum Gr. Finn DN9 86 B4
Laburnum Gr. Kill S31 156 C5
Laburnum Gr. Stock S30 92 B8
Laburnum Par. Maltby S66 118 D5
Laburnum Pl. Ben DN5 41 B2
Laburnum Rd. Don DN4 82 F7
Laburnum Rd. Lan S81 136 F4
Laburnum Rd. Maltby S66 118 D5
Laburnum Rd. Mex S64 79 F6
Laceby Cl. Roth S66 117 D7
Laceby Ct. Barn S70 54 C7
Lacy St. Hem WF9 17 C7
Ladies Spring Ct. Dron S17 152 A7
Ladies Spring Dr. Shef S17 152 A7
Ladies Spring Gr. Shef S17 152 A7
Ladock Cl. Barn S71 34 B3
Lady Croft La. Hoy S73 77 C7
Lady Croft. W up D S63 78 E6
Lady Field Rd. Th Sa S80 158 D8
Lady Gap La. Burg DN6 21 D5
Lady Ida's Dr. Eck S19, S31 155 C4
Lady Ida's Dr. Shef S19, S31 155 C5
Lady Mary View. Hick DN5 59 B7
Lady Oak Rd. Roth S65 116 C8
Lady Wharncliffe's Rd. Stock S30 93 D4
Lady Wharncliffe's Rd. Wort S30 93 D6
Lady's Bridge. Shef S3 129 B4
Ladybank Rd. Shef S19 155 D6
Ladybank View. Eck S31 155 D4
Ladybower Ct. Shef S17 152 A5 4
Ladybower Dr. Hath S30 149 A7
Ladycroft. Dearne S63 58 C2
Ladycroft Rd. Arm DN3 64 C4
Ladysmith Ave. Shef S7 140 D6
Ladywood Fst Sch. Grime The. 36 B6
Ladywood Rd. Grime S72 36 B6
Laird Ave. Shef S6 112 A1
Laird Dr. Shef S6 112 A1
Laird Rd. Shef S6 112 A1
Laithe Croft. Dod S75 53 F7
Laithes Cl. Barn S71 34 B7
Laithes Cres. Barn S71 33 F7
Laithes La. Barn S71 34 A7
Lake Cl. N Edl DN12 82 A1
Lake Ct. Ad I S DN6 40 C4
Lake Rd. Ad I S DN6 40 C3
Lakeen Rd. Don DN2 63 A4
Lakeland Cl. Cud S72 35 C5
Lakeland Dr. Din S31 146 E7
Lakeland Dr. N Anst S31 146 F7
Lamb Dr. Shef S5 112 D3
Lamb Hill. Bfield S6 110 B4
Lamb Hill Cl. Shef S13 142 D7
Lamb La. Barn S71 34 C5
Lamb La. Fir S81 136 C5
Lamb Rd. Shef S5 112 D3
Lambcote Way. Maltby S66 119 B6
Lambcroft La. Shef S13 143 C6
Lambcroft View. Shef S13 143 C6
Lambe Flatt. Kex S75 32 C8
Lambert Fold. Dod S75 54 A7
Lambert Rd. Barn S70 55 C7
Lambert St. Shef S3 129 A4
Lambert Wlk. Barn S70 55 C8
Lamberts La. Roth S65 98 F3
Lambeth Rd. Don DN4 83 B7
Lambra Rd. Barn S70 33 F1
Lambrell Ave. Wales S31 145 C2
Lambrell Gn. Wales S31 145 C2
Lanark Dr. Mex S64 80 C6
Lanark Gdns. Don DN2 63 C5
Lancaster Ave. Don DN3 42 F4
Lancaster Ave. Don DN2 63 C4
Lancaster Cl. Tick DN11 121 B7
Lancaster Cres. Tick DN11 121 B7
Lancaster Dr. Bawtry DN10 122 F8
Lancaster Dr. Hat DN7 66 A8
Lancaster Gate. Barn S70 33 E2 6
Lancaster Rd. Stock S30 73 B1
Lancaster St. Barn S70 33 D1
Lancaster St. Dearne S63 37 E1
Lancaster St. Shef S3 128 F5
Lancing Rd. Shef S2 129 B1
Lancing Rd. Shef S2 141 A8
Land Ends Rd. Thorne DN8 8 F2
Landsdown Ave. S Kirk WF9 18 A1
Landseer Cl. Dron S18 152 E1 4
Landseer Cl. Shef S14 141 D2
Landseer Ct. Roth S66 117 B6
Landseer Dr. Shef S14 141 E2
Landseer Pl. Shef S14 141 E2
Landseer Wlk. Shef S14 141 E2
Lane Cotts. Roy S71 15 C3
Lane End Rd. Roth S60 116 A3
Lane Hackings. D Dale HD8 29 E7
Lane Hackings Gn. D Dale HD8 29 E7
Lane Head Cl. Mapp S75 14 A2
Lane Head Cl. Rawm S62 98 A6
Lane Head Rd. Bfield S6 109 A4
Lane Head Rd. Caw S75 31 D3
Lane Head Rd. Shef S17 151 C4
Lane Head Rd. Shep HD8 28 E7
Lane Head Rise. Mapp S75 14 A2
Lane The. Eck S31 156 D1
Laneham Cl. Don DN4 84 D6
Lanes The. Roth S65 116 B7
Laneside Cl. Don DN4 62 A1
Lang Ave. Barn S71 34 E2
Lang Cres. Barn S71 34 E2
Langar Cl. Ben DN5 41 A4
Langcliffe Cl. Mapp S75 14 A2
Langdale Cl. Tick DN11 121 B8
Langdale Dr. Ben DN5 61 F8
Langdale Dr. Dron S18 153 C3
Langdale Dr. Tick DN11 121 B8
Langdale Rd. Ad le S DN6 21 C1
Langdale Rd. Barn S75 32 E5
Langdale Rd. Barn S71 34 A1
Langdale Rd. Shef S8 140 E5
Langdale Way. Din S31 146 F7
Langdon Rd. Roth S61 114 E8
Langdon St. Shef S11 140 F8
Langdon Wlk. Barn S70 33 D2 1
Langer St. Don DN4 62 A1
Langley Cl. Roth S65 116 D7
Langleys Rd. Norton DN6 4 D1
Langold Ctry Pk. C in L 136 E1
Langsett Ave. Shef S6 112 A3
Langsett Cl. Shef S6 128 D7
Langsett Cres. Shef S6 128 D7
Langsett Gr. Shef S6 128 D6
Langsett Rd. Barn S71 33 E7
Langsett Rd N. Ought S30 111 D8
Langsett Rd N. Wharn S30 111 D8
Langsett Rd S. Ought S30 111 E6
Langsett Rd. Shef S6 128 D7
Langsett Rise. Shef S6 128 D7
Langsett Wlk. Shef S6 128 D7
Langthwaite Grange Ind Est.
S Kirk 18 D2
Langthwaite La. Ben DN5 40 E2
Langthwaite La. S Elm WF9 18 E2
Langthwaite Rd. Ben DN5 40 E1
Langthwaite Rd. S Kirk WF9 18 D2
Langton Gdns. Bran DN3 85 E8
Lansbury Ave. Chap S30 94 F5
Lansbury Ave. Maltby S66 119 B3
Lansbury Ave. Ross DN11 104 A8
Lansbury Pl. Rawm S62 98 C6
Lansbury Rd. Eck S31 155 D2
Lansdowne Cl. Dearne S63 58 C8
Lansdowne Cres. Kex S75 32 D7
Lansdowne Cres. Swint S64 79 D2
Lansdowne Rd. Don DN2 63 C5
Lanyon Way. Barn S71 34 B3
Lapwater Rd. Roth S61 96 F3
Lapwater Wlk. Roth S61 96 F3
Lapwing Vale. Roth S61 96 A6
Larch Ave. Finn DN9 85 F3
Larch Ave. Kill S31 156 C5
Larch Ave. Roth S66 117 C5
Larch Dr. Arm DN3 64 B6
Larch Gr. Chap S30 95 A4
Larch Gr. Con DN12 100 A8
Larch Hill. Shef S9 130 E3
Larch Pl. Barn S70 55 C6
Larch Rd. Eck S31 155 B2
Larch Rd. Maltby S66 118 D6
Larch Sq. Finn DN9 86 B4
Larches The. Swint S64 79 C3
Larchfield Pl. Barn S71 34 D5
Larchfield Rd. Don DN4 82 F7
Large Sq. Stai DN7 24 E4
Lark Ave. Brin S60 131 D8
Lark St. Shef S6 128 B6
Larkspur Cl. Don DN3 42 F1
Larkspur Cl. Swint S64 98 C8
Larwood Gr. N Edl DN12 82 C3
Latham Sq. Don DN3 42 F5
Latham Sq. Shef S11 139 E5
Lathe Rd. Roth S60 116 D3
Lathkill Cl. Shef S13 142 C7
Lathkill Rd. Shef S13 142 C7
Latimer Cl. Wales S31 145 F2
Latin Gdns. Ben DN5 61 C7
Lauder Rd. Ben DN5 62 A6
Lauder St. Shef S4 113 E2
Laudsdale Cl. Roth S65 116 D7
Laudsdale Rd. Roth S65 116 D7
Laughton Common Rd. Thurcr S66 134 B4
Laughton Rd. Din S31 134 F1
Laughton Rd. Don DN4 62 B2
Laughton Rd. Shef S9 114 B2
Laughton Rd. Thurcr S66 134 A5
Launce Rd. Shef S5 112 F4
Laurel Ave. Barn S70 55 D7
Laurel Ave. Ben DN5 61 E5
Laurel Ave. Roth S66 117 D5
Laurel Ave. Thorne DN8 9 C3
Laurel Cl. S Anst S31 146 D3
Laurel Ct. Shef S10 128 B1
Laurel Dr. Kill S31 156 C5
Laurel Rd. Arm DN3 64 B7
Laurel Sq. Finn DN9 86 A4
Laurel Terr. Ad le S DN6 21 B1
Laurel Terr. Don DN4 83 A7
Laurold Ave. Hat DN7 45 A6
Lavenham Pl. Ad le S DN6 20 E2
Laverack St. Shef S13 130 F1
Laverdene Ave. Shef S17 151 F4
Laverdene Cl. Shef S17 151 E4
Laverdene Dr. Shef S17 151 F4
Laverdene Rd. Shef S17 151 E4
Laverdene Way. Shef S17 151 F4
Laverock Way. Shef S5 113 D5
Lavinia Rd. Shef S30 112 E8
Law Common Rd. Carl HD7 48 E5
Law Common Rd. Dun Br HD7 48 E5
Law Slack Rd. Holmfi HD7 48 D6
Lawn Ave. Ad le S DN6 39 F6
Lawn Ave. Don DN1 62 E3
Lawn Garth. Ben DN5 62 A7
Lawn La. Fenw DN6 6 C5
Lawn Rd. C in L S81 148 E8
Lawn Rd. Don DN1 62 E3
Lawn The. Dron S18 153 B2
Lawndale. Ad le S DN6 20 F2
Lawndale Fold. Mapp S75 13 F1
Lawns The. Shef S10 128 B2
Lawns The. Shef S11 140 B6
Lawnswood Ct. Don DN4 84 C8
Lawrence Briggs Inf Sch. Barn 33 E8
Lawrence Cl. Barn S75 32 E3
Lawrence Cl. Roth S66 117 B5
Lawrence Ct. Swint S64 79 C1
Lawrence Dr. Swint S64 79 C1
Lawrence St. Shef S9 129 F6
Lawson Rd. Shef S10 128 C2
Lawton La. Roth S60 115 F3
Laxey Rd. Shef S6 127 E5
Laxton Rd. Barn S71 33 F8
Laycock Ave. Aston S31 144 E7
Le Brun Sq. C in L S81 148 E7
Lea Dr. Shep HD8 28 F8
Lea Rd. Barn S71 34 B7
Lea Rd. Dron S18 153 A1
Lea The. Shef S19 143 D2
Lea The. Swint S64 79 B2
Leabrook Rd. Dron S18 152 C1
Leach La. Mex S64 80 B4
Leadbeater Dr. Shef S12 142 A5
Leadbeater Rd. Shef S12 142 A4
Leader Ct. Shef S6 112 B1
Leader Rd. Shef S6 112 B1
Leadley St. Dearne S63 58 E5
Leadmill Rd. Shef S1, S2 129 B1
Leadmill Rd. Shef S1 129 B2
Leadmill St. Shef S1 129 B2
Leaf Cl. Maltby S66 119 B6
Leak Hall La. D Dale HD8 30 A6
Leak Hall Rd. D Dale HD8 29 F6
Leake Rd. Shef S6 112 C2
Leamington Gdns. Don DN2 63 B5
Leamington St. Shef S10 128 C4
Leas The. Ben DN5 61 F5
Lease Gate Rd. Roth S60 116 B2
Leaton Cl. Shef S6 111 D1
Leavy Greave. Shef S10 128 E3 2
Leavygreave Rd. Shef S3 128 E3 1
Leawood Pl. Shef S6 127 D6
Ledbury Gdns. Ben DN5 61 D5
Ledbury Rd. Barn S71 33 F6
Ledger Cl. Wales S31 145 C2
Ledsham Ct. Hoy S74 77 B6
Ledsham Rd. Roth S60 116 A4
Ledstone Rd. Shef S8 140 E4
Lee Ave. Stock S30 73 D1
Lee Brook La. W up D S62 77 F2
Lee Croft. Maltby S66 119 C4
Lee Croft. Shef S1 129 A4
Lee Hill Inf Sch. Barn 56 A8
Lee House La. Stock S30 92 A8
Lee La. Bfield S30 91 D3
Lee La. Mapp S71 14 E2
Lee La. Pen S30 50 B3
Lee La. Roy S71 14 E2
Lee La. Wh Com S30 49 F4
Lee Moor La. Shef S6 126 F7
Lee Rd. Shef S6 111 D1
Leech Row. Thurgo S30 73 F5
Leedham Cl. Shef S5 113 F4
Leedham Rd. Roth S65 116 D4
Leedham Rd. Shef S5 113 F4
Leeds Ave. N Anst S31 146 E7
Leeds Rd. Shef S9 130 A6
Leeds Rd. Shire S81 159 F7
Lees Ave. Pen S30 51 D3
Lees Hall Ave. Shef S8 141 B5
Lees Hall Golf Course. Shef 141 D3
Lees Hall Pl. Shef S8 141 B5
Lees Hall Rd. Shef S8 141 B4
Lees House Ct. Shef S8 141 A4
Lees Nook. Shef S8 141 A4
Leger Way. Don DN2 63 C4
Legion Dr. Aston S31 144 E7
Leicester Ave. Don DN2 63 A3
Leicester Rd. Din S31 135 A1
Leicester Wlk. Shef S3 128 F4 9
Leigh St. Shef S9 130 A7
Leighton Cl. Barn S71 33 F3
Leighton Dr. Shef S14 141 F3
Leighton Pl. Shef S14 141 F3
Leighton Rd. Shef S14 141 E4
Leinster Ave. Don DN2 63 A5
Lemont Rd. Shef S17 151 E4
Lennox Rd. Don DN2 63 B5
Lennox Rd. Shef S6 112 B1
Lenny Balk. H Pag DN6 38 E7
Lenthall Cty Inf Sch. Dron 153 B3
Lenton St. Shef S2 129 B1
Leonard Cl. Shef S2 142 A7
Leopold Ave. Din S31 146 F8
Leopold St. Barn S70 54 D8
Leopold St. Din S31 146 F8
Leopold St. Shef S1 129 A3
Leppings La. Shef S6 112 C2
Lepton Gdns. Barn S70 55 D6
Lescar La. Shef S11 140 C8
Lesley Rd. Dearne S63 58 E5
Leslie Ave. Con DN12 81 A2
Leslie Ave. Maltby S66 118 D5
Leslie Rd. Barn S70 55 D7
Leslie Rd. Shef S6 112 B1
Lesmond Cres. G Hou S72 57 E6
Lestermoor Ave. Wales S31 145 C2
Letard Dr. Brin S60 115 C1
Levels La. Blax DN9 86 F8
Leverick Dr. Rawm S62 98 C7
Leverstock Gn. Hat DN7 44 A7
Leverton Dr. Shef S11 128 F1
Leverton Gdns. Shef S11 128 F1
Leverton Way. Roth S65 98 E1
Leveson St. Shef S4 129 D5
Levet Rd. Don DN4 63 F1
Lewdendale. Barn S70 55 A4
Lewes Rd. Con DN12 81 B1
Lewis Rd. Barn S71 34 E4
Lewis Rd. Shef S13 142 C7
Lewyns Dr. Don DN4 63 F1
Ley End. Barn S70 54 F4
Leybourne Rd. Roth S61 96 E1
Leybrook Croft. Hem WF9 17 E7
Leyburn Cl. Don DN4 84 F7
Leyburn Dr. Aston S31 144 C8
Leyburn Gr. Chap S30 95 A6
Leyburn Rd. Ad le S DN6 20 F2
Leyburn Rd. Shef S8 140 F6
Leyfield Ct. Arm DN3 64 C5
Leyfield Rd. Shef S17 151 D7
Leyland Ave. Hat DN7 44 C7
Leys Cl. Don DN4 82 F5
Leys La. Din S31 135 C2
Leys La. Ham DN6 20 C2
Leys La. K Smea WF8 3 C7
Liberty Cl. Shef S6 127 E5
Liberty Dr. Shef S6 127 E5
Liberty Hill. Shef S6 127 E5
Liberty La. Wort S30 74 D3
Liberty Pl. Shef S6 127 E5
Liberty Rd. Shef S6 127 E5
Library Cl. Roth S61 97 A3
Lichen Cl. Don DN3 42 F1
Lichfield Gdns. N Edl DN12 82 A1
Lichfield Rd. Don DN2, 62 F6
Lichfield Rd. Hat DN7 44 A8
Lichfield Wlk. C in L S81 148 E7
Lichford Rd. Shef S2 141 C6
Lidgate Cres. S Kirk WF9 18 E2
Lidgate La. Shaf S72 16 B3
Lidgate. Snaith DN14 1 C8
Lidget Cl. Don DN4 84 E7
Lidget Gdns. Auck DN9 86 A6
Lidget La. Dearne S63 58 F7
Lidget La. Hick DN5 59 A7
Lidget La. Roth S65 117 E7
Lidgett La. Din S31 146 F8
Lidgett La. Pilley S75 75 D5
Lifestyle House. Shef S10 128 C2 2
Liffey Ave. Don DN2 63 A5
Lifford Pl. Hoy S74 77 B5
Lifford Rd. Don DN2 62 F5
Lifford St. Shef S9 114 E3
Lightwood House Hospl. Shef 141 E1
Lightwood La. Eck S8 141 F1
Lightwood La. Uns S31 154 E1
Lightwood Rd. Eck S31 154 E2
Lilac Ave. Stock S30 92 B8
Lilac Cl. S Anst S31 146 D4
Lilac Cres. Hoy S74 76 F7
Lilac Cres. N Edl DN12 82 B1
Lilac Gr. Bawtry DN10 122 F7
Lilac Gr. C in L S81 148 E7
Lilac Gr. Con DN12 81 A1
Lilac Gr. Don DN4 84 F8
Lilac Gr. Finn DN9 86 A4
Lilac Gr. Maltby S66 118 D5
Lilac Gr. Roth S66 117 C5
Lilac Rd. Arm DN3 64 C7
Lilac Rd. Shef S19 143 F3
Lilac Rd. Shef S5 113 E3
Lilacs The. Roy S71 15 E4
Liley La. Pen S30 50 D1
Lilian St. Roth S60 115 E5
Lilian St S. Roth S60 115 E5
Lilley St. Hem WF9 17 D6
Lilley Terr. S Kirk WF9 18 B2
Lillford Rd. Bran DN3 85 E8
Lilly Hall Cl. Maltby S66 118 D6
Lilly Hall Jun Mix Sch. Maltby 118 E5
Lilly Hall Rd. Maltby S66 118 E5
Lily Terr. Hoy S74 76 F7
Lilydene Ave. Grime S72 35 F7
Limb La. Shef S17 139 D1
Limbrick Cl. Shef S6 128 C7
Limbrick Rd. Shef S6 128 C7
Lime Ave. Finn DN9 86 A4
Lime Ave. Fir S81 136 A6
Lime Cl. Roth S65 99 D2
Lime Cres. S Elm WF9 18 E1
Lime Ct. Sprot DN5 61 D1
Lime Gr. Chap S30 95 A4
Lime Gr. Maltby S66 119 B5
Lime Gr. Roy S71 15 C1
Lime Gr. S Elm WF9 18 E1
Lime Gr. Stock S30 92 B8
Lime Gr. Swint S64 79 D2
Lime Rd. Eck S31 155 B2
Lime St. Shef S6 128 E6
Lime St. Shef S19 143 F4
Lime Tree Ave. Arm DN3 64 B7
Lime Tree Ave. C in L S81 148 E7
Lime Tree Ave. Don DN4 62 F2
Lime Tree Ave. Kill S31 156 C5
Lime Tree Cl. Cud S72 35 B7
Lime Tree Cres. Bawtry DN10 122 F7
Lime Tree Cres. Rawm S62 98 B6
Lime Tree Cres. Ross DN11 104 A8
Lime Tree Ct. Don DN4 62 F1
Lime Tree Ct. Hem WF9 17 C6
Lime Tree Gr. Thorne DN8 26 B8
Lime Tree Wlk. Con DN12 80 F4
Limedale View. B Dun DN3 43 A6
Limegrove. Roth S60 116 A4
Limekiln La. Ston S66 120 A6
Limekiln La. Ston S66 101 E2
Limekilns. N Anst S31 146 D6
Limelands Rd. Din S31 146 E8
Limes Ave. Barn S75 33 B3
Limes Ave. Mapp S75 14 C2
Limes Cl. Mapp S75 14 C2
Limestone Cl. Woods S81 147 E3
Limestone Cottage La. Shef S6 112 B4
Limesway. Barn S75 33 B3
Limesway. Maltby S66 118 F5
Limetree Ave. Thurcr S66 133 F6
Limetree Ave. Wales S31 145 C3
Limpool Cl. Don DN4 84 F7
Limpsfield Community
Mid Sch. Shef 114 A2
Limpsfield Rd. Shef S9 114 A2
Linaker Rd. Shef S6 128 B5
Linburn Cl. Roy S71 15 A4
Linburn Rd. Shef S8 140 F2
Linby Rd. Barn S71 33 F8
Lincoln Cl. Con DN12 80 F2
Lincoln Cres. S Elm WF9 19 A4
Lincoln Gdns. Dearne S63 58 D5
Lincoln Rd. Don DN2 62 F6
Lincoln Rd. Hat DN7 66 A8
Lincoln St. Maltby S66 119 B4
Lincoln St. Ross DN11 84 E2
Lincoln St. Roth S60 115 D8
Lincoln St. Shef S9 114 B2
Lindale Cl. N Anst S31 146 F5
Lindale Gdns. Dearne S63 58 F4
Lindales The. Barn S75 33 C2 3
Linden Ave. Dron S18 153 B3
Linden Ave. Roth S66 117 C6
Linden Ave. Shef S8 140 E2
Linden Cl. Hat DN7 44 B8
Linden Cres. Stock S30 73 B1
Linden Ct. Shef S10 128 B1
Linden Ct. Shef S30 95 B1

Linden Gr. Maltby S66 118 D5
Linden Gr. N Edl DN12 82 B1
Linden Rd. Shef S30 95 B1
Linden Rd. W up D S63 78 B6
Linden Wlk. Ben DN5 41 A4
Lindholme Bank Rd. Hat DN7 45 D2
Lindholme Dr. Ross DN11 85 B1
Lindholme Gdns. Shef S19 143 C2
Lindhurst Rd. Barn S71 33 F8
Lindley Cres. Dearne S63 58 D7
Lindley Rd. Finn DN9 86 E3
Lindley Rd. Shef S5 113 D2
Lindley St. Roth S65 115 E8
Lindley's Croft. Tod S31 145 F5
Lindrick Ave. Swint S64 79 E2
Lindrick Cl. C in L S81 148 F6
Lindrick Cl. Con DN12 81 E3
Lindrick Cl. Cud S72 16 C1
Lindrick Cl. Don DN4 84 D6
Lindrick Cl. Tick DN11 120 F6
Lindrick Ct. Woods S81 147 F3
Lindrick Dr. Arm DN3 64 B5
Lindrick Golf Course. Woods 147 D2
Lindrick La. Tick DN11 120 F6
Lindrick Rd. Hat DN7 44 F6
Lindrick Rd. Woods S81 147 E3
Lindrick. Tick DN11 121 A6
Lindsay Ave. Shef S5 113 B5
Lindsay Cl. Shef S5 113 B5
Lindsay Cres. Shef S5 113 B5
Lindsay Dr. Shef S5 113 B5
Lindsay Pl. Aston S31 144 D7
Lindsay Rd. Shef S5 113 B5
Lindsay Road Infant & Jun Sch. Shef 113 B5
Lindsey Cl. Don DN4 84 D5
Lindsey Rd. Har DN11 122 A5
Lindum Dr. Roth S66 117 C4
Lindum St. Don DN4 62 B2
Lindum Terr. Roth S65 115 E6 1
Ling Field Rd. Brod DN5 39 B3
Ling House La. B Dun DN7 24 C2
Lingamore Leys. Dearne S63 37 D1
Lingard Ct. Barn S75 33 D2
Lingard St. Barn S75 33 D2
Lingfield Dr. Ben DN5 61 D5
Lingfield Wlk. Mex S64 80 C6
Lingfoot Ave. Shef S8 153 B6
Lingfoot Cl. Shef S8 153 B6
Lingfoot Cres. Shef S8 153 C6
Lingfoot Dr. Shef S8 153 C6
Lingfoot Pl. Shef S8 153 B6
Lingfoot Wlk. Shef S8 153 C6
Lingmoor Cl. Don DN4 82 E6
Lingodell Cl. Laugh S31 134 E4
Lings La. Hat DN7 44 B5
Lings La. Roth S66 117 C4
Lings La. Upton DN6 20 A8
Lings The. Arm DN3 64 D5
Lings The. Roth S66 117 E4
Link Rd. Roth S65 99 A2
Link Row. Shef S2 129 C4
Link The. Dod S75 54 A6
Links View. Mapp S75 14 B2
Linkswood Ave. Don DN2 63 C6
Linkthwaite. Dod S75 54 A7
Linkway. Don DN2 63 B6
Linkway. Hat DN7 44 F6
Linkway. Norton DN6 4 D3
Linley La. Shef S12, S13 142 E5
Linnet Mount. Roth S61 95 F5
Linscott Rd. Shef S8 140 E2
Linshaws Rd. Dun Br HD7 47 E5
Linthwaite La. Hoy S62 77 C4
Linton Cl. Barn S70 54 B8
Lion Cott. Caw S75 31 E4
Lipp Ave. Kill S31 156 C7
Liskeard Pl. Ad l S DN6 40 A5
Lisle Rd. Roth S60 116 A4
Lismore Rd. Shef S8 141 B5
Lister Ave. Don DN4 83 B8
Lister Ave. Rawm S62 97 E7
Lister Ave. Shef S12 142 B3
Lister Cl. Shef S12 142 B3
Lister Cres. Shef S12 142 B3
Lister Ct. Don DN2 63 A5
Lister Dr. Shef S12 142 B3
Lister La. Shef S3 128 F5 2
Lister Pl. Shef S12 142 B3
Lister Rd. Shef S6 128 C7
Lister Row. G Hou S72 36 D3
Lister St. Roth S65 115 F6
Lister Way. Shef S12 142 B3
Listerdale Sh Ctr. Roth S65 116 E4
Litherop La. Emley HD8 12 C5
Litherop Rd. H Hoy S75 12 D3
Little Attercliffe. Shef S9 130 B5
Little Common La. Roth S61 114 D7
Little Common La. Roth S60 116 E1
Little Common La. Shef S11 139 F5
Little Haynooking La. Maltby S66 118 F5
Little Hemsworth. Hem WF9 17 E6
Little La. Don DN2 42 C1
Little La. K Smea WF8 4 A7
Little La. S Elm WF9 18 F3
Little La. S Elm WF9 19 B3
Little La. Shef S12 142 B6
Little La. Shef S4 113 F1
Little La. Sprot DN5 61 A4
Little La. Th Sa S80 159 B6
Little La. Upton WF9 19 B7
Little La. Went S30 95 E6
Little Leeds. Hoy S74 76 E6
Little London La. Snaith DN14 1 A7
Little London Pl. Shef S8 140 F6
Little London Rd. Shef S8 140 F5
Little Matlock Gdns. Shef S6 127 D6
Little Matlock Way. Shef S6 127 D6
Little Norton Ave. Shef S8 153 A8
Little Norton Dr. Shef S8 153 A8
Little Norton La. Shef S8 153 A8
Little Norton Way. Shef S8 153 A7
Little Wood Dr. Shef S12 142 A3
Little Wood Rd. Shef S12 142 A3
Littledale Rd. Shef S9 130 C2
Littlefield La. Dar S73 56 D3
Littlehey Cl. Maltby S66 118 D6
Littlemoor Ave. Wales S31 145 C2
Littlemoor. Eck S31 155 E4
Littlemoor La. Don DN4 62 B1
Littlemoor St. Don DN4 62 B1
Littlewood Rd. Thorne DN8 26 C7
Littlewood St. Don DN4 62 B2
Littlewood Way. Maltby S66 119 B6
Littleworth Cl. Ross DN11 85 B1
Littleworth La. Barn S71 34 D3
Littleworth La. Ross DN11 85 C1
Littleworth Lane Inf Sch. Barn 34 D3
Litton Wlk. Barn S70 33 D2 2
Liverpool Ave. Don DN2 62 F6
Liverpool Pl. Shef S9 129 F7
Liverpool St. Shef S9 130 A7
Livingston Rd. Shef S9 129 E6
Livingstone Ave. Don DN2 42 D1
Livingstone Cres. Barn S71 34 B5
Livingstone Rd. Chap S30 94 E5
Livingstone Terr. Barn S70 54 E8 4
Llewelyn Cres. Askern DN6 21 F7
Lloyd St. Rawm S62 97 F3
Lloyd St. Shef S4 113 E1
Lloyds Terr. Hat DN7 24 F1
Load Field Rd. Bfield S30 91 F2
Loakfield Dr. Shef S5 112 F7
Lobelia Cres. Don DN3 42 F3
Lobelia Ct. S Anst S31 146 D4
Lobwood. Barn S70 55 B5
Lobwood La. Barn S70 55 B5
Locarno Rd. Thorne DN8 9 D3
Lock Hill. Thorne DN8 26 A7
Lock House Rd. Shef S9 114 C1
Lock La. Shef S9 114 E3
Lock La. Thorne DN8 26 A7
Lock St. Shef S6 128 E6
Locke Ave. Barn S70 54 E8
Locke Ave. Barn S70 54 F6
Locke Rd. Dod S75 54 A6
Locke St. Barn S70 54 D7
Lockeaflash Cres. Barn S70 55 D7
Lockesley Ave. Con DN12 81 A1
Lockgate Rd. Bal M DN6 5 F8
Locking Dr. Arm DN3 64 D5
Locksley Ave. Don DN3 42 F2
Locksley Dr. Thurcr S66 133 E6
Locksley Gdns. Norton DN6 4 C1
Lockton Cl. Chap S30 94 C8
Lockton Way. Con DN12 81 D3
Lockwood Ave. S Anst S31 146 D3
Lockwood Cl. Roth S65 116 C7
Lockwood Cl. Thorne DN8 26 D7
Lockwood La. Barn S70 54 F7 11
Lockwood La. Dearne S63 58 E7
Lockwood Rd. Dearne S63 58 E6
Lockwood Rd. Don DN1 62 E5
Lockwood Rd. Roth S65 116 C7
Lodge Ct. Hat DN7 44 B7
Lodge Dr. Went S62 76 D1
Lodge Farm Cl. N Anst S31 146 D6
Lodge Hill Dr. Wales S31 145 B3
Lodge La. Aston S31 144 D7
Lodge La. Din S31 135 B1
Lodge La. K Bram DN7 24 B6
Lodge La. Roth S61 95 F3
Lodge La. Shef S10, S6 127 A2
Lodge La. Snaith DN14 1 A8
Lodge La. Wort S30 93 D5
Lodge Moor Hospl. Shef 126 F1
Lodge Moor Rd. Shef S10 138 F8
Lodge Rd. Ad le S DN6 21 C2
Lodge St. Hem WF9 17 D8
Lodge The. Shef S11 140 A5
Lodge Way. Brin S60 115 C1
Logan Rd. Shef S9 130 D4
Loicher La. Shef S30 95 D1
Lomas Cl. Shef S6 127 C7
Lomas Lea. Shef S6 127 B6
Lombard Cl. Barn S75 33 E3
Lombard Cres. Dar S73 56 E5
London La. Moss DN6 6 B1
London Rd. Shef S2 140 F8
London Way. Roth S61 95 E4
Long Acre View. Shef S19 156 A8
Long Cl. Don DN4 84 E6
Long Close La. Holmfi HD8 28 C7
Long Close La. S Elm WF9 19 C6
Long Croft. Mapp S75 14 B1
Long Croft Rd. Dron S18 152 C2
Long Cswy. Barn S71 34 D3
Long Cswy. Hath S10 137 C5
Long Edge La. Ben DN5 40 E1
Long Field Dr. Don DN3 43 B3
Long Field Rd. Don DN3 43 A3
Long Gate. Wad DN12 101 F5
Long Gr. Stai DN7 24 E4
Long Henry Row. Shef S2 129 C3 6
Long Ing Rd. Holmfi HD7 48 A7
Long La. C in L S81 148 F6
Long La. K Smea WF8 3 D3
Long La. Kill S31 156 F6
Long La. Ought S30 111 C7
Long La. Ought S30 111 D2
Long La. Oxspr S30 73 F3
Long La. Roth S60 132 A7
Long La. Shef S6 126 D5
Long La. Shef S10 127 F4
Long La. Shef S6 111 D2
Long La. Shep HD8 28 E8
Long La. Sprot DN5 61 B4
Long La. Stock S30 91 E8
Long La. Treet S60 132 A7
Long La. Uns S31 154 C1
Long Lands La. Ad le S DN5 39 E5
Long Leys La. Braith S66 101 A5
Long Line. Shef S11 139 B2
Long Rd. Thurcr S66 133 E6
Long Royd La. Shep HD8 29 B8
Longacre Cl. Shef S19 144 A1
Longacre Way. Shef S19 144 B1
Longcar Jun & Inf Sch. Barn 54 D8
Longcar La. Barn S70 54 D8
Longcroft Ave. Dron S18 152 C2
Longcroft Cres. Dron S18 152 C2
Longdale Dr. S Elm WF9 18 E4
Longfellow Dr. Roth S65 116 B5
Longfellow Rd. Don DN4 83 C6
Longfield Cl. Wombw S73 56 B4
Longfield Dr. Don DN4 84 D6
Longfield Dr. Mapp S75 14 B1
Longfield Dr. Roth S65 117 D8
Longfield Rd. Shef S10 128 B5
Longfields Cres. Hoy S74 76 D6
Longford Cl. Shef S17 152 A5
Longford Cres. Shef S17 152 A5
Longford Dr. Shef S17 151 F4
Longford Rd. Shef S17 152 A4
Longford Spinney. Shef S17 151 F4
Longlands Ave. Wales S31 145 C2
Longlands Dr. Mapp S75 33 B8
Longlands Dr. Roth S65 99 A3
Longley Ave W. Shef S5 112 F2
Longley Cl. Barn S75 32 E4
Longley Cl. Shef S5 113 B2
Longley Cres. Shef S5 113 B3
Longley Dr. Shef S5 113 B2
Longley Edge Rd. Holmfi HD7 48 B8
Longley Hall Gr. Shef S5 113 C2
Longley Hall Rd. Shef S5 113 C2
Longley Hall Rise. Shef S5 113 B3
Longley Hall Way. Shef S5 113 C2
Longley Jun & Inf Sch. Shef 113 A2
Longley La. Holmfi HD7 48 A8
Longley La. Shef S5 113 B3
Longley St. Barn S75 32 E4
Longman Rd. Barn S70 33 E2
Longridge Rd. Barn S71 34 D6
Longshaw Ctry Pk. Grin 150 A3
Longside Way. Barn S75 33 A1
Longsight Rd. Mapp S75 14 A1
Longstone Cres. Shef S12 142 D4
Longthwaite Cl. Lough S31 134 E4
Longton Rd. Don DN3 43 A4
Lonsbrough Way. S Elm WF9 19 A4
Lonsdale Ave. Barn S71 56 B8
Lonsdale Ave. Don DN2 63 D4
Lonsdale Cl. N Anst S31 146 F6
Lonsdale House. Don DN2 63 C5
Lonsdale Rd. Shef S6 128 C7
Loosemore Dr. Shef S12 141 F5
Lopham St. Shef S3 129 B5
Lord St. Barn S71 34 C2
Lord St. Roth S65 116 A7
Lord St. Stai DN7 24 E3
Lord's Head La. Don DN4 82 D4
Lordens Hill. Din S31 135 A1
Lords Cl. N Edl DN12 82 C3
Lorna Rd. Mex S64 80 A5
Lorne Cl. Dron S18 152 D2
Lorne Rd. Dearne S63 58 C8
Lothian Rd. Don DN2 63 C5
Louden Cl. Roth S61 96 B2
Louden Rd. Roth S61 96 B2
Lound Inf Sch. Chap 94 F6
Lound Jun Sch. Chap 95 A6
Lound La. H Pag DN5 38 F5
Lound Rd. Shef S9 130 D3
Lound Side. Chap S30 95 A5
Lounde Cl. Sprot DN5 61 C1
Louth Rd. Shef S11 140 B8
Love La. Shef S3 129 A4
Love St. Shef S3 129 A4
Lovell St. Shef S4 129 D5
Loversall Cl. Don DN4 83 C5
Loversall. Don 83 C5
Lovetot Ave. Aston S31 144 D8
Lovetot Rd. Roth S61 96 E2
Lovetot Rd. Shef S9 129 E5
Low Bradfield Cty Prim Sch. Bfield 110 A4
Low Cudworth. Cud S72 35 B5
Low Cudworth Gn. Cud S72 35 B5
Low Deeps La. Misson DN10 87 E1
Low Field La. Aust DN10 105 C1
Low Fisher Gate. Don DN1 62 D4
Low Gate. S Elm WF9 19 A3
Low Grange Sq. Dearne S63 58 C8
Low La. K Bram DN7 23 F4
Low La. Maltby S66 118 C2
Low La. Roth S61 115 A8
Low La. Thurcr S66 118 C2
Low Laithes View. Wombw S73 56 B4
Low Levels Bank. Hat DN8 46 C6
Low Matlock La. Shef S6 127 E8
Low Moor La. Midhop S30 71 D3
Low Pastures Cl. Dod S75 54 A7
Low Rd. Con DN12 81 D3
Low Rd. Don DN4 83 A7
Low Rd E. Don DN4 82 D6
Low Rd. Ought S30 111 D7
Low Rd. Scro DN10 123 A2
Low Rd. Shef S6 128 A6
Low Rd. Thurgo S30 52 D1
Low Rd W. Don DN4 82 C6
Low Row. Mapp S75 13 E3
Low St. Dod S75 54 B6
Low View. Dod S75 53 F7
Lowburn Rd. Shef S13 142 C7
Lowe La. Hd Gr S75 53 F3
Lowedges Cres. Shef S8 152 F6
Lowedges Dr. Shef S8 152 F6
Lowedges Pl. Shef S8 153 A6
Lowedges Rd. Shef S8 152 E6
Lowell Ave. Don DN4 83 B6
Lower Boundary Rd. T in B DN5 42 B7
Lower Castlereagh St. Barn S70 33 E1 6
Lower Common La. Clay W HD8 30 D8
Lower Denby La. D Dale HD8 30 B4
Lower Dolcliffe Rd. Mex S64 79 F5
Lower Kenyon St. Thorne DN8 26 B8
Lower Malton Rd. Ben DN5 61 E6
Lower Maythorn La. Wh Com HD7 49 D8
Lower Mill Cl. Dearne S63 58 C4
Lower Northcroft. S Elm WF9 19 A3
Lower Northfield La. S Kirk WF9 18 C3
Lower Putting Mill. D Dale HD8 30 B7
Lower Thomas St. Barn S70 54 E8 3
Lower Unwin St. Pen S30 51 D2
Lower York St. Wombw S73 56 D3
Lowfield Ave. Eck S12 154 E8
Lowfield Ave. Roth S61 97 C3
Lowfield Cl. B Dun DN3 43 A6
Lowfield Cres. Hem WF9 17 E7
Lowfield Ct. Shef S2 141 A7 4
Lowfield Jun & Inf Sch. Shef 141 A7
Lowfield Rd. Dearne S63 58 D2
Lowfield Rd. Don DN2 63 C7
Lowfield Wlk. Con DN12 80 F4
Lowgate. Bal M DN6 6 A8
Lowgate. Ben DN5 61 E7
Lowgreave. Roth S65 116 C8
Lowhill. Thorne DN8 8 F1
Lowhouse Rd. Shef S5 113 E7
Lowlands Cl. Barn S71 34 D5
Lowlands Wlk. Askern DN6 22 B7
Lowry Dr. Dron S18 152 F1
Lowther Rd. Don DN1 62 E5
Lowther Rd. Shef S6 112 D1
Lowther Sq. C in L S81 148 E7
Lowton Way. Maltby S66 118 A5
Loxley Ave. Wombw S73 56 C2
Loxley Coll. Stock 73 B2
Loxley Ct. Shef S6 128 C7
Loxley Jun & Inf Sch. Shef 111 E1
Loxley Mount. Norton DN6 4 C1
Loxley New Rd. Shef S6 128 B7
Loxley Rd. Barn S71 34 F3
Loxley Rd. Bfield S6 110 C4
Loxley Rd. Shef S6 127 E8
Loxley View Rd. Shef S10 128 B5
Loy Cl. Roth S61 97 A3
Lucas St. Shef S4 129 C7
Lucknow Ct. Shef S7 140 E6
Ludgate Cl. Ross DN11 104 A7
Ludwell Hill. Bnbur DN5 59 E2
Lugano Gr. Dar S73 56 E6
Luke La. Shef S6 111 F1
Lulworth Cl. Barn S70 55 B8 6
Lumb La. Wharn S30 110 E8
Lumley Cl. Maltby S66 119 C4
Lumley Cres. Maltby S66 119 C4
Lumley Dr. Laugh S31 134 C2
Lumley Dr. Maltby S66 119 C4
Lumley Dr. Tick DN11 121 B7
Lumley St. Shef S4, S9 129 D4
Lumley St. Shef S9 129 F4
Lump La. Shef S30 94 C1
Luna Croft. Shef S12 141 F2
Lunbreck Rd. Don DN4 82 C5
Lund Ave. Barn S71 34 F3
Lund Cl. Barn S71 34 F3
Lund Cres. Barn S71 34 F3
Lund Hill La. Roy S71 15 F5
Lund Hill La. Ryhill S71 15 F5
Lund La. Barn S71 34 F3
Lund Rd. Ought S30 111 D5
Lundhill Cl. Wombw S73 56 E1
Lundhill Gr. Wombw S73 56 E1
Lundhill Rd. Wombw S73 56 E1
Lundwood Cl. Shef S19 143 C2
Lundwood Dr. Shef S19 143 C2
Lundwood Gr. Shef S19 143 C2
Lundwood House. Don DN1 62 C2 18
Lunn Rd. Cud S72 35 B6
Lupton Bdlgs. Swint S64 79 D4
Lupton Cres. Shef S8 152 F6
Lupton Dr. Shef S8 152 F6
Lupton Rd. Shef S8 152 F6
Luterel Dr. Aston S31 144 D8
Lutterworth Dr. Ad l S DN6 40 A6
Lych Gate Cl. Don DN4 85 A7
Lydgate Cty Jun Sch. Shef 128 A3
Lydgate Ct. Shef S10 128 B3
Lydgate Hall Cres. Shef S10 128 A3
Lydgate La. Shef S10 128 B3
Lydgate Mid Sch. Shef 128 A2
Lydgate Rd. Shep HD8 28 F8
Lyme St. Roth S60 115 C6
Lyme Terr. Ad le S DN6 20 E1
Lyminster Rd. Shef S6 112 D4
Lymister Ave. Roth S60 115 F1
Lyndale Ave. Don DN3 42 F1
Lynden Ave. Ad l S DN6 40 A6
Lyndhurst Cl. Norton DN6 4 E3
Lyndhurst Cl. Shef S11 140 C6
Lyndhurst Cl. Thorne DN8 25 F8
Lyndhurst Cres. Don DN3 42 E3
Lyndhurst Dr. Norton DN6 4 E3
Lyndhurst Rd. Shef S11 140 D6
Lyndhurst Rise. Norton DN6 4 E3
Lynmouth Rd. Shef S7 140 E5
Lynn Pl. Shef S9 130 B8
Lynton Ave. Roth S60 116 B3
Lynton Dr. Don DN3 42 E2
Lynton Pl. Kex S75 32 D8
Lynton Rd. Shef S11 140 D8 9
Lynwood Cl. Dron S18 152 D1 1
Lynwood Dr. Roy S71 15 C2
Lynwood La. Roy S71 15 C2
Lyons Rd. Shef S4 129 C7
Lyons St. Shef S4 129 D7
Lytham Ave. Barn S71 34 D5
Lytham Ave. Din S31 146 F7
Lytham Cl. Don DN4 85 B6
Lyttleton Cres. Pen S30 51 C1
Lytton Ave. Shef S5 112 E5
Lytton Cl. Don DN4 83 B6
Lytton Cres. Shef S5 112 E5
Lytton Dr. Shef S5 112 F5
Lytton Rd. Shef S5 112 E5

Mabel St. Roth S60 115 F5
Macaulay Cres. Arm DN3 64 C6
Machin Dr. Rawm S62 97 D8
Machin La. Stock S30 72 E2
Machins Ct. Dron S18 153 A2
Machon Bank Rd. Shef S7 140 E6
Machon Bank. Shef S7 140 E6
Mackenzie Cres. Chap S30 94 E4
Mackenzie Cres. Shef S10 128 E2
Mackenzie St. Shef S11 140 E8
Mackey Cres. Bri S72 16 F3
Macmanus Ave. Rawm S62 97 F8
Macnaghten Rd. Pilley S75 75 F5
Macro Rd. Wombw S73 56 F2
Madam La. B Dun DN3 42 E8
Madehurst Gdns. Shef S2 141 B7
Madehurst Rd. Shef S2 141 B7
Madehurst Rise. Shef S2 141 B7
Madehurst View. Shef S2 141 B7
Madingley Cl. Don DN4 83 A5
Mafeking Pl. Chap S30 95 A6
Magellan Rd. Maltby S66 118 E6
Maggot La. Thurgo S75 52 D2
Magna Cl. Roth S66 117 B6
Magna Cres. Roth S66 117 A6
Magna La. Roth S65 98 E1
Magnolia Cl. Don DN3 42 F3
Magnolia Cl. S Anst S31 146 D3
Magnolia Cl. Shaf S72 16 D2
Magnolia Ct. Shef S10 139 E8
Magpie Gr. Shef S2 129 E2
Mahon Ave. Rawm S62 97 F6
Maidstone Rd. Shef S6 112 D4
Main Ave. N Edl DN12 82 B3
Main Ave. Shef S17 151 E4
Main Rd. Dron S18 152 B1
Main Rd. Eck S31 154 F3
Main Rd. Eck S12 154 E8
Main Rd. Eck S31 156 B1
Main Rd. Hath S30 149 A8
Main Rd. Shef S9 130 C4
Main Rd. Shef S9 130 D4
Main Rd. Shef S6 110 D1
Main Rd. Wharn S30 93 B2
Main St. Aston S31 132 C2
Main St. Aston S31 144 C7
Main St. Auck DN9 86 A6
Main St. Bran DN3 64 B1
Main St. Dearne S63 58 E6
Main St. Fish DN7 25 A7
Main St. Ham DN6 20 B1
Main St. Har DN11 121 E4
Main St. Hat DN7 44 F6
Main St. K Smea WF8 3 D6
Main St. Mex S64 79 F4
Main St. N Anst S31 146 D6
Main St. Old S81 136 F6
Main St. Rawm S62 98 A6
Main St. Roth S60 115 D6
Main St. Roth S66 117 D5
Main St. Roth S61 97 C3
Main St. Roth S65 99 D2
Main St. S Hie S72 16 D6
Main St. Shef S12 143 B3
Main St. Shef S30 112 C8
Main St. Sprot DN5 82 B8
Main St. Styr DN11 121 D1
Main St. Treet S60 131 D6
Main St. Ulley S31 132 E4
Main St. Upton WF9 19 D8
Main St. Wad DN11 102 C7
Main St. Went S62 77 B1
Main St. Wombw S73 56 C3
Main View. Stai DN7 25 B4
Makin St. Mex S64 80 C4
Malcolm Cl. Barn S70 55 D8
Malham Cl. Bawtry DN10 122 F8
Malham Cl. Shaf S72 16 C3
Malham Ct. Barn S70 33 D2 3
Malham Gdns. Shef S19 155 D7
Malham Gr. Shef S19 155 E7
Malham Pl. Chap S30 94 F6
Malin Bridge Jun & Inf Schs. Shef 128 B8
Malin Rd. Roth S65 116 D8
Malin Rd. Shef S6 128 A7
Malinda St. Shef S3 128 F5
Mallard Ave. B Dun DN3 42 F6
Mallard Cl. Don DN4 82 F6
Mallard Cl. Kill S31 156 B7
Mallard Cl. Roth S61 96 A5
Mallin Dr. N Edl DN12 82 B1
Mallory Ave. Rawm S62 97 E6
Mallory Dr. Mex S64 80 D6
Mallory Rd. Roth S65 116 C8
Mallory Way. Cud S72 35 C7
Malpas Hill. Old DN11 120 F1
Maltas Ct. Barn S70 55 C5
Maltby Comp Sch. Maltby 118 F5
Maltby Crags Jun Mix & Inf Sch. Maltby 119 A4
Maltby Hall Inf Sch. Maltby 118 E5
Maltby House. Don DN1 62 C2 17
Maltby La. Maltby S66 118 F8
Maltby Rd. Old S81 136 E6
Maltby St. Shef S9 130 A7
Malthouse Rd. Barn S70 33 F1 18
Malting La. Shef S4 129 C4
Maltings The. Roth S60 115 D5
Maltkiln St. Roth S60 115 D5
Maltkin Cotts. Don DN3 42 F5
Maltkin Dr. W Bret WF4 12 F8
Malton Dr. Aston S31 144 E7
Malton Pl. Barn S71 33 E7
Malton Rd. Ben DN5 61 D7
Malton Rd. Don DN2 63 B5
Malton Rd. Upton WF9 19 D8
Malton St. Shef S4 129 C7
Maltravers Cl. Shef S2 129 E2
Maltravers Cres. Shef S2 129 E3
Maltravers Pl. Shef S2 129 E3
Maltravers Rd. Shef S2 129 E3
Maltravers St. Shef S4 129 C4
Maltravers Terr. Shef S2 129 E2
Maltravers Way. Shef S2 129 E3
Malvern Ave. Ben DN5 61 E5
Malvern Cl. Barn S75 33 B2
Malvern Cl. Thorne DN8 26 A6
Malvern Rd. Don DN2 63 C4
Malvern Rd. Shef S9 130 B5
Malwood Way. Maltby S66 119 B6
Manchester Rd. Pen S30 50 D3
Manchester Rd. Shef S10 127 D3
Manchester Rd. Stock S30 73 B2
Manchester Rd. Stock S30 73 E1
Mandale Rd. B Dun DN3 42 F8
Mandeville St. Shef S9 130 C5
Mangham La. Tick DN11 121 A8
Mangham Rd. Roth S61, S62 97 E2
Mangham Way. Roth S61 97 D1
Mannering Rd. Don DN4 82 E6
Manners St. Shef S3 128 F6
Manor App. Roth S61 114 F7
Manor Ave. Dearne S63 58 E5
Manor Cl. B Dun DN3 42 E7
Manor Cl. K Smea WF8 3 D5
Manor Cl. Maltby S66 118 F5
Manor Cl. Norton DN6 4 C3
Manor Cl. Notton WF4 14 F7
Manor Cl. Rawm S62 97 C8
Manor Cl. Tod S31 145 F5
Manor Cl. W up D S63 78 B7
Manor Cl. Wad DN11 102 C6
Manor Cres. Brin S60 131 B8
Manor Cres. Dron S18 152 F1
Manor Cres. Grime S72 36 A8
Manor Croft. S Hie S72 16 D6
Manor Ct. Con DN12 80 E3
Manor Dr. Cade DN5 81 D5
Manor Dr. Don DN2 62 F3
Manor Dr. Roth S60 116 C1
Manor Dr. Roy S71 15 B3
Manor Dr. S Hie S72 16 D6
Manor Dr. Tod S31 145 F5

Manor End. Barn S70 54 F5
Manor Est. Ben DN5 40 F4
Manor Farm Cl. Ad I S DN6 40 B6
Manor Farm Cl. Aston S31 132 D2
Manor Farm Cl. Roy S71 34 D8
Manor Farm Ct. Roth S65 98 F4
Manor Farm Dr. Swint S64 79 C2
Manor Farm Est. Rawm S62 97 C8
Manor Farm Est. S Elm WF9 19 A3
Manor Farm Gdns. S Anst S31 146 D4
Manor Farm La. Syke DN14 7 A5
Manor Fields. Roth S61 114 E8
Manor Garth. Norton DN6 4 E3
Manor Gdns. Barn S71 56 B8
Manor Gdns. Hat DN7 44 C7
Manor Gdns. Sprot DN5 61 B1
Manor Gr. Grime S72 35 F8
Manor Gr. Roy S71 15 B3
Manor Gr. S Kirk WF9 18 A1
Manor House Cl. Hoy S74 76 E6
Manor House Ct. Ben DN5 40 F1
Manor House Rd. Roth S61 114 E8
Manor House. Shef S6 127 C6
Manor Inf Sch. Maltby 119 A5
Manor Jun Sch. Maltby 119 A6
Manor La. Din S31 135 A3
Manor La. Mex S64 80 A7
Manor La. Oxspr S30 52 C1
Manor La. Shef S2 129 F2
Manor Laith Rd. Shef S2 129 D2
Manor Lodge Fst & Mid Schs. Shef 129 E1
Manor Oaks Cl. Shef S2 129 E3
Manor Oaks Gdns. Shef S2 129 D3
Manor Oaks Pl. Shef S2 129 E2
Manor Oaks Rd. Shef S2 129 D3
Manor Occupation Rd. Roy S71 15 B4
Manor Park Ave. Shef S2 129 F1
Manor Park Cl. Shef S2 129 F1
Manor Park Cres. Shef S2 129 F1
Manor Park Ct. Shef S2 129 F1
Manor Park Ctr. Shef S2 129 F2
Manor Park Dr. Shef S2 129 F1
Manor Park Pl. Shef S2 129 F2
Manor Park Rd. Shef S2 129 F2
Manor Park Rise. Shef S2 129 F2
Manor Park Way. Shef S2 129 F1
Manor Pk. Silk S75 52 F8
Manor Pl. Rawm S62 98 A5
Manor Rd. Askern DN6 21 F7
Manor Rd. B Dun DN3 42 F8
Manor Rd. Ben DN5 41 A4
Manor Rd. Bnbur DN5 59 C2
Manor Rd. Brin S60 131 B8
Manor Rd. Clay W HD8 12 A4
Manor Rd. Cud S72 35 A6
Manor Rd. Dearne S63 58 C8
Manor Rd. Din S31 134 F2
Manor Rd. Hart S31 157 F8
Manor Rd. Hat DN7 44 C7
Manor Rd. Kill S31 156 E5
Manor Rd. Maltby S66 119 A5
Manor Rd. Scro DN10 123 A2
Manor Rd. Swint S64 79 D2
Manor Rd. W up D S63 78 B7
Manor Rd. Wales S31 145 B3
Manor Sq. Dearne S63 58 C8
Manor St. Roy S71 34 D8
Manor View. Shaf S72 16 C2
Manor View. Shef S19 155 E7
Manor Way. Askern DN6 21 F6
Manor Way. Hoy S74 76 E6
Manor Way. Shef S31 129 F3
Manor Way. Tod S31 145 F5
Manor Wlk. Wad DN11 102 B6
Manse Cl. Don DN4 85 A8
Mansel Ave. Shef S5 112 E6
Mansel Cres. Shef S5 112 D6
Mansel Ct. Shef S5 112 E6
Mansel Jun & Inf Schs. Shef 112 E7
Mansel Rd. Shef S5 112 E6
Mansfield Cres. Ad le S DN6 21 B2
Mansfield Cres. Arm DN3 63 F7
Mansfield Dr. Shef S12 142 C6
Mansfield Rd. Aston S31 144 F3
Mansfield Rd. Barn S71 33 F8
Mansfield Rd. Don DN4 62 B1
Mansfield Rd. Kill S31 156 F6
Mansfield Rd. Roth S60 115 E6
Mansfield Rd. Wales S31 144 F3
Mansion Court Gdns. Thorne DN8 26 C8
Manton House. Don DN1 62 C2 19
Manton St. Shef S2 129 B1
Manvers Cl. Aston S31 144 D7
Manvers Cl. N Anst S31 146 E7
Manvers Rd. Aston S31 144 C7
Manvers Rd. Mex S64 79 E5
Manvers Rd. Shef S6 128 C7
Manvers Rd. Shef S19 143 F4
Maori Ave. Dearne S63 58 A2
Maple Ave. Don DN4 84 F8
Maple Ave. Finn DN9 86 A4
Maple Ave. Maltby S66 118 D5
Maple Cl. Barn S70 55 B7
Maple Croft Cres. Shef S9 114 A3
Maple Croft Rd. Shef S9 113 F3
Maple Dr. Auck DN9 86 A7
Maple Dr. Kill S31 156 C5
Maple Dr. Roth S66 117 B6
Maple Gr. Arm DN3 64 B7
Maple Gr. Aston S31 144 F8
Maple Gr. Bawtry DN10 122 F7
Maple Gr. Con DN12 100 A8
Maple Gr. Shef S9 130 E3
Maple Gr. Stock S30 92 B8
Maple Leaf Ct. Mex S64 79 F5
Maple Pl. Chap S30 95 A4
Maple Rd. Mapp S75 14 A1
Maple Rd. Mex S64 79 F6
Maple Rd. Pilley S75 75 D3
Maple Rd. Thorne DN8 9 C1
Maple Rd. Wales S31 145 C3
Maple Wlk. Thorne DN8 9 C1
Maplebeck Dr. Shef S9 114 F2
Maplebeck Rd. Shef S9 114 F2
Mapperley Rd. Dron S18 152 C1
Mappin Art Gal. Shef 128 D3
Mappin St. Shef S1 128 F3
Mappin's Rd. Treet S60 131 D5
Mapplebeck Rd. Chap S30 94 E7
Mapplewell Inf Sch. Mapp 14 C1
Mapplewell Jun Mix Sch. Mapp 14 C1
Maran Ave. Dar S73 57 C5
March Bank. Roth S65 99 A3
March Flatts Rd. Roth S65 99 A2
March Gate. Con DN12 81 C1
March St. Con DN12 81 C2
March St. Shef S9 130 B7
March Vale Rise. Con DN12 81 C1
Marcham Dr. Shef S19 144 A4
Marchwood Ave. Shef S6 127 E6
Marchwood Dr. Shef S6 127 E7
Marchwood Rd. Shef S6 127 E7
Marcliff Cl. Roth S66 116 F4
Marcliff Cres. Roth S66 116 F4
Marcliff La. Roth S66 116 F4
Marcus Dr. Shef S3 129 B5
Mardale Wlk. Don DN2 63 C6
Marden Rd. Shef S7 140 E6
Margaret Cl. Aston S31 144 D6
Margaret Cl. Dar S73 56 F5
Margaret Rd. Dar S73 56 F5
Margaret Rd. Wombw S73 56 E2
Margaret St. Maltby S66 119 B3
Margaret St. Shef S1 129 A1
Margate Dr. Shef S4 129 D8
Margate St. Grime S72 36 A7
Margate St. Shef S4 129 E8
Margetson Cres. Shef S5 112 F6
Margetson Dr. Shef S5 112 F6
Margetson Rd. Shef S5 112 F6
Marian Cres. Askern DN6 21 E8
Marian Rd. Don DN3 42 E2
Marigold Cl. Shef S5 113 E3
Marina Rise. Dar S73 56 E5
Marina View. Thorne DN8 26 B5
Marion Rd. Shef S6 112 B2
Mark Gr. Roth S66 117 B5
Mark La. Shef S10 139 A6
Mark St. Barn S70 33 E1 8
Markbrook Dr. Chap S30 94 C8
Market Cl. Barn S71 34 A1
Market Hill. Barn S70 33 E1 3
Market Par. Barn S70 33 F1 6
Market Pl. Askern DN6 22 A8
Market Pl. Bawtry DN10 123 A7
Market Pl. Chap S30 95 B5
Market Pl. Cud S72 35 B7
Market Pl. Din S31 134 F1
Market Pl. Don DN1 62 D3
Market Pl. Pen S30 51 D3
Market Pl. Shef S1 129 B4
Market Pl. Thorne DN8 26 B7
Market Rd. Don DN1 62 D4
Market Sq. Dearne S63 58 E5
Market Sq. Roth S65 115 E7 9
Market Sq. Shef S13 143 C6
Market St. Ad I S DN6 40 B2
Market St. Barn S70 33 E1
Market St. Chap S30 95 B5
Market St. Cud S72 35 B7
Market St. Dearne S63 58 C8
Market St. Dearne S63 58 E5
Market St. Eck S31 155 E3
Market St. Hem WF9 17 D7
Market St. Hoy S74 76 E6
Market St. Mex S64 80 A4
Market St. Pen S30 51 D3
Market St. Roth S60 115 D6
Market St. Shef S13 143 C6
Market St. Swint S64 79 E3
Markfield Dr. Roth S66 117 B5
Markham Ave. Ad le S DN6 21 C1
Markham Ave. Arm DN3 64 A7
Markham Ave. Con DN12 81 A2
Markham Ct. Con DN12 81 A2
Markham Rd. Lan S81 136 E3
Markham Rd. N Edl DN12 82 C2
Markham Sq. N Edl DN12 82 C2
Markham Terr. N Edl DN12 82 B2
Markham Terr. Shef S8 140 F6
Marlborough Ave. Ben DN5 61 F4
Marlborough Cl. Dearne S63 58 C8
Marlborough Cl. N Anst S31 146 D7
Marlborough Cres. Askern DN6 22 B7
Marlborough Croft. S Elm WF9 18 F4
Marlborough Rd. Askern DN6 22 B8
Marlborough Rd. Don DN2 62 F4
Marlborough Rd. Shef S10 128 D3
Marlborough Rd. Thorne DN8 26 C6
Marlborough Rise. Aston S31 144 E6
Marlborough Terr. Barn S70 54 E8 8
Marlcliffe Jun & Inf Sch. Shef 112 B2
Marlcliffe Rd. Shef S6 112 B2
Marley Rd. Shef S2 129 E1
Marlow Cl. Don DN2 63 C5
Marlow Cl. Roth S66 117 D4
Marlow Rd. Don DN2 63 C5
Marlowe Dr. Roth S65 116 B5
Marlowe Rd. B Dun DN3 42 F8
Marlowe Rd. Roth S65 116 B5
Marmion Rd. Shef S11 140 B8
Marples Cl. Shef S8 140 F7 7
Marples Dr. Shef S8 140 F7 8
Marquis Gdns. B Dun DN3 42 F7
Marr Grange La. Marr DN5 60 E7
Marr Terr. Shef S10 127 F1
Marrick Ct. Chap S30 94 F5
Marrion Rd. Rawm S62 98 A6
Marriott La. Shef S7 140 D3
Marriott Pl. Rawm S62 97 D7
Marriott Rd. Shef S7 140 D3
Marriott Rd. Swint S64 79 E4
Marrison Dr. Kill S31 156 C6
Marsala Wlk. Dar S73 56 F6
Marsden Gr. Thorne DN8 26 A8
Marsden La. Shef S3 128 F4
Marsden Rd. Stock S30 73 C1
Marsh Ave. Dron S18 153 B3
Marsh Cl. Shef S19 155 C6
Marsh Gate. Don DN5 62 B4
Marsh Hill. Braith S66 100 D1
Marsh Hill La. Syke DN14 7 F7
Marsh House Rd. Shef S11 140 A5
Marsh La. Ben DN5 41 C4
Marsh La. Ben DN3 42 C6
Marsh La. Shef S10 128 A3
Marsh La. Shep HD8 28 D7
Marsh La. T in B DN3 23 C1
Marsh La. T in B DN3 42 C7
Marsh La. Thorne DN8 9 A4
Marsh Lane Prim Sch. Eck 154 E3
Marsh Lea Grove. Hem WF9 17 F7
Marsh Rd. Ben DN5 62 B5
Marsh Rd. T in B DN6 23 D4
Marsh St. Roth S60 115 C5
Marsh St. Stock S30 73 D1
Marsh St. Wombw S73 56 E3
Marsh View. Eck S31 155 B2
Marsh Wlk. Shef S2 129 D4
Marshall Ave. Don DN4 83 A7
Marshall Cl. Rawm S62 97 F4
Marshall Dr. S Elm WF9 18 F3
Marshall Gr. W up D S63 78 F5
Marshall Rd. Shef S8 140 F2
Marshfield. Barn S70 54 F1
Marshland Rd. Thorne DN8 9 C3
Marson Ave. Ad le S DN6 39 F5
Marston Cres. Barn S71 33 F6
Marston Rd. Shef S10 128 B4
Marstone Cres. Shef S17 151 F5
Martin Beck La. Tick DN11 104 A1
Martin Cl. Aston S31 132 C2
Martin Cl. Barn S70 75 F8
Martin Cres. Shef S5 113 B6
Martin Croft. Silk S75 52 F8
Martin Ct. Eck S31 155 C3
Martin La. Bawtry DN10 122 E8
Martin La. Hoy S74 55 D1
Martin Rise. Eck S31 155 C3
Martin Rise. Roth S61 96 A6
Martin St. Shef S6 128 E5
Martin Wells Rd. N Edl DN12 82 C1
Martin's Rd. Barn S71 34 F3
Martindale Wlk. Ad I S DN6 40 C8
Marton Ave. Hem WF9 17 C6
Marton Dr. Hat DN7 44 B7
Marton Rd. Ben DN5 40 F5
Marvell Rd. Ben DN5 61 D6
Mary Ann Cl. Barn S71 34 D2
Mary La. Dar S73 57 B5
Mary St. Barn S75 32 D4
Mary St. Eck S31 155 D3
Mary St. G Hou S72 57 E7
Mary St. Roth S60 115 C7 5
Mary St. Shef S1 129 A1
Mary Tozer House. Shef S10 128 B3
Mary's Pl. Barn S75 33 C2 2
Marys Wlk. Shef S2 129 D4
Masbrough St. Roth S60 115 C6
Masefield Ct. Din S31 147 A8
Masefield Rd. Don DN2 63 C7
Masefield Rd. Shef S13 142 C6
Masefield Rd. W up D S63 78 C7
Masham Rd. Don DN4 84 E7
Mason Ave. Aston S31 132 D1
Mason Cres. Shef S13 142 D6
Mason Dr. Aston S31 132 D1
Mason Gr. Shef S13 142 D7
Mason Lathe Rd. Shef S5 113 E6
Mason St. Dearne S63 58 E5
Mason Way. Hoy S74 76 D7
Masons Cotts. Eck S31 155 A1
Masons Way. Barn S70 55 C6
Massey Rd. Shef S13 143 D5
Mastall La. Ben DN5 41 F2
Masters Cres. Shef S5 113 B5
Masters Rd. Shef S5 113 B5
Mather Ave. Shef S9 130 D5
Mather Cres. Shef S9 130 B3
Mather Dr. Shef S9 130 B3
Mather Rd. Shef S9 130 B3
Matilda La. Shef S1 129 B2
Matilda St. Shef S1 129 A2
Matilda Way. Shef S1 129 A2
Matlock Rd. Barn S71 34 B6
Matlock Rd. Shef S6 128 C5
Mattersey Cl. Don DN4 84 E5
Matthew St. Shef S3 128 F5
Matthews Ave. W up D S63 78 E6
Matthews Cl. W up D S63 78 E5
Matthews Dr. Roth S66 117 B3
Matthews La. Shef S8 141 C1
Maud Maxfield Sch. Shef 139 E5
Maugerhay. Shef S8 141 C1
Maun Way. Shef S5 113 C3
Mauncer Cres. Shef S13 143 B7
Mauncer Dr. Shef S13 143 B7
Mauncer La. Shef S13 143 B6
Maunche St. Rawm S62 97 F3
Mawfa Ave. Shef S14 141 D2
Mawfa Cres. Shef S14 141 D2
Mawfa Dr. Shef S14 141 D2
Mawfa Rd. Shef S14 141 D2
Mawfield Rd. Barn S75 33 A4
Mawson Green La. Syke DN14 7 F6
Maxey Pl. Shef S8 141 A6
Maxfield Ave. Shef S10 128 C3
Maxwell St. Shef S4 129 C6
Maxwell Way. Shef S4 129 C6
May Ave. Don DN4 83 A6
May Day Gn. Barn S70 33 F1 3
May Day Green Arc. Barn S70 33 F1 7
May Rd. Shef S6 128 B8
May Terr. Barn S70 33 C1
May Tree Cl. Shef S19 143 E1
May Tree Croft. Shef S19 143 E1 3
May Tree La. Shef S19 143 E1
Mayberry Dr. Silk S75 31 F1
Maycock Ave. Roth S61 96 D2
Mayfair Cl. Har DN11 121 F4
Mayfair Pl. Hem WF9 17 D7
Mayfield. Askern DN6 22 A8
Mayfield Ave. Stai DN7 25 B4
Mayfield. Barn S71 34 B4
Mayfield Cres. Barn S70 54 E6
Mayfield Cres. Ross DN11 103 F8
Mayfield Croft. Shef S30 113 B8
Mayfield Ct. Oxspr S30 73 C8
Mayfield Ct. Shef S10 139 C8
Mayfield. Oxspr S30 73 B8
Mayfield Rd. Ben DN5 62 A4
Mayfield Rd. Shef S10 139 A6
Mayfield Special Sch. Shef 139 A7
Mayfield Terr. Askern DN6 22 A8
Mayfield Terr. Hath S30 149 A8
Mayfields. Ben DN5 40 D1
Mayfields Way. S Kirk WF9 18 B1
Mayflower Ave. Scro DN10 123 A2
Mayflower Cl. Bawtry DN10 123 A8
Mayflower Cres. Don DN4 82 C5
Mayflower Jun & Inf Sch. Bawtry 123 A8
Mayflower Rd. Don DN4 82 C5
Maynard Rd. Grin S30 149 D1
Maynard Rd. Roth S60 116 C2
Maythorne Cl. Mapp S75 33 C8
Maytree Cl. Dar S73 57 A5
McConnel Cres. Ross DN11 84 D1
McIntyre Rd. Stock S30 73 B1
McLaren Ave. Upton WF9 19 D8
McLaren Cres. Maltby S66 119 A4
McLintock Way. Barn S70 33 D1
Meaburn Cl. Don DN4 84 F8
Meadow Ave. Cud S72 35 D4
Meadow Ave. Rawm S62 97 D7
Meadow Bank Ave. Shef S7 140 D7
Meadow Bank Rd. Roth S61 114 C4
Meadow Bank Rd. Roth S61 114 E5
Meadow Bank Rd. Roth S61 115 A6
Meadow Bank Rd. Shef S11 140 D7
Meadow Cl. Dron S18 153 C4
Meadow Cl. Hem WF9 17 C6
Meadow Cl. Roth S65 98 E1
Meadow Cl. Wales S31 145 F3
Meadow Cres. Grime S72 36 A7
Meadow Cres. Roy S71 15 D3
Meadow Cres. Shef S19 155 B7
Meadow Croft. Don DN3 43 A2
Meadow Croft. Hem WF9 17 E5
Meadow Croft. Shaf S72 16 C3
Meadow Croft. Sprot DN5 82 D8
Meadow Croft. Swint S64 98 C8
Meadow Ct. Ross DN11 103 E8
Meadow Ct. Roy S71 15 D3
Meadow Ct. S Elm WF9 19 B3
Meadow Dr. Barn S71 34 D4
Meadow Dr. Chap S30 94 E5
Meadow Dr. Swint S64 79 C2
Meadow Dr. Tick DN11 121 B6
Meadow Field Rd. B Dun DN3 43 A6
Meadow Gate Ave. Shef S19 144 B2
Meadow Gate Cl. Shef S19 144 B2
Meadow Gate La. Shef S19 144 B1
Meadow Gr. Shef S17 151 E4
Meadow Grove Rd. Shef S17 151 D4
Meadow Head Ave. Shef S8 152 F8
Meadow Head Dr. Shef S8 152 F8
Meadow House Dr. Shef S10 127 D1
Meadow La. Con DN12 80 B3
Meadow La. Dar S73 57 B5
Meadow La. Kex S75 32 E7
Meadow La. Maltby S66 119 A4
Meadow La. Rawm S62 97 D8
Meadow Rd. Roy S71 15 D3
Meadow Rise. B Dun DN3 43 A7
Meadow Rise. Hem WF9 17 C7
Meadow Rise. Wad DN11 102 C6
Meadow St. Barn S71 33 F2
Meadow St. Laugh S31 134 C2
Meadow St. Roth S61 115 A6
Meadow St. Shef S3 128 F4
Meadow Terr. Shef S11 140 C8 2
Meadow View. Askern DN6 22 C7
Meadow View. Barn S70 55 A5
Meadow View Cl. Hoy S74 76 D5
Meadow View. Pen S30 51 F6
Meadow View Rd. Shef S8 152 F8
Meadow View Rd. Swint S64 98 D8
Meadow Way. Har DN11 121 F5
Meadow Wlk. Don DN3 43 A3
Meadowbank Cl. Roth S61 115 A6
Meadowbrook Ind Est. Shef 156 A8
Meadowcourt. Shef S9 114 B2
Meadowcroft Cl. Roth S60 132 B8
Meadowcroft Gdns. Shef S19 155 E8
Meadowcroft Glade. Shef S19 155 E8
Meadowcroft Rise. Shef S19 155 E8 2
Meadowfield Dr. Hoy S74 76 E4
Meadowgates. Dearne S63 58 C3
Meadowhall Interchange. Shef S9 114 C3
Meadowhall Rd Jun Sch. Roth 114 E6
Meadowhall Rd. Roth S61 114 D5
Meadowhall Rd. Shef S9 114 B2
Meadowhall Ret Pk. Shef 114 C1
Meadowhall Retail Pk. Shef 130 C8
Meadowhall Sta. Shef 114 B3
Meadowhall Way. Shef S9 114 C2
Meadowhead. Shef S8 152 F8
Meadowland Rise. Cud S72 35 C5
Meadowpark Croft. Din S31 146 E8
Meadows The. D Dale HD8 29 F5
Meadows The. Tod S31 145 F5
Meads The. Shef S8 153 B8
Meadstead Dr. Roy S71 15 B3
Meadway Dr. Shef S17 151 D7
Meadway The. Shef S17 151 D7
Meal Hill La. Holmfi HD7 28 A3
Mears Cl. Pen S30 51 E3
Measham Dr. Stai DN7 25 B5
Mede The. Ad le S DN6 39 F5
Medina Way. Barn S75 32 F5
Medley View. Con DN12 81 D1
Medlock Cl. Shef S13 131 A1
Medlock Cres. Shef S13 131 A2
Medlock Croft. Shef S13 131 A2
Medlock Dr. Shef S13 131 A1
Medlock Rd. Shef S13 131 A1
Medlock Way. Shef S13 131 A2
Medway Cl. Barn S75 32 F5
Medway Pl. Wombw S73 56 F1
Meersbrook Ave. Shef S8 140 F5
Meersbrook Bank Sch. Shef 140 F5
Meersbrook Park Rd. Shef S8 141 A5
Meersbrook Rd. Shef S8 141 B5
Meetinghouse Croft. Shef S13 143 C6
Meetinghouse La. Shef S1 129 B4 2
Meetinghouse La. Shef S13 143 C6
Mekyll Cl. Roth S66 117 B6
Melbeck Ct. Chap S30 94 E5
Melbourn Rd. Shef S10 128 C4
Melbourne Ave. Aston S31 144 E8
Melbourne Ave. Dearne S63 58 B2
Melbourne Ave. Dron S18 152 B1
Melbourne Ave. Shef S10 128 C2
Melbourne Gr. Har DN11 121 F4
Melbourne Rd. Don DN4 82 E6
Melbourne Rd. Stock S30 73 A1
Melciss Rd. Roth S66 117 A4
Meld Cl. Ross DN11 103 F7
Melford Cl. Mapp S75 14 B1
Melford Dr. Don DN4 83 A5
Melfort Glen. Shef S10 127 E3
Mell Ave. Hoy S74 76 E6
Mellinder La. Marr DN5 60 C6
Melling Ave. Ben DN5 61 F3
Mellington Cl. Shef S8 141 C2
Mellish Rd. Lan S81 136 F2
Mellor Rd. Wombw S73 56 D2
Mellow Fields Rd. Lough S31 134 D5
Mellwood Gr. Hoy S73 77 C8
Mellwood La. S Elm WF9 18 F3
Melrose Cl. Don DN4 82 E7
Melrose Cl. Thurcr S66 133 D6
Melrose Gr. Roth S60 116 A2
Melrose Rd. Shef S3 129 B7
Melrose Way. Barn S71 34 D2
Melton Ave. Dearne S63 58 E5
Melton Ave. W up D S73 78 B8
Melton Cl. S Elm WF9 19 A5
Melton Ct. Con DN12 80 F4
Melton Gdns. Sprot DN5 61 B1
Melton Gn. W up D S63 78 C6
Melton Gr. Shef S19 143 A2
Melton Hall Doncaster Training Coll. H Mel 81 B8
Melton High St. W up D S63 78 D6
Melton Mill La. H Mel DN5 80 F8
Melton Rd. Ben DN5 61 C1
Melton Rd. H Mel DN5 60 E1
Melton Rd. Sprot DN5 61 C1
Melton St. Mex S64 80 C4
Melton St. W up D S73 78 B8
Melton Terr. Barn S70 55 C5
Melton View. Bnbur DN5 59 C3
Melton Wood Gr. Sprot DN5 61 B1
Meltonfield Cl. Arm DN3 64 C5
Melville Ave. Don DN4 83 B7
Melville St. Wombw S73 56 D3
Melvinia Cres. Barn S75 33 D4
Melwood Ct. Arm DN3 64 C4
Memoir Gr. Ross DN11 103 E7
Mendip Cl. Barn S75 33 B2
Mendip Cl. Ben DN5 61 E5
Mendip Ct. C in L S81 148 E7
Mendip Rise. Brin S60 131 D7
Menson Dr. Hat DN7 44 B8
Merbeck Dr. Chap S30 75 E1
Merbeck Gr. Chap S30 94 E8
Mercel Ave. Arm DN3 64 C7
Mercia Dr. Shef S17 151 E6
Mere Gr. Arm DN3 64 A7
Mere La. Arm DN3 64 A7
Meredith Cres. Don DN4 83 B6
Meredith Rd. Shef S6 128 B8
Merlin Cl. Barn S70 75 F8
Merlin Way. Roth S61 96 A6
Merlin Way. Shef S5 113 C3
Merrill Rd. Dearne S63 37 C1
Merton La. Shef S9 114 B4
Merton Rd. Shef S9 114 B4
Merton Rise. Shef S9 114 B4
Metcalfe Ave. Kill S31 156 C6
Methley Cl. Shef S12 141 F6
Methley House. Don DN1 62 C2 2
Methley St. Cud S72 35 B6
Mexborough Grammar Sch. Swint 79 F6
Mexborough Rd. Dearne S63 58 D1
Mexborough Sch. Mex 80 B5
Mexborough St John's CE Jun & Inf Sch. Mex 80 B6
Mexborough Sta. Mex 80 A4
Mexborough Windhill Jun & Inf Sch. Mex 80 C6
Meynell Cres. Shef S5 112 D4
Meynell Rd Fst & Mid Sch. Shef 112 E4
Meynell Rd. Shef S5 112 D4
Meynell Way. Kill S31 156 C6
Meyrick Dr. Kex S75 32 D7
Michael Croft. W up D S63 78 D6
Michael Rd. Barn S71 34 F2
Michael's Est. Grime S72 36 A7
Mickelden Way. Barn S75 33 A1
Micklebring Gr. Con DN12 100 A8
Micklebring La. Braith S66 100 E2
Micklebring Way. Maltby S66 118 B7
Micklethwaite Gr. Thorne DN8 9 C4
Micklethwaite Rd. Thorne DN8 9 C4
Mickley La. Shef S17, S18 151 F4
Middle Ave. Rawm S62 97 F6
Middle Bank. Don DN4 62 E1
Middle Cl. Kex S75 13 C1
Middle Dr. Roth S60 115 F1
Middle Field La. Wool WF4 13 F6
Middle Hay Cl. Shef S14 141 E4
Middle Hay Pl. Shef S14 141 E4
Middle Hay Rise. Shef S14 141 E4
Middle Hay View. Shef S14 141 E4
Middle La. Askern DN5 22 D2
Middle La. Roth S65 116 A6
Middle La S. Roth S65 116 A5
Middle La. Shef S6 128 A6
Middle La. Shef S30 94 B1
Middle Ox Gdns. Shef S19 155 F6
Middle Pl. Roth S65 116 B7
Middlebrook La. Thorne DN8 26 B7
Middleburn Cl. Barn S70 55 A7
Middlecliff Cl. Shef S19 143 E1
Middlecliff Cotts. G Hou S72 57 E7
Middlecliff Ct. Shef S19 143 E1 2
Middlecliff La. G Hou S72 57 D7
Middlecliff Rise. Shef S19 143 E1 1
Middlecliffe Dr. Wh Com S30 49 D5
Middlefield Cl. Shef S17 151 C7
Middlefield Croft. Shef S17 151 C7
Middlefield La. K Smea WF8 3 B4
Middlefield Rd. Don DN4 84 D7
Middlefield Rd. Roth S60 116 B2
Middlefields Dr. Roth S60 116 C1
Middlegate. Ben DN5 40 E1
Middleham Rd. Don DN4 84 E7
Middlesex St. Barn S70 54 F7
Middleton Ave. Din S31 146 E8
Middleton La. Shef S30 112 D8
Middleton Rd. Roth S65 115 F6
Middlewood Hall. Dar S73 57 C6
Middlewood Hospl. Shef 111 F3
Middlewood Rd N. Ought S30 111 F5
Middlewood Rd N. Shef S30 111 F5
Middlewood Rd. Shef S6 112 B3
Middlewoods. Dod S75 54 A7
Midfield Rd. Shef S10 128 B4

Midhill Rd. Shef S2 141 B7
Midhope Cliff La. Lang S30 71 C5
Midhope Cliff La. Midhop S30 71 C5
Midhope Hall La. Midhop S30 71 F4
Midhope La. Midhop S30 71 D4
Midhope Way. Barn S75 33 A1
Midhopestones Fst & Mid Sch. Midhop 72 B4
Midhurst Gr. Barn S75 32 E5
Midhurst Rd. Shef S6 112 B5
Midland Rd. Roth S61 115 B6
Midland Rd. Roy S71 15 D4
Midland Rd. Swint S64 79 E3
Midland St. Barn S70 33 F1
Midland St. Roth S62 97 F2
Midland St. Shef S1 129 A1
Midland Sta. Shef 129 B2
Milano Rd. Dar S73 56 F5
Milbanke St. Don DN1 62 D4
Milburn Ct. Shef S19 144 A1 3
Milburn Gr. Shef S19 144 A1
Milcroft Cres. Hat DN7 44 B8
Milden Pl. Barn S70 55 A7
Milden Rd. Shef S6 112 A2
Mile End Ave. Hat DN7 44 A5
Mile Oak Rd. Roth S60 116 A3
Milefield Mid Sch. Grime 35 F7
Milefield View. Grime S72 35 F7
Miles Cl. Shef S5 113 A1
Miles Rd. Chap S30 94 E7
Miles Rd. Shef S5 113 A1
Mileswood Cl. G Hou S72 36 D3
Milethorn La. Don DN1 62 D5
Milford Ave. Hoy S74 77 B6
Milford St. Shef S9 130 B8
Milgate St. Roy S71 15 D4
Milgrove Cres. Chap S30 94 D8
Mill Cl. Laugh S31 134 D6
Mill Cl. Roth S60 115 C4
Mill Cl. S Kirk WF9 18 A1
Mill Cl. Tod S31 145 F4
Mill Field Ct. B Dun DN3 43 A6
Mill Field Rd. Fish DN7 7 F1
Mill Fields. Tod S31 145 E4
Mill Gate. Ben DN5 62 B8
Mill Hill Cl. Ben DN5 61 F3
Mill Hill Rd. Hat DN7 44 C6
Mill Hill. Roth S60 116 C1
Mill Hill. Wombw S73 56 B4
Mill Hills. Tod S31 145 F5
Mill La. Ad l S DN6 40 C6
Mill La. Ad le S DN6 20 F2
Mill La. Bfield S30 91 F4
Mill La. Bnbur DN5 59 C1
Mill La. Don DN4, DN5 82 C7
Mill La. Dron S18 153 B1
Mill La. Eck S31 156 A2
Mill La. Ingb S30 50 E8
Mill La. Mapp S75 13 E1
Mill La. N Anst S31 146 D5
Mill La. Notton WF4 14 D8
Mill La. Pen S30 50 F3
Mill La. Rawcl DN14 2 A8
Mill La. Ryhill WF4 16 B8
Mill La. S Anst S31 146 D5
Mill La. S Elm WF9 19 B4
Mill La. S Kirk WF9 18 A2
Mill La. Scro DN10 123 A3
Mill La. Shef S3 129 B4
Mill La. Shef S17 151 F5
Mill La. Stock S30 73 F1
Mill La. Treet S60 131 D4
Mill La. W up D S63 78 C5
Mill La. Went S62 76 F2
Mill Lee La. Bfield S6 110 A3
Mill Lee Rd. Bfield S6 110 A4
Mill Meadow Cl. Shef S19 144 B1
Mill Meadow Gdns. Shef S19 144 B1
Mill Rd. Eck S31 155 E4
Mill Rd. Shef S30 95 B1
Mill Rd. Treet S60 131 D4
Mill Road Cl. Shef S30 95 B1
Mill Shaw La. Holmfi HD7 28 B1
Mill St. Arm DN3 64 B6
Mill St. Roth S60 115 D5
Mill St. Roth S61 97 B4
Mill St. S Kirk WF9 18 A2
Mill View. Dearne S63 58 B1
Mill View. Hem WF9 17 C6
Mill View. Stai DN7 24 E3
Mill Wood View. Shef S6 127 C7
Millais Rise. Roth S66 117 B7
Millard Ave. Hat DN7 44 B8
Millard La. Maltby S66 119 A5
Millard Nook. Hat DN7 44 B7
Millbank Cl. Chap S30 94 D6
Milldale Rd. Shef S17 151 F5
Milldyke Cl. Roth S60 116 D1
Miller Cl. Thorne DN8 26 C6
Miller Croft. Shef S13 143 A6
Miller Dale Dr. Brin S60 131 D7
Miller Hill Bank. D Dale HD8 30 A5
Miller Hill. D Dale HD8 30 A5
Miller La. Midhop S30 72 B4
Miller La. Thorne DN8 26 C6
Miller Rd. Shef S8 140 F7 6
Miller St. Stock S30 73 F1
Millers Dale. Barn S70 55 A4
Millfield Rd. Ben DN5 42 C8
Millfield Rd. Thorne DN8 26 B8
Millhill Cl. Arm DN3 64 C4
Millhouse Glen. Shef S11 140 B4
Millhouse Prim Sch. Pen 50 D3
Millhouses La. Shef S11, S7 140 B4
Millhouses St. Hoy S74 76 F5
Millicent Sq. Maltby S66 119 A3
Millindale. Maltby S66 119 A5
Millmoor Ct. Dar S73 56 F4
Millmoor La. Roth S60 115 B6
Millmoor Rd. Dar S73 56 F4
Millmoor Rd. Don DN4 84 E8
Millmount Rd. Hoy S74 76 F5
Millmount Rd. Shef S8 140 F5
Millrace Dr. Dearne S63 58 C4
Mills Dr. Hat DN7 66 A7
Millsands. Shef S3 129 B4
Millside. Shaf S72 16 C3
Millside Wlk. Shaf S72 16 C3
Millstone Cl. Dron S18 152 D2 1
Millstone Dr. Aston S31 144 D7
Millthorpe Rd. Shef S5 113 D4
Millwood Rd. Don DN4 82 F5
Milne Ave. Bir DN11 122 C4
Milne Dr. Bir DN11 122 D4
Milne Gr. Bir DN11 122 C4
Milne Rd. Bir DN11 122 D4
Milne St. Barn S75 32 E4
Milner Ave. Pen S30 51 B4
Milner Cl. Roth S66 117 E6
Milner Gate. Con DN12 81 E3
Milner Gate Ct. Con DN12 81 E2
Milner Rd. Don DN4 82 F7
Milnes St. Barn S70 55 A8 9
Milnrow Cres. Shef S5 112 F6
Milnrow Dr. Shef S5 112 F6
Milnrow Rd. Shef S5 112 F6
Milnrow View. Shef S5 112 F6
Milton Ave. Ben DN5 61 F4
Milton Cl. Hoy S74 76 F7
Milton Cl. Roth S61 97 B4
Milton Cl. W up D S63 78 C8
Milton Cres. Hoy S74 76 E5
Milton Ct. Don DN1 62 D2
Milton Ct. Swint S64 79 C3
Milton Gr. Arm DN3 64 C6
Milton Gr. Don DN3 42 F2
Milton Gr. Wombw S73 56 E2
Milton La. Shef S1 128 F2
Milton Rd. Ad le S DN6 21 C1
Milton Rd. Bran DN3 85 E8
Milton Rd. Chap S30 94 D5
Milton Rd. Din S31 147 A8
Milton Rd. Hoy S74 76 E5
Milton Rd. Mex S64 80 A5
Milton Rd. Roth S65 115 F8
Milton Rd. Shef S7 140 F7
Milton Sch The. Swint 79 D3
Milton St. G Hou S72 36 D2
Milton St. Maltby S66 118 F4
Milton St. Roth S60 115 D8
Milton St. Shef S1, S3 128 F2
Milton St. Swint S64 79 C3
Milton Wlk. Don DN1 62 D2
Minden Cl. Roth S66 117 B4
Minden Ct. Ben DN5 62 B8
Minna Rd. Shef S3 129 B7
Minneymoor Hill. Con DN12 81 D2
Minneymoor La. Con DN12 81 D2
Minster Cl. Don DN4 85 A7
Minster Cl. Shef S30 113 C8
Minster Rd. Shef S30 113 B8
Minster Way. Barn S71 34 D3
Minsthorpe High Sch & Comm Coll. S Elm 19 A5
Minsthorpe La. S Elm WF9 18 E4
Minsthorpe La. S Kirk WF9 18 E4
Minsthorpe Vale. S Elm WF9 18 F4
Minto Rd. Shef S6 128 B8
Mission Field. W up D S73 78 A8
Misson Bank. Misson DN10 87 F5
Mitchell Cl. Barn S70 55 D5
Mitchell Cl. Hat DN7 25 A1
Mitchell Rd. Shef S8 140 F2
Mitchell Rd. Wombw S73 56 C5
Mitchell St. Shef S3 128 E4
Mitchell's St. Barn S73 55 E5
Mitchells Enterprise Ctr. Wombw 56 C5
Mitchelson Ave. Dod S75 53 E7
Moat Hills Ct. Ben DN5 41 B1
Moat La. Roth S66 117 D1
Modena Ct. Dar S73 56 E6
Moffat Gdns. Don DN2 42 D1
Moffatt Rd. Shef S2 141 B7
Moira Cl. Stai DN7 25 B5
Molineaux Cl. Shef S5 113 D5
Molineaux Rd. Shef S5 113 D5
Molloy Pl. Shef S8 141 A6 12
Molloy St. Shef S8 141 A6 11
Molly Hurst La. Wool WF4 13 F7
Mona Ave. Shef S10 128 C4
Mona Rd. Don DN4 83 B8
Mona Rd. Shef S10 128 C4
Mona St. Barn S75 33 D2
Mona Terr. Tod S31 145 D7
Monckton Rd. Bir DN11 122 C4
Monckton Rd. Shef S5 113 F3
Moncrieffe Rd. Shef S7 140 E6
Monk Bretton Priory. Barn 34 E2
Monk Terr. Barn S71 34 E5
Monk's Bridge Rd. Laugh S31 134 D2
Monk's Bridge Trad Est. Lough 134 D2
Monks Cl. Roth S61 96 C2
Monks Way. Barn S71 34 D3
Monks Way. Shire S81 159 F7
Monkspring. Barn S70 55 C5
Monkwood Rd. Rawm S62 97 E7
Monmouth Rd. Don DN2 63 A6
Monmouth St. Shef S3 128 E2
Mons St. Shef S9 114 B1
Monsal Cres. Barn S71 34 A7
Monsal St. Dearne S63 58 C8
Mont Wlk. Wombw S73 56 A4
Montagu Hospl. Mex 80 B6
Montagu Jun Sch. Mex 80 A6
Montagu Rd. Ben DN5 61 E3
Montagu St. Mex S64 80 C4
Montague Ave. Con DN12 81 A2
Montague St. Cud S72 35 C8
Montague St. Don DN1 62 D4
Montague St. Shef S11 128 E1
Monteney Cres. Shef S5 113 A8
Monteney Fst Sch. Shef 113 A7
Monteney Mid Sch. Shef 113 A7
Monteney Rd. Shef S5 113 A8
Montfort Dr. Shef S3 129 B6
Montgomery Ave. Shef S7 140 E7
Montgomery Ct. Shef S11 140 A5
Montgomery Dr. Shef S7 140 E7
Montgomery Gdns. Don DN2 63 C6
Montgomery Rd. Shef S7 140 E7
Montgomery Rd. W up D S63 78 E6
Montgomery Sq. W up D S63 78 F5
Montgomery Terrace Rd. Shef S6 128 F5
Montrose Ave. Don DN2 63 C5
Montrose Ave. Mapp S75 13 F1
Montrose Ct. Shef S11 139 F4
Montrose Pl. Dron S18 152 D2
Montrose Rd. Shef S7 140 C5
Moonpenny Way. Dron S18 153 A1
Moonshine La. Shef S5 112 F3
Moor Cres. Shef S19 155 C7
Moor Dike Rd. Hat DN7 45 B4
Moor Dike Rd. Hat DN7 66 A7
Moor Edges Rd. Thorne DN8 26 E7
Moor End Houses. Silk S75 53 B5
Moor End Rd. Shef S10 128 C4
Moor Farm Ave. Shef S19 155 B8
Moor Farm Garth. Shef S19 155 C8
Moor Farm Rise. Shef S19 155 B8
Moor Gap. Bran DN3 85 D8
Moor Green Cl. Barn S75 33 A1
Moor Head. Shef S1 129 A2
Moor La. Barn S70 75 F5
Moor La. Bfield S30 91 D4
Moor La. Braith S66 100 C1
Moor La. Don DN3 42 E5
Moor La. G Hou S72 36 E4
Moor La. Hat DN8 46 A6
Moor La. N. Roth S65 99 D1
Moor La S. Roth S65 117 D7
Moor La. Syke DN14 7 B7
Moor La. Thorne DN8 9 D2
Moor La. Wroot DN9 66 F4
Moor Oaks Rd. Shef S10 128 C3
Moor Owners Rd. Thorne DN8 27 B7
Moor Rd. Rawcl DN8 2 E5
Moor Rd. Roth S65 116 B6
Moor Rd. Shef S6 110 F4
Moor Rd. Thorne DN8 26 E5
Moor Rd. W up D S63 78 F7
Moor The. Shef S1 129 A2
Moor Top Dr. Hem WF9 17 D5
Moor Top Rd. Har DN11 121 F5
Moor Valley. Shef S19 143 A1
Moor View. Bran DN3 85 E8
Moor View Dr. Shef S8 140 E2
Moor View Rd. Shef S8 140 E2
Moor View Terr. Shef S11 139 E5
Moorbank Cl. Barn S75 33 C4
Moorbank Cl. Shef S10 127 D2
Moorbank Cl. Wombw S73 56 B4
Moorbank Dr. Shef S10 127 E3
Moorbank Rd. Shef S10 127 D3
Moorbank Rd. Wombw S73 56 B5
Moorbank View. Wombw S73 56 B5
Moorbridge Cres. W up D S73 57 B1
Moorcrest Rise. Mapp S75 14 B2
Moorcroft Ave. Shef S10 139 B7
Moorcroft Cl. Shef S10 139 B7
Moorcroft Dr. Shef S10 139 B7
Moorcroft Rd. Shef S10 139 B7
Moordale View. Rawn S62 98 C7
Moore St. Shef S3 128 F2
Moorend La. Silk S75 53 A5
Moorends Fst Sch. Thorne 9 D3
Moorends Rd. Thorne DN8 9 C7
Moorfield Ave. Roth S65 117 D7
Moorfield Cl. Roth S65 117 D7
Moorfield Cres. Hem WF9 17 C6
Moorfield Dr. Arm DN3 64 C5
Moorfield Gr. Roth S65 117 D7
Moorfield Pl. Hem WF9 17 C6
Moorfields Flats. Shef S3 129 A5
Moorfields. Shef S3 129 A4 1
Moorgate Ave. Roth S60 115 E4
Moorgate Ave. Shef S10 128 D4
Moorgate Chase. Roth S60 115 E5
Moorgate Gr. Roth S60 115 F4
Moorgate La. Roth S60 115 E4
Moorgate Rd. Roth S60 115 E4
Moorgate St. Roth S60 115 D6
Moorhouse Cl. Roth S60 116 D1
Moorhouse Ct. S Elm WF9 19 A1
Moorhouse Gap. H Pag DN6 19 F1
Moorhouse La. H Pag WF9 19 D1
Moorhouse La. Roth S60 116 D1
Moorhouse La. Wool S75 13 C5
Moorhouse View. S Elm WF9 19 B2
Moorland Ave. Barn S70 54 B8
Moorland Ave. Mapp S75 14 B2
Moorland Cres. Mapp S75 14 B2
Moorland Ct. W up D S63 78 C8
Moorland Dr. Stock S30 73 A1
Moorland Gr. Don DN4 63 C1
Moorland Pl. Shef S6 127 C6
Moorland Pl. Silk S75 53 A5
Moorland Rd. Hath S30 149 A7
Moorland Terr. Cud S72 35 C5
Moorland View. Aston S31 144 F7
Moorland View. Clay W HD8 12 A2
Moorland View. Shef S12 142 A2
Moorland View. Uns S18 154 A1
Moorlands Cres. Roth S60 116 D1
Moorlands. Roth S66 116 F4
Moorshutt Rd. Hem WF9 17 C6
Moorside Ave. Pen S30 51 D1
Moorside Cl. Mapp S75 33 B8
Moorside Cl. Shef S19 155 C8
Moorside. Shef S10 139 A8
Moorsyde Ave. Shef S10 128 B5
Moorsyde Cres. Shef S10 128 B5
Moorthorpe Gdns. Shef S19 143 A2 2
Moorthorpe Gn. Shef S19 142 F2
Moorthorpe Sta. S Elm 18 E3
Moorthorpe Way. Shef S19 143 A2
Moorthorpe Way. Shef S19 143 C2
Moortop Rd. Uns S18 154 B1
Moortown Ave. Din S31 147 A7
Moorview Ct. Shef S17 152 B5 2
Moorview. Roth S61 114 D6
Moorwood La. Hol S17 151 C1
Moorwood La. Shef S6 126 D4
Moorwoods Ave. Chap S30 95 A5
Moorwoods La. Chap S30 95 A5
Moray Pl. Dron S18 152 D2
Mordaunt Rd. Shef S2 141 F6
More Hall La. Stock S30 93 A4
More Hall View. Wharn S30 93 B3
Morgan Ave. Shef S5 112 F3
Morgan Cl. Shef S5 112 F3
Morgan Rd. Don DN2 63 C4
Morgan Rd. Shef S5 112 F2
Morland Cl. Shef S14 141 F3
Morland Dr. Shef S14 141 F3
Morland Pl. Shef S14 141 F3
Morland Rd. Shef S14 141 F3
Morley Cl. Dron S18 152 C1
Morley Fold. D Dale HD8 29 F5
Morley Pl. Shef S7 140 C8
Morley Pl Jun Mix Sch. Con 81 B2
Morley Rd. Don DN1 62 E5
Morley Rd. Roth S61 96 E1
Morley St. Rawm S62 97 F4
Morley St. Shef S6 128 C7
Morpeth Gdns. Shef S3 128 F4 3
Morpeth St. Roth S65 115 E6
Morpeth St. Shef S3 128 F4
Morrell St. Maltby S66 119 A4
Morris Ave. Rawm S62 97 F8
Morris Cres. Don DN4 82 E6
Morris Rd. Don DN4 82 E6
Morrison Ave. Maltby S66 119 A6
Morrison Dr. Ross DN11 104 A8
Morrison Pl. Dar S73 57 A6
Morrison Rd. Dar S73 57 A6
Mortain Rd. Roth S60 115 F2
Mortains. Tod S31 145 F6
Morthen Hall La. Roth S66 133 C8
Morthen La. Roth S66 133 B8
Morthen La. Ulley S60 132 E6
Morthen Rd. Roth S66 117 C3
Mortimer Dr. Pen S30 51 C1
Mortimer Rd. Bfield S30 91 C4
Mortimer Rd. Lang S30 72 D6
Mortimer Rd. Maltby S66 119 C4
Mortimer Rd. Midhop S30 72 A2
Mortimer Rd. Pen S30 51 C1
Mortimer St. Shef S1 129 B2 1
Mortlake Rd. Shef S5 113 D2
Mortomley Cl. Chap S30 94 E7
Mortomley Hall Gdns. Chap S30 94 E8
Mortomley La. Chap S30 94 E7
Morton Cl. Barn S71 34 D5
Morton La. Uns S31 154 C1
Morton Pl. Shef S30 112 C8
Morton Rd. Mex S64 80 C5
Morvern Meadows. Hem WF9 17 F7
Mosborough Hall Dr. Shef S19 155 E6
Mosborough Jun & Inf Sch. Shef 155 D7
Mosborough Moor. Shef S19 155 B8
Mosborough Rd. Shef S13 142 B7
Moscar Cross Rd. Bfield S6 125 A5
Mosham Cl. Blax DN9 86 D5
Mosham Rd. Blax DN9 86 C5
Moss Beck Ct. Eck S31 155 C2
Moss Cl. Roth S66 117 B4
Moss Dr. Kill S31 156 D5
Moss Edge Rd. Holme HD7 47 C8
Moss & Fenwick Cty Prim Sch. Moss 5 F2
Moss Gr. Shef S12 143 D3
Moss Haven. Moss DN6 6 B1
Moss La. T in B DN6 23 C5
Moss Rd. Askern DN6 22 C8
Moss Rd. Moss DN6 6 C1
Moss Rd. Shef S17 151 B4
Moss Rise Pl. Eck S31 155 C3
Moss Terr. Thorne DN8 9 C5
Moss View. Shef S19 155 C6
Moss Way. Shef S19 143 C2
Mossbrook Sch. Shef 153 C8
Mosscroft La. Hat DN7 44 D5
Mossdale Ave. Shef S19 155 D7
Mossdale Cl. Ben DN5 61 E7
Mossley Rd. Lang S30 72 C6
Motehall Dr. Shef S2 130 A1
Motehall Pl. Shef S2 130 B1
Motehall Rd. Shef S2 130 B1
Motehall Way. Shef S2 130 A1
Motte The. Roth S61 114 F8
Mottram St. Barn S71 33 F2
Mount Ave. G Hou S72 36 E1
Mount Ave. Grime S72 36 A8
Mount Ave. Hem WF9 17 D7
Mount Cl. Barn S70 54 F7 10
Mount Cl. Har DN11 121 F5
Mount Cres. Hoy S74 76 D7
Mount Pleasant. Barn S70 55 B4
Mount Pleasant Cl. Chap S30 95 A6
Mount Pleasant. Don DN4 83 A7
Mount Pleasant. Grime S72 36 A8
Mount Pleasant. K Smea WF8 3 F6
Mount Pleasant Rd. Roth S61 115 B7
Mount Pleasant Rd. Shef S11 140 F8
Mount Pleasant Rd. W up D S63 78 F4
Mount Pleasant. Thurgo S30 74 C8
Mount Rd. Chap S30 94 E5
Mount Rd. Grime S72 36 A8
Mount Rd. Shef S3 128 F7
Mount St. Barn S70 54 E8
Mount St. Barn S71 55 F8
Mount St Mary's RC Coll. Eck 156 C2
Mount St. Roth S61 115 B7
Mount St. Shef S11 128 F1
Mount Terr. W up D S63 78 C6
Mount Terr. Wombw S73 56 C3
Mount The. Don DN3 43 A1
Mount Vernon Ave. Barn S70 54 F7
Mount Vernon Cres. Barn S70 55 A6
Mount Vernon Day Special Sch. Barn 54 F6
Mount Vernon Hospl. Barn 54 F6
Mount Vernon Rd. Barn S70 55 A6
Mount View Ave. Shef S8 141 A3
Mount View Gdns. Shef S8 141 A3
Mount View. N Edl DN12 82 B1
Mount View Rd. Shef S8 141 B3
Mountbatten Dr. Chap S30 94 D5
Mountenoy Rd. Roth S60 115 E5
Mountfield Wlk. S Kirk WF9 18 B1
Mountford Croft. Shef S17 151 E5
Mouse Park Gate. Wharn S30 93 F2
Mousehole Cl. Roth S65 98 E1
Mousehole La. Roth S65 98 E1
Mowbray Gdns. Roth S65 116 C8
Mowbray Pl. Roth S65 116 C8
Mowbray Rd. Thorne DN8 26 C6
Mowbray St. Roth S65 116 C8
Mowbray St. Shef S3 129 A5
Mowson Cres. Ought S30 111 D5
Mowson Dr. Ought S30 111 D5
Mowson La. Ought S30 111 D5
Moxon Cl. Stock S30 92 E8
Mucky La. Barn S71 35 A1
Mucky La. Stock S30 73 A4
Mucky La. Stock S30 91 F7
Muglet La. Maltby S66 119 B4
Muirfield Ave. Don DN4 85 B6
Muirfield Ave. Swint S64 79 E2
Muirfield Cl. Cud S72 16 C1
Muirfields The. Mapp S75 14 A1
Mulberry Ave. Thorne DN8 9 C2
Mulberry Cl. Ben DN5 61 D5
Mulberry Cres. C in L S81 148 F7
Mulberry Rd. Eck S31 155 B2
Mulberry Rd. N Anst S31 146 E6
Mulberry St. Shef S1 129 B3
Mulberry Way. Kill S31 156 B5
Mulehouse Rd. Shef S10 128 B4
Mundella Jun & Inf Sch. Shef 141 A3
Mundella Pl. Shef S8 141 A3
Munro Cl. Kill S31 156 D6
Munsbrough La. Roth S61 97 B2
Munsbrough Rise. Roth S61 97 B3
Munsdale. Roth S61 97 B3
Murdoch Pl. Barn S71 33 E7
Murdock Rd. Shef S5 112 F4
Murray Rd. Kill S31 156 E7
Murray Rd. Rawm S62 98 A6
Murray Rd. Shef S11 140 B7
Murrayfield Dr. Shef S19 155 E6 6
Musard Way. Kill S31 156 C6
Musgrave Cres. Shef S5 113 A1
Musgrave Dr. Shef S5 113 A1
Musgrave Pl. Shef S5 113 A1
Musgrave Rd. Shef S5 112 F1
Musgrove Ave. Roth S65 99 A2
Mushroom La. Shef S10 128 D4
Muskoka Ave. Shef S11 139 E5
Muskoka Dr. Shef S11 139 E5
Mutual St. Don DN4 62 B2
Myers Ave. Ought S30 111 D8
Myers Grove La. Shef S6 127 E7
Myers Grove Sch. Shef 127 F7
Myers La. Shef S6 111 B3
Myers St. Wombw S73 56 C4
Mylnhurst Convent Sch. Shef 140 B4
Mylnhurst Rd. Shef S11 140 B5
Mylor Ct. Barn S71 34 C3
Mylor Rd. Shef S11 140 A6
Myndon Wlk. Con DN12 81 A3
Myrtle Cres. Roth S66 117 C5
Myrtle Gr. Auck DN9 86 A7
Myrtle Gr. Wales S31 145 C2
Myrtle Rd. Hat DN7 43 F8
Myrtle Rd. Shef S2 141 B7
Myrtle Rd. Wombw S73 56 C3
Myrtle Springs. Shef S12 141 F5
Myrtle St. Barn S75 33 C2
Myton Rd. Shef S9 130 A4

Nab La. Fish DN7 24 F7
Nairn Dr. Dron S18 152 D1
Nairn St. Shef S10 128 B3
Nan Sampson Bank. Blax DN9 87 D8
Nancy Cres. Grime S72 36 B6
Nancy Rd. Grime S72 36 B6
Nanny Hill. Stock S30 73 C1
Nanny Marr Rd. Dar S73 57 B6
Napier Mount. Barn S70 54 F6
Napier St. Shef S11 128 F1
Narrow Balk. H Pag DN5 38 E5
Narrow La. Askern DN5 22 D4
Narrow La. Bawtry DN10 123 B8
Narrow La. N Anst S31 146 E5
Narrow La. Tick DN11 102 E2
Naseby Ave. Ben DN5 61 D6
Naseby Cl. Hat DN7 44 A5
Naseby St. Shef S9 114 A2
Nathan Ct. Shef S19 143 F1
Nathan Dr. Shef S19 143 F2
Nathan Gr. Shef S19 143 E2
Navan Rd. Shef S2 142 A7
Navy La. Ryhill S71 15 D7
Naylor Gr. Dod S75 53 F7
Naylor Gr. Ought S30 111 C6
Naylor Rd. Ought S30 111 C7
Naylor St. Rawm S62 97 F3
NCB Offices. W up D 79 C5
Neale Rd. Don DN2 63 B8
Nearcroft Rd. Roth S61 114 F8
Nearfield Rd. Don DN4 84 D7
Needham Way. Shef S7 140 C5
Needlewood. Dod S75 53 F6
Neepsend La. Shef S3 128 F6
Neild Rd. Hoy S74 76 F6
Neill Rd. Shef S11 140 C8
Nelson Ave. Barn S71 34 B4
Nelson Cl. Brin S60 131 D8
Nelson Mandela Wlk. Shef S2 130 B1 2
Nelson Pl. Chap S30 94 D5
Nelson Rd. Maltby S66 119 B5
Nelson Rd. N Edl DN12 82 B2
Nelson Rd. Ross DN11 84 E1
Nelson Rd. Shef S6 127 F6
Nelson Sq. Stai DN7 24 E3
Nelson St. Barn S70 33 E1 5
Nelson St. Don DN4 62 D1
Nelson St. Roth S65 115 E7
Nelson St. S Hie S72 16 E5
Nemesia Cl. S Anst S31 146 C4
Nene Gr. Auck DN9 86 A7
Nesfield Way. Shef S5 113 D4
Nether Ave. Kill S31 156 C6
Nether Ave. Shef S30 94 D1
Nether Cantley La. Bran DN3 64 B1
Nether Cres. Shef S30 94 D1
Nether Edge Hospl. Shef 140 D6
Nether Edge Rd. Shef S7 140 E6
Nether Green Mid Sch. Shef 139 E8
Nether Green Sch. Shef 139 D8
Nether Hall Rd. Don DN1 62 D4
Nether House La. Lang S30 71 D7
Nether La. Chap S30 95 B3
Nether Ley Ave. Chap S30 95 A5
Nether Ley Croft. Chap S30 95 A5
Nether Ley Ct. Chap S30 95 A5
Nether Ley Gdns. Chap S30 95 A5
Nether Oak Cl. Shef S19 144 B2
Nether Oak Dr. Shef S19 144 B2
Nether Oak View. Shef S19 144 B2
Nether Rd. Silk S75 32 A1
Nether Royd View. Silk S75 53 B5
Nether Shire La. Shef S4 113 D6
Nether Thorpe Rd. Th Sa S80 159 B5
Netherfield Cl. Stock S30 73 F1
Netherfield La. Rawm S62 97 F4
Netherfield Rd. Shef S10 128 B4
Netherfield. Roth S65 116 B8 5
Netherfield View. Roth S65 116 D8
Nethergate. Shef S6 127 C5

St Mary's Sch. Don 84 D8
Sandall Rise. Don DN2 .... 63 B6
Scampton Lodge. Shef S5 .... 113 B2
Seagrave Rd. Shef S12 .... 142 B4
Sheaf Sq. Shef S1 .... 129 B2
St Mary's St. Pen S30 .... 51 D3
Sandall Stones Rd. Don DN3 ...... 42 D3
Scar Hole La. Holmfi HD7 ...... 28 A3
Searby Rd. Roth S66 .... 117 D7
Sheardown St. Don DN4 .... 67 B2
St Mary's View. Roth S61 .... 97 B3
Sandall View. Lough S81 .... 134 C3
Scar La. Barn S71 .... 55 F8
Seaton Cl. Shef S2 .... 129 F2
Sheards Cl. Dron S18 .... 152 E1
St Marys Cl. Cud S72 .... 35 B6
Sandall Wood Sch. Don 63 D5
Scarborough Cl. N Anst S31 ...... 146 E7
Seaton Cres. Shef S2 .... 129 F2
Sheards Dr. Dron S18 .... 152 E1
St Marys Rd. Wombw S73 .... 56 C2
Sandbeck La. Barn S71 .... 33 F3
Scarborough La. Roth S66 .... 117 A5
Seaton Gdns. Ross DN11 .... 103 F7
Sheards Way. Dron S18 .... 152 E1
St Matthew's Inf Sch. Barn 33 C2
Sandbeck House. Don DN1 .... 62 C2 4
Scarborough Rd. Roth S66 .... 117 A5
Seaton Pl. Shef S2 .... 129 F2
Shearman Ave. Roth S61 .... 96 E2
St Matthews Way. Barn S71 .... 34 C3
Sandbeck La. Maltby DN11 .... 120 B2
Scarborough Rd. Shef S9 .... 130 C5
Seaton Way. Shef S2 .... 129 F2
Shearwood Rd. Shef S10 .... 128 E3
St Matthias Rd. Stock S30 .... 92 E8
Sandbeck La. Tick DN11 .... 120 B3
Scarfield Cl. Barn S71 .... 55 F8
Sebastion View. Brin S60 .... 115 C2
Sheep Bridge Rd. Ross DN11 ...... 85 B2
St Michael's Ave. Barn S71 .... 34 D6
Sandbeck Pl. Shef S11 .... 140 D8
Scarlett Oak Meadow. Shef S6 ...... 127 C6
Seckar La. Wool WF4 .... 14 B8
Sheep Cote La. Hat DN7 .... 44 C4
St Michael's Ave. Swint S64 .... 79 D4
Sandbeck Rd. Shef S6 .... 128 B7
Scarll Cl. Don DN4 .... 62 A1
Second Ave. Ad I S DN6 .... 40 C4
Sheep Cote Rd. Roth S60 .... 116 E3
St Michael's C of E Sch. Barn 33 C2
Sandbeck St. Shef S6 .... 128 E7
Scarll Croft. Shef S5 .... 129 B6
Second Ave. S Kirk WF9 .... 17 F1
Sheep Dike La. Roth S66 .... 133 C7
St Michael's C of E Sch. Ross 85 B1
Sandbergh Rd. Roth S61 .... 96 E2
Scarsdale Cross. Dron S18 .... 153 B1
Second Ave. Upton WF9 .... 19 A8
Sheep Dip La. Hat DN7 .... 44 A7
St Michael's Cl. Shef S5 .... 113 B8
Sandby Croft. Shef S14 .... 141 E2
Scarsdale Rd. Dron S18 .... 153 B1
Second La. S Anst S31 .... 146 E3
Sheep La. H Mel DN5 .... 60 D3
St Michael's Cl. Thorne DN8 ...... 26 D6
Sandby Ct. Shef S14 .... 141 E2
Scarsdale Rd. Shef S8 .... 140 F3
Second La. Stai DN7 .... 24 E4
Sheepcote Rd. Kill S31 .... 156 C6
St Michael's Cres. Shef S5 .... 113 B8
Sandby Dr. Shef S14 .... 141 E2
Scarsdale St. Din S31 .... 135 A1
Second Sq. Stai DN7 .... 24 E4
Sheephill Rd. Shef S11 .... 139 A2
St Michael's Dr. Thorne DN8 ...... 26 D6
Sandcliffe Rd. Don DN2 .... 63 B6
Scarth Ave. Don DN4 .... 83 B8
Sedan St. Shef S4 .... 129 C7
Sheepwalk La. Upton WF9 .... 19 E8
St Michael's RC Prim Sch. Dar 56 F7
Sandcroft Cl. Hoy S74 .... 76 C5
Scarsdale St. Din S31 .... 135 A1
Sedge Cl. Roth S66 .... 117 E4
Sheepwash La. Tick DN11 .... 103 D1
St Michael's Rd. Don DN4 .... 63 B1
Sandeby Dr. Roth S65 .... 117 D7
Scawsby La. Ben DN5 .... 61 B8
Sedgefield Way. Mex S64 .... 80 B6
Sheerien Cl. Barn S71 .... 33 E8
St Michael's Rd. Shef S5 .... 113 B8
Sanderson's Bank. Misson DN10 ...87 F4
Scawsby Ridgewood Comp Sch.
Sedgley Rd. Shef S6 .... 128 C8
Sheffield Amateur Sports Club.
St Michael's St. Barn 34 B7
Sanderson's Bank. Misson DN10 ...87 F4
Ben 61 C7
Sefton Ct. Shef S10 .... 139 D7
Shef 152 A7
St Michaels Ave. Ross DN11 .... 85 A2
Sandford Cl. Barn S70 .... 54 D8
Scawsby Rosedale Fst Sch. Ben ...61 D7
Sefton Rd. Shef S10 .... 139 D7
Sheffield Arena. Shef 130 B7
St Michaels Cl. Dearne S63 .... 58 D5
Sandford Grove Rd. Shef S7 ...... 140 E6
Scawsby Rosedale Mid Sch. Ben ... 61 D7
Selborne Rd. Shef S10 .... 128 A3
Sheffield Childrens Hospl. Shef ...128 D3
St Nicholas Cl. Thorne DN8 ...... 42 E2
Sandford Rd. Don DN4 .... 83 A7
Scawsby Saltersgate Fst Sch. Ben . 61 E6
Selborne St. Roth S65 .... 115 E8
Sheffield City Polytechnic. Shef ...140 C7
St Nicholas Rd. Thorne DN8 ...... 26 E2
Sandford Rd. S Elm WF9 .... 19 A5
Scawthorpe Ave. Roth S60 ...... 116 B1
Selbourne Cl. Barn S75 .... 32 E5
Sheffield City Polytechnic. Shef ...151 D4
St Nicolas Wlk. Rawm S62 .... 98 B6
Sandhill Cl. Rawm S62 .... 98 B7
Scawthorpe Cotts. Ben DN5 .... 61 C8
Selby Cl. Aston S31 .... 144 C7
Sheffield Hallam Univ. Shef 129 B3
St Oswald's Dr. Finn DN9 .... 86 D3
Sandhill Gr. Grim S72 .... 17 D3
Sceptone Gr. Shaf S72 .... 16 C3
Selby Cl. Askern DN6 .... 5 A4
Sheffield High Sch (girls). Shef ...128 C2
St Oswald's Dr. Don DN3 .... 42 F2
Sandhill Rd. Rawm S62 .... 98 B7
Sceptre Gr. Ross DN11 .... 103 E7
Selby Cl. Barn S71 .... 33 F7
Sheffield La. Treet S60 .... 131 C5
St Oswald's Dr. Finn DN9 .... 86 E3
Sandhill Rise. Auck DN9 .... 86 A7
Schofield Dr. Dar S73 .... 57 A6
Selby Cl. Don DN2 .... 63 A5
Sheffield La. Treet S60 .... 131 B6
St Oswald's RC Sch. Shef 129 E2
Sandhurst Rd. Don DN4 .... 85 A6
Schofield Pl. Dar S73 .... 57 A6
Selby Cl. Norton DN6 .... 5 A4
Sheffield Parkway. Shef S9 .... 130 D2
St Owens Dr. Barn S75 .... 33 B2
Sandown Cl. Eck S31 .... 155 B2
Schofield Rd. Stock S30 .... 92 D8
Selby Cl. Shef S4 .... 113 D1
Sheffield Parkway. Treet S60 .... 131 B6
St Patrick Rd. Stock S30 .... 92 E8
Sandown Gdns. Don DN4 .... 63 D2
Schofield St. Mex S64 .... 79 E5
Selby Rd. Thorne DN8 .... 8 E1
Sheffield Polytechnic. Shef 128 F1
St Patrick's Jun & Inf Sch. Shef ...113 C4
Sandown Rd. Mex S64 .... 80 B6
Schofied Technical Coll. Mex 80 A6
Selby Rd. W Stub DN6 .... 5 A4
Sheffield Rd. Aston S31 .... 144 B4
St Patrick's RC Prim Sch. Har ...122 A4
Sandpiper Rd. Roth S61 .... 95 F6
Scole Ave. Pen S30 .... 51 C3
Selby Rd. Womer DN6 .... 5 A4
Sheffield Rd. Barn S70 .... 75 F7
St Patrick's Rd. Don DN2 .... 63 A5
Sandpit Hill. Bran DN3 .... 85 C5
Schole Hill La. Pen S30 .... 51 B3
Selhurst Cres. Don DN4 .... 84 E7
Sheffield Rd. Con DN12 .... 81 C5
St Patrick's Way. Ben DN5 .... 61 E5
Sandringham Ave. Roth S60 ...... 116 B1
Scholes Gn. Roth S61 .... 96 C3
Selkirk Ave. Don DN4 .... 82 D6
Sheffield Rd. Con DN12 .... 81 F3
St Paul Cl. Stock S30 .... 92 E8
Sandringham Cl. Pen S30 .... 51 A4
Scholes La. Roth S61 .... 96 B4
Selkirk Rd. Don DN2 .... 63 C6
Sheffield Rd. Don DN12 .... 82 B4
St Paul Cl. Tod S31 .... 145 E5
Sandringham Ct. Har DN11 .... 122 B5
Scholes Moor Rd. Holmfi HD7 .... 28 A8
Sellars Rd. Roth S61 .... 96 E1
Sheffield Rd. Dron S18 .... 152 F3
St Paul's C of E Fst Sch. Bri 17 A3
Sandringham Fst Sch. Don 63 B6
Scholes View. Hoy S74 .... 76 E5
Sellers St. Shef S8 .... 140 F7
Sheffield Rd. Eck S31 .... 155 E5
St Paul's Cl. Upton WF9 .... 19 D8
Sandringham Pl. Roth S65 ...... 117 D8
Scholes View. Hoy S74 .... 76 F7
Selly Oak Gr. Shef S8 .... 153 C6
Sheffield Rd. Hath S30 .... 149 A7
St Paul's Par. Barn S71 .... 55 F8
Sandringham Rd. Don DN2 .... 63 B4
Scholes View. Shef S30 .... 95 B1
Selly Oak Rd. Shef S8 .... 153 C6
Sheffield Rd. Hoy S74 .... 76 B4
St Paul's Par. Shef S1 .... 129 A3 13
Sandringham Rd. Shef S9 .... 114 A4
Scholey Ave. Woods S81 .... 147 E3
Selwood. Roth S65 .... 115 E8
Sheffield Rd. Kill S31 .... 156 D7
St Peter and St Paul's Cath. Shef . 129 A3
Sandrock Dr. Roth S66 .... 84 E7
Scholey Rd. Roth S66 .... 117 B5
Selwyn St. Roth S65 .... 115 E8
Sheffield Rd. Oxspr S30 .... 52 B1
St Peter Ave. Stock S30 .... 92 F8
Sandrock Rd. Har DN11 .... 121 F5
Scholey St. Shef S3 .... 129 B5
Senior Rd. Roth S61 .... 96 E2
Sheffield Rd. S Anst S31 .... 146 D4
St Peter's Cl. Bnbur DN5 .... 59 C4
Sands Cl. Shef S14 .... 141 E4
School Cl. Shef S19 .... 155 F7
Senior Rd. Shef S9 .... 130 C4
Sheffield Rd. Shef S9 .... 114 E3
St Peter's Cl. Brin S60 .... 131 A8
Sands The. Bfield S6 .... 110 A4
School Cl. Wales S31 .... 145 B2
Sennen Croft. Barn S71 .... 34 B3
Sheffield Rd. Shef S9 .... 114 C1
St Peter's Cl. Shef S1 .... 129 A4 18
Sandstone Cl. Shef S9 .... 114 A3
School Gr. Aston S31 .... 144 E7
Serlby Dr. Hart S31 .... 157 F2 5 6
Sheffield Rd. Shef S12, S9 .... 143 A3
St Peter's Gate. Dearne S63 .... 37 C1
Sandstone Dr. Shef S9 .... 114 A3
School Green La. Shef S10 ...... 139 B7
Serlby House. Don DN1 .... 62 C2 6
Sheffield Rd. Shef S13 .... 143 B6
St Peter's High Sch. Don 85 A8
Sandstone Rd. Shef S9 .... 114 A3
School Hill. Cud S72 .... 35 B7
Serlby La. Hart S31 .... 157 F2
Sheffield Rd. Shef S31 .... 155 E5
St Peter's Rd. Con DN12 .... 81 B1
Sandtoft Rd. Hat DN7 .... 45 C8
School La. Auck DN9 .... 86 A6
Serpentine Wlk. Shef S8 .... 153 B8
Sheldon Ave. Con DN12 .... 81 B3
St Peter's Rd. Don DN4 .... 82 E7
Sandwith Rd. Tod S31 .... 145 E5
School La. D Dale HD8 .... 30 A6
Setcup La. Eck S31 .... 155 D2
Sheldon La. Shef S6 .... 127 C6
St Peter's Rd. Th Sa S80 .... 158 E7
Sandy Acres Cl. Shef S19 .... 143 F1
School La. Dron S18 .... 153 A1
Seth Terr. Barn S70 .... 55 A8
Sheldon Rd. Shef S7 .... 140 E6
St Peter's Terr. Barn S70 .... 55 A8 1
Sandy Acres Dr. Shef S19 .... 143 F1
School La. Eck S31 .... 154 E3
Sevenfields Ct. Shef S6 .... 112 A1
Sheldon Rd. Stock S30 .... 73 C1
St Peters R C School. Shef 113 A7
Sandy La. Don DN4 .... 63 A1
School La. Hath S30 .... 149 A8
Sevenfields La. Shef S6 .... 112 A1
Sheldon Row. Shef S3 .... 128 B4
St Philip's La. Shef S3 .... 128 E5
Sandy La. Hoy S73 .... 55 F2
School La. Rawm S62 .... 97 E3
Severn Ct. Shef S10 .... 128 D3
Sheldon St. Shef S2 .... 129 A1
St Philip's Rd. Shef S3 .... 128 E4
Sandy La. Hoy S73 .... 55 F2
School La. Roth S65 .... 98 F3
Severn Rd. Shef S10 .... 128 D3
Sheldrake Cl. Roth S61 .... 95 F5
St Philip's Rd. Shef S3 .... 128 E5
Sandy La. Shef S2 .... 129 C3
School La. Shef S2 .... 129 C3
Severnside Dr. Shef S13 .... 143 A7
Shelley Ave. Don DN4 .... 83 B6
St Philip's Cl. Maltby S66 .... 118 E4
Sandy La. Thurcr S66 .... 133 F7
School La. Shef S8 .... 152 F7
Severnside Pl. Shef S13 .... 143 A7
Shelley Cl. Pen S30 .... 51 D4
St Quentin Cl. Shef S17 .... 152 B5
Sandy Mount E. Har DN11 .... 122 A4
School La. Shef S8 .... 94 C1
Severnside Wlk. Shef S13 .... 143 A6
Shelley Dr. Arm DN3 .... 64 C6
St Quentin Dr. Shef S17 .... 152 B5
Sandy Mount W. Har DN11 .... 122 A4
School La. Ston S66 .... 119 B8
Sewell Rd. Shef S19 .... 155 F6
Shelley Dr. Barn S71 .... 34 B3
St Quentin Mount. Shef S17 ...... 152 B5
Sandybridge La. Shaf S72 .... 16 B4
School La. Wharn S30 .... 93 B1
Sexton Dr. Roth S66 .... 117 D4
Shelley Dr. Din S31 .... 147 B8
St Quentin Rise. Shef S17 .... 152 B5
Sandyfields View. Ad le S DN6 ... 21 B1
School Lane Cl. Shef S8 .... 141 C1
Seymore Rd. Aston S31 .... 144 E6
Shelley Dr. Roth S65 .... 116 B6
St Quentin View. Shef S17 .... 152 B5
Sandygate Cres. W up D S63 ...... 78 F4
School Rd. Chap S30 .... 94 F6
Seymour Rd. Maltby S66 .... 119 B5
Shelley Gr. Ben DN5 .... 61 F4
St Ronan's Rd. Shef S7 .... 140 F7
Sandygate Gr. Shef S10 .... 127 D2
School Rd. Lan S81 .... 136 E3
Shackleton Rd. Don DN2 .... 42 D1
Shelley Rd. Roth S65 .... 116 B6
St Sepulchre Gate. Don DN1 .... 62 C3
Sandygate. Hem WF9 .... 17 C7
School Rd. Lough S31 .... 134 D4
Shackleton View. Pen S30 .... 51 D2
Shelley Rise. Ad I S DN6 .... 40 A5
St Sepulchre Gate W.
Sandygate Park Cres. Shef S10 ...127 D2
School Rd. Shef S10 .... 128 C4
Shady Side. Don DN4 .... 62 A1
Shelley Way. W up D S63 .... 78 D7
Don DN1, DN4 .... 62 C2
Sandygate Park Rd. Shef S10 ...... 127 D2
School Rd. Shef S19 .... 144 B3
Shaftesbury Ave. Don DN2 .... 63 B4
Shelley Woodhouse La. Skel HD8 .. 29 C8
St Stephen's Dr. Aston S31 .... 144 D8
Sandygate Pk. Shef S10 .... 127 D2
School Rd. Thurcr S66 .... 133 F6
Shaftesbury St. Barn S70 .... 55 E8
Shelley Cl. Hat DN7 .... 44 A6
St Stephen's Rd. Roth S65 .... 115 E7
Sandygate Rd. Shef S10 .... 127 E2
School Rd. Wales S31 .... 145 A2
Shaftholme Rd. Ben DN5 .... 41 C6
Shenstone Dr. Roth S65 .... 116 B6
St Stephen's Wlk. Shef S3 .... 128 E4
Sandygate. W up D S63 .... 78 F5
School St. Aston S31 .... 144 C7
Shafton Hall Dr. Shaf S72 .... 16 B3
Shenstone Rd. Roth S65 .... 116 B4
St Theresa's RC Prim Schs. Shef . 142 B7
Sandymount E. Har DN11 .... 122 A4
School St. Barn S75 .... 33 D3
Shafton Rd. Roth S60 .... 116 A1
Shenstone Rd. Shef S6 .... 112 C2
St Thomas More's R C Sch. Shef . 112 C7
Sandymount Rd. W up D S63 ...... 79 A6
School St. Barn S70 .... 55 E8
Shafton Two Gates Fst Sch. Shaf .. 16 C2
Shepcote La. Shef S9 .... 130 C8
St Thomas of Canterbury Prim Sch.
Sandymount W. Har DN11 .... 122 A4
School St. Cud S72 .... 35 B8
Shaftsbury Ave. Ad le S DN6 ...... 39 F5
Shepcote Way. Shef S9 .... 130 D7
Shef 152 F8
Sankey Sq. Dearne S63 .... 58 C2
School St. Dar S73 .... 57 B6
Shaftsbury Sq. Roth S65 .... 115 E7
Shepherd's Cl. Con DN12 .... 80 F3
St Thomas Rd. Shef S10 .... 128 B3
Saracens La. Scro DN10 .... 122 F2
School St. Dearne S63 .... 58 D8
Shakepeare Ave. Ben DN5 .... 61 C6
Shepherd Dr. Chap S30 .... 94 F6
St Thomas St. Shef S1 .... 128 F3 2
Sarah St. Mex S64 .... 80 A4
School St. Din S31 .... 134 F1
Shakespeare Ave. Norton DN6 ...... 4 C1
Shepherd La. Dearne S63 .... 58 D7
St Thomas's Cl. Don DN4 .... 82 E6
Sarah St. Roth S61 .... 115 B6
School St. Eck S31 .... 155 D3
Shakespeare Dr. Din S31 .... 147 A8
Shepherd St. Shef S3 .... 128 E4
St Thomas's Rd. Barn S75 .... 33 A4
Sark Rd. Shef S2 .... 141 A7
School St. G Hou S72 .... 36 E2
Shakespeare Rd. Ben DN5 .... 41 B1
Shepherds Croft. Blax DN9 .... 86 F6
St Ursula's Rd. Don DN4 .... 63 A2
Saunders Pl. Shef S2 .... 129 E3
School St. Hoy S73 .... 77 C8
Shakespeare Rd. W up D S63 ...... 78 D7
Shepley Croft. Chap S30 .... 94 F6
St Veronica Rd. Stock S30 .... 92 F7
Saunders Rd. Shef S2 .... 129 E3
School St. Mapp S75 .... 13 C1
Shaldon Gr. Aston S31 .... 144 D7
Shepley Fst Sch. Shep 28 E8
St Vincent Ave. Ad le S DN6 .... 39 F6
Saunders Row. Wombw S73 .... 56 C2
School St. Mapp S75 .... 14 C1
Shalesmoor. Shef S3 .... 128 F5
Sheppard Rd. Don DN4 .... 83 D4
St Vincent Rd. Don DN1 .... 62 E4
Saunderson Rd. Pen S30 .... 51 B8
School St. Roth S65 .... 98 E2
Shambles St. Barn S70 .... 33 E1
Shepperson Rd. Shef S6 .... 112 B1
St Vincent's Ave. Bran DN3 .... 85 C8
Savage La. Shef S17 .... 151 D7
School St. Shef S19 .... 155 D7
Shardlow Gdns. Don DN4 .... 84 F6
Sherburn Cl. Ad le S DN6 .... 20 E2
St Vincent's RC Jun & Inf Sch.
Savile St E. Shef S4 .... 129 D6
School St. Upton WF9 .... 19 D8
Sharlston Gdns. Ross DN11 .... 85 B1
Sherburn Gate. Chap S30 .... 94 F6
Shef 128 F4
Savile St E. Shef S4 .... 129 D6
School Terr. Con DN12 .... 81 B2
Sharman Cl. Uns S18 .... 154 A1
Sherburn Rd. Barn S71 .... 33 E7
St Wandrilles Cl. Shef S30 .... 95 B1
Savile St. Shef S4 .... 129 C6
School Wlk. Bawtry DN10 ...... 123 A4
Sharman Wlk. Uns S18 .... 154 A1
Sherde Rd. Shef S6 .... 128 E5
St Wilfrid's Gdns. Don DN4 .... 84 E7
Savile Ct. Hoy S74 .... 76 F7
School Wlk. Con DN12 .... 81 A4
Sharp Rd Nook. Oxspr S30 .... 73 C5
Sheridan Ave. Don DN4 .... 83 C6
St Wilfrid's RC Jun & Inf Sch.
Savile Hall La. Dod S75 .... 53 F6
School Wlk. Maltby S66 .... 119 A5
Sharpe Ave. Shef S8 .... 152 E8
Sheridan Ct. Barn S71 .... 34 B3
Shef 140 C4
Savile La. Pen S30 .... 51 B8
Scholfield Dr. Rawm S62 .... 97 D7
Sharpfield Ave. Rawm S62 .... 97 F8
Sheridan Dr. Roth S65 .... 116 C6
St Wilfrid's Rd. Don DN4 .... 84 D8
Savile Rd. Dod S75 .... 54 A6
Scorah's La. Swint S64 .... 79 A3
Sharrard Cl. Shef S12 .... 142 B5
Sheridan Rd. B Dun DN3 .... 42 F8
St Wilfrid's Rd. Shef S2 .... 141 A8 11
Savile Rd. W up D S63 .... 78 E6
Scorcher Hills La. Burg DN6 .... 20 E5
Sharrard Dr. Shef S12 .... 142 B5
Sheringham Cl. Chap S30 .... 94 D7
St Withold Ave. Thurcr S66 .... 133 E1
Savile St. Cud S72 .... 35 B7
Scot La. Bawtry DN10 .... 123 A4
Sharrard Gr. Shef S12 .... 142 B5
Sheringham Gdns. Chap S30 .... 94 D7
Salcombe Gr. Bawtry DN10 .... 122 F8
Savile St. Roth S65 .... 98 C1
Scot La. Don DN1 .... 62 D3
Sharrard Rd. Shef S12 .... 142 B5
Sherwood Ave. Askern DN6 .... 21 E7
Sale Hill. Shef S10 .... 128 B2
Savile Terr. Barn S70 .... 54 E8 7
Scotch Spring La. Ston S66 ...... 119 E7
Sharrow Inf Sch. Shef 140 E8
Sherwood Ave. Ben DN5 .... 61 D6
Sale St. Hoy S74 .... 76 A5
Scotia Cl. Shef S2 .... 141 F8
Scotia Cl. Shef S2 .... 141 F8
Sharrow La. Shef S11 .... 140 D8
Sherwood Ave. Con DN12 .... 81 A1
Salerno Way. Dar S73 .... 56 E6
Scotia Dr. Shef S2 .... 141 F8
Scotia Dr. Shef S2 .... 141 F8
Sharrow Vale Rd. Shef S11 .... 140 D8
Sherwood Ave. Don DN3 .... 42 F2
Sales La. Syke DN14 .... 7 D5
Scotland St. Shef S3 .... 129 A4
Scotland St. Shef S3 .... 129 A4
Sharrow View. Shef S7 .... 140 D8
Sherwood Chase. Shef S17 .... 151 E5
Salisbury Rd. Don DN4 .... 62 A1
Scott Ave. Bnbur DN5 .... 59 C2
Scott Ave. Bnbur DN5 .... 59 C2
Shaw Cl. S Elm WF9 .... 19 A4
Sherwood Cres. Roth S60 .... 115 C6
Salisbury Rd. Maltby S66 .... 119 A6
Scott Ave. Con DN12 .... 81 A2
Scott Ave. Con DN12 .... 81 A2
Shaw La. Arm DN3 .... 64 C5
Sherwood Dr. Ad le S DN6 .... 20 E2
Salisbury Rd. Shef S10 .... 128 B4
Scott Cl. Thurcr S66 .... 133 E6
Scott Cl. Thurcr S66 .... 133 E6
Shaw La. Cud S71 .... 15 D1
Sherwood Dr. Don DN2 .... 82 E5
Salisbury St. Barn S75 .... 33 D3
Scott Cres. Don DN3 .... 42 E3
Scott Cres. Don DN3 .... 42 E3
Shaw La. Don DN2 .... 63 A4
Sherwood Glen. Shef S7 .... 140 A1
Salisbury Wlk. C in L S81 .... 148 E7
Scott Hill. Sprot DN5 .... 82 B8
Scott Hill. Sprot DN5 .... 82 B8
Shaw La. Fenw DN6 .... 6 A4
Sherwood Pl. Dron S18 .... 152 D1 2
Salmon St. Shef S11 .... 140 F8 5
Scott Rd. Shef S4 .... 129 C8
Scott Rd. Shef S4 .... 129 C8
Shaw La. Mapp S75 .... 14 C2
Sherwood Rd. Dron S18 .... 152 D1
Salt Hill. Fir S81 .... 136 B5
Scott St. Shef S4 .... 129 B1
Scott St. Shef S4 .... 129 B1
Shaw La. Midhop S30 .... 71 D3
Sherwood Rd. Har DN11 .... 121 F5
Salt Hill Rd. Fir S81 .... 136 C4
Scott Way. Chap S30 .... 94 F4
Scott Way. Chap S30 .... 94 F4
Shaw La. Roy S71 .... 15 E1
Sherwood Rd. Kill S31 .... 156 F7
Salter's Way. Pen S30 .... 51 D2
Scott Wlk. Maltby S66 .... 118 C8
Scott Wlk. Maltby S66 .... 118 C8
Shaw Lane Ind Est. Don 63 D8
Sherwood Rd. Ross DN11 .... 104 A8
Saltersbrook. Dearne S63 .... 58 D5
Scout Dike Outdoor Ed Cntr Pen .. 51 B6
Shaw Rd. N Edl DN12 .... 82 C3
Sherwood St. Barn S71 .... 33 F1 15
Saltersbrook Rd. Dar S73 .... 57 A7
Scovell Ave. Rawm S62 .... 97 D7
Scovell Ave. Rawm S62 .... 97 D7
Shaw Rd. Roth S65 .... 116 A8
Sherwood Way. Cud S72 .... 16 A2
Samson St. Shef S2 .... 129 C2 5
Scovell House. Rawm S62 .... 97 D7
Scovell House. Rawm S62 .... 97 D7
Shaw St. Barn S70 .... 54 D8
Shetland Gdns. Don DN2 .... 63 D5
Samuel Cl. Shef S2 .... 141 D7
Scowerdons Cl. Shef S12 .... 142 F5
Scowerdons Cl. Shef S12 .... 142 F5
Shaw St. Dron S18 .... 153 A4
Shield Ave. Barn S70 .... 55 A5
Samuel Dr. Shef S2 .... 141 D7
Scowerdons Dr. Shef S12 .... 142 F5
Scowerdons Dr. Shef S12 .... 142 F5
Shaw St. Roth S65 .... 116 A8
Shildon Dr. Thorne DN8 .... 9 E3
Samuel Pl. Shef S2 .... 141 D7
Scraith Wood Dr. Shef S5 .... 112 E2
Scraith Wood Dr. Shef S5 .... 112 E2
Shaw Wood Jun & Inf Sch. Arm ... 64 A7
Shinwell Dr. Upton WF9 .... 19 D8
Samuel Rd. Barn S75 .... 33 B3
Scratta La. Whit S80 .... 159 C2
Scratta La. Whit S80 .... 159 C2
Shawfield Cl. Shef S19 .... 143 F3
Ship Hill. Roth S60 .... 115 D6
Samuel Rd. Shef S2 .... 141 D7
Scrooby Dr. Roth S61 .... 97 D3
Scrooby Dr. Roth S61 .... 97 D3
Shawfield Rd. Barn S71 .... 34 C6
Shipcroft Cl. Wombw S73 .... 56 F2
Samuel Sq. Barn S75 .... 33 B3
Scrooby La. Roth S62 .... 97 D3
Scrooby La. Roth S62 .... 97 D3
Shawlands Jun & Inf Sch. Barn 54 D8
Shipman Ct. Shef S19 .... 155 D7
Samuel St. Don DN4 .... 83 A6
Scrooby Pl. Roth S61 .... 97 C3
Scrooby Pl. Roth S61 .... 97 C3
Shawsfield Rd. Roth S60 .... 115 F3
Shipman St. Shef S19 .... 155 D7
Sanctuary Fields. N Anst S31 ...... 146 D7
Scrooby Rd. Bir DN11 .... 122 C4
Scrooby Rd. Bir DN11 .... 122 C4
Shay House La. Stock S30 .... 92 B8
Shipston Dr. Chap S30 .... 94 D7
Sand La. Wroot DN9 .... 66 F4
Scrooby Rd. Har DN11 .... 121 F5
Scrooby Rd. Har DN11 .... 121 F5
Shay Rd. Stock S30 .... 73 C1
Shipton St. Shef S6 .... 128 E5
Sandal Rd. Con DN12 .... 81 B1
Scrooby Rd. Roth S61 .... 97 C3
Scrooby Rd. Roth S61 .... 97 C3
Shay The. Don DN4 .... 84 E7
Shirburn Gdns. Don DN4 .... 63 F1
Sandall Beat La. Don DN2 .... 63 D5
Sayers Cl. Bnbur DN5 .... 59 C2
Sayers Cl. Bnbur DN5 .... 59 C2
Sheaf Bank. Shef S2 .... 141 A7
Shirebrook Fst & Mid Schs. Shef .. 143 C5
Sandall Beat Rd. Don DN2 .... 63 C3
Scafell Pl. N Anst S31 .... 146 F6
Scafell Pl. N Anst S31 .... 146 F6
Sheaf Cl. Con DN12 .... 81 D1
Shirebrook Rd. Shef S8 .... 141 A6
Sandall Carr Rd. Don DN3 .... 42 E4
Scaftworth Cl. Don DN4 .... 84 C7
Scaftworth Cl. Don DN4 .... 84 C7
Sheaf Cres. Dearne S63 .... 58 D1
Shirecliffe Cl. Shef S3 .... 129 B7
Sandall La. Don DN3 .... 42 E4
Scaly Gate. Holmfi HD7 .... 28 A2
Scaly Gate. Holmfi HD7 .... 28 A2
Sheaf Ct. Barn S70 .... 55 D7
Shirecliffe Coll of F Ed. Shef 129 A8
Sandall Park Dr. Don DN2 .... 63 C7
Scammadine Cl. Brin S60 .... 131 D8
Scammadine Cl. Brin S60 .... 131 D8
Sheaf Gdns. Shef S2 .... 129 B1
Shirecliffe Inf Sch. Shef 112 E2
Sheaf Gdns. Shef S2 .... 129 B1
Shirecliffe Jun Sch. Shef 112 E2

Union St. Hem WF9 17 E6
Union St. Roth S61 115 B6
Union St. Shef S1 129 A2
Unity Pl. Roth S60 115 D6
Univ of Sheffield. Shef 128 E3
Unsliven Rd. Stock S30 72 F3
Unstone St. Shef S1 129 A1
Unstone-Dronfield By-Pass.
Dron S18 152 F3
Unwin Cres. Pen S30 51 D2
Unwin St. Pen S30 51 D2
Uplands Ave. Kex S75 32 C8
Uplands Rd. Arm DN3 64 C6
Uplands Way. Rawm S62 97 E6
Upper Albert Rd. Shef S8 141 B5
Upper Allen St. Shef S3 128 F4
Upper Ash Gr. S Elm WF9 19 B3
Upper Clara St. Roth S61 114 F6
Upper Cliffe Rd. Dod S75 53 E8
Upper Common La. Clay W HD8 12 A1
Upper Common La. Clay W HD8 30 F8
Upper Cumberworth C of E Aided
Fst Sch. D Dale 29 B6
Upper Field La. H Hoy S75 12 E1
Upper Field La. Kex S75 12 E1
Upper Folderings. Dod S75 53 F7
Upper Gate Rd. Shef S6 127 C6
Upper Hanover St. Shef S3 128 E2
Upper Hanover St. Shef S3 128 E3
Upper House Rd. Holmfi HD7 48 C8
Upper Hoyland Rd. Hoy S74 76 C7
Upper Kenyon St. Thorne DN8 26 B8
Upper Ley Ct. Chap S30 95 A5
Upper Ley Dell. Chap S30 95 A5
Upper Maythorn La. Wh Com HD7 49 D8
Upper Mill Gate. Roth S60 115 D6
Upper New St. Barn S70 54 F8 1
Upper Norcroft. Caw S75 31 F3
Upper Rye Cl. Roth S60 116 D1
Upper School La. Dron S18 153 A1
Upper Sheffield Rd. Barn S70 55 A6
Upper Valley Rd. Shef S8 141 B5
Upper Whiston La. Ulley S60 132 D7
Upper Wortley Rd. Roth S61 96 B2
Upperfield Cl. Maltby S66 118 F6
Upperfield Rd. Maltby S66 118 E6
Upperthorpe Fst Sch. Shef 128 E5
Upperthorpe Glen. Shef S6 128 D5
Upperthorpe Mid Sch. Shef 128 E5
Upperthorpe Rd. Kill S31 156 D4
Upperthorpe Rd. Shef S6 128 E5
Upperthorpe. Shef S6 128 D5
Upperthorpe Villas. Kill S31 156 D5
Upperwood Hall. Dar S73 56 E6
Upperwood Rd. Dar S73 56 E6
Upton Cl. Maltby S66 118 E7
Upton Cl. Wombw S73 56 B4
Upton Mid Sch. Upton 18 F7
Upwell Hill. Shef S4 113 E1
Upwell La. Shef S4 113 E1
Upwell St. Shef S4 113 F1
Upwood Rd. Shef S6 112 B1
Urban Rd. Don DN4 62 A1
Urch Cl. Con DN12 81 C1
Uttley Cl. Shef S9 130 B6
Uttley Croft. Shef S9 130 B6
Uttley Dr. Shef S9 130 B6
Uttoxeter Ave. Mex S64 80 C6

Vaal St. Barn S70 55 B8
Vainor Rd. Shef S6 112 A2
Vale Ave. Roth S65 98 F2
Vale Cl. Dron S18 153 B1
Vale Cres. Roth S65 98 F2
Vale Gr. Shef S6 127 E8
Vale Rd. Roth S65 99 A2
Vale Rd. Shef S3 128 F7
Valentine Cl. Shef S5 113 C5
Valentine Cres. Shef S5 113 C5
Valentine Rd. Shef S5 113 C5
Valestone Ave. Hem WF9 17 E7
Valetta House. Rawm S62 97 F4
Valiant Gdns. Ben DN5 61 E3
Valley Ave. S Elm WF9 19 B3
Valley Dr. Bran DN3 85 D8
Valley Dr. Kill S31 156 D7
Valley Dr. W up D S63 78 E6
Valley Rd. Chap S30 94 E6
Valley Rd. Dar S73 56 E3
Valley Rd. Kill S31 156 D7
Valley Rd. Mapp S75 14 A1
Valley Rd. Shef S8 141 A6
Valley Rd. Shef S12 143 C3
Valley Rd. Swint S64 79 B1
Valley St. S Elm WF9 18 F2
Valley View Cl. Eck S31 155 C2
Valley View. S Elm WF9 19 B3
Valley Way. Hoy S74 76 E5
Vancouver Dr. Dearne S63 58 B2
Varley Gdns. Roth S66 117 B6
Varney Rd. W up D S63 78 E4
Varsity Cl. Hat DN7 66 A7
Vaughan Rd. Barn S75 33 B3
Vaughan Rd. Norton DN6 4 D1
Vaughan St. Don DN1 62 D4
Vaughan Terr. G Hou S72 36 E2
Vaughton Hill. Stock S30 73 F1
Vauxhall Cl. Shef S9 114 B4
Vauxhall Rd. Shef S9 114 B4
Velvet Wood Cl. Barn S75 33 A3
Venetian Cres. Dar S73 56 F5
Ventnor Cl. Don DN4 82 F7
Ventnor Ct. Shef S7 140 F8 13
Ventnor Pl. Shef S7 140 F8
Venus Ct. Brin S60 115 C2
Verdant Way. Shef S5 113 D5
Verdon St. Shef S3 129 B5
Vere Rd. Shef S6 112 C2
Verelst Ave. Aston S31 144 D8
Verger Cl. Ross DN11 85 B1
Vermuyden Rd. Thorne DN8 9 D3
Vernon Cl. Barn S70 54 F7
Vernon Cres. Barn S70 54 F5
Vernon Delph. Shef S10 127 F3
Vernon Dr. Chap S30 95 A5
Vernon Rd. Barn S70 55 A4
Vernon Rd. Roth S60 116 B3
Vernon Rd. Shef S17 151 F6
Vernon St. Barn S71 33 F2
Vernon St. Barn S70 75 F6
Vernon St. Hoy S74 76 C5
Vernon St N. Barn S71 33 F2 3
Vernon Terr. Shef S10 128 A2
Vernon Way. Barn S75 33 B3
Vernon Way. Maltby S66 118 E6
Verona Rise. Dar S73 57 A5
Vesey St. Rawm S62 97 F4
Vicar Cres. Dar S73 57 B5
Vicar La. Shef S1 129 A3
Vicar La. Shef S13 143 B7
Vicar Rd. Dar S73 57 B5
Vicar Rd. W up D S63 78 E7
Vicarage Cl. Don DN4 85 A7
Vicarage Cl. Hoy S74 76 E6
Vicarage Cl. Mex S64 80 C4
Vicarage Cl. Roth S65 116 D8
Vicarage Cl. S Kirk WF9 18 C3
Vicarage Cres. Shef S30 112 C8
Vicarage Dr. Wad DN11 102 B7
Vicarage La. Roth S60 115 D6
Vicarage La. Roy S71 15 C3
Vicarage La. Shef S17 151 D7
Vicarage Rd. Shef S9 129 F6
Vicarage Rd. Shef S30 112 C8
Vicarage Way. Ben DN5 41 E2
Vicarage Wlk. Pen S30 51 D3
Vickers Ave. S Elm WF9 18 E1
Vickers Dr. Shef S5 113 D3
Vickers Rd. Chap S30 94 D7
Vickers Rd. Shef S5 113 D2
Victor Rd. S Kirk WF9 18 C2
Victor Rd. Shef S17 151 F7
Victor St. Ad I S DN6 40 B8
Victor St. S Elm WF9 18 F2
Victor St. Shef S6 128 D7
Victor Terr. Barn S70 55 A8 3
Victoria Ave. Barn S70 33 E2 1
Victoria Ave. Hat DN7 44 C8
Victoria Ave. Roth S65 115 F6
Victoria Cl. Stai DN7 24 F2
Victoria Cl. Stock S30 73 B1
Victoria Cl. Wales S31 145 E2
Victoria Cres. Barn S70, S75 33 D2
Victoria Cres. Barn S70 75 E7
Victoria Cres W. Barn S75 33 D2
Victoria Ct. Ben DN5 41 B3
Victoria Ct. Upton WF9 19 A7
Victoria Ct. Wales S31 145 E2
Victoria La. Ross DN11 84 E1
Victoria Rd. Ad I S DN6 40 D6
Victoria Rd. Askern DN6 21 F6
Victoria Rd. Barn S70 33 E2
Victoria Rd. Ben DN5 41 B3
Victoria Rd. Don DN4, 83 B8
Victoria Rd. Mex S64 80 A5
Victoria Rd. N Edl DN12 82 B3
Victoria Rd. Norton DN6 4 C3
Victoria Rd. Rawm S62 97 F4
Victoria Rd. Rawm S62 98 A4
Victoria Rd. Roy S71 15 D4
Victoria Rd. Shef S10 128 E1
Victoria Rd. Shef S19 143 F4
Victoria Rd. Stock S30 73 C1
Victoria Rd. W up D S63 78 D7
Victoria Rd. Wombw S73 56 D3
Victoria St. Barn S70 33 E2
Victoria St. Barn S70 55 D8
Victoria St. Cud S72 35 B7
Victoria St. Dar S73 57 B6
Victoria St. Dearne S63 58 E5
Victoria St. Din S31 135 A1
Victoria St. Dron S18 152 F2
Victoria St. Hem WF9 17 E6
Victoria St. Hoy S74 76 F6
Victoria St. Maltby S66 119 A3
Victoria St. Mex S64 79 E5
Victoria St. Pen S30 51 D3
Victoria St. Roth S60 115 B6
Victoria St. Shef S3 128 F3
Victoria St. Stock S30 73 C1
Victoria St. Swint S62 98 E7
Victoria St. Treet S60 131 D6
Victoria Station Rd. Shef S4 129 C4
Victoria Terr. Barn S70 55 A8 11
Victoria Way. Maltby S66 118 D6
Victorian Cres. Don DN2 62 F4
View Rd. Pen S30 51 A4
View Rd. Roth S65 116 A8
View Rd. Shef S2 141 A7
Viewland Cl. Cud S72 35 C5
Viewlands Cl. Pen S30 51 D5
Viewlands. Silk S75 53 A5
Viewtree Cl. Went S62 76 D1
Viking Way. Wales S31 145 F3
Vikinglea Cl. Shef S2 142 B8
Vikinglea Dr. Shef S2 142 B8
Vikinglea Glade. Shef S2 130 B1
Vikinglea Rd. Shef S2 130 B1
Villa Gdns. Ben DN5 41 A5
Villa Park Rd. Don DN4 84 E8
Villa Rd. Ad I S DN6 40 B5
Village St. Ad I S DN6 40 C6
Village St. Ben DN6 61 D5
Villiers Cl. Shef S2 141 E6
Villiers Dr. Shef S2 141 E6
Vincent Rd. Barn S71 34 F3
Vincent Rd. Roth S65 117 D7
Vincent Rd. Shef S7 140 F8
Vincent Terr. Dearne S63 58 F7
Vine Cl. Barn S71 34 C4
Vine Cl. Roth S60 115 C6
Vine Rd. Tick DN11 121 C7
Vineyard Cl. Tick DN11 120 F8
Viola Bank. Stock S30 73 B1
Violet Ave. N Edl DN12 82 B1
Violet Ave. Shef S19 143 F3
Violet Bank Rd. Shef S7 140 E6
Vissett Cl. Hem WF9 17 B6
Vissitt La. Hem WF9 17 B6
Vivian Rd. Shef S5 113 D2
Vizard Rd. Hoy S74 76 F6
Vizard Rd. Hoy S74 77 A6
Vulcan House. Roth S65 116 A7 2
Vulcan Rd. Shef S9 114 B2
Vulcan Rd. Shef S9 114 D2
Vulcan Way. Hat DN7 44 F1
Vulcan Way. Hat DN7 45 A1

Wadbrough Rd. Shef S11 128 D1
Waddington Rd. Barn S75 33 B2
Wade Cl. Roth S60 115 F4
Wade Meadow. Shef S6 112 A1
Wade St. Barn S75 33 B2
Wade St. Shef S4 113 E1
Wadsley La. Shef S6 112 B2
Wadsley Park Cres. Shef S6 112 A1
Wadsworth Ave. Shef S12 142 D5
Wadsworth Cl. Shef S12 142 D5
Wadsworth Dr. Rawm S62 97 C8
Wadsworth Dr. Shef S12 142 D5
Wadsworth Rd. Roth S66 117 D4
Wadsworth Rd. Shef S12 142 C5
Wadworth Ave. Ross DN11 85 B1
Wadworth Cl. Bnbur DN5 59 C3
Wadworth Hill. Wad DN11 102 C8
Wadworth Jun & Inf Sch. Wad 102 C6
Wadworth Rise. Roth S65 98 E1
Wadworth St. Con DN12 81 A4
Waggon La. Upton WF9 19 C8
Wagon Rd. Roth S61 97 B2
Waingate. Shef S3 129 B4
Wainwright Ave. Shef S13 142 D8
Wainwright Ave. Wombw S73 56 C3
Wainwright Cres. Shef S13 142 D8
Wainwright Pl. Wombw S73 56 B3
Wainwright Rd. Don DN4 62 E2
Wainwright Rd. Roth S61 96 F1
Wake Rd. Shef S7 140 E7
Wakefield District Coll. Hem 17 E7
Wakefield Rd. Barn S71, S75 33 E7
Wakefield Rd. Barn S71 34 A5
Wakefield Rd. D Dale HD8 30 B7
Wakefield Rd. Hem WF9 17 D8
Wakefield Rd. Mapp S75 14 C2
Walbank Rd. Arm DN3 64 C6
Walbert Ave. Dearne S63 58 C7
Walbrook. Barn S70 55 B4
Walden Ave. Ben DN5 40 E1
Walden Rd. Shef S2 141 B7
Walden Stubbs Rd. Norton DN6 4 D4
Walders Ave. Shef S6 112 A2
Wales Comp Sch. Wales 145 C3
Wales Jun & Inf Sch. Wales 145 B2
Wales Pl. Shef S6 128 D6
Wales Rd. Wales S31 145 C2
Walesmoor Ave. Wales S31 145 C2
Waleswood Rd. Wales S31 144 C4
Waleswood View. Aston S31 144 D6
Waleswood Villas. Wales S31 144 F3
Walford Rd. Kill S31 156 C6
Walk Royd Hill. Kex S75 13 B2
Walk The. Barn S70 75 E6
Walker Cl. Shef S30 112 C8
Walker Edge. Bfield S30 92 A3
Walker La. Roth S65 115 E7
Walker Rd. Pilley S75 75 F5
Walker Rd. Roth S61 96 F1
Walker St. Rawm S62 98 B6
Walker St. Shef S3 129 B5
Walker St. Swint S64 79 E3
Walker View. Rawm S62 98 B6
Walkers La. Kill S31 156 D6
Walkers Terr. Barn S71 34 C5
Walkley Bank Cl. Shef S6 128 C7
Walkley Bank Rd. Shef S6 128 B7
Walkley Crescent Rd. Shef S6 128 B6
Walkley Inf Sch. Shef 128 D6
Walkley Jun Sch. Shef 128 D6
Walkley La. Shef S6 128 C7
Walkley Rd. Shef S6 128 C6
Walkley St. Shef S6 128 D5
Walkley Terr. Shef S6 128 A6
Wall Nook La. Holmfi HD8 28 D6
Wall St. Barn S70 54 E8
Wallace Rd. Don DN4 82 E6
Wallace Rd. Shef S3 128 F7
Walled Garden The. Wool WF4 14 A7
Waller Rd. Shef S6 128 A5
Walling Cl. Shef S9 114 B2
Walling Rd. Shef S9 114 B2
Wallingwells La. Gild S81 147 F6
Wallroyds. D Dale HD8 29 F5
Walmsley Dr. Upton WF9 19 B7
Walney Fold. Barn S71 34 D6
Walnut Ave. Finn DN9 86 A4
Walnut Ave. Shire S81 159 F7
Walnut Ave. Tick DN11 121 B7
Walnut Dr. Din S31 146 F8
Walnut Dr. Kill S31 156 C5
Walnut Gr. Mex S64 79 F6
Walnut Pl. Chap S30 94 F6
Walnut St. S Elm WF9 18 F1
Walnut Tree Hill. Wad DN11 102 C7
Walpole Cl. Don DN4 82 F5
Walpole Gr. Aston S31 132 D1
Walseker La. Hart S31 157 C7
Walsham Dr. Ben DN5 61 E5
Walshaw Rd. Ought S30 111 D5
Walter St. Roth S60 115 C7
Walter St. Shef S6 128 D7
Walters Rd. Maltby S66 119 B5
Waltham Dr. Ad le S DN6 20 E2
Waltham Gdns. Shef S19 144 A2 1
Waltham St. Barn S70 54 F8 7
Waltheof Rd. Shef S2 142 A8
Waltheof Sch Darnall Road
Annexe. Shef 130 B5
Waltheof Sch. Shef 130 B2
Walton Cl. Chap S30 94 C8
Walton Cl. Dron S18 152 C2
Walton Ct. Shef S8 152 E8
Walton Rd. Shef S11 128 D1
Walton Rd. Upton WF9 19 D8
Walton St. Barn S75 33 C3
Walton St N. Barn S75 33 C3
Wannop St. Rawm S62 97 F3
Wansfell Rd. Shef S4 113 F1
Wansfell Terr. Barn S71 34 A1
Wapping The. H Rob S65 99 D7
Warburton Cl. Shef S2 141 C7
Warburton Gdns. Shef S2 141 C7
Warburton Rd. Shef S2 141 C7
Ward Green Prim Sch. Barn 54 F5
Ward La. Barl S43 157 B2
Ward Pl. Shef16 S7 140 F8
Ward St. Pen S30 51 D2
Ward St. Shef S3 129 A5
Warde Ave. Don DN4 82 F6
Warde-Aldam Cres. Roth S66 117 A5
Warden Cl. Don DN4 85 A8
Warden St. Roth S60 115 D3
Wardlow Rd. Shef S12 142 D5
Wardsend Rd N. Shef S6 112 C3
Wardsend Rd. Shef S6 112 D2
Wareham Ct. Shef S19 144 A2
Wareham Gr. Dod S75 54 A8
Warehouse La. W up D S63 78 E6
Warminster Cl. Shef S8 141 A4
Warminster Dr. Shef S8 141 B3
Warminster Gdns. Shef S8 141 B4
Warminster Pl. Shef S8 141 B2
Warminster Rd. Shef S8 141 A3
Warmsworth C of E Fst Sch. Don 82 D5
Warmsworth Ct. Don DN4 82 D6
Warmsworth Halt. Don DN12 82 B4
Warmsworth Halt Ind Est. Don 82 C4
Warmsworth Mid Sch. Don 82 C6
Warmsworth Rd. Don DN4 82 E6
Warner Ave. Barn S75 33 B2
Warner Pl. Barn S75 33 C2
Warner Rd. Barn S75 33 B2
Warner Rd. Shef S6 112 B1
Warning Tongue La. Don DN4 85 B6
Warning Tongue La. Ross DN4 85 B6
Warnington Dr. Ross DN4 85 B5
Warren Ave. Rawm S62 97 E7
Warren Cl. Don DN2 63 A4
Warren Cl. Roy S71 15 D5
Warren Cl. Woods S81 147 E4
Warren Cres. Barn S70 54 F7
Warren Cres. Eck S31 154 E2
Warren Dr. Roth S61 114 F8
Warren Gdns. Chap S30 95 B8
Warren Hill. Roth S61 114 F8
Warren House Cl. Roth S66 117 D5
Warren La. Chap S30 75 F1
Warren La. Chap S30 95 B8
Warren La. Don DN4 84 F5
Warren La. Mapp S75 14 C4
Warren La. Ross DN11 85 A3
Warren La. Wool S75 14 C4
Warren Mount. Roth S61 114 F8
Warren Pl. Barn S70 54 F7 14
Warren Quarry La. Barn S70 54 F7
Warren Rd. Con DN12 81 B1
Warren Rd. Roth S66 117 B5
Warren Rd. Thorne DN8 26 C6
Warren Rise. Dron S18 153 C3
Warren St. Shef S4 129 D5
Warren St. Shef S4 129 E5
Warren Vale. Rawm S62 98 A7
Warren Vale Rd. Swint S64 79 A2
Warren Vale. Swint S64 79 A1
Warren View. Hoy S74 76 C4
Warren Wlk. Eck S31 154 E2
Warreners Dr. Roth S65 99 A2
Warrenne Cl. Hat DN7 44 A7
Warrenne Rd. Hat DN7 44 A8
Warrington Rd. Shef S10 128 D4
Warris Cl. Roth S61 96 E1
Warris Pl. Shef S2 129 D3
Warsop Rd. Barn S71 14 E1
Warwick Ave. C in L S81 148 F6
Warwick Cl. Hat DN7 45 A6
Warwick Rd. Barn S71 34 B4
Warwick Rd. Don DN2 63 B5
Warwick St. Roth S60 115 E5
Warwick St S. Roth S60 115 E5
Warwick St. Shef S10 128 C4
Warwick Terr. Shef S10 128 C4
Warwick Way. N Anst S31 146 E7
Wasdale Ave. Shef S19 155 E6 5
Wasdale Cl. Shef S19 155 E6
Washfield La. Treet S60 131 E4
Washford Rd. Shef S9 129 E5
Washfield Cres. Treet S60 131 E4
Washington Ave. Con DN12 81 A2
Washington Ave. Wombw S73 56 B2
Washington Gr. Ben DN5 62 A7
Washington Rd. Ad I S DN6 40 C5
Washington Rd. Dearne S63 58 D4
Washington Rd. Shef S11 140 F8
Washington Rd. Shef S30 95 B1
Washington St. Mex S64 80 B5
Wasteneys Rd. Tod S31 145 F5
Watch House La. Ben DN5 62 A7
Watch St. Shef S13 143 E8
Watchley La. H Pag DN5 38 B3
Water Bank. Wroot DN9 67 C2
Water Hall La. Pen S30 51 D4
Water La. Hoy S74 77 A3
Water La. K Smea WF8 3 E6
Water La. Roth S60 115 D5
Water La. S Kirk WF9 17 F4
Water La. Shef S17 151 F7
Water La. Stai DN7 24 E5
Water La. Tick DN11 121 A5
Water La. Wool WF4 14 A8
Water Royd Dr. Dod S75 54 A7
Water Slacks Cl. Shef S13 143 B6
Water Slacks Dr. Shef S13 143 B6
Water Slacks Rd. Shef S13 143 B5
Water Slacks Wlk. Shef S13 143 B6
Water St. Shef S3 129 A4
Waterdale. Don DN1 62 D3
Waterdale Rd. Barn S70 54 F4
Waterfield Mews. Shef S19 143 E1 8
Waterfield Pl. Barn S70 55 E8
Waterford Rd. Shef S3 128 E7
Waterhall View. Pen S30 51 D4
Waterhouse Cl. Roth S65 98 E1
Watering Place Rd. Pen S30 51 A3
Waterloo Rd. Barn S70 33 D1 7
Waterloo Wlk. Shef S3 128 F5
Watermead. Dearne S63 58 D1
Watermead Fst Sch. Shef 112 F2
Watermeade. Eck S31 155 B2
Waterside Gdns. Ought S30 111 D7
Waterside. Thorne DN8 25 E8
Waterslack Rd. Bir DN11 122 B4
Watersmeet Rd. Shef S6 128 B7
Waterthorpe Cl. Shef S19 155 F8 4
Waterthorpe Cres. Shef S19 155 F8
Waterthorpe Fst Sch. Shef 143 E1
Waterthorpe Gdns. Shef S19 155 F8 3
Waterthorpe Glade. Shef S19 155 F8 5
Waterthorpe Glen. Shef S19 155 F8 2
Waterthorpe Greenway.
Shef S19 143 D3
Waterthorpe Rise. Shef S19 155 F8 1
Waterton Cl. S Kirk WF9 18 D3
Waterton La. Hat DN7 44 C3
Watery St. Shef S3 128 F5
Wath C of E Jun & Inf Sch. W up D 78 E7
Wath Comp Sch Park Rd Annexe.
W up D 78 E5
Wath Golf Course. W up D 78 D3
Wath Rd. Dearne S63 58 C1
Wath Rd. Hoy S74 77 C5
Wath Rd. Mex S64 79 D5
Wath Rd. Shef S7 140 E6
Wath Rd. W up D S73 57 A1
Wath Rd. W up D S64 79 E5
Wath Rd. Wombw S73 56 F1
Wath upon Dearne Central Sch.
W up D 78 F5
Wath upon Dearne Grammar Sch.
W up D 78 F5
Wath Victoria Jun Mix & Inf Sch.
W up D 79 A6
Wath West Ind Est. W up D 78 C8
Wath Wood Bottom. W up D S63 78 F3
Wath Wood Dr. Swint S64 78 F3
Wath Wood Rd. Swint S63 78 F3
Wathwood Hospl. Swint 78 F3
Watkinson Gdns. Shef S19 143 F1
Watnall Rd. Barn S71 33 F8
Watson Cl. Roth S61 114 F8
Watson Glen. Roth S61 114 C8
Watson Rd. Roth S61 114 F8
Watson Rd. Shef S10 128 D2
Watson St. Hoy S74 76 B5
Watt La. Shef S10 127 F2
Waulkmill Cl. Upton WF9 19 A7
Waveney Dr. Barn S75 32 E3
Waverley Ave. Con DN12 81 C2
Waverley Ave. Don DN4 82 E7
Waverley Ave. Thurcr S66 133 F6
Waverley Ave. Wales S31 145 E3
Waverley Cotts. Shef S13 130 F3
Waverley Ct. Ben DN5 41 A4
Waverley Rd. Shef S9 130 C4
Waverley View. Treet S60 131 C5
Waycliffe. Barn S71 34 C3
Wayford Ave. Roth S66 117 E6
Wayland Ave. Barn S70 54 F5
Wayland Rd. Shef S11 140 D8
Weakland Cl. Shef S12 142 F3
Weakland Cres. Shef S12 142 F3
Weakland Dr. Shef S12 142 F3
Weakland Way. Shef S12 142 F3
Weather Hill La. Holme HD7 47 E8
Weatherall Pl. Ad le S DN6 20 F2
Weaver Cl. Barn S75 32 E3
Weavers Cl. Shef S30 94 C1
Weavers Wlk. D Dale HD8 30 B7
Webb Ave. Stock S30 92 E8
Webbs Ave. Shef S6 127 E6
Webster Cl. Roth S61 114 D8
Webster Cres. Roth S61 114 D8
Webster St. Shef S9 114 B1
Wedgewood Cl. Rawm S62 97 F5
Weedon St. Shef S9 114 B1
Weet Shaw La. Cud S72 16 B1
Weetwood Dr. Shef S11 140 B5
Weetwood Rd. Roth S60 116 A2
Weigh La. Shef S2 129 C3 4
Weir Cl. Hoy S74 76 F4
Weir Head. Shef S9 114 B1
Weirside. Old S81 136 F6
Welbeck Cl. Dron S18 152 C2
Welbeck Dr. Aston S31 144 F7
Welbeck Pl. Roth S65 116 B8 4
Welbeck Rd. Don DN4 62 F2
Welbeck Rd. Har DN11 122 A5
Welbeck Rd. Shef S6 128 B6
Welbeck St. Barn S75 33 D2
Welbury Gdns. Shef S19 155 E6
Welby Pl. Shef S8 140 F5
Welfare Ave. Con DN12 81 A2
Welfare Rd. Ad I S DN6 40 C4
Welfare Rd. Dearne S63 58 D8
Welfare View. Dearne S63 58 D4
Welfare View. Dod S75 53 F8
Welham Dr. Roth S60 115 E4
Well Croft. Chap S30 94 D7
Well Ct. Shef S12 143 B3
Well Dr. Roth S65 99 A2
Well Green Rd. Shef S6 127 B5
Well Hill Gr. Roy S71 15 C4
Well Hill Rd. Stock S30 73 F4
Well House La. Pen S30 51 D5
Well Houses La. Wort S30 74 D5
Well La. Aston S31 132 C2
Well La. Barn S71 34 C5
Well La. Roth S60 116 B1
Well La. Shef S6 111 F2
Well La. Treet S60 131 E5
Well La. Ulley S60 132 D7
Well La. Wad DN11 102 C7
Well Lane Ct. G Hou S72 57 F6
Well Meadow Dr. Shef S3 128 F4 6
Well Meadow St. Shef S3 128 F4
Well Pl. Shef S8 141 A6
Well Rd. Shef S8 141 A6
Well St. Barn S70 33 D1 6
Well View Rd. Roth S61 114 D8
Welland Cl. Shef S3 128 F6
Welland Cres. Hoy S74 77 B6
Welland Ct. Barn S75 32 E3
Wellbourne Cl. Chap S30 95 C4
Wellcarr Rd. Shef S8 141 A2
Wellcliffe Cl. Roth S66 117 C6
Wellcroft Cl. Don DN2 63 C6
Wellesley Rd. Shef S10 128 D3
Wellfield Cl. Eck S12 142 E1
Wellfield Cl. Shef S6 128 D5
Wellfield Cres. Woods S81 147 E3
Wellfield Gr. Pen S30 51 D5
Wellfield Rd. Barn S75 33 D3
Wellfield Rd. Roth S61 96 E2
Wellfield Rd. Shef S6 128 D5
Wellgate. Con DN12 81 C2
Wellgate. Mapp S75 14 B1
Wellgate Mount. Roth S60 115 E6
Wellgate. Roth S60 115 E6
Wellgate Terr. Roth S60 115 E6 4
Wellhead Rd. Shef S8 141 A6 4
Wellhouse Way. Pen S30 51 D5
Welling Way. Roth S61 114 E7
Wellingley La. Tick DN11 102 F2

Wellingley La. Wad DN11 102 E5
Wellington Ave. N Anst S31 146 D7
Wellington Cl. Barn S71 34 B4
Wellington Cres. Barn S70 55 C5
Wellington Gr. Bawtry DN10 122 F8
Wellington Gr. Ben DN5 62 A7
Wellington Pl. Barn S70 33 D1 8
Wellington Pl. Shef S9 130 C4
Wellington Rd. Hat DN7 66 A8
Wellington Rd. N Edl DN12 82 B2
Wellington Rd. Shef S6 127 E6
Wellington St. Barn S70 33 E1
Wellington St. Dearne S63 58 E5
Wellington St. Mex S64 80 A5
Wellington St. Shef S1 128 F2
Wellington St. Shef S1 129 A3
Wellington St. Stai DN7 24 F4
Wellingtonia Dr. Norton DN6 4 C1
Wells Mount. D Dale HD8 29 A6
Wells Rd. Don DN2 62 F6
Wells St. Cud S72 35 B6
Wells St. Kex S75 32 E8
Wells The. N Anst S31 146 D5
Wellsyke Rd. Ad I S DN6 40 D7
Wellthorne Ave. Ingb S30 29 E1
Wellthorne La. Ingb S30 29 D1
Wellway The. Roth S66 117 C7
Welney Pl. Shef S6 112 C4
Welton Cl. Don DN4 84 C6
Welwyn Cl. Shef S12 142 B4
Welwyn Rd. Shef S12 142 B4
Wembley Ave. Con DN12 81 A2
Wembley Cl. Don DN2 63 C5
Wembley Rd. Lan S81 136 F3
Wembley Rd. Thorne DN8 9 D3
Wenchirst La. Fish DN7 8 A2
Wendan Rd. Thorne DN8 26 B5
Wendel Gr. Hoy S74 77 B6
Wenlock St. Shef S13 130 F1
Wensley Cl. Shef S4 113 E1
Wensley Cres. Don DN4 84 F7
Wensley Croft. Shef S4 113 E2
Wensley Ct. Shef S4 113 E2
Wensley Dale Dr. Brin S60 131 D7
Wensley Gdns. Shef S4 113 E2
Wensley Gn. Shef S4 113 E2
Wensley Rd. Barn S71 33 E7
Wensley St. Dearne S63 58 B8
Wensley St. Shef S4 113 E2
Wensleydale Rd. Ben DN5 61 D7
Wensleydale Rd. Roth S61 96 F3
Went Edge Rd. K Smea WF8 3 B6
Wentdale. K Smea WF8 3 E6
Wentworth Ave. Aston S31 144 F7
Wentworth Ave. Shef S11 140 A2
Wentworth Cl. Roth S61 95 E5
Wentworth Cl. Wool WF4 13 F7
Wentworth Cres. Mapp S75 33 D8
Wentworth Cres. Pen S30 51 D3
Wentworth Ct. Roth S61 97 B4
Wentworth Dr. S Kirk WF9 18 C3
Wentworth Gdns. Swint S64 79 C1
Wentworth Hospl (Almshouses).
Went S74 77 A1
Wentworth House. Don DN1 62 C2 9
Wentworth Ind Pk. Pilley 75 D4
Wentworth Pl. Roth S61 96 C2
Wentworth Rd. Don DN2 62 F5
Wentworth Rd. Dron S18 152 C1
Wentworth Rd. Hoy S74 55 D2
Wentworth Rd. Hoy S74 77 A4
Wentworth Rd. Hoy S74 77 A7
Wentworth Rd. Kex S75 32 D8
Wentworth Rd. Mapp S75 33 C8
Wentworth Rd. Pen S30 51 D4
Wentworth Rd. Rawm S62 97 D8
Wentworth Rd. Roth S61 96 A5
Wentworth Rd. Swint S64 98 C8
Wentworth St. Barn S71 33 E3
Wentworth St. Barn S70 75 F7
Wentworth View. Hoy S74 76 E5
Wentworth View. Wombw S73 56 D1
Wentworth Way. Din S31 147 A7
Wentworth Way. Dod S75 53 F6
Wentworth Way. Pilley S75 75 D4
Wescoe Ave. G Hou S72 36 F1
Wesley Ave. Aston S31 144 D8
Wesley Ct. Roth S61 95 F5
Wesley La. Shef S10 128 B3
Wesley Pl. S Anst S31 146 D4
Wesley Rd. Chap S30 94 C7
Wesley Rd. Wales S31 145 D3
Wesley St. Barn S70 33 F1
Wesley St. S Elm WF9 18 E2
Wesley Terr. D Dale HD8 29 F6
Wessenden Cl. Barn S75 33 A1
Wessex Gdns. Shef S17 151 D5
West Ave. Ad le S DN6 39 F4
West Ave. Dearne S63 58 B1
West Ave. Don DN4 83 A7
West Ave. Rawm S62 97 F6
West Ave. Roy S71 15 D4
West Ave. S Elm WF9 19 B4
West Ave. Stai DN7 24 F4
West Ave. Wombw S73 56 B3
West Bank. K Bram DN7 24 D5
West Bank Rise. S Anst S31 146 D4
West Bar. Shef S3 129 A4
West Bawtry Rd. Roth S60 115 D1
West Bretton Jun & Inf School.
W Bret 12 F8
West Circuit. T in B DN3 42 C8
West Cl. Roth S61 114 E8
West Cres. Oxspr S30 52 A2
West Cres. Stock S30 73 A1
West Don St. Shef S6 128 E6
West End Ave. Ben DN5 62 A7
West End Ave. Pen S30 50 D3
West End Ave. Roy S71 15 A3
West End Cres. Roy S71 15 A3
West End La. Ross DN11 84 E1
West End Rd. Norton DN6 4 C3
West End Rd. W up D S63 78 B7
West End View. Eck S31 155 C2
West Garth Cl. Din S31 134 F1
West Gate. Holme HD7 47 F8
West Gate. Mex S64 80 C5
West Gate. Tick DN11 120 F6
West Gr. Don DN2 63 A5
West Gr. Roy S71 15 A4
West Hill. Roth S61 114 C6
West Kirk La. G Hou S72 57 F7
West La. Aston S31 132 B1
West La. Bfield S6 109 F1
West La. Shef S6 111 A2
West La. Syke DN14 6 F4
West La. Thurcr S66 118 B1
West Laith Gate. Don DN1 62 C3 4
West Melton Jun & Inf Sch.
W up D 78 C7
West Moor Cres. Barn S75 33 A1
West Moor La. Arm DN3 64 D8
West Moor La. Hat DN3 43 E1
West Park Dr. Aston S31 144 B7
West Pinfold. Roy S71 15 C2
West Pl. Ben DN5 41 B1
West Quadrant. Shef S5 113 D3
West Rd. Barn S75 33 C2
West Rd. Mex S64 79 F5
West Rd. Thorne DN8 9 D3
West Service Rd. T in B DN3 42 C8
West St. Barn S70 55 B4
West St. Con DN12 81 C2
West St. Dar S73 57 A5
West St. Dearne S63 58 E5
West St. Don DN1 62 C3
West St. Dron S18 152 F2
West St. Eck S31 155 C2
West St. Har DN11 122 A5
West St. Hoy S74 76 D6
West St. Mex S64 80 A4
West St. Roy S71 15 D4
West St. S Anst S31 146 D4
West St. S Elm WF9 19 B4
West St. S Hie S72 16 E5
West St. S Kirk WF9 18 A2
West St. Shef S1 128 F3
West St. Shef S19 144 A3
West St. Thorne DN8 26 B6
West St. Thurcr S66 133 F6
West St. W up D S63 78 E6
West St. Wombw S73 56 C3
West Street La. Shef S1 129 A3 3
West Vale Gr. Roth S65 98 F2
West View. Barn S70 54 E7
West View. C in L S81 148 F8
West View Cl. Shef S17 151 F6
West View Cres. Dearne S63 58 D4
West View. Cud S72 35 C5
West View La. Shef S17 151 F6
West View Rd. Mex S64 80 A4
West View Rd. Roth S61 114 C6
West View. Silk S75 53 A6
West View Terr. Barn S70 55 B4
West Way. Barn S70 33 E1
West Wood Est. Bawtry DN10 122 F6
Westbank Cl. Dron S18 153 B4
Westbank Dr. S Anst S31 146 C4
Westbar Gn. Shef S1, S3 129 A4
Westbourne Gdns. Don DN4 82 F5
Westbourne Gr. Barn S75 33 D3
Westbourne Prep Sch. Shef 128 C2
Westbourne Rd. Shef S10 128 C2
Westbourne Terr. Barn S70 33 C1
Westbrook Bank. Shef S11 140 D8
Westbrook Rd. Chap S30 95 A5
Westbury Ave. Chap S30 95 B4
Westbury Cl. Barn S75 33 B4
Westbury St. Shef S9 129 F5
Westby Cl. Roth S65 117 E8
Westby Cres. Roth S60 116 B1
Westby Wlk. Roth S66 117 E5
Westcroft Cres. Shef S19 155 E8
Westcroft Dr. Shef S19 155 E7
Westcroft Gdns. Shef S19 155 E8
Westcroft Glen. Shef S19 155 E7
Westcroft Gr. Shef S19 155 E7
Westcroft Rd. Hem WF9 17 D7
Westerdale Rd. Ben DN5 61 D6
Western Ave. Din S31 146 F8
Western Bank. Shef S10 128 D3
Western Cl. Din S31 146 F8
Western Rd. Roth S65 116 B6
Western Rd. Shef S10 128 C4
Western St. Barn S70 33 E2
Western Terr. Wombw S73 56 C3
Westfield Ave. Aston S31 132 C1
Westfield Ave. Pen S30 51 A4
Westfield Ave. Shef S12 143 C3
Westfield Bglws. S Elm WF9 19 A2
Westfield Campus. Shef 155 D8
Westfield Cl. Tick DN11 120 F7
Westfield Cres. Askern DN6 22 B8
Westfield Cres. Dearne S63 37 C1
Westfield Cres. Shef S19 155 C8
Westfield Ctr. Shef S19 155 E8
Westfield Gr. Ingb S30 29 D1
Westfield Gr. Shef S12 143 B3 4
Westfield La. Bnbur DN5 59 B3
Westfield La. Fish DN7 7 C1
Westfield La. Norton WF8 3 F3
Westfield La. Pen S30 50 F4
Westfield La. S Elm WF9 18 F2
Westfield Northway. Shef S19 155 E8
Westfield Rd. Arm DN3 64 A6
Westfield Rd. Don DN4 83 B8
Westfield Rd. Fish DN7 24 D8
Westfield Rd. Hat DN7 44 C8
Westfield Rd. Hem WF9 17 D7
Westfield Rd. Kill S31 156 C5
Westfield Rd. Rawm S62 97 E4
Westfield Rd. Roth S66 117 D5
Westfield Rd. Tick DN11 120 F7
Westfield Rd. W up D S63 78 A7
Westfield Southway. Shef S19 155 E8
Westfield St. Barn S70 33 D1
Westfield Terr. Shef S1 128 F3
Westfield Villas. Hat DN7 44 C8
Westfields. Barn S70 55 A4
Westfields. Roy S71 15 A4
Westgate. Barn S70 33 E1
Westgate. Barn S71 34 B4
Westgate. Hem WF9 17 C6
Westgate. Pen S30 51 E2
Westgate. Roth S60 115 D6
Westhaven. Cud S72 35 C5
Westhill La. Shef S3 128 F3
Westholme Rd. Don DN4 62 B1
Westland Cl. Shef S19 143 E1
Westland Gdns. Shef S19 143 D1
Westland Gr. Shef S19 155 E8 3
Westland Rd. Shef S19 155 E8 1
Westminster Ave. Shef S10 127 B1
Westminster Cl. Shef S10 127 B1
Westminster Cres. Don DN2 63 C5
Westminster Cres. Shef S10 127 B1
Westminster House. Don DN2 63 C5
Westmoreland St. Shef S6 128 E5 2
Westmorland Ct. Bir DN11 122 D4
Westmorland Dr. C in L S81 148 F8
Westmorland La. Con DN12 80 F3
Westmorland St. Don DN4 82 F6
Westmorland Way. Sprot DN5 61 B1
Westmount Ave. W up D S63 78 C8
Westnall Rd. Shef S5 113 D7
Westnall Terr. Shef S5 113 D7
Westoff La. S Hie S72 16 D7
Weston Park Hospl. Shef 128 D3
Weston Park Mus. Shef 128 D3
Weston Rd. Don DN4 83 B6
Weston St. Shef S3 128 E4
Westover Rd. Shef S10 127 E2
Westpit Hill. W up D S63 78 A7
Westside Grange. Don DN4 83 A8
Westthorpe Gr. Kill S31 156 D4
Westthorpe Rd. Kill S31 156 D5
Westville Rd. Barn S75 33 D3
Westways Prim Sch. Shef 128 C4
Westwell Pl. Shef S19 155 D6
Westwick Cres. Shef S8 152 D7
Westwick Gr. Shef S8 152 E7
Westwick Rd. Shef S8 152 E7
Westwood Ct. Barn S70 33 E2
Westwood Ctry Pk. Chap 75 E2
Westwood La. Wort S75 75 C3
Westwood New Rd. Chap S30 94 C7
Westwood New Rd. Pilley S75 75 D3
Westwood New Rd. Pilley S75 75 E5
Westwood Rd. Chap S30 94 D8
Westwood Rd. Shef S11 139 F8
Wet Moor La. W up D S63 78 D7
Wet Moor La. W up D S63 78 F7
Wet Shaw La. Bfield S6 109 E1
Wetherby Cl. Ben DN5 61 D5
Wetherby Ct. Shef S9 130 C4
Wetherby Dr. Aston S31 144 C6
Wetherby Dr. Mex S64 80 B6
Whaley Rd. Barn S75 33 A5
Whams Rd. Carl S30 49 F2
Wharf Cl. Swint S64 79 E3
Wharf Rd. Don DN1 62 D5
Wharf Rd. Shef S9 114 D3
Wharf Rd. Swint S62 98 E7
Wharf St. Barn S71 34 A3
Wharf St. Bawtry DN10 123 A7
Wharf St. Shef S2 129 B4
Wharf St. Swint S64 79 E3
Wharfedale Dr. Chap S30 94 E5
Wharfedale Rd. Barn S75 33 B2
Wharncliffe Ave. Aston S31 144 E8
Wharncliffe Ave. W up D S63 78 E6
Wharncliffe Ave. Wharn S30 93 B3
Wharncliffe Cl. Hoy S74 76 D4
Wharncliffe Cl. Rawm S62 97 D8
Wharncliffe. Dod S75 54 A6
Wharncliffe Rd. Chap S30 94 D7
Wharncliffe Rd. Shef S10 128 E2
Wharncliffe Side Cty Prim Sch.
Wharn 93 B1
Wharncliffe Side Jun & Inf Sch.
Wharn 93 B2
Wharncliffe St. Barn S70 33 D1
Wharncliffe St. Don DN4 62 A2
Wharncliffe St. Roth S65 115 E6
Wharncliffe St. Roy S71 34 D8
Wharton Ave. Aston S31 132 D1
Wheat Croft. Con DN12 81 E2
Wheat Holme La. Askern DN5 41 D8
Wheata Dr. Shef S5 113 B7
Wheata Pl. Shef S5 113 A7
Wheata Rd. Shef S5 113 A7
Wheatacre Rd. Stock S30 73 C1
Wheatcroft Rd. Rawm S62 98 B6
Wheatfield Cl. B Dun DN3 43 A6
Wheatfield Cres. Shef S5 113 D6
Wheatfield Dr. Dearne S63 58 D7
Wheatfield Dr. Tick DN11 121 B8
Wheatfields. Thorne DN8 26 B7
Wheathill St. Roth S60 115 D5
Wheatley Cl. Barn S71 33 F4
Wheatley Golf Course. Don 63 D7
Wheatley Gr. Shef S13 130 E1
Wheatley Hall Rd. Don DN2 62 F6
Wheatley High Sch for Girls. Don 62 E5
Wheatley Hill La. Clay W HD8 30 E8
Wheatley Hills Mid Sch. Don 63 D7
Wheatley La. Don DN1 62 D4
Wheatley Pl. Con DN12 80 F3 7
Wheatley Rd. Barn S70 55 E7
Wheatley Rd. Ben DN5 41 A2
Wheatley Rd. Roth S61 96 E1
Wheatley Rd. Swint S62 98 E7
Wheatley Rise. Mapp S75 14 B2
Wheatley St. Con DN12 80 F3
Wheats La. Shef S1 129 A4 17
Wheel La. Ought S30 111 C7
Wheel La. Ought S30 111 D6
Wheel La. Shef S30 112 D8
Wheel The. Shef S30 112 F8
Wheeldon St. Shef S1 128 F3
Wheldrake Rd. Shef S5 113 D2
Whernside Ave. Chap S30 94 F6
Whih Moor La. Silk S75 52 C7
Whin Cl. Hem WF9 17 D5
Whin Gdns. Dearne S63 37 D1
Whin Hill Rd. Don DN4 84 D8
Whinacre Cl. Shef S8 153 B6
Whinacre Pl. Shef S8 153 A6
Whinacre Wlk. Shef S8 153 A6
Whinby Croft. Dod S75 53 F7
Whinfell Cl. Ad I S DN6 40 B6
Whinfell Ct. Shef S11 139 E2
Whinmoor Cl. Silk S75 31 F1
Whinmoor Ct. Silk S75 31 F1
Whinmoor Dr. Silk S75 31 F1
Whinmoor Rd. Chap S30 94 C7
Whinmoor Rd. Shef S5 113 F3
Whinmoor Sch. Barn 32 D4
Whinmoor View. Silk S75 31 F1
Whinmoor Way. Silk S75 31 F1
Whins The. Rawm S62 97 C5
Whinside Cres. Dearne S63 37 C1
Whiphill Cl. Don DN4 84 E7
Whiphill La. Arm DN3 64 C5
Whirlow Brook Sch. Shef 139 D1
Whirlow Court Rd. Shef S11 139 F2
Whirlow Gr. Shef S11 139 F2
Whirlow La. Shef S11 139 F3
Whirlow Mews. Shef S11 139 F3
Whirlow Park Rd. Shef S11 139 F1
Whirlowdale Cl. Shef S11 139 F2
Whirlowdale Cres. Shef S7 140 B3
Whirlowdale Rd. Shef S11, S7 140 B3
Whirlowdale Rise. Shef S11 139 F2
Whiston Brook View. Roth S60 116 D1
Whiston Gr. Roth S60 115 F4
Whiston Grange. Roth S60 116 A1
Whiston Grange Sch. Roth 116 B1
Whiston Jun & Inf Sch. Roth 116 B1
Whiston Vale. Roth S60 132 B8
Whiston Worrygate Prim Sch.
Roth 116 D1
Whitaker Cl. Ross DN11 103 F7
Whitbeck Cl. Wad DN11 102 B7
Whitburn Rd. Don DN1 62 E2
Whitby Rd. Har DN11 122 A5
Whitby Rd. Ross DN11 103 F8
Whitby Rd. Shef S9 130 C5
Whitcomb Dr. Ross DN11 103 F7
White Apron St. S Kirk WF9 18 B2
White Ave. Lan S81 136 E3
White Croft. Shef S1 129 A4
White Cross Gdns. S Hie S72 16 D6
White Cross La. Barn S70 55 D5
White Cross La. Don DN11 83 B1
White Cross La. Wad DN11 102 B8
White Cross Rd. Cud S72 35 B5
White Cross Rise. Barn S70 55 D5
White Gate. N Anst S31 146 F6
White Gate Rd. Holme HD7 47 D7
White Hill Ave. Barn S70 33 B1
White Hill Gr. Barn S70 33 B1
White Hill Terr. Barn S70 33 B1
White House Cl. Hat DN7 44 A7
White House Cl. Stai DN7 24 E5
White House Dr. Bir DN11 122 C4
White House Rd. Bir DN11 122 C4
White La. Chap S30 95 B7
White La. Eck S12 142 C2
White La. H Pag DN5 38 E4
White La. Shef S12 142 B3
White La. Thorne DN8 25 F8
White Lee La. Bfield S6 92 B3
White Ley Bank. Holmfi HD7 28 A7
White Ley Rd. Norton WF8 3 E1
White Rose Ct. Ben DN5 41 C1
White Rose Way. Don DN4 83 F7
White Thorns Cl. Shef S8 153 B5
White Thorns Dr. Shef S8 153 B5
White Thorns View. Shef S8 153 B6
White's La. Shef S2 129 D3
Whitecroft Cres. Brin S60 131 C8
Whitegate Wlk. Roth S61 96 F3
Whitehall Rd. Roth S61 97 A3
Whitehall Way. Roth S61 97 A3
Whitehead Ave. Stock S30 73 D1
Whitehead Cl. Din S31 134 E1
Whitehill Ave. Brin S60 131 C8
Whitehill Dr. Brin S60 131 C7
Whitehill La. Brin S60 131 D7
Whitehill La. Treet S60 131 D7
Whitehill Rd. Brin S60 131 C8
Whitehouse Ct. Bir DN11 122 C4
Whitehouse La. Shef S6 128 D6
Whitehouse Rd. Shef S6 128 D6
Whitelea Gr. Mex S64 79 F4
Whitelee Rd. Swint S64 79 E4
Whiteley La. Shef S10 139 C7
Whiteley Wood Cl. Shef S11 139 F7
Whiteley Wood Rd. Shef S11 139 E7
Whiteleys Ave. Rawm S62 97 E7
Whitelow La. Shef S17 151 B7
Whiteways Cl. Shef S4 129 D8
Whiteways Dr. Shef S4 129 D8
Whiteways Gr. Shef S4 129 D8
Whiteways Mid Sch. Shef 129 D8
Whiteways Rd. Shef S4 129 D8
Whitewood Cl. Roy S71 15 B3
Whitfield Rd. Rawm S62 97 D7
Whitfield Rd. Shef S10 139 C7
Whiting St. Shef S8 141 A6 9
Whitley Carr. Shef S30 94 E2
Whitley La. Shef S30 94 E2
Whitley Terr. Wh Com S30 49 D5
Whitley View Rd. Roth S61 114 B6
Whitney Cl. Don DN4 82 E5
Whittier Rd. Don DN4 83 A6
Whittington St. Don DN1 62 D5
Whitton Cl. Don DN4 84 C6
Whitwell Cres. Stock S30 73 B1
Whitwell La. Stock S30 92 A8
Whitwell Rd. Th Sa S80 159 A4
Whitwell St. Shef S9 130 D4
Whitwell View. Ross DN11 85 B1
Whitworth La. Shef S9 130 A7
Whitworth Rd. Shef S10 127 F2
Whitworth St. Dearne S63 58 E5
Whitworth Way. W up D S63 78 E7
Whitworth's Terr. Dearne S63 58 E8
Whybourne Gr. Roth S60 115 E5
Whybourne Terr. Roth S60 115 E6 5
Whyn View. Dearne S63 58 E8
Wicker La. Shef S3 129 B4
Wicker. Shef S3 129 B4
Wickersley High Sch. Roth 117 C4
Wickersley Northfield Inf Sch.
Roth 117 B5
Wickersley Northfield Jun Sch.
Roth 117 B5
Wickersley Rd. Roth S60 116 C4
Wicket Way. N Edl DN12 82 C3
Wickett Hern Rd. Arm DN3 64 C6
Wickfield Cl. Shef S12 142 F5
Wickfield Dr. Shef S12 142 F5
Wickfield Gr. Shef S12 142 E4
Wickfield Pl. Shef S12 142 F5
Wickfield Rd. Shef S12 142 F5
Wicklow Rd. Don DN2 63 B5
Widdop Cl. Shef S13 142 D8
Widdop Croft. Shef S13 142 D8
Widford Gn. Hat DN7 44 A6
Wigfield Dr. Barn S70 54 F5
Wigfull Rd. Shef S11 128 C1
Wignall Ave. Roth S66 116 F4
Wike Gate Cl. Thorne DN8 26 D6
Wike Gate Gr. Thorne DN8 26 D6
Wike Gate Rd. Thorne DN8 26 D6
Wike Rd. Barn S71 34 E2
Wilberforce Rd. Don DN2 42 D1
Wilberforce Rd. S Anst S31 146 D5
Wilbrook Rise. Barn S75 33 A4
Wilby Carr High Sch. Don 63 E1
Wilby La. Barn S70 55 A8
Wilcox Cl. Shef S6 112 D5
Wilcox Rd. Shef S6 112 D5
Wild Ave. Rawm S62 97 C7
Wildflower Cl. Ross DN11 103 F7
Wilding Cl. Roth S61 114 E8
Wilding Way. Roth S61 114 E8
Wilford Rd. Barn S71 14 E1
Wilfred Cl. Shef S9 130 A5
Wilfred Dr. Shef S9 130 A5
Wilfred St. Roth S60 115 D6
Wilfrid Rd. Shef S9 130 A5
Wilkinson Ave. Ross DN11 104 A8
Wilkinson Ave. Thorne DN8 9 C2
Wilkinson La. Shef S10 128 E3
Wilkinson Rd. Hoy S74 77 A5
Wilkinson St. Barn S70 54 F8 17
Wilkinson St. Shef S10 128 E3 3
Willan Dr. Treet S60 131 C5
Willbury Dr. Shef S12 142 A6
Willey St. Shef S3 129 B4
William Bradford Cl. Aust DN10 105 C1
William Cl. Shef S19 155 D6
William Cres. Shef S19 155 D6
William La. Ross DN11 84 E1
William Levick Cty Prim Sch.
Dron 152 B2
William Nuttall Cott Homes.
Don DN2 62 F2
William St. Barn S70 55 A5
William St. Dearne S63 58 C5
William St. Eck S31 155 D3
William St. Rawm S62 98 A4
William St. Roth S60 115 E6
William St. Shef S10 128 E2
William St. Swint S64 79 E3
William St. W up D S63 78 F6
William St. Wombw S73 56 C3
Williams Rd. Ben DN5 61 E6
Williams St. Lan S81 136 E3
Williamson Rd. Shef S11 140 D7
Willingham Cl. Shef S19 144 A1
Willingham Gdns. Shef S19 144 A2
Willington Rd. Ad le S DN6 21 B1
Willington Rd. Shef S5 113 C4
Willis Rd. Shef S6 112 B1
Willman Rd. Barn S71 34 E3
Willoughby St. Shef S4 113 E2
Willow Ave. C in L S81 148 E7
Willow Ave. Don DN4 84 F8
Willow Ave. Rawm S62 98 A6
Willow Ave. Thorne DN8 9 B2
Willow Bank. Barn S75 33 E4
Willow Beck. Notton WF4 15 A6
Willow Bridge La. K Bram DN6 23 E6
Willow Bridge La. T in B DN6 23 E6
Willow Bridge Rd. Ben DN5 62 B5
Willow Brook Rd. Mapp S75 33 A8
Willow Cl. Brin S60 131 D7
Willow Cl. Cud S72 35 B7
Willow Cl. Hoy S74 76 C5
Willow Cl. Roth S66 117 C6
Willow Cl. S Anst S31 146 D3
Willow Cotts. Fish DN7 24 E8
Willow Cres. Braith S66 101 A2
Willow Cres. Chap S30 95 A4
Willow Cres. Finn DN9 85 F4
Willow Cres. Thorne DN8 9 C1
Willow Dene Rd. Grime S72 36 A7
Willow Dr. Hem WF9 17 D5
Willow Dr. Mex S64 79 F5
Willow Dr. Roth S66 117 C6
Willow Dr. Shef S9 130 E3
Willow Garth La. Norton DN6 5 C1
Willow Garth. Rawm S62 98 A6
Willow Garth. S Elm WF9 19 B2
Willow Gr. Aston S31 144 F8
Willow Gr. Thorne DN8 9 C1
Willow Inf Sch. Don 84 D6
Willow La. Dearne S63 58 D1
Willow La. Ross DN11 85 A2
Willow Pl. Braith S66 101 A2
Willow Rd. Arm DN3 64 C7
Willow Rd. Dearne S63 37 D1
Willow Rd. Kill S31 156 C5
Willow Rd. Maltby S66 118 D5
Willow Rd. Norton DN6 4 D1
Willow Rd. Stock S30 92 B7
Willow Rd. Thorne DN8 9 B1
Willow Rd. W up D S63 79 A4
Willow St. Barn S70 54 D8
Willow St. Con DN12 81 C2
Willow Wlk. Ben DN5 41 A3
Willowbridge Rd. K Smea WF8 4 A6
Willowbrook. Ad le S DN6 20 F2
Willowdale Cl. Sprot DN5 82 D8
Willowgarth Ave. Brin S60 131 C8
Willowgarth High Sch. Grim 17 A1
Willowgarth House. Rawm S62 98 A6
Willowlees Ct. Don DN4 84 E7
Willows The. Oxspr S30 52 B1
Willows The. Roth S61 96 D2
Wilsden Gr. Barn S75 33 B4
Wilsic Hall Sch. Wad 102 A4
Wilsic La. Wad DN11 102 D2
Wilsic Rd. Tick DN11 120 F8
Wilsic Rd. Wad DN11 102 A5
Wilson Ave. Pen S30 51 D2
Wilson Ave. Rawm S62 97 E6
Wilson Dr. Roth S65 98 E1
Wilson Gr. Barn S71 34 F4
Wilson Pl. Shef S8 141 A7 6
Wilson Rd. Dron S18 153 C4
Wilson Rd. Shef S11 140 C8
Wilson Rd. Stock S30 92 F8
Wilson St. Shef S3 129 A6
Wilson St. Wombw S73 56 B4
Wilson Wlk. Dod S75 54 A6
Wilthorpe Ave. Barn S75 33 C4

Wilthorpe Cres. Barn S75 33 C4
Wilthorpe Farm Rd. Barn S75 33 C4
Wilthorpe Gdns. Shef S19 143 A3 7
Wilthorpe Gn. Barn S75 33 C4
Wilthorpe Inf Sch. Barn 33 D4
Wilthorpe Jun Sch. Barn 33 D4
Wilthorpe La. Barn S75 33 B4
Wilthorpe Rd. Barn S75 33 B4
Wilton Cl. Rawm S62 97 F5
Wilton Ct. Roth S61 115 A7
Wilton Gdns. Roth S61 115 A7
Wilton La. Roth S61 115 A6
Wilton Pl. Shef S10 128 E2
Wiltshire Ave. Con DN12 80 F3
Wiltshire Rd. Don DN2 63 C4
Winberry Ave. N Anst S31 146 E5
Wincanton Cl. Mex S64 80 B6
Winchester Ave. Don DN2 63 A6
Winchester Ave. Shef S10 139 B8
Winchester Cres. Shef S10 139 B8
Winchester Ct. Roth S65 115 E7 4
Winchester Dr. Shef S10 139 B8
Winchester Flats. Hat DN7 44 A8
Winchester House. Ben DN5 61 E6
Winchester Mews. Bir DN11 122 C4
Winchester Rd. Hat DN7 44 A8
Winchester Rd. Shef S10 139 B8
Winchester Way. Barn S71 56 A7
Winchester Way. Ben DN5 61 E6
Winchester Way. Brin S60 115 A1
Winchester Way. S Elm WF9 19 A4
Winco Rd. Shef S4 113 F1
Winco Wood La. Shef S5 113 F3
Wincobank Ave. Shef S5 113 F3
Wincobank Cl. Shef S5 113 F3
Wincobank Fst Sch. Shef 114 A4
Wincobank La. Shef S4 113 F1
Wincobank Rd. Shef S5 113 F3
Wind Hill La. Stock S30 91 C8
Wind Mill La. Pen S30 51 A3
Windam Dr. B Dun DN3 42 F8
Windermere Ave. Don DN2 63 C5
Windermere Ave. Dron S18 152 E1
Windermere Ave. Har DN11 121 F4
Windermere Cl. Ad le S DN6 21 A1
Windermere Cres. Don DN3 42 F3
Windermere Ct. N Anst S31 146 E6
Windermere Grange. N Edl DN12 82 B1
Windermere Rd. Barn S71 34 A1
Windermere Rd. Pen S30 51 D4
Windermere Rd. Shef S8 140 E5 3
Winders Pl. Wombw S73 56 D2
Windgate Hill. Con DN12 81 D3
Windham Cl. Barn S71 33 F3
Windhill Ave. Mapp S75 14 A3
Windhill Ave. Mex S64 80 C5
Windhill Cres. Mapp S75 14 A3
Windhill Cres. Mex S64 80 C6
Windhill Dr. Mapp S75 14 A3
Windhill La. Mapp S75 14 A3
Windhill Mount. Mapp S75 14 A3
Windhill Terr. Mex S64 80 C6
Windle Edge. Dun Br S30 69 B7
Windle Rd. Don DN4 62 A1
Windle Sq. Don DN3 42 F4
Windlestone Sq. Thorne DN8 9 D3
Windmere Ave. Dearne S63 58 E4
Windmere Cl. Mex S64 80 D6
Windmill Ave. Con DN12 81 D1
Windmill Ave. Grime S72 36 A8
Windmill Balk La. Ad I S DN6 40 B5
Windmill Cotts. Norton DN6 4 B2
Windmill Dr. Wad DN11 102 B6
Windmill Greenway. Shef S19 155 E5
Windmill Hill Inf Sch. Chap 94 F4
Windmill Hill Jun Sch. Chap 94 F4
Windmill Hill La. Chap S30 94 F4
Windmill La. Norton DN6 4 C2
Windmill La. Shef S5 113 E3
Windmill La. Wh Com HD7 28 D3
Windmill Rd. N Anst S31 146 E6
Windmill Rd. Wombw S73 56 B2
Windses Est. Grin S30 149 D2
Windsor Ave. Kex S75 32 C8
Windsor Ave. Pen S30 51 A4
Windsor Cl. Askern DN6 22 C8
Windsor Cl. Bnbur DN5 59 C2
Windsor Cl. Roth S66 117 D6
Windsor Cres. Barn S71 34 B3
Windsor Cres. G Hou S72 57 D7
Windsor Ct. Har DN11 122 B5
Windsor Ct. Shef S11 139 F4
Windsor Dr. Bnbur DN5 59 C3
Windsor Dr. Dod S75 53 F7
Windsor Dr. Dron S18 152 C1
Windsor Dr. Mex S64 80 C6
Windsor Gdns. C in L S81 148 E6
Windsor Rd. C in L S81 148 E6
Windsor Rd. Con DN12 81 B3
Windsor Rd. Don DN2 62 F4
Windsor Rd. Hem WF9 17 F6
Windsor Rd. Roth S61 95 F4
Windsor Rd. Shef S8 140 F6
Windsor Rd. Stai DN7 24 E3
Windsor Rise. Aston S31 144 E6
Windsor Sq. Dearne S63 58 E8
Windsor Sq. Stai DN7 24 E3
Windsor St. Dearne S63 58 E8
Windsor St. Hoy S74 76 D6
Windsor St. S Elm WF9 19 A2
Windsor St. Shef S4 129 D6
Windsor St. Shef S4 129 E5
Windsor Wlk. Ben DN5 61 E6
Windsor Wlk. S Anst S31 146 D3
Windy Bank. Bfield S6 109 E6
Windy House La. Shef S2 142 A8
Windy Ridge. Aston S31 132 C1
Winfield Rd. W up D S63 78 F5
Wingerworth Ave. Shef S8 152 D8
Wingfield Cl. Dron S18 152 C1 6
Wingfield Cl. Roth S61 97 A3
Wingfield Comp Sch. Roth 97 A2
Wingfield Cres. Shef S12 142 C5
Wingfield Rd. Barn S71 34 A7
Wingfield Rd. Roth S61 96 F2
Winholme. Arm DN3 64 B6
Winifred St. Roth S60 115 C7
Winkley Terr. Shef S5 113 E5
Winlea Ave. Roth S65 116 E4
Winmarith Ct. Roy S71 15 B3
Winn Cl. Shef S6 112 B3
Winn Dr. Shef S6 112 B3
Winn Gdns. Shef S6 112 B3
Winn Gr. Shef S6 112 B3
Winnery Cl. Tick DN11 121 A8
Winney Hill. Hart S31 157 E5
Winney La. Hart S31 157 E3
Winnifred Rd. W up D S63 79 B6
Winnipeg Rd. Ben DN5 41 B1
Winsford Rd. Shef S6 112 C5
Winster Cl. Barn S70 54 F1
Winster Rd. Shef S6 112 C1
Winston Ave. Stock S30 72 F2
Winston Gn. Matt DN10 123 F1
Winter Ave. Barn S75 33 C2
Winter Hill La. Roth S61 114 E7
Winter Rd. Barn S75 33 C2
Winter St. Shef S3 128 E4
Winter Street Hospl. Shef 128 E4
Winter Terr. Barn S75 33 C2
Winterhill Rd. Roth S61 114 D6
Winterton Cl. Don DN4 84 D6
Winterton Gdns. Shef S12 143 C3
Winterwell Rd. W up D S63 78 C7
Winton Cl. Barn S70 55 A7
Winton Rd. Don DN2 63 B4
Wiseton Rd. Shef S11 140 C8 1
Wisewood Ave. Shef S6 128 A8
Wisewood La. Shef S6 128 A8
Wisewood Pl. Shef S6 128 A8
Wisewood Prim Sch. Shef 112 A1
Wisewood Rd. Shef S6 128 A8
Wisewood Sch. Shef 112 A1
Witham Ct. Barn S75 32 E3
Witham Rd. Shef S10 128 D3
Withens Ave. Shef S6 112 B2
Withens Ct. Mapp S75 14 A1
Withyside. D Dale HD8 30 A6
Witmore St. S Elm WF9 19 A3
Witney St. Shef S8 141 A8
Wivelsfield Rd. Don DN4 82 E6
Woburn Cl. Don DN4 82 E5
Woburn Pl. Dod S75 53 F6
Woburn Pl. Shef S11 139 F2
Wolfe Dr. Shef S6 112 D5
Wolfe Rd. Shef S6 112 D5
Wollaton Ave. Shef S17 152 A5
Wollaton Cl. Barn S71 33 E8
Wollaton Dr. Shef S17 152 A5
Wollaton Rd. Shef S17 152 A5
Wolseley Rd. Shef S8 141 A7 2
Wolsey Ave. Don DN2 63 B4
Wolverley Rd. Shef S13 143 A6
Wombwell Aldham Prim Sch.
Wombw 56 B3
Wombwell Ave. W up D S63 78 E5
Wombwell Hemingfield Ellis
C of E Sch. Hoy 77 C8
Wombwell High Sch. Wombw 56 E1
Wombwell Highfields Jun Sch.
Wombw 56 C3
Wombwell John Street Inf Sch.
Wombw 56 C3
Wombwell Jump Cty Prim Sch. Hoy 76 F7
Wombwell Kings Road Inf Sch.
Wombw 56 E2
Wombwell La. Barn S73 55 F7
Wombwell La. Hoy S73 55 E2
Wombwell Park Street Prim Sch.
Wombw 56 E2
Wombwell Rd. Hoy S74 76 E7
Wombwell Sta. Wombw 56 B1
Wong La. Tick DN11 120 F7
Wood Cl. Chap S30 95 C4
Wood Cl. Rawm S62 97 E7
Wood Cl. Roth S65 117 C8
Wood Cliffe. Shef S10, S11 139 B6
Wood Croft. Roth S61 96 F1
Wood End Ave. Pen S30 51 C1
Wood End La. Shep HD8 28 C7
Wood End. Shef S30 94 D2
Wood Fall La. Bfield S6 110 A5
Wood Fold. Shef S3 129 A7
Wood La. Brin S60 131 A7
Wood La. D Dale HD8 29 E6
Wood La. Don DN12 82 F2
Wood La. Fish DN7 8 E2
Wood La. Fish DN7 25 B8
Wood La. Grime S72 36 A6
Wood La. Mapp S71 14 E2
Wood La. N Edl DN12 101 C7
Wood La. Roth S60 115 D3
Wood La. Roth S66 117 C3
Wood La. Roy S71 15 C1
Wood La. Shef S6 127 E6
Wood La. Ston S66 101 E1
Wood La. Thurcr S66 133 C5
Wood La. Treet S60 132 A3
Wood Lane Cl. Shef S6 127 E6
Wood Moor Rd. Hem WF9 17 F7
Wood Rd. Roth S61 96 F1
Wood Rd. Shef S6 128 B8
Wood Royd Hill La. Holmfi HD7 49 B8
Wood Royd Rd. Stock S30 92 E8
Wood Seats. Shef S30 94 D3
Wood Spring Ct. Shef S4 129 E8
Wood St. Barn S70 54 F8
Wood St. Don DN1 62 D3
Wood St. Mex S64 79 F5
Wood St. Roth S65 98 E2
Wood St. S Hie S72 16 F6
Wood St. Shef S6 128 E6
Wood St. Swint S64 79 E3
Wood St. Wombw S73 56 C2
Wood Syke. Dod S75 54 A7
Wood Terr. Roth S60 115 D3
Wood View. Barn S70 75 F5
Wood View. Con DN12 81 E1
Wood View. Hoy S74 77 A5
Wood View. N Edl DN12 82 C2
Wood View Pl. Roth S60 115 D3
Wood Wlk. Mex S64 79 F6
Wood's Riding. Don DN2 63 D4
Woodall La. Hart S31 157 D6
Woodall Rd. Kill S31 156 F5
Woodall Rd. Roth S65 116 C5
Woodall Rd S. Roth S65 116 C4
Woodbank Cres. Shef S8 140 F5
Woodbank Ct. Dron S17 152 A7
Woodbank Rd. Shef S6 126 F4
Woodbine Rd. Shef S9 129 F7
Woodbourn Hill. Shef S9 129 F5
Woodbourn Rd. Shef S9 129 F4
Woodburn Dr. Chap S30 95 C4
Woodbury Cl. Shef S9 114 A5
Woodbury Rd. Shef S9 114 A5
Woodcock Cl. Roth S61 96 F2
Woodcock Pl. Shef S2 129 D3
Woodcock Rd. Hoy S74 76 E5
Woodcock Way. S Elm WF9 19 A4
Woodcross Ave. Don DN4 85 A7
Woodend Cl. Shef S6 128 A7
Woodend Dr. Shef S6 128 A7
Woodfarm Ave. Shef S6 127 F6
Woodfarm Cl. Shef S6 127 E6
Woodfarm Dr. Shef S6 127 E6
Woodfarm Pl. Shef S6 127 E6
Woodfield Ave. Mex S64 80 B5
Woodfield Cl. Dar S73 57 A6
Woodfield Mid Sch. Don 82 F6
Woodfield Primary Schs. Don 83 B6
Woodfield Rd. Arm DN3 64 C5
Woodfield Rd. Don DN4 83 A6
Woodfield Rd. Don DN4 83 C6
Woodfield Rd. Norton DN6 20 E8
Woodfield Rd. Shef S10 128 B5
Woodfield Rd. W up D S63 78 C6
Woodfoot Rd. Roth S60 115 F1
Woodford Rd. B Dun DN3 42 F8
Woodgrove Rd. Roth S65 116 C7
Woodgrove Rd. Shef S9 114 B4
Woodhall Flats. Dar S73 57 A6
Woodhall Rd. Dar S73 57 A6
Woodhall Rise. Swint S64 79 D2
Woodhead Dr. Hoy S74 55 D1
Woodhead La. Hoy S74 55 E1
Woodhead Rd. Shef S2 141 A8
Woodhead Rd. ShefS30 94 B3
Woodhead Rd. Wort S30 93 E6
Woodholm Pl. Shef S11 140 B5
Woodholm Rd. Shef S11 140 B5
Woodhouse Ave. Shef S19 143 F4
Woodhouse Cl. Rawm S62 97 D8
Woodhouse Cres. Shef S19 143 F4
Woodhouse Ct. Shef S19 143 F4
Woodhouse Gdns. Shef S13 143 C6
Woodhouse Gn. Thurcr S66 133 E7
Woodhouse Green Rd.
K Bram DN7 24 D7
Woodhouse La. Emley HD8 12 A7
Woodhouse La. Hat DN7 44 B4
Woodhouse La. Shef S19 143 F5
Woodhouse La. Wombw S73,WF4 14 B5
Woodhouse Rd. Don DN2 62 F5
Woodhouse Rd. Hoy S74 76 E5
Woodhouse Rd. Shef S12 142 B6
Woodhouse Sta. Shef 143 D7
Woodhouse West Cty Prim Sch.
Shef 143 A6
Woodhouse West Fst & Mid Sch.
Shef 143 A6
Woodland Ave. N Anst S31 146 E5
Woodland Cl. Roth S66 117 C3
Woodland Cl. Treet S60 131 C5
Woodland Dr. Barn S70 54 B8
Woodland Dr. N Anst S31 146 F5
Woodland Dr. Shef S12 142 B2
Woodland East RC Inf & Jun Sch.
Ad le S 40 C4
Woodland Gdns. Maltby S66 119 B5
Woodland Gr. W up D S63 78 F4
Woodland Pl. Shef S17 151 F5
Woodland Rd. Shef S8 141 B3
Woodland Rd. W up D S63 78 F4
Woodland Rise. Silk S75 53 A5
Woodland Terr. Grime S72 36 B5
Woodland View. Cud S72 35 B5
Woodland View. Dron S17 152 A7
Woodland View. Mex S64 80 C4
Woodland View Rd. Shef S6 128 A6
Woodland View. Shef S12 142 B2
Woodland View. Silk S75 53 A5
Woodland Way. Roth S65 116 D4
Woodlands Ave. Shef S19 143 F5
Woodlands Cl. Aston S31 132 D1
Woodlands Cl. D Dale HD8 30 A6
Woodlands Cres. Hem WF9 17 E8
Woodlands Cres. Swint S64 79 B2
Woodlands Fst Sch. Ad le S 40 A4
Woodlands Mid Sch. Ad le S 40 A4
Woodlands Rd. Ad I S DN6 40 B4
Woodlands Rd. Hoy S74 76 E8
Woodlands Rise. Norton DN6 4 C1
Woodlands Terr. N Edl DN12 82 B2
Woodlands The. Shef S10 128 A2
Woodlands View. Ad I S DN6 40 A4
Woodlands View. G Hou S72 36 E2
Woodlands View. Hoy S74 76 E7
Woodlands View. Hoy S73 77 A8
Woodlands Way. Con DN12 80 F3
Woodlea Gdns. Don DN4 85 A7
Woodlea Gr. Arm DN3 64 B6
Woodlea. S Elm WF9 18 F2 6
Woodlea Way. Don DN2 63 C7
Woodleys Ave. Rawm S62 97 E8
Woodman Dr. Swint S64 79 A2
Woodmoor St. Roy S71 34 D8
Woodnook Gr. Eck S31 154 E2
Woodpecker Cl. Aston S31 144 E6
Woodrove Ave. Shef S13 142 B7
Woodrove Cl. Shef S13 142 B7
Woodroyd Ave. Roy S71 15 C1
Woodroyd Cl. Roy S71 15 C1
Woodseats House Rd. Shef S8 140 F2
Woodseats Jun & Inf Sch.
Shef 140 F3
Woodseats Rd. Shef S8 140 F4
Woodsett Wlk. Con DN12 81 E3
Woodsetts Inf Sch. Woods 147 E4
Woodsetts La. Work S81 148 A1
Woodsetts Lindrick Road
Jun Sch. Woods 147 E4
Woodsetts Rd. Gild S81 147 F6
Woodsetts Rd. N Anst S31 147 B5
Woodside Ave. Kill S31 156 F7
Woodside Ave. W up D S63 78 F6
Woodside Cl. Maltby S66 119 B4
Woodside Ct. Ad I S DN6 40 A4
Woodside Ct. Roth S66 117 C3
Woodside. D Dale HD8 30 A6
Woodside La. Shef S3 129 A6
Woodside La. Shef S30 94 C1
Woodside La. Wroot DN9 67 B3
Woodside Rd. Ad I S DN6 40 A4
Woodside Rd. Ben DN5 61 F8
Woodside Rd. Shire S81 159 F7
Woodside View. Bir DN11 122 B4
Woodside Villas. Wroot DN9 67 B2
Woodside Wlk. Roth S61 97 B3
Woodstock Rd. Barn S75 33 D4
Woodstock Rd. Don DN4 82 E7
Woodstock Rd. Shef S7 140 E6
Woodthorpe Cl. Shef S2 142 A8
Woodthorpe Cres. Shef S13 142 C8
Woodthorpe Rd. Shef S13 142 C7
Woodvale Rd. Shef S10 128 B1
Woodview La. Barn S75 33 B3
Woodview Rd. Shef S6 128 C7
Woodview. Sprot DN5 61 B1
Woodview Terr. Shef S10 139 E8
Woodway The. Roth S66 117 B7
Woofindin Ave. Shef S11 139 E7
Woofindin Rd. Shef S10 139 D7
Wooldale Ave. Shef S19 143 A2 12
Wooldale Cl. Shef S19 143 A2
Wooldale Croft. Shef S19 143 A2
Wooldale Dr. Shef S19 143 B2
Wooldale Gdns. Shef S19 143 A2
Wooley Ave. Wombw S73 56 C2
Woollen Wlk. Shef S6 128 E6 2
Woolley C of E Sch. Wool 14 A7
Woolley Colliery Rd. Mapp S75 13 E2
Woolley Edge La. Wool WF4 13 E6
Woolley Fst Sch. Mapp 13 E3
Woolley Hall Coll. Wool 14 B7
Woolley House. Don DN1 62 C1 6
Woolley Low Moor La. Wool WF4 13 D8
Woolley Park Gdns. Wool WF4 14 A7
Woolley Rd. Stock S30 73 A1
Woolley Wood Rd. Shef S5 113 F7
Woolley Wood Special Sch. Shef 113 E6
Woolstocks La. Caw S75 31 E3
Wootton Ct. Roth S65 98 E2
Worcester Ave. Don DN2 63 A7
Worcester Cl. Shef S10 127 B1
Worcester Dr. Shef S10 127 B1
Worcester Rd. Shef S10 127 B1
Wordsworth Ave. Din S31 147 A8
Wordsworth Ave. Don DN4 83 B6
Wordsworth Ave. Norton DN6 4 C1
Wordsworth Ave. Pen S30 51 C2
Wordsworth Ave. Shef S5 112 E5
Wordsworth Cl. Shef S5 112 E6
Wordsworth Cres. Shef S5 112 F4
Wordsworth Dr. Ben DN5 61 F4
Wordsworth Dr. Roth S65 116 A6
Wordsworth Dr. Shef S5 112 E4
Wordsworth Rd. Barn S71 34 B4
Wordsworth Rd. W up D S63 78 C7
Work Bank La. Pen S30 51 B4
Workhouse La. Shef S3 129 A4 6
Worksop Rd. Aston S31 144 E7
Worksop Rd. Shef S9 130 A6
Worksop Rd. Th Sa S80 158 E7
Worksop Rd. Tick DN11 120 F6
Worksop Rd. Tod S31 145 C7
Worksop Rd. Woods S81 147 D2
Worksop Rd. Woods S81 147 F3
Wormley Hill La. Syke DN14 8 D5
Worral Ave. Treet S60 131 E4
Worral Cl. Barn S70 54 F6
Worrall Dr. Ought S30 111 D5
Worrall Rd. Chap S30 94 F7
Worrall Rd. Ought S30 111 E3
Worrall Rd. Shef S30 111 E3
Worry Goose La. Roth S60 116 D2
Worsbrough View. Pilley S75 75 D6
Worsbrough Bank End
Cty Prim Sch. Barn 55 C6
Worsbrough Blacker Cty Inf Sch.
Hoy 76 D8
Worsbrough Bridge RC Sch. Barn 55 B5
Worsbrough C of E Jun & Inf Sch.
Barn 54 F1
Worsbrough Common Cty Prim Sch.
Barn 54 F6
Worsbrough Common Inf Sch.
Barn 54 F7
Worsbrough Ctry Pk. Barn 54 E3
Worsbrough Lobwood Inf Sch.
Barn 55 B5
Worsbrough Manor Inf Sch. Barn 54 F5
Worsbrough Rd. Barn S70 54 F1
Worsley Pl. Ad le S DN6 20 F2
Worthing Cres. Con DN12 81 D2
Worthing Rd. Shef S9 129 E5
Wortley Ave. Con DN12 81 A2
Wortley Ave. Swint S64 79 D3
Wortley Ave. Wombw S73 56 B4
Wortley Dr. Ought S30 111 E7
Wortley Pl. Hem WF9 17 C7
Wortley Rd. Chap S30 94 D8
Wortley Rd. Roth S61 114 F8
Wortley Rd. Stock S30 74 A1
Wortley Sch. Wort 74 D3
Wortley St. Barn S70 33 E1 7
Wortley Top Forge (Mus). Stock 74 B4
Wortley View. Hoy S74 55 D1
Wostenholm Rd. Shef S7 140 F8
Wragby Rd. Shef S11 140 A8
Wragg La. Aston S31 144 B5
Wragg Rd. Shef S2 129 E2
Wrancarr La. T in B DN6 23 A6
Wrangbrook La. Ham WF9 19 D7
Wrangbrook Rd. Upton WF9 19 D8
Wreakes La. Dron S18 152 F2
Wrelton Cl. Roy S71 15 B3
Wren Bank. Shef S2 129 E2
Wren Park Cl. Eck S12 154 E8
Wrens Way. Barn S70 75 F8
Wright Cres. Wombw S73 56 D2
Wright St. N Anst S31 146 E6
Wright's Hill. Shef S2 140 F8 2
Wrightson Ave. Don DN4 82 C5
Wrightson Terr. Ben DN5 62 B6
Wroot Rd. Finn DN9 87 B6
Wroot Travis Charity Sch
(Jun Mix & Inf). Wroot 67 A2
Wroxham Cl. Roth S66 117 E5
Wroxham Dr. Roth S66 117 E5
Wroxham Way. Ben DN5 61 E5
Wroxham Way. Roth S66 117 E6
Wulfric Cl. Shef S2 141 F8
Wulfric Pl. Shef S2 141 F8
Wulfric Rd. Eck S31 155 C3
Wulfric Rd. Shef S2 142 A8
Wyatt Ave. Shef S11 140 C6
Wybourn Fst Sch. Shef 129 E3
Wybourn House Rd. Shef S2 129 E3
Wybourn Mid Sch. Shef 129 E3
Wybourn Terr. Shef S2 129 E3
Wychwood Cl. Don DN4 82 F4
Wychwood Croft. Shef S19 144 A2 8
Wychwood Glenn. Shef S19 144 A2 7
Wychwood Gr. Shef S19 144 A2 9
Wycombe St. Barn S71 34 E2
Wyedale Croft. Shef S19 143 F4
Wyming Brook Dr. Hal M S10 126 B2
Wyn Gr. W up D S73 78 A8
Wyndthorpe Ave. Don DN4 84 E7
Wynford Dr. S Elm WF9 19 A3
Wynlea Dr. Old S81 136 F6
Wynmoor Cres. W up D S73 78 A7
Wynyard Rd. Shef S6 112 B1
Wyvern Gdns. Shef S17 151 E6

Yarborough Terr. Ben DN5 62 B5
Yardley Sq. Shef S3 128 E4
Yarmouth St. Shef S9 114 B1
Yarwell Dr. Maltby S66 118 E6
Yates Cl. Roth S66 117 A3
Yealand Cl. Ad I S DN6 40 B6
Yearling Chase. Swint S64 79 B3
Yeomans Rd. Shef S6 128 E5
Yeomans Way. S Anst S31 146 D4
Yew Greave Cres. Shef S5 112 F7
Yew La. Shef S5 112 F7
Yew Tree Ave. N Anst S31 146 F5
Yew Tree Cres. Ross DN11 85 A2
Yew Tree Dr. Bawtry DN10 122 F7
Yew Tree Dr. Finn DN9 86 B4
Yew Tree Dr. Kill S31 156 C5
Yew Tree Dr. Shef S9 114 F1
Yew Tree Rd. Maltby S66 118 D6
Yew Tree Rd. Shep HD8 28 F8
Yewdale. Barn S70 55 B5
Yewlands Sch. Shef 112 E7
Yews Ave. Barn S70 55 B5
Yews Cl. Ought S30 111 D4
Yews Hospl The. Ought 111 E4
Yews La. Barn S70 55 B7
Yews La. Shef S6 126 D8
Yews Pl. Barn S70 55 B7
Yews The. Roth S65 115 F7
Yewtrees La. Stock S30 92 B5
Yoredale Ave. Chap S30 94 F6
York Bldgs. N Edl DN12 82 B3
York Cl. S Elm WF9 19 A4
York Gdns. Don DN4 63 D1
York Gdns. W up D S63 78 D7
York La. Roth S66 133 B8
York Pl. Shire S81 159 F7
York Rd. Ben DN5 61 E7
York Rd. Don DN5 62 B4
York Rd. Har DN11 122 A4
York Rd. Hat DN7 44 A8
York Rd. Roth S65 115 E7
York Rd. Shef S9 130 C5
York Rd. Stock S30 73 B1
York Rd. Tick DN11 121 B7
York Rise. Aston S31 144 C7
York Sq. Mex S64 80 A4
York St. Barn S70 33 E1
York St. Cud S72 35 B6
York St. Dearne S63 37 F1
York St. Hem WF9 17 E5
York St. Hoy S74 76 E7
York St. Mex S64 79 F5
York St. Ross DN11 84 E2
York St. Shef S1 129 A4
York St. Wombw S73 56 D3
York Terr. Dearne S63 58 E8
York Way. Con DN12 81 E3
Yorkshire Residential Sch
for the Deaf. Don 63 A3
Yorkshire Sculpture Pk. W Bret 12 E7
Youlgreave Dr. Shef S12 142 D5
Young St. Don DN1 62 D3
Young St. Shef S3 128 F1
Yvonne Gr. Wombw S73 56 B3

Zamor Cres. Thurcr S66 133 E5
Zetland Rd. Don DN2 63 A4
Zetland Rd. Hoy S74 77 B5
Zion Dr. Mapp S75 14 B1
Zion La. Shef S9 129 F6
Zion Pl. Shef S9 129 F6

Ordnance Survey

STREET ATLASES

The Ordnance Survey Street Atlases provide unique and definitive mapping of entire counties

Street Atlases available

- Berkshire
- Bristol and Avon
- Buckinghamshire
- Cardiff
- Cheshire
- Derbyshire
- Edinburgh
- East Essex
- West Essex
- Glasgow
- North Hampshire
- South Hampshire
- Hertfordshire
- East Kent
- West Kent
- Nottinghamshire
- Oxfordshire
- Staffordshire
- South Yorkshire
- Surrey
- East Sussex
- West Sussex
- Warwickshire
- West Yorkshire

The Street Atlases are revised and updated on a regular basis and new titles are added to the series. Each title is available in three formats and as from 1996 the atlases are produced in colour. All contain Ordnance Survey mapping except Surrey which is by Philip's.

The series is available from all good bookshops or by mail order direct from the publisher. However, the order form on the following pages may not reflect the complete range of titles available so it is advisable to check by telephone before placing your order. Payment can be made in the following ways:

By phone *Phone your order through on our special Credit Card Hotline on* **01933 414000.** *Speak to our customer service team during office hours (9am to 5pm) or leave a message on the answering machine, quoting T604N99CO2, your full credit card number plus expiry date and your full name and address.*

By post *Simply fill out the order form (you may photocopy it) and send it to: Cash Sales Department, Reed Book Services, PO Box 5, Rushden, Northants, NN10 6YX.*

Ordnance Survey STREET ATLASES ORDER FORM

NEW COLOUR EDITIONS

T604N99CO2	HARDBACK Quantity @ £10.99 each	SPIRAL Quantity @ £8.99 each	POCKET Quantity @ £4.99 each	£ Total
BERKSHIRE Publication May 1996	0 540 06170 0	0 540 06172 7	0 540 06173 5	➤

	Quantity @ £12.99 each	Quantity @ £9.99 each	Quantity @ £4.99 each	£ Total
HERTFORDSHIRE Publication May 1996	0 540 06330 4	0 540 06331 2	0 540 06332 0	➤
SOUTH YORKSHIRE	0 540 06329 0	0 540 06327 4	0 540 06328 2	➤
WEST YORKSHIRE	0 540 06174 3	0 540 06175 1	0 540 06176 X	➤

BLACK AND WHITE EDITIONS

T604N99CO2	HARDBACK Quantity @ £12.99 each	SOFTBACK Quantity @ £8.99 each	POCKET Quantity @ £4.99 each	£ Total
BERKSHIRE	0 540 05992 7	0 540 05993 5	0 540 05994 3	➤
BUCKINGHAMSHIRE	0 540 05989 7	0 540 05990 0	0 540 05991 9	➤
EAST ESSEX	0 540 05848 3	0 540 05866 1	0 540 05850 5	➤
WEST ESSEX	0 540 05849 1	0 540 05867 X	0 540 05851 3	➤
NORTH HAMPSHIRE	0 540 05852 1	0 540 05853 X	0 540 05854 8	➤
SOUTH HAMPSHIRE	0 540 05855 6	0 540 05856 4	0 540 05857 2	➤
HERTFORDSHIRE	0 540 05955 1	0 540 05996 X	0 540 05997 8	➤
EAST KENT	0 540 06026 7	0 540 06027 5	0 540 06028 3	➤
WEST KENT	0 540 06029 1	0 540 06031 3	0 540 06030 5	➤
NOTTINGHAMSHIRE	0 540 05858 0	0 540 05859 9	0 540 05860 2	➤
OXFORDSHIRE	0 540 05986 2	0 540 05987 0	0 540 05988 9	➤
EAST SUSSEX	0 540 05875 0	0 540 05874 2	0 540 05873 4	➤
WEST SUSSEX	0 540 05876 9	0 540 05877 7	0 540 05878 5	➤

	Quantity @ £10.99 each	Quantity @ £8.99 each	Quantity @ £4.99 each	£ Total
SURREY	0 540 05983 8	0 540 05984 6	0 540 05985 4	➤
WARWICKSHIRE	0 540 05642 1			➤

See more titles overleaf

Ordnance Survey STREET ATLASES ORDER FORM

BLACK AND WHITE EDITIONS

T604N99C02	HARDBACK Quantity @ £12.99 each	SOFTBACK Quantity @ £9.99 each	POCKET Quantity @ £4.99 each	£ Total
BRISTOL AND AVON	☐ 0 540 06140 9	☐ 0 540 06141 7	☐ 0 540 06142 5	➤
CARDIFF	☐ 0 540 06186 7	☐ 0 540 06187 5	☐ 0 540 06207 3	➤
CHESHIRE	☐ 0 540 06143 3	☐ 0 540 06144 1	☐ 0 540 06145 X	➤
DERBYSHIRE	☐ 0 540 06137 9	☐ 0 540 06138 7	☐ 0 540 06139 5	➤
EDINBURGH	☐ 0 540 06180 8	☐ 0 540 06181 6	☐ 0 540 06182 4	➤
GLASGOW	☐ 0 540 06183 2	☐ 0 540 06184 0	☐ 0 540 06185 9	➤
STAFFORDSHIRE	☐ 0 540 06134 4	☐ 0 540 06135 2	☐ 0 540 06136 0	➤

Name..

Address..

....

....Postcode

◆ Free postage and packing

◆ All available titles will normally be dispatched within 5 working days of receipt of order but please allow up to 28 days for delivery

☐ Please tick this box if you do not wish your name to be used by other carefully selected organisations that may wish to send you information about other products and services

I enclose a cheque / postal order, for a **total** of ☐
made payable to *Reed Book Services*, or please debit my

☐ Access ☐ American Express ☐ Visa

account by ☐

Account no ☐☐☐☐ ☐☐☐☐ ☐☐☐☐ ☐☐☐☐
Expiry date ☐☐ ☐☐

Signature..

Registered Office: Michelin House, 81 Fulham Road, London SW3 6RB. Registered in England number: 1974080

T604N99C02